The Revised Handbook for Analyzing Jobs

U.S. Department of Labor
Lynn Martin, Secretary

Employment and Training Administration
Roberts T. Jones
Assistant Secretary for Employment Training
1991

This book is a complete reprint of *The Handbook for Analyzing Jobs* as produced by the U.S. Department of Labor. It includes all the content of the original book and is published by JIST Works, Inc., Indianapolis, IN 46202.

from

PUBLISHER'S NOTE

This edition of *The Handbook for Analyzing Jobs* is the first widely available revision of this importnt book since 1972. This version is an *exact* duplicate of the book produced by the U.S. Department of Labor, plus 36 pages (9-1 through 9-36) in chapter 9 that were accidentally omitted in the version released by the government. These pages include information on definitions, interpretive data, and examples of the "Aptitudes" provided as an important component of the "Worker Characteristics" which is widely used by the U.S. Employment Service for job analysis.

Please observe that, while pages 9-1 through 9-36 are quite readable, they are based on copies of pages missing from the government's edition rather than more legible typeset page proofs. For this reason, the printing quality of these 36 pages is compromised. Still, we think that the inclusion of these pages is quite important and thank the staff of the U.S. Department of Labor for providing them to us.

This edition distributed by JIST Works, Inc. is an unabridged reprint of *The Handbook for Analyzing Jobs*, 1991 compiled by the United States Department of Labor, Employment and Training Administration.

Manufactured in the United States of America

Contact your distributor or the publisher for quanitity discounts.

See list of other JIST titles on order form at the end of this book.

JIST Works, Inc.
720 North Park Avenue
Indianapolis, IN 46202-3431
Phone: **1-800-648-5478** (most areas) or **1-317-264-3720**
Fax: **1-800-JIST-FAX** or **1-317-264-3709**

ISBN: 1-56370-051-4

INTRODUCTION

The *Handbook for Analyzing Jobs* (HAJ) contains the methodology and benchmarks used by the cooperative Federal-State Occupational Analysis Program in gathering and recording information about jobs. Major Occupational Analysis products include the *Dictionary of Occupational Titles* which contains occupational definitions of some 13,000 occupations, *Selected Characteristics of Occupations Defined in the Dictionary of Occupational Titles*, and the *Guide for Occupational Exploration*. All of these publications are available from the U.S. Government Printing Office.

Since the first edition of the *Handbook* was published in 1944, changes and improvement in occupational analysis methodology have resulted in periodic revisions. This, the fourth revision, has been used by staff of State Occupational Analysis Field Centers since 1984. During this time, analysts have continued to refine the *Handbook* in order to reduce ambiguities and further refine procedures to facilitate accurate and consistent gathering, synthesis, interpretation, and reporting of occupational information. The methodology documented here was used in the *Dictionary of Occupational Titles, 4th Edition (Revised)* published in 1991.

Although many individuals made invaluable contributions, the lead Occupational Analysis Field Center in North Carolina is primarily responsible for formulating and refining this edition of the *Handbook for Analyzing Jobs*.

CONTENTS

CHAPTER 1

JOB ANALYSIS: WHAT IT IS AND ITS USES

Job information is the basic data used by industry, governmental and private agencies, and employee organizations for many human resource programs. The nature of the required job information varies in type and approach according to program needs. Regardless of the ultimate use for which it is intended, however, the data must be accurate; inclusive, omitting nothing pertinent to the program; and presented in a form suitable for study and use. The techniques for obtaining and presenting this information are known as "job analysis".

In the United States Employment Service, job analysis involves a systematic study of a specific job in terms of:

> The worker's relationship to data, people, and things (Worker Functions);
>
> The methodologies and techniques employed (Work Fields);
>
> The machines, tools, equipment, and work aids used (MTEWA);
>
> The materials, products, subject matter, or services which result (MPSMS); and
>
> The worker attributes that contribute to successful job performance (Worker Characteristics).

This *Handbook for Analyzing Jobs* (HAJ) is devoted to an explanation of the procedures and techniques used in the public employment service to analyze jobs and record the analyses. These procedures were developed to meet the occupational information needs of various human resource programs, and are applicable to any job analysis program, regardless of the intended utilization of the data.

Job analyses are basic for supplying occupational information needed for human resource development and utilization programs in the public employment service, industry, and other non-government establishments. Some of the major areas of use are:

Recruitment and Placement - Providing meaningful and correct job data for the recruitment and selection of workers.

Better Utilization of Workers - Determining job relationships useful in the transfer and promotion of workers to facilitate the opening of job opportunities at the entry level. Determining actual physical demands of the job and suggesting job adjustments to facilitate improved utilization of workers with a disability.

Job Restructuring - Restructuring jobs to make better use of the available work force; and to assist in opening job opportunities for people who are less than fully qualified, in facilitating the placement of workers in hard-to-fill jobs, and in providing trainee jobs.

Vocational Counseling - Furnishing the Vocational Counselor with an assessment of the tasks and requirements of jobs and of the avocations, training, and experiences that lead to them, as a basis for vocational counseling.

Training - Determining training needs and developing training programs. The content of the training curriculum, the amount of time required for training, and the basis for the selection of trainees are dependent, in part, upon knowledge of the jobs.

Performance Evaluation - Providing an objective basis for developing performance standards.

Occupational Safety - Improving safety through the identification of job hazards.

CHAPTER 2

CONCEPTS AND PRINCIPLES OF JOB ANALYSIS

In modern usage, the word "job" has different meanings depending on how, when, or by whom it is used. Moreover, "job" is often used interchangeably with the words "occupation", "position", and "task". To eliminate this confusion and to clarify terms, the United States Employment Service (USES) developed definitions for the following terms for use in job analysis:

1. An **Element** is the smallest step into which it is practical to subdivide any work activity without analyzing separate motions, movements, and mental processes involved.

2. A **Task** is one or more elements and is one of the distinct activities that constitute logical and necessary steps in the performance of work by the worker. A task is created whenever human effort, physical or mental, is exerted to accomplish a specific purpose.

3. A **Position** is a collection of tasks constituting the total work assignment of a single worker. There are as many positions as there are workers in the country.

4. A **Job** is a group of positions within an establishment[1] which are identical with respect to their major or significant tasks and sufficiently alike to justify their being covered by a single analysis. There may be one or many persons employed in the same job.

5. An **Occupation** is a group of jobs, found at more than one establishment, in which a *common* set of tasks are performed or are related in terms of similar objectives, methodologies, materials, products, worker actions, or worker characteristics.

Element, task, and job are relative concepts; an activity that is an element in one job could be a task in another job, and could be a job in and of itself for a third worker. The following example illustrates this point. "Slices cold meats and cheese" is an element in the job of a Short Order Cook, a task in the job of a Sandwich Maker, and the total job of a Deli Cutter-Slicer.

Job, Task, and Element as Relative Concepts

JOB TITLE	SHORT ORDER COOK	SANDWICH MAKER	DELICUTTER-SLICER
JOB	Prepares and cooks, to order, food requiring short preparation time	Prepares sandwiches	Slices cold meats and cheese by hand or machine
TASK	Prepares sandwiches	Slices cold meats and cheese by hand or machine	
ELEMENT	Slices cold meats and cheese by hand or machine		

DETERMINING JOB LIMITS

In the analysis of jobs it is necessary to determine where jobs begin and where they end. The analyst must be able to analyze a group of positions, determine the number of jobs existing among the positions, and then determine the exact nature of these jobs.

Jobs must be analyzed as they exist; therefore, each completed Job Analysis Report (JAR) must report the job as it exists at the time of the analysis, not as it should exist, not as it has existed in the past, and not as it exists in similar establishments.

---

[1]Establishment: A public or private employing unit that produces, provides, and/or sells goods or services at a single, physical location. An establishment may range in size from a single, self-employed worker to thousands of workers.

Basically, every job analysis should represent a description of one job; no more and no less. Tasks temporarily assigned to a given worker in addition to regular duties should not be considered part of the basic job. The following examples are the kinds of situations which the analyst may encounter in job analysis studies:

A. **The worker performs a specific cycle or sequence of operations.** The analyst should begin with the first task the worker is called upon to do and consider the work steps successively. For example, tasks for some machine operating jobs may be arranged in the following order: (1) sets up machine; (2) operates machine; (3) removes workpieces; (4) maintains tools; and (5) maintains machine.

B. **The worker has no regular cycle of operations.** This situation is usually more difficult to analyze since it frequently involves a considerable variety of tasks. Therefore, the analyst should organize the information according to function.

   For example, a chemist could (1) test and analyze raw materials or manufactured products for conformance to plant standards; (2) conduct controlled experiments for purposes of devising new methods for improving production or testing and analyzing raw materials and products, of adapting substances to new uses, and of recovering and utilizing by-products; and (3) supervise workers engaged in manufacturing processes and operations, including the measuring and mixing of ingredients and the control of chemical reactions during processing.

C. **The worker frequently changes from one set of duties to another.** For example, four workers are found performing a set of duties which include (1) weighing out specified amounts of loose tobacco; (2) packing the weighed tobacco into shape boxes in which the tobacco is compressed into cakes in a mashing machine; (3) taking shape boxes from mashing machine and removing the cakes of pressed tobacco from the shape boxes; and (4) cutting the tobacco cakes into large squares. Since the workers frequently rotate to relieve monotony, the duties involved actually constitute one job, all phases of which are performed by all the workers.

D. **The worker performs a given set of duties although in emergencies the worker performs duties involved in other jobs.** For example, in an aircraft factory a group of workers are known as fuselage frame builders, rib frame builders, and spar builders. The workers are engaged in framework assembly. Each assembles various members of a unit fuselage, wing, rib, or wing spar in a jig, and then temporarily secures the assembly with screws, bolts, or tack welds prior to final riveting or welding operations. Although the jobs are interchangeable to the extent that any one of the workers performs the duties of any one of the others in emergencies, the workers perform their respective jobs in regular production work. Situations such as these should be considered separate jobs.

DIMENSIONS OF A JOB: THE JOB ANALYSIS COMPONENTS

All job analysis methods require that certain categories of information about jobs be collected, analyzed, and recorded in a systematic way. The method used by the USES recognizes two major areas of job information: Work Performed and Worker Characteristics. The specific categories of information under each are the job analysis components. Each job analysis component has a specific number of factors, which are defined subcomponents. Factors are assigned to a given job based on an evaluation of the activities and requirements of the job.

Work Performed Components

Work Performed includes those job analysis components that relate to the actual work activities of a job and constitute information that should be reflected in the job summary and the body of a well-written job description. The Work Performed components consist of:

Worker Functions: The ways in which a job requires the worker to function in relation to Data, People, and Things, as expressed by mental, interpersonal, and physical worker actions. Every job is assigned the three Worker Functions that best characterize the worker's primary involvement with Data, People, and Things, and the predominance of each function is indicated. These estimates provide useful information about the Work Performed. This job analysis component contains 24 identifying functions and is defined and discussed in Chapter 3.

Work Fields: These are groupings of technologies and socioeconomic objectives that reflect how work gets done and what gets done as the result of the work activities of a job, or in other words, the purpose of the job. They summarize and classify the overall objectives of work, such as processing of materials, fabricating products, utilizing data, and providing services. The 96 Work Fields are defined and discussed in Chapter 4.

Materials, Products, Subject Matter, and Services (MPSMS): MPSMS include (a) basic materials being processed, such as fabric, metal, or wood; (b) final products being made, such as automobiles or baskets; (c) data, when being dealt with or applied, such as in dramatics or physics; and (d) services being rendered, such as barbering or dentistry. Chapter 5 contains information about this component.

Worker Characteristics Components

The Worker Characteristics component includes job analysis components which reflect worker attributes that contribute to successful job performance. The Worker Characteristics components consist of:

General Educational Development (GED): Education of a general nature which contributes to reasoning development and to the acquisition of mathematical and language skills that are required of the worker to achieve average satisfactory job performance. GED is estimated on the basis of discrete scales for reasoning, mathematical, and language development and is discussed in Chapter 7.

Specific Vocational Preparation (SVP): Vocational preparation that involves acquiring information, learning the techniques, and developing the facility for acceptable performance in a specific job. The application of SVP in job analysis is discussed in Chapter 8.

Aptitudes: Capacities or abilities required of an individual in order to facilitate the learning of some task or job duty. The 11 Aptitudes included in this component are defined and discussed in Chapter 9.

Temperaments: Adaptability requirements made on the worker by the job-worker situation. This component consists of 11 factors, which are defined and discussed in Chapter 10.

GOE (Interest Areas): A liking or preference for an activity. The 12 Interest factors used by the USES in job analysis are explained in Chapter 11.

Physical Demands and Environmental Conditions: Physical Demands are defined as the physical requirements made on the worker by the specific job-worker situation. Environmental Conditions are the surroundings in which a job is performed. This component is defined and discussed in Chapter 12.

SENTENCE ANALYSIS

The technique of sentence analysis has been devised to help the analyst express a job-worker situation in standard, concise form. Use of this technique makes it easier for an analyst to collect complete job information, to assign correct ratings for the ratable Work Performed components (Worker Functions, Work Fields, and MPSMS), and to write the job summary section of the job description. Application of the sentence analysis technique in job analysis is discussed in Chapter 6.

MACHINES, TOOLS, EQUIPMENT, AND WORK AIDS

Machines, Tools, Equipment, and Work Aids (MTEWA) are instruments and devices used to carry out work activities and are defined as follows:

1. **Machines:** Devices which are a combination of mechanical parts with the framework and fastenings to support and connect them, and are designed to apply a force to do work on or move materials or to process data. A machine may be activated by hand or foot power applied through levers or treadles, or outside power sources, such as electricity, steam, or compressed air. Included are printing presses, drill presses, casting machines, forging machines, conveyors, hoists, locomotives, and automobiles.

2. **Tools:** Devices or implements which are manipulated by hand to do work on or move materials. Included are common handtools, plus those manipulated by the worker and activated by outside power sources, such as electricity or compressed air. Examples are pneumatic hammers, cutting torches, paint-spray guns, electric-powered screwdrivers, and electric cutters.

3. **Equipment:** Devices which generate power, communicate signals, or have an effect upon materials through application of light, heat, electricity, steam, chemicals, or atmospheric pressure. Examples are ovens, stills, forges, cameras, and power-generating devices. Also included in this category are nonprocessing devices, such as PBX switchboards, radio transmitters, ammeters, and signal-light systems.

4. **Work Aids:** Miscellaneous items which cannot be considered as machines, tools, or equipment, and yet are necessary for carrying out the work. Included are (1) supportive devices, such as jigs, fixtures, clamps, vises, or anvils; (2) special measuring, hand-manipulated devices, such as micrometers, calipers, gauges, rules, squares, and tapes; (3) graphic instructions, such as blueprints, sketches, maps, charts, wiring diagrams, manuals, and formalized job instructions; (4) substances used in the processing or fabrication of materials and products, such as glue and paint; and (5) musical instruments.

CHAPTER 3

WORKER FUNCTIONS

Worker Functions, one of the three components of Work Performed, are activities which identify worker relationships to data, people, and things. The following 24 Worker Functions are used in job analysis to express these relationships.

WORKER FUNCTIONS

Data	People	Things
0 Synthesizing	0 Mentoring	0 Setting Up
1 Coordinating	1 Negotiating	1 Precision Working
2 Analyzing	2 Instructing	2 Operating-Controlling
3 Compiling	3 Supervising	3 Driving-Operating
4 Computing	4 Diverting	4 Manipulating
5 Copying	5 Persuading	5 Tending
6 Comparing	6 Speaking-Signaling	6 Feeding-Off Bearing
	7 Serving	7 Handling
	8 Taking Instructions-Helping	

NOTE:

1. The hyphenated functions Speaking-Signaling, Taking Instructions-Helping, Operating-Controlling, Driving-Operating, and Feeding-Off Bearing are single functions.

2. The functions Setting Up, Operating-Controlling, Tending, and Feeding-Off Bearing include the situation in which the worker is part of the setup of the machine, as the holder and guider of the material or the tool.

3. Feeding-Off Bearing and Tending, Operating-Controlling and Driving-Controlling, and Setting Up are special cases involving machines and equipment of Handling, Manipulating, and Precision Working, respectively.

4. When a worker becomes part of the machine function by reason of holding and guiding the material or the tool, the Worker Function should be interpreted as machine-related. In these cases the worker is Setting Up, Operating-Controlling, Tending, or Feeding-Off Bearing.

5. When a worker is involved primarily with non-machine activities, but also has a minor relationship to a machine, the appropriate non-machine Things Worker Function should be assigned.

Each Worker Function depicts a broad action which summarizes what the worker does in relation to Data, People, and Things. The selection of three Worker Functions, which represent the most characteristic worker relationships in the job to Data, People, and Things, respectively, provides a device to structure the analysis of the job. Worker Function code numbers are also reflected in DOT definition codes, i.e., the middle three digits of a 9-digit code.

STRUCTURE OF WORKER FUNCTIONS

Although the arrangement within each of the three relationships (Data, People, Things) is structured to suggest an upward progression from the less complex to the more complex, there are instances where hierarchical relationships are limited.

Data Functions are an arrangement of different kinds of activities involving information, knowledge, or concepts. Some are broad in scope and others are narrow. There is considerable overlap in complexity among the Functions. Computing and Copying are more specialized types of functional activities than the other Data Functions.

People Functions are also activities that have little or no hierarchical arrangement. Beyond the generalization that Taking Instructions-Helping is usually the least complex People Function, the remaining Functions have no specific order denoting levels.

Things Functions can be divided into relationships based upon the worker's involvement with either machines and equipment (machine-related) or with tools and work aids (non-machine related). [For clarification, Machines, Tools, Equipment and Work Aids (MTEWA) are defined in Chapter 2, Concepts and Principles of Job Analysis.] As shown in the following chart, Things Functions also represent levels of complexity based on the worker's decisions or judgments.

LEVELS OF JUDGMENT OF THINGS WORKER FUNCTIONS

Levels of Judgment	Nonmachine-Related Levels	Machine-Related Levels
Considerable judgment	1 Precision Working	0 Setting Up
Some latitude for judgment	4 Manipulating	2 Operating-Controlling 3 Driving-Operating
Little or no latitude for judgment	7 Handling	5 Tending 6 Feeding-Off Bearing

PROCEDURE FOR RATING WORKER FUNCTIONS

Read the definitions of the Worker Functions and the examples that follow each definition, and compare them with the activities of the job studied. Select the Data, People, and Things Worker Functions that best characterize the job. The Worker Functions selected should reflect the Data, People, and Things levels needed to accomplish the overall purpose of the job and the important worker activities in the job.

The Worker Function assigned that best characterizes the job is not necessarily the Function which is the "highest" Function present in the job. In some cases, the amount of time spent in an activity will determine which particular Worker Function is most characteristic. In other cases, the contribution of an activity to the completion of the overall purpose of the job, rather than the frequency of the activity, will determine the selection of a Worker Function. In short, the analyst must differentiate the incidental from the essential work activities.

When selecting the appropriate Things Worker Function, consider the following: (1) determine the highest appropriate level of complexity of the worker's relationship to Things based on the degree of judgment involved as depicted in the previous chart; then (2) decide whether the worker relates to several items, in which machines sometimes are one of the items, or whether the situation is a special case in which the worker is concerned almost exclusively with one or more machines or pieces of equipment.

After determining the highest appropriate level of the worker's relationship to Data, People, and Things, evaluate which of the Functions is relatively the most important. Enter in Item 8 of the JAR the appropriate number in each space provided. Circle the "Data", "People", and "Things" caption(s) to indicate which relationship(s) best exemplify the job.

DEFINITIONS AND EXAMPLES OF WORKER FUNCTIONS

DATA: Information, knowledge, and conceptions related to data, people, or things obtained by observation, investigation, interpretation, visualization, and mental creation. Data are intangible and include numbers, words, symbols, ideas, concepts, and oral verbalization.

0   **Synthesizing:** Integrating analyses of data to discover facts or develop knowledge concepts or interpretations.

0:1   Creates satirical or humorous cartoons based on personal interpretations of current news events.

0:2   Writes critical reviews of literary, musical, or artistic works and performances for broadcast and publication.

0:3   Interprets play scripts and conducts rehearsals for stage presentation.

0:4   Formulates hypotheses and experimental designs to investigate problems of growth, intelligence, learning, personality, and sensory processes.

0:5 Directs choral group rehearsals and performances to achieve desired effects, such as tonal and harmonic balance, dynamics, rhythms, tempos, and shadings.

0:6 Conducts research to discover new uses for chemical byproducts, and devises new procedures for preparing organic compounds.

0:7 Creates musical compositions, using knowledge of harmonic, rhythmic, melodic, and tonal structure and other elements of music theory.

0:8 Formulates editorial policies of newspaper and originates plans for special features or projects.

0:9 Interprets serious or comic parts by speech or gesture to portray role in theatrical production.

0:10 Creates and teaches original dances for ballet, musical, or revue to be performed for stage, television, nightclub, or motion picture production.

1 **Coordinating:** Determining time, place, or sequence of operations or activities on the basis of analysis of data; executing determinations or reporting on events.

1:1 Plans, directs, and coordinates activities of designated project to ensure that aims, goals, or objectives are accomplished in accordance with prescribed priorities, time limitations, and funding conditions.

1:2 Plans and arranges for activities of radio or television studio and control room personnel to ensure technical quality of pictures and sound for programs originating in studio or from remote pickup points.

1:3 Coordinates movement of air traffic between altitude sectors and control centers to provide maximum separation and safety for aircraft.

1:4 Directs the routing and controlling of oil through pipelines from wells and storage tanks to delivery points in accordance with delivery obligations and deadlines.

1:5 Plans advertising campaign to promote sale of merchandise.

1:6 Plans and establishes collection routes and directs assignment of personnel and equipment in the operation of a municipal sanitation department.

1:7 Authorizes number and frequency of buses traveling over established city routes to meet the transportation needs of patrons.

1:8 Arranges activities of public and private housing projects to relocate residents in accordance with relocation regulations, facilities, and services.

1:9 Plans and directs milk plant activities, such as pasteurizing, separating, evaporating, drying, cooling, and bottling, in the processing of milk products.

2 **Analyzing:** Examining and evaluating data. Presenting alternative actions in relation to the evaluation is frequently involved.

2:1 Examines food service records and tastes food and beverage samples to determine sales appeal and cost of preparing and serving meals and beverages in food establishments.

2:2 Observes and listens to engine to diagnose causes of engine malfunction.

2:3 Evaluates student loan applications and determines eligibility based on need and academic standing.

2:4 Examines incoming weather data and plots anticipated weather developments on maps and charts.

2:5 Reviews and evaluates scouting reports in preparing defensive plans for football team.

2:6   Assays mineral samples taken from outcrops, floats, and stream channels for preliminary quantitative estimates of mineral content.

2:7   Investigates and evaluates customers' bill complaints for electric or gas-power service.

2:8   Studies blueprints and operation of machinery or equipment in plant and evaluates deviations from original specifications to resolve problems.

2:9   Analyzes water in purification plant to control chemical processes which soften water or make it suitable for drinking.

2:10   Examines works of art, such as paintings, sculpture, and antiques, to determine their authenticity and value.

3   **Compiling:** Gathering, collating, or classifying information about data, people, or things. Reporting or carrying out a prescribed action in relation to the information is frequently involved.

3:1   Operates wire-drawing machine, observing operation of machine as work progresses and making adjustments to conform to written specifications.

3:2   Classifies aircraft flight data and submits data to Dispatcher for approval and flight authorization.

3:3   Collects, classifies, and records forest data, such as rainfall, stream flow, and soil moisture, to develop information tables.

3:4   Summarizes details of transactions in separate ledgers and transfers data to general ledger to maintain records of financial transactions of an establishment.

3:5   Collects and arranges flight arrival and departure times at specified points to construct flight schedule.

3:6   Receives telephone complaints from public concerning crimes or other emergencies, records complaints, and files them for future processing.

3:7   Catalogs library materials, such as books, films, and periodicals, according to subject matter.

3:8   Sells footwear, such as shoes, boots, overshoes, and slippers, in department store.

3:9   Sets up metal-stamping machines for other workers according to product specifications and prescribed procedures.

3:10   Prepares specialty foods, such as tacos and fish and chips, according to recipe using specific methods applicable to type of cookery.

3:11   Inspects precision optical and ophthalmic lenses at various stages of production to determine lenses meet company standards, according to work order and prescription specifications, using precision measuring instruments.

4   **Computing:** Performing arithmetic operations and reporting on or carrying out a prescribed action in relation to them. Does not include counting.

4:1   Calculates cost of customers' laundry by pricing each item on customers' lists, using adding machine or calculating machine.

4:2   Calculates interest and principal payments on mortgage loans, using calculating machine.

4:3   Computes and quotes repair cost estimates for hosiery and gloves.

4:4   Calculates daily wages of miners from production records.

4:5   Totals payments and proves daily transactions in car-rental establishment.

4:6   Calculates change due for payment received for food bill, cashes checks, and issues receipts or tickets to customers.

4:7   Calculates freight or passenger charges payable to participating carriers, using rate table and calculating machine.

4:8 Calculates customer telephone charge according to time consumed, type of call, and mileage zone rate.

4:9 Calculates cost to customer of water conditioner based on frequency of service and size of unit required.

5   Copying: Transcribing, entering, or posting data.

5:1 Enters information on manifest, such as name of shipper, tonnage, and destination, from bills of lading and shipper's declaration.

5:2 Records meter readings, such as oil, steam, temperature, and pressure, on company operating chart.

5:3 Enters data from production records into computer system terminal.

5:4 Enters test scores of applicants on permanent office record form.

5:5 Transcribes addresses from mailing list to envelopes, cards, advertising literature, packages, and similar items.

5:6 Records quantity and length of hides from tag on bundle.

5:7 Types letters, reports, stencils, forms, or other straight copy material from corrected rough draft.

5:8 Records color, quantity, material, and part number from work ticket onto production report.

5:9 Posts totals of checks and drafts to clearing-house settlement sheets.

5:10 Records odometer reading and amount of gas and oil used during refueling in vehicle logbook.

6   Comparing: Judging the readily observable functional, structural, or compositional characteristics (whether similar to or divergent from obvious standards) of data, people, or things.

6:1 Inspects loaded freight cars to ascertain that materials and goods, such as automobiles, lumber, or containers of explosives, are securely braced and blocked according to loading specifications.

6:2 Sorts and inspects telephone charge tickets for such billing information as destination of telegraph message and accuracy of telephone number to which charges are made.

6:3 Compares invoices of incoming articles with actual numbers and weights of articles.

6:4 Grades dressed poultry according to size and physical appearance.

6:5 Sorts burned clay products, such as brick, roofing tile, and sewer pipe, according to form, color, and surface characteristics.

6:6 Examines wood of designated logs to determine that moisture content of logs is within limits specified on work ticket.

6:7 Inspects candy in containers or on conveyor to ensure that it is formed, coated, cupped, wrapped, or packed according to plant standards.

6:8 Examines painted surfaces of automobile to detect scratches, blemishes, and thin spots.

6:9 Sorts and stacks hats according to color, size, and style specified.

6:10 Inspects washed automobiles at end of automatic carwash line to ensure completeness of wash job.

PEOPLE: Human beings; also animals dealt with on an individual basis as if they were human.

0   Mentoring: Dealing with individuals in terms of their total personality in order to advise, counsel, or guide them with regard to problems that may be resolved by legal, scientific, clinical, spiritual, or other professional principles.

0:1 Counsels individuals in debt to provide financial information and advice concerning resolution of financial problems.

0:2 Confers with and advises parents, teachers, and children in order to develop plans for overcoming behavioral, personality, or scholastic problems in children.

0:3 Counsels clients in legal matters.

0:4 Counsels and aids individuals and families requiring assistance of social service agency.

0:5 Provides treatment for individuals with mental and emotional disorders.

0:6 Provides individuals with vocational and educational planning services based on appraisal of their interests, aptitudes, temperaments, and other personality factors.

0:7 Diagnoses or evaluates mental and emotional disorders of individuals, and administers programs of treatment.

0:8 Assists foreign students in making academic, social, and environmental adjustments to campus and community life.

0:9 Provides spiritual and moral guidance and assistance to congregation members.

0:10 Diagnoses and treats diseases and disorders of animals.

1 **Negotiating:** Exchanging ideas, information, and opinions with others to formulate policies and programs or arrive jointly at decisions, conclusions, or solutions.

1:1 Negotiates with property owners and public officials to secure purchase or lease of land and right-of-way for utility lines, pipelines, and other construction projects.

1:2 Contacts landowners and representatives of oil-producing firms in attempt to complete agreements, such as leases, options, and royalty contracts covering oil exploration, drilling, and production activities in specified oil fields.

1:3 Arranges with officials of various organizations in each locality to rent premises for circus, to arrange for distribution of publicity and promotional materials, and to hire musicians for circus band.

1:4 Participates in talks to settle labor disputes. Confers with union members and prepares cases for presentation. Meets with employers to negotiate or arbitrate.

1:5 Confers with foreign shippers to agree upon reciprocal freight-handling contract.

1:6 Contracts with hospitals and other institutional agencies for students to obtain clinical experience in school of nursing.

1:7 Meets with representatives of entertainment attractions, such as troupes, performers, or motion picture distributors, to arrange terms of contract and fees to be paid for engagement in establishments, such as nightclubs, theaters, or dancehalls.

1:8 Contracts with farmers to raise or purchase fruit or vegetable crops.

1:9 Consults with members of welfare board to plan activities and expenditures.

1:10 Confers with editorial committee and heads of production, advertising, and circulation departments of newspaper to develop editorial and operating procedures and negotiate decisions affecting publication of newspaper.

2 **Instructing:** Teaching subject matter to others, or training others (including animals) through explanation, demonstration, and supervised practice; or making recommendations on the basis of technical disciplines.

2:1 Trains nursing staff in techniques of industrial nursing. Conducts classes in first aid and home nursing for employees.

2:2 Conducts classes in instrumental or vocal music for individuals or groups in public or private school.

2:3 Provides training for police recruits in police science investigative methods and techniques, government, law, community life, proficiency in firearms, self-defense, and care of firearms.

2:4 Trains wild animals, such as lions, tigers, bears, and elephants, to perform tricks for entertainment of audience at circus or other exhibitions.

2:5 Teaches one or more subjects in college or university classroom.

2:6 Coaches groups at playgrounds and schools in fundamentals and rules of competitive sports. Demonstrates techniques of game and drills players in fundamentals until they are familiar with all phases.

2:7 Lectures, demonstrates, and uses audiovisual teaching aids to present subject matter to class.

2:8 Lectures and demonstrates job fundamentals to flight attendants of passenger airline.

2:9 Instructs workers in painting decorations on plates, bowls, saucers, and other dinnerware.

3 **Supervising:** Determining or interpreting work procedures for a group of workers, assigning specific duties to them, maintaining harmonious relations among them, and promoting efficiency. A variety of responsibilities is involved in this function. (NOTE: The activities may include training workers; evaluating workers' performance; assisting workers in solving work problems; initiating and recommending personnel actions, such as hiring, firing, promoting, transferring, and disciplining; enforcing company regulations; and maintaining or directing maintenance of production and personnel records.)

3:1 Assigns guard force personnel to station or patrols. Interprets security rules and supervises subordinates in carrying out rules. Reports irregularities and hazards to appropriate personnel. Selects and trains subordinates. Ensures that safety standards are maintained.

3:2 Supervises and coordinates activities of workers engaged in loading ships' cargoes. Studies bills of lading to determine sequence of loading operations, calculates number of hours and personnel required, and assigns tasks to workers. Oversees workers to ensure cargo is loaded in proper sequence.

3:3 Issues oral and written orders to newspaper workers engaged in gathering, writing, and publishing one type of news, such as sports, society, music, or drama.

3:4 Directs activities of workers engaged in distributing materials to other workers and keeping records of parts worked on and completed.

3:5 Inspects engines and other equipment and orders ship's crew to repair or replace defective parts.

3:6 Assigns duties to typists and examines typed material for accuracy, neatness, and conformance to standards.

3:7 Interviews, hires, and gives instructions to crew of fishing vessel, and assigns crew to watches and quarters. Directs fishing operations, using knowledge of fishing grounds and work load capacities of vessel and crew.

3:8 Establishes work procedures for workers engaged in loading and unloading kiln to dry green hops. Examines hops on kiln floor to determine distribution for drying, and gives instructions to workers concerning depth hops may be piled in kiln bay and kiln temperature and air volume to be maintained.

3:9 Directs workers engaged in maintaining grounds and turf on golf course. Determines work priority and assigns workers to tasks, such as fertilizing, seeding, mowing, raking, and spraying. Observes employees' work and demonstrates more efficient work methods.

3:10 Assigns bricklayers to specific duties. Inspects work in progress to determine conformance to specifications and trains new workers.

4 **Diverting**: Amusing others, usually through the medium of stage, screen, television, or radio.

4:1 Portrays role in dramatic production to entertain audience.

4:2 Sings classical, opera, church, or folk music in musical programs.

4:3 Performs classical, modern, or acrobatic dances alone, with partner, or in groups to entertain audience.

4:4 Induces hypnotic trance in subjects, occasionally using members of audience as subjects, and commands hypnotized subjects to perform specific activities.

4:5 Speaks in such manner that voice appears to come from source other than own vocal chords, such as from dummy or hand puppet.

4:6 Pilots airplane to perform stunts and aerial acrobatics at fairs and carnivals.

4:7 Drives racing car over track in competition with other drivers.

4:8 Performs difficult and spectacular feats, such as leaping, tumbling, and balancing, alone or as member of team.

4:9 Impersonates Santa Claus during Christmas season.

4:10 Performs original and stock tricks of illusion and sleight of hand to mystify audience, using props such as cards and cigarettes. Frequently uses members of audience in act.

5 Persuading: Influencing others in favor of a product, service, or point of view.

5:1 Sells services of industrial psychology firms to management officials.

5:2 Calls on farmers to solicit repair business and to sell new milking equipment. Demonstrates milking machines.

5:3 Offers articles at auction, asking for bids, attempting to stimulate buying desire of bidders and closing sales to highest bidder.

5:4 Sells all types of life insurance by pointing out company programs that meet clients' insurance needs.

5:5 Solicits membership for club or trade association. Visits or contacts prospective members to explain benefits and cost of membership and to describe organization and objective of club or association.

5:6 Contacts individuals and firms by telephone and in person to solicit funds for charitable organization.

5:7 Sells home appliances to customer after pointing out salable features of merchandise.

5:8 Calls on retail outlets to suggest merchandising advantages of company's trading stamp plan.

5:9 Promotes use of and sells ethical drugs and other pharmaceutical products to doctors, dentists, hospitals, and retail and wholesale drug establishments.

5:10 Purchases merchandise or commodities for resale.

6 Speaking-Signaling: Talking with and signaling people to convey or exchange information. Includes giving assignments and directions to helpers or assistants.

6:1 Manages program to ensure that implementation and prescribed activities are carried out in accordance with specified objectives.

6:2 Directs and coordinates through subordinate supervisory personnel activities of production department(s) in processing materials or manufacturing products in industrial establishment.

6:3 Directs traffic by motioning with flag when construction work obstructs normal traffic route.

6:4 Gives property coordinator verbal directions in placing of items on stage or set.

6:5 Informs public on library activities, facilities, rules, and services.

6:6 Indicates customer bid by word, mannerism, hand, or other characteristic signal.

6:7 Interviews job applicants in employment agency.

6:8 Answers questions from passengers concerning train routes, stations, and timetable information.

6:9   Informs tourists concerning size, value, and history of establishment; points out features of interest; and gives other information peculiar to establishment.

6:10   Answers telephone to give information about company's special services to potential customers.

6:11   Signals or relays signals to operators of hoisting equipment engaged in raising or lowering loads and pumping or conveying materials.

6:12   Explains hunting and fishing laws to sporting groups.

7   **Serving:** Attending to the needs or requests of people or animals or the expressed or implicit wishes of people. Immediate response is involved.

7:1   Accompanies and assists ambulance driver on calls. Assists in lifting patient onto wheeled cart or stretcher and into and out of ambulance. Renders first aid, such as bandaging, splinting, and administering oxygen.

7:2   Renders variety of personal services conducive to safety and comfort of airline passengers during flight.

7:3   Carries golf bags around golf course for players, handing clubs to players as requested.

7:4   Cares for elderly, handicapped, or convalescent people. Acts as aide or friend by attending to employer's personal, business, or social needs.

7:5   Arranges wearing apparel and checks personal effects for performers and other personnel when they are on set.

7:6   Feeds and waters animals in zoo.

7:7   Mixes and serves alcoholic and nonalcoholic drinks to patrons of bar, following standard recipes.

7:8   Bathes and gives alcohol rubs to hospital patients.

7:9   Cleans and polishes footwear for customers.

7:10   Escorts hotel guests to rooms, assists them with luggage, and offers information pertaining to available services and facilities of hotel.

8   **Taking Instructions-Helping:** Attending to the work assignment instructions or orders of supervisor. (No immediate response required unless clarification of instructions or orders is needed.) Helping applies to "non-learning" helpers.

8:1   Drives forklift to move, hoist, and stack cartons of materials in warehouse, following oral instructions of supervisor and written work orders.

8:2   Tests ballpoint pen cartridges to determine conformity to company specifications, referring to test procedures.

8:3   Folds garments for bagging or boxing, following guide marks on table or using folding board.

8:4   Records financial transactions in ledgers or accounts books to maintain establishment records.

8:5   Inspects, assembles, and packs mounted or unmounted negatives, color film transparencies, and photographic prints.

8:6   Weighs and mixes seasonings and other ingredients to prepare spice mixes according to formula.

THINGS: Inanimate objects as distinguished from human beings; substances or materials; and machines, tools, equipment, work aids, and products. A thing is tangible and has shape, form, and other physical characteristics.

0   **Setting Up:** Preparing machines (or equipment) for operation by planning order of successive machine operations, installing and adjusting tools and other machine components, adjusting the position of workpiece or material, setting controls, and verifying accuracy of machine functions and work produced, applying knowledge of machine capabilities, properties of materials, and shop practices. Uses tools, equipment, and work aids, such as precision gauges and measuring instruments. Workers who set up one or a number of machines for other workers or who set up and personally operate a variety of machines are included here.

0:1   Selects, positions, and secures cutters in toolhead, in spindle, or on arbor of gear cutting machines, such as gear shapers, hobbers, and generators. Sets feed rates and rotation speeds of cutters and workpiece in relation to each other by selecting and mounting gears, cams, or templates or by moving levers. Moves controls to set cutting speeds and depth of stroke and cut for reciprocating cutters and to position tools and workpieces.

0:2   Selects and secures tool in spindle, using wrenches. Positions workpiece in fixture or on machine table, securing it with clamps and wrenches, and verifies positions with instruments, such as surface gauges and dial indicators. Selects feed rate, honing tool rotation speed, and depth of cut according to knowledge of metal properties and abrasives. Moves controls to position tool in relation to workpiece and to set feed rate and spindle speed. Positions and tightens stops, using wrench, to control length of honing tool stroke. Starts machine and turns handwheels to feed tool to workpiece. Measures first-run workpiece for conformance to specifications, using micrometers and fixed gauges.

0:3   Selects and positions, aligns, and secures electrodes, jigs, holding fixtures, guides, and stops on resistance welding and brazing machines.

0:4   Lifts specified die sections into die-casting machines that cast parts, such as automobile trim, carburetor housing, and motor parts, from nonferrous metals. Secures die sections in position and adjusts stroke of rams. Connects water hoses to cooling system of die. Preheats die sections. Turns valves and sets dials to regulate flow of water circulating through dies. Starts machine to produce sample casting and examines casting to verify setup.

0:5   Selects, installs, and adjusts saw blades, cutter heads, boring bits, and sanding belts in variety of woodworking machines, using handtools and rules. Operates machines to saw, smooth, shape, bore, and sand lumber and wood parts. Periodically verifies dimensions of parts for adherence to specifications, using gauges and templates.

0:6   Aligns and bolts specified dies to ram and anvil of presses and hammers. Installs impression and gripping dies and synchronizing cams on upsetting machines. Sets and bolts roll dies into self-positioning slots or dogs on roll shafts of forging rolls. Aligns and bolts positioning fixtures and stops, and turns handles or knobs to synchronize conveyor speed with forging-machining action and heating cycle of furnace. Starts machine and inspects work to verify conformance of die setup to specifications.

1   **Precision Working:** Using body members and/or tools or work aids to work, move, guide, or place objects or materials in situations where ultimate responsibility for the attainment of standards occurs and selection of appropriate tools, objects, or materials, and the adjustment of the tool to the task, require considerable judgment.

1:1   Repairs and maintains production machinery in accordance with blueprints, diagrams, operation manuals, and manufacturer's specifications, using handtools, power tools, and precision-measuring and testing instruments.

1:2   Lays out position of parts on metal, using scribe and handtools.

1:3   Locates and marks reference lines and marks location of holes to be drilled, using scribe.

1:4   Sketches original designs for textile cloth patterns on graph paper, using water colors, brushes, pen, and rulers.

1:5   Carves statues, monuments, and ornaments from stone, concrete, and wood, using chisels, hammers, and knives.

1:6   Fits and assembles machine components according to assembly blueprints, manuals, engineering specifications, sketches, and knowledge of machine construction procedures, using handtools and power tools. Shapes parts for precision fit, using metalworking machines.

1:7   Lays out, cuts, shapes, and finishes wood, plastics, plexiglass, and hardboard parts of displays, using handtools.

1:8   Drafts full- or reduced-scale drawings for use by building contractors and craft workers.

1:9   Diagnoses electrical malfunctions, using test lights, ohmmeter, voltmeters, circuit simulators, and wiring diagrams.

1:10   Cuts, trims, and tapers hair, using clippers, comb, and scissors.

1:11   Measures, marks, and cuts carpeting and linoleum with knife to get maximum number of usable pieces from standard size rolls, following floor dimensions and diagrams.

1:12   Forms sand molds for production of metal castings, using handtools, power tools, patterns, and flasks and applying knowledge of variables, such as metal characteristics, molding sand, contours of patterns, and pouring procedures.

2   **Operating-Controlling:** Starting, stopping, controlling, and adjusting the progress of machines or equipment. Operating machines involves setting up and adjusting the machine or material(s) as the work progresses. Controlling involves observing gauges, dials, etc. and turning valves and other devices to regulate factors such as temperature, pressure, flow of liquids, speed of pumps, and reactions of materials.

2:1   Turns controls on television camera, observes scenes through camera monitor, adjusts lens to maintain scenes in focus, and moves levers to alter angle or distance of shot to photograph scenes for broadcasting.

2:2   Types alphabetic or numeric input data on keyboard of computer terminal from source documents. Inserts paper into carriage, presses key to obtain printout or video display of data, and backspaces and strikes over original material, using keyboard, to correct errors. Presses code key to transmit corrected data via telephone lines to computer.

2:3   Moves lever to regulate speed of turntable of tape recorder machines. Turns knobs on cutting arms to shift or adjust weight of stylus. Moves switches to open microphone and tune in live or recorded programs.

2:4   Places wooden barrel horizontally on barrel rest of barrel-lathe machine. Clamps barrel between two chucks of lathe. Starts machine and holds barrel plane against surface of revolving barrel while guiding tool along its length to scrape and smooth it.

2:5   Places glass blanks and tube components in chuck or tailstock of lathes and depresses pedals of compressed air devices that lock parts in lathes. Starts lathes, lights gas-torch heating elements, and turns valves to regulate flames. Turns handwheels or pushes levers to control heating of specified areas of glass parts.

2:6   Places spool on spindle of floor-mounted sewing machines. Draws thread through machine guides, tensions, and needle eye. Inserts bobbins into shuttles and draws thread through slots in shuttle walls or draws thread through guides and looper eyes. Presses knee levers, depresses pedals, or moves hand levers to raise presser foot or spread feed cups. Positions parts to be joined and lowers presser foot. Starts, stops, and controls speed of machines with pedals or knee levers and guides parts under needles.

2:7   Moves switches on central control panel of switchboard to regulate converters. Observes demand meters, gauges, and recording instruments and moves controls to ensure efficient power utilization, equipment operation, and maintenance of power distribution. Monitors gauges, alarms, and oscilloscopes to detect and prevent damage to equipment and disruption of power.

2:8   Fires furnace or kiln, observes gauges, and adjusts controls to maintain specified temperature for drying coal and ore before or after washing, milling, or pelletizing operations.

2:9   Regulates flow and pressure of gas from mains to fuel feed lines of gas-fired boilers, furnaces, kilns, soaking pits, smelters, and related steam-generating or heating equipment. Opens valve on feed lines to supply adequate gas for fuel and closes valves to reduce gas pressure. Observes, records, and reports flow and pressure gauge readings on gas mains and fuel feed lines.

3   **Driving-Operating:** Starting, stopping, and controlling the actions of machines or equipment for which a course must be steered or which must be guided to control the movement of things or people for a variety of purposes. Involves such activities as observing gauges and dials, estimating distances and determining speed and direction of other objects, turning cranks and wheels, and pushing or pulling gear lifts or levers. Includes such machines as cranes, conveyor systems, tractors, furnace-charging machines, paving machines, and hoisting machines. Excludes manually powered machines, such as handtrucks and dollies, and power-assisted machines, such as electric wheelbarrows and handtrucks.

3:1   Steers vessel over course indicated by electronic equipment, such as radio and land radar, to transport passengers to fishing locations for catching fish and other marine life.

3:2   Pushes pedals and pulls levers to move, control speed, and stop crane boom, and raise or lower cables attached to load. Adjusts controls to move and position load by sight or at direction of other worker.

3:3   Pilots airplane or helicopter over agricultural fields at low altitudes to dust or spray fields with seeds, fertilizers, or pesticides.

3:4   Operates throttle, air brakes, and other controls to transport passengers or freight on electric, diesel-electric, steam, or gas-turbine-electric locomotive. Interprets train orders, block or semaphore signals, and railroad rules and regulations.

3:5   Fastens attachments, such as graders, plows, and rollers, to tractor with hitchpins. Releases brake, shifts gears, and depresses accelerator or moves throttle to control forward and backward movement of machine. Steers tractor by turning steering wheel and depressing brake pedals.

3:6   Pushes levers and pedals to move machine; to lower and position dipper into material; and to lift, swing, and dump contents of dipper into truck, car, or onto conveyor or stockpile.

3:7   Moves control levers, cables, or other devices to control movement of elevator. Opens and closes safety gate and door of elevator of each floor where stop is made.

3:8   Controls movement and stops railroad or mine cars by switching, applying brakes, placing sprags (rods) between wheel spokes, or placing wooden wedges between wheel and rail. Positions cars under loading chutes by inserting pinch bar under car wheels, using bar as fulcrum and lever to move car. Hooks cable drum brake to ease car down incline.

3:9   Moves controls to drive armored car to deliver money and valuables to business establishments.

3:10   Controls action of rail-mounted trackmobile to spot railroad cars on ramp above chip storage bins for unloading, and releases bottom doors of cars allowing chips to fall into bin.

3:11   Drives street sweeper and moves controls to activate rotary brushes and spray so that sweeping machine picks up dirt and trash from paved street and deposits it in rear of machine.

4   **Manipulating:** Using body members, tools, or special devices to work, move, guide, or place objects or materials. Involves some latitude for judgment with regard to precision attained and selecting appropriate tools, object, or material although this is readily manifest.

4:1 Shapes knitted garments after cleaning by shrinking or stretching garments by hand to conform to original measurements.

4:2 Trims and smooths edges, surfaces, and impressed or raised designs of jewelry articles and jewelry findings, using files, chisels, and saws.

4:3 Scrapes, files, and sands machine-shaped gunstocks to remove excess wood and impart finished appearance to surface, using files, sandpaper, and emery cloth.

4:4 Moves rotating disk of powered, portable grinder against surface of stationary workpiece to remove scratches, excess weld material, and burrs. Changes disks to ones with progressively finer abrasives to obtain specified finish on workpiece.

4:5 Draws colored strips of material, such as fabric or leather, between slits in shoe upper to weave decorative design according to specifications.

4:6 Turns sprayer valves and nozzle to regulate width and pressure of spray, pulls trigger, and directs spray onto work surface to apply prime or finish coat according to knowledge of painting techniques.

4:7 Guides tip of soldering iron along seam of metal plates to heat plates to bonding temperature and dips bar or wire of soft solder in seam to solder joint.

4:8 Mixes soldering flux in crock or vat according to formula, using paddle, and tests consistency of flux with hydrometer.

4:9 Repacks parachutes that have been opened in use, or unopened ones that are to be repacked in interest of safety.

4:10 Attaches cables to buildings, installs supports, and cuts or drills holes in walls and partitions through which cables are extended, using wrenches, pliers, screwdrivers, saws, and drills.

5 **Tending:** Starting, stopping, and observing the functioning of machines and equipment. Involves adjusting materials or controls of the machine, such as changing guides, adjusting timers and temperature gauges, turning valves to allow flow of materials, and flipping switches in response to lights. Little judgment is involved in making these adjustments.

5:1 Positions and secures scoring disks on machine shaft, turns handwheel to adjust pressure on disks, and feeds cardboard blanks into machine hopper.

5:2 Turns controls to regulate amount of coal, pushes air-blower controls that blow coal into furnaces, and observes air gauges and feed of coal.

5:3 Presses pedal or button and moves lever on packaging machine. Observes operation to detect malfunctions. Opens valves, changes cutting dies, sets guides, and clears away damaged products or containers.

5:4 Holds and turns wood shoe last against revolving sanding wheel to remove specified amount of material and to smooth surface of last while retaining original contours. Verifies contours of sanded last, using template.

5:5 Lights fire and opens valves to regulate fuel supply to asphalt-heater. Screws hose connections to heater to connect circulating system and uses pump to circulate asphalt through heating unit. Observes temperature gauge and adjusts blower and damper controls to regulate heat and maintain required temperature.

5:6 Adjusts control that regulates stroke of paper pusher on machine that assembles pages of printed material in numerical sequence. Places pages to be assembled in holding tray. Turns controls manually to start machine and removes assembled pages from machine.

5:7 Depresses pedal to start, stop, and control speed of yarn winding machine. Observes yarn to detect slubs and broken or tangled ends, cuts out slubs, using scissors, and ties broken yarn ends.

5:8 Positions spring on bed of machine, turns hand gauges to regulate travel of flattening ram, and pulls lever to lower ram that compresses spring under specified pressure.

5:9   Places tack in holder on machine bed. Positions premarked article over tack on bed and positions button on garment over tack and under machine ram. Depresses pedal that lowers ram to join button to article.

5:10   Shovels coal or coke into firebox of boiler, turns valves to regulate flow of gas, oil, or pulverized coal into firebox, or moves controls to regulate feeding speed of automatic stoker. Reads gauges and moves controls to maintain specified steam pressure, temperature, and water level in boiler.

6   Feeding-Off Bearing: Inserting, throwing, dumping, or placing materials in or removing them from machines or equipment which are automatic or tended or operated by other workers.

6:1   Inserts milled rubber stock into rolls of calendering machine to maintain continuous supply.

6:2   Places molded lens blanks into automatic burr-grinding machines. Catches ejected blanks and stacks them in trays prior to polishing.

6:3   Removes cartons of bottles from conveyor and stacks them on pallet.

6:4   Picks up and dumps specified dry materials into feeder hopper of crutcher equipment which forms slurry for processing into soap.

6:5   Hangs toy parts in specified positions on hooks of overhead conveyor that passes through painting operations and lifts painted parts from hooks.

6:6   Places eggs in holder that carries them into machine that removes earth, straw, and other residue from egg surface prior to shipment. Removes cleaned eggs and packs them in cases.

6:7   Places plate glass onto conveyor of glass silvering machine or automatic washing and drying machines and removes silvered or cleaned mirror from conveyor.

6:8   Shovels scrap tobacco onto screens of cleaning machine, picks out stems and dirt from tobacco, and shovels tobacco dust from receptacle under screen into containers.

6:9   Picks up handfuls of glass pipettes from conveyor and packs them into boxes.

6:10   Dumps dyed cotton fiber into hopper of extractor that removes liquid by forcing cotton through rollers.

6:11   Places soiled garments into washing machine, extractor, and tumbler, and removes garments at completion of cleaning cycle.

6:12   Removes stacks of paper cups accumulating at collection rack at end of pneumatic tube leading from automatic cup-forming machine and packs cups into cardboard tubes.

7   Handling: Using body members, handtools, or special devices to work, move, or carry objects or materials. Involves little or no latitude for judgment with regard to attainment of standards or in selecting appropriate tool, object, or materials.

7:1   Loads and pushes handtruck to move metal molds of pipemaking concrete from forming area to steam-cooking area.

7:2   Hammers steel pins into holes in ends of logs preparatory to skidding.

7:3   Drives herd of goats to fresh pastures during day and back to corral at night.

7:4   Files documents in alphabetical or numerical order or according to subject matter and removes documents from files upon request.

7:5   Clears stumps, trees, brush, cactus, mesquite, or other growth from land so land can be used as pasture, for cultivation, or for proposed construction project.

7:6   Weighs materials in chemical plant and writes or stencils identifying information on containers. Fastens caps or covers on containers, or screws bungs in place. Cleans stills and other equipment, using detergents. Loads railroad cars or trucks.

7:7   Distributes work cards containing instructions to workers.

7:8 Mops, sweeps, and dusts halls and corridors.

7:9 Digs ditches that drain excess moisture from land, using pick and shovel.

7:10 Transfers fingerprints from persons onto cards for purposes of identification.

7:11 Cuts candy into squares, using knife.

7:12 Folds and stacks cuffs preparatory to sewing cuffs to sleeves of garments.

7:13 Scrapes or knocks mortar from bricks, using hammer.

7:14 Copies production data, using pen.

CHAPTER 4

WORK FIELDS

Work Fields, a component of Work Performed, are categories of technologies that reflect how work gets done and what gets done as a result of the work activities of a job: the purpose of the job. There are 96 Work Fields identified for use by the USES for classification of all jobs in the economy in terms of what gets done on the job.

Work Fields range from the specific to the general and are organized into homogeneous groups, based on related technologies or objectives, such as the movement of materials, the fabrication of products, the use of data, and the provision of services. Each Work Field is identified by a three-digit code, a brief descriptive title, and a definition. In many cases, a comment is included which enlarges upon the definition and limits or extends the application of the Work Field. Also, cross-references are frequently included which distinguish one Work Field from other related Work Fields.

Following the definition is a list of methods verbs which illustrate the application of the Work Field. This list is not intended to be exhaustive, but merely representative, of the ways in which the objective of the Work Field can be accomplished. Note that the methods verbs listed as examples do not include those appearing in the title or definition for that Work Field, inasmuch as they are implicit in the Work Field. Some methods verbs are used as illustrative examples in more than one Work Field; however, their meanings may differ in the various listings.

It is important to understand that the concept of Work Fields involves consideration not only of the overall objective or purpose of a job, but also how the objective is attained; that is, the means by which the objective of the job is met. MTEWA are instruments and devices used by the worker to achieve the objective of the job. MTEWA are directly related to, and help describe, specific methods verbs.

The job of a worker who performs in a first-line supervisory or helper capacity is assigned the same Work Field(s) as that of the jobs of the workers supervised or helped, because the technological objectives are the same as those of the workers supervised or helped. It is incorrect to assign Work Field 295-Administering to such supervisory jobs; or 011-Material Moving to helper jobs. For Things jobs that are machine-related, the Work Field is based upon what the machine does. For example, the job of a worker who tends a machine that smooths and polishes bores of shotgun barrels is assigned Work Field 051-Abrading. Prefixes, such as **un** or **re**, are implicit in the definition of a Work Field. For example, **Material Moving** includes unloading and removing; **Filling-Packing-Wrapping** includes unpacking, unwrapping, etc.

COMBINATION WORK FIELDS

Combination Work Fields are general categories of Work Fields that contain combinations of Work Fields to cover jobs involving various technologies. For example, Structural Fabricating-Installing-Repairing includes combinations of such specific Work Fields as Abrading, Nailing, Riveting, and Welding. However, in some situations, the analyst may elect to assign the specific Work Fields, rather than a combination Work Field, to express the overall objective of a job.

PROCEDURE FOR ASSIGNING WORK FIELDS

The core of the procedure for assigning Work Fields is the sentence analysis technique. The object of such assignment is to formulate sentences containing words illustrative of the Work Field(s). The resulting sentence must provide an integrated picture that answers the ''how'' and ''why'' sufficiently for classification purposes. The sentence analysis technique is outlined in Chapter 6.

Experienced analysts have found the following steps to be helpful in assigning Work Fields.

Step 1. Study the job-worker situation to determine the method(s) specific to the accomplishment of the overall job objective. As has been pointed out in this section, many verbs are used to signify specific methods which relate to quite different objectives. Thus it is essential to check the particular use of the verb against the definition of the Work Field which is supposed to include it. The listing of methods verbs accompanying each Work Field definition is by no means exhaustive, and it is entirely possible that the analyst will use others. However, make certain that they have methodological value in a particular context and are not simply explanatory or reflective of the end results of the job. The analyst must always keep in mind that Work Fields are broader in scope than the intermediate objectives reflected in individual work element statements in a description of a job. The total of all the intermediate objectives contained in the Description of Tasks should lead to an understanding of the assigned Work Field(s).

Step 2. Select the Work Field that most adequately encompasses the specific methodology of the job-worker situation. Although it is possible to select more than one Work Field for almost any job-worker situation (e.g., nearly all job-worker situations involving Things require Material Moving in addition to whatever else is done), this will not be necessary if the primary Work Field is adequately comprehensive. However, there will be instances where it is necessary to assign more than one Work Field. When a combination Work Field best reflects the overall objective of the job, specific Work Fields encompassed by the Combination Work Field are not assigned.

Step 3. Record in Item 8 of the JAR the code number(s) and title(s) of the Work Field(s) selected that reflect(s) the analysis of the data.

051	Abrading	272	Litigating
291	Accommodating	004	Logging
295	Administering	057	Lubricating
298	Advising-Counseling	033	Machining*
002	Animal Propagating	091	Masoning
211	Appraising	011	Material Moving
262	Artistic Painting-Drawing	121	Mechanical Fabricating-Installing-Repairing*
141	Baking-Drying	131	Melting
071	Bolting-Screwing	292	Merchandising-Sales
053	Boring	055	Milling-Turning-Planing
153	Brushing-Spraying	005	Mining-Quarrying-Earth Boring
034	Butchering-Meat Cutting	143	Mixing
094	Caulking	136	Molding
132	Casting	072	Nailing
052	Chipping	232	Numerical Recording-Recordkeeping
031	Cleaning	095	Paving
161	Combing-Napping	201	Photographing
263	Composing-Choreographing	003	Plant Cultivating
146	Cooking-Food Preparing	134	Pressing-Forging
142	Crushing-Grinding	191	Printing
233	Data Processing	147	Processing-Compounding*
135	Die Sizing	293	Protecting
202	Developing-Printing	014	Pumping
144	Distilling	251	Researching
242	Drafting	073	Riveting
111	Electrical-Electronic Fabricating-Installing Repairing*	152	Saturating
		056	Sawing
154	Electroplating	145	Separating
244	Engineering	171	Sewing-Tailoring
183	Engraving	054	Shearing-Shaving
297	Entertaining	083	Soldering-Brazing
182	Etching	162	Spinning
007	Excavating-Clearing-Foundation Building	021	Stationary Engineering
062	Fastening	221	Stock Checking
041	Filling-Packing-Wrapping	102	Structural Fabricating-Installing-Repairing*
061	Fitting-Folding	264	Styling
082	Flame Cutting-Arc Cutting-Beam Cutting	032	Surface Finishing
063	Gluing-Laminating	243	Surveying
294	Health Caring-Medical	281	System Communicating
133	Heat Conditioning	296	Teaching
001	Hunting-Fishing	013	Transporting
151	Immersing-Coating	166	Tufting
192	Imprinting	101	Upholstering*
282	Information Giving	231	Verbal Recording-Record Keeping
212	Inspecting-Measuring-Testing	164	Weaving
271	Investigating	081	Welding
165	Knitting	163	Winding
092	Laying-Covering	261	Writing
241	Laying Out		

*Combination Work Fields

WORK FIELDS ORGANIZATION

The Work Fields have been organized into the following groups on the basis of similar technologies. This arrangement may be helpful in ensuring the applicability of the Work Field(s) selected for the job being analyzed.

	ORGANIZATION	DESCRIPTION
001	Hunting-Fishing	Securing, producing, and cultivating raw materials,
002	Animal Propagating	products, and animals (livestock or game) on and
003	Plant Cultivating	below the surface of the earth; usually outdoor work.
004	Logging	
005	Mining-Quarrying-Earth Boring	
007	Excavating-Clearing-Foundation Building	Grading surfaces and building foundations.
011	Material Moving	Moving materials and people by hand and machine
013	Transporting	power.
014	Pumping	
021	Stationary Engineering	Producing and distributing heat, power, and conditioned air.
031	Cleaning	Industrial, commercial, and domestic cleaning.
032	Surface Finishing	Shaping, pressing, and stretching articles, usually with heat and steam, under tension or pressure.
033	Lubricating	Coating objects with liquid or dry lubricants.
034	Butchering-Meat Cutting	Slaughtering livestock and preparing meats for marketing.
041	Filling-Packing-Wrapping	Packaging materials and products for distribution and storage.
051	Abrading	Working with machines and handtools to cut and
052	Chipping	shape materials and objects usually made from wood,
053	Boring	metal, and plastics. Can also involve assembly of ob-
054	Shearing-Shaving	jects.
055	Milling-Turning-Planing	
056	Sawing	
057	Machining	
061	Fitting-Folding	Folding and assembling parts and materials, usually
062	Fastening	light, by means of fitting together or joining with sticky
063	Gluing-Laminating	compounds and fastening devices, such as staples, grommets, and snaps.
071	Bolting-Screwing	Assembling parts and materials, usually of metal,
072	Nailing	wood, and plastics, by means of screws, nails, rivets,
073	Riveting	or other fasteners.
081	Welding	Joining or cutting materials by means of a gas flame,
082	Flame Cutting-Arc Cutting-Beam Cutting	electric arc, laser beam, combination welding process, and soldering.
083	Soldering-Brazing	

ORGANIZATION		DESCRIPTION
091	Masoning	Building and repairing structures and surfaces, and assembling structural parts, usually working with brick, cement, mortar, stone, and other building materials.
092	Laying-Covering	
094	Caulking	
095	Paving	
101	Upholstering	All-around fabricating, installing, and repairing of structures, interior fittings, and electrical, electronic, and mechanical units.
102	Structural Fabricating-Installing-Repairing	
111	Electrical-Electronic Fabricating-Installing-Repairing	
121	Mechanical Fabricating-Installing-Repairing	
131	Melting	Compounding, melting, heat conditioning, and shaping objects, usually metal and plastics, by methods which involve heat or pressure or force.
132	Casting	
133	Heat Conditioning	
134	Pressing-Forging	
135	Die Sizing	
136	Molding	
141	Baking-Drying	Processing various materials, in solid, fluid, semifluid, and gaseous states, during production process.
142	Crushing-Grinding	
143	Mixing	
144	Distilling	
145	Separating	
146	Cooking-Food Preparing	
147	Processing-Compounding	
151	Immersing-Coating	Coating and impregnating materials and products to impart decorative and protective finish and other specific qualities.
152	Saturating	
153	Brushing-Spraying	
154	Electroplating	
161	Combing-Napping	Converting fiber raw stock into yarn and thread, and interlacing and otherwise working yarns to form woven, nonwoven, knitted, and tufted fabrics. Winding also includes coiling any material about an object.
162	Spinning	
163	Winding	
164	Weaving	
165	Knitting	
166	Tufting	
171	Sewing-Tailoring	Joining, mending, and fastening materials, usually with needle and thread, and fitting and adjusting parts.
182	Etching	Cutting designs and letters into materials and products by sandblasting, applying acids (Etching), and action of sharp pointed tools (Engraving).
183	Engraving	
191	Printing	Transferring letters and designs onto paper and other material, by use of ink and pressure; includes setting type and preparing plates.
192	Imprinting	
201	Photographing	Taking pictures and processing film.
202	Developing-Printing	
211	Appraising	Evaluating and estimating the quality, quantity, and value of things and data; ascertaining the physical characteristics of materials and objects.
212	Inspecting-Measuring-Testing	

ORGANIZATION		DESCRIPTION
221	Stock Checking	Receiving, storing, issuing, shipping, requisitioning, and accounting for stores of materials.
231	Verbal Recording-Record Keeping	Preparing and maintaining verbal and numerical records.
232	Numerical Recording-Record Keeping	
233	Data Processing	Planning, developing, testing, evaluating, and executing a systematic sequence of activities or operations to process alphabetic, numeric, and symbolic data or to solve problems by means of computer systems.
241	Laying Out	Plotting, tracing, and drawing diagrams and other directive graphic information for use in design and production; designing and constructing machinery, structures, and systems.
242	Drafting	
243	Surveying	
244	Engineering	
251	Researching	Controlled exploration of fundamental areas of knowledge, by means of critical and exhaustive investigation and experimentation.
261	Writing	Creating, expressing, or depicting one's own ideas in various media.
262	Artistic Painting-Drawing	
263	Composing-Choreographing	
264	Styling	
271	Investigating	Obtaining and evaluating data for purposes of completing business and legal procedures.
272	Litigating	
281	System Communicating	Providing and effecting the transmission of information to other persons, indirectly (by electrical or electronic media) and directly (by voice or written statement).
282	Information Giving	
291	Accommodating	Dealing with people to provide services of various types.
292	Merchandising-Sales	
293	Protecting	
294	Health Caring-Medical	
295	Administering	
296	Teaching	
297	Entertaining	
298	Advising-Counseling	

LIST OF COMBINATION WORK FIELDS

The following is a list of combination Work Fields and the corresponding component Work Fields of which they are comprised.

COMBINATION WORK FIELDS		COMPONENT WORK FIELDS
057	Machining	Abrading (051), Boring (053), Chipping (052), Milling-Turning-Planing (055), Sawing (056), and Shearing-Shaving (054).
101	Upholstering	Bolting-Screwing (071), Gluing-Laminating (063), Nailing (072), Sewing-Tailoring (171), and Shearing-Shaving (054).
102	Structural Fabricating-Installing-Repairing	Abrading (051), Bolting-Screwing (071), Boring (053), Brushing-Spraying (153), Caulking (094), Chipping (052), Fastening (062), Fitting-Folding (061), Flame Cutting-Arc Cutting-Beam Cutting (082), Gluing-Laminating (063), Immersing-Coating (151), Laying-Covering (092), Masoning (091), Milling-Turning-Planing (055), Molding (136), Nailing (072), Paving (095), Sawing (056), Sewing-Tailoring (171), Shearing-Shaving (054), Soldering-Brazing (083), and Welding (081).
111	Electrical-Electronic Fabricating-Installing-Repairing	Abrading (051), Bolting-Screwing (071), Boring (053), Fitting-Folding (061), Nailing (072), Riveting (073), Soldering-Brazing (083), Welding (081), and Winding (163).
121	Mechanical Fabricating-Installing-Repairing	Abrading (051), Bolting-Screwing (071), Boring (053), Brushing-Spraying (153), Chipping (052), Fastening (062), Fitting-Folding (061), Flame Cutting-Arc Cutting-Beam Cutting (082), Gluing-Laminating (063), Immersing-Coating (151), Milling-Turning-Planing (055), Nailing (072), Pressing-Forging (134), Riveting (073), Sawing (056), Sewing-Tailoring (171), Shearing-Shaving (054), Soldering-Brazing (083), and Welding (081).
147	Processing-Compounding	Baking-Drying (141), Distilling (144), Heat Conditioning (133), Melting (131), Mixing (143), Saturating (152), and Separating (145).

WORK FIELDS DESCRIPTIONS

001 HUNTING-FISHING

Capturing and killing wild land and marine animals for such purposes as bounty, conservation, research, and for their value as meat or skin.

Baiting	Dredging	Seining	Tonging
Dipping	Hooking	Shooting	Trapping
Dragging	Raking	Spearing	Trawling

Typical Occupations: Fisher; Trapper; Dredger; Fishing-Boat Captain; Deckhand.

002 ANIMAL PROPAGATING

Raising and caring for livestock, poultry, fish, and other animal life and collecting eggs, milk, wool, honey, and other animal products by methods which may include those specific to other work fields.

Bailing	Feeding	Netting	Spawning
Branding	Fumigating	Pelting (mink)	Sterilizing
Candling	Grooming	Rounding Up	Training
Caponizing	Hatching	Separating	Vaccinating
Castrating	Herding	Sexing (poultry)	Washing (eggs)
Debeaking	Incubating	Shearing (sheep)	Watering
Dehorning	Inseminating	Shoeing (horses)	
Disinfecting	Milking	Skinning	
Dredging (shellfish)	Milting	Sowing	

Typical Occupations: Animal Breeder; Dairy Farmer; Poultry-Farm Worker; Beekeeper; Artificial Inseminator; Milker; Animal Herder.

003 PLANT CULTIVATING

Planting, nurturing, harvesting, and otherwise caring for plant life by methods which may include those specific to other work fields.

Bailing	Fertilizing	Plowing	Stringing
Budding	Gathering	Potting	Thinning
Conditioning (soil)	Grading	Propagating	Threshing
Culling	Grafting	Pruning	Tilling
Curing (tobacco)	Harrowing	Raking	Transplanting
Cutting	Hoeing	Reaping	Watering
Detasseling	Husking	Shelling	Weeding
Digging	Irrigating	Sorting	Winnowing
Disking	Mowing	Sowing	
Drying	Mulching	Spading	
Dusting	Picking	Spraying	

Typical Occupations: Farm-Equipment Operator; Landscaper; Gardener; Crop Farmer; Farm Hand; Harvest Worker; Nursery Worker.

004 LOGGING

Extracting wood and forest products from woodlands, including felling and cutting of trees into logs or other products and collecting gums, saps, or resins.

Boxing	Felling	Riving	Towing
Bucking	Hewing	Sawing	
Chopping	Notching	Skidding	
Cruising	Rafting	Splitting	

Typical Occupations: Logger; Tree-Shear Operator; River; Laborer, Tree Tapping; Supervisor, Felling Bucking.

005 MINING-QUARRYING-EARTH BORING

Extracting minerals, oil, gas, water, and stone from the earth. Includes drilling earth formations to obtain core samples.

Blasting	Chipping	Digging	Perforating
Breaking	Crushing	Panning	

Typical Occupations: Miner; Driller; Blaster; Quarry Supervisor; Mine Supervisor; Well Driller; Quarry Worker; Prospector.

007 EXCAVATING-CLEARING-FOUNDATION BUILDING

Removing and distributing earth materials, such as dirt, gravel, rock, and sand; grading surfaces; dredging ditches, canals, and marine channels; drilling holes in earth and through rock formations for purposes other than blasting and mineral extractions; and driving pilings and shafts into earth for structural footings. Includes clearing away obstacles preparatory to construction and logging, and controlling growth of weeds, trees, bushes, etc., to facilitate maintenance of utility lines and rights-of-way.

Backfilling	Cutting	Raking
Burning	Digging	Trimming

Typical Occupations: Tree Trimmer; Pile-Driver Operator; Dredge Operator; Dredging Inspector; Brush Clearer; Grade Operator; Levee Superintendent; Pile-Driving Supervisor; Motor Grader Operator; Bulldozer Operator.

011 MATERIAL MOVING

Conveying materials manually and by use of machines and equipment, such as cranes, hoists, conveyors, industrial trucks, elevators, winches, and handtrucks. Distinguish from Transporting (013), which involves conveyance of passengers and materials by common carrier.

Carrying	Forking	Relaying	Unloading
Dragging	Hanging	Shackling	Wheeling
Drawing	Hoisting	Shoveling	
Dumping	Lifting	Skidding	
Floating	Loading	Throwing	

Typical Occupations: Fork-Lift Operator; Crane Operator; Stevedore; Freight-Elevator Operator; Hoist Operator; Conveyor Worker.

013 TRANSPORTING

Conveying passengers and materials by truck, bus, airplane, train, ship, automobile, and other vehicles. Distinguish from Material Moving (011), which involves moving materials by conveyances other than common carriers.

Driving	Landing	Steering	Taking Off
Flying	Piloting	Stoking	

Typical Occupations: Vehicle Driver; Airplane Pilot; Marine-Vessel Captain; Locomotive Engineer.

014 PUMPING

Raising, lowering, and moving gases, liquids, and solids by suction, pressure, and vacuum within a piping system.

Draining	Expelling	Siphoning
Drawing (off or out)	Propelling	Sucking

Typical Occupations: Pump Operator-Gauger; Terminal Supervisor; Oil Dispatcher.

021 STATIONARY ENGINEERING

Producing and distributing heat, power, and conditioned air.

Compressing (air)	Firing	Humidifying	Refrigerating
Cooling	Generating	Purifying	Ventilating

Typical Occupations: Boiler Operator; Stationary Engineer; Compressor Operator; Powerhouse Attendant; Power Dispatcher.

031 CLEANING

Cleaning objects and premises by methods such as washing with water, steam, and cleaning agents; brushing, wiping, sweeping, raking, and scraping; using suction, compressed air, and ultrasonic equipment.

Agitating	Fluffing	Scrubbing	Spotting
Beating	Flushing	Shaking	Steaming
Blowing	Hosing	Shoveling	Straining
Chipping	Immersing	Soaking	Tumbling
Dusting	Mopping	Sopping	
Filtering	Scalding	Sponging	

Typical Occupations: Laundry Worker; Dishwasher; Equipment Cleaner; Janitor; Housekeeper; Cleaning Supervisor.

032 SURFACE FINISHING

Removing wrinkles from, restoring shape to, and giving finish to articles made of fabric, fur, leather, straw, paper, and similar materials by application of tension or pressure (usually accompanied by heat or steam). Includes burning excess materials from surfaces of articles.

Blocking (hats)	Gassing	Rubbing	Stretching
Brushing	Ironing	Singeing	Texturing
Calendering	Pressing	Steaming	

Typical Occupations: Ironer; Presser (Hand and Machine); Hat Blocker; Tenter-Frame Operator; Singeing-Machine Operator; Calender-Machine Operator.

033 LUBRICATING

Coating objects with lubricants to reduce friction of moving parts and to prevent sticking.

Dusting	Greasing	Spraying	Waxing
Graphiting	Oiling	Swabbing	

Typical Occupations: Oiler; Greaser; Automobile Lubricator.

034 BUTCHERING-MEAT CUTTING

Killing and cutting up animals, poultry, finfish, and shellfish, and dressing or processing meats for marketing.

Bleeding	Flushing	Scraping	Skinning
Boning	Gutting	Shackling	Striking
Cleaving	Plucking	Shaving	Stripping
Eviscerating	Sawing	Singeing	Trimming

Typical Occupations: Butcher; Meat Cutter; Poultry Worker; Slaughterhouse Worker; Hide Puller; Dehairing-Machine Operator; Fish Cleaner.

041 FILLING-PACKING-WRAPPING

Pouring dry and liquid materials and products into containers; enveloping and enclosing materials and products in paper, cellophane, burlap, and other materials; putting materials and products into containers; or closing and sealing containers. Includes unpacking, unwrapping, and refilling.

Banding	Dropping	Moistening	Strapping
Boxing	Dumping	Padding	Stripping
Bunching	Folding	Peeling Off	Twisting
Channeling	Funneling	Securing	Tying
Covering	Injecting	Spooning	
Draping	Inserting	Stacking	

Typical Occupations: Packager; Filling-Machine Operator; Baling-Machine Operator; Wrapping-Machine Operator; Packaging Supervisor; Bagger.

051 ABRADING

Smoothing, polishing, sharpening, or cutting materials by use of abrasives; and cutting letters and designs into objects and structures by the wearing-away action of abrasives. Distinguish from Cleaning (031), in which abrasives may be used to remove foreign substances.

Blowing	Frosting	Pouncing	Sandpapering
Buffing	Grinding	Rubbing	Scraping
Filing	Honing	Sandblasting	
Finishing	Lapping	Sanding	

Typical Occupations: Sandblaster; Grinder; Polisher; Honer; Glass Beveler; Tumbling-Machine Operator; Bit Sharpener; Sander.

052 CHIPPING

Cutting away flakes and fragments with hatchets and chisels struck with hammers or similarly activated by a power source, such as compressed air. Distinguish from Milling-Turning-Planing (055), in which rotary or chisel-like cutters are used but without percussion.

Breaking Up	Chiseling	Gouging	Striking
Broaching	Chopping	Hewing	Wedging

Typical Occupations: Chiseler; Chipper; Air-Hammer Operator.

053 BORING

Making, enlarging, and threading holes in material (other than earth) by means of rotary cutting tools advanced into the material. Distinguish from piercing by Pressing-Forging (134), in which tools do not rotate.

Countersinking	Piercing	Tapping
Drilling	Reaming	

Typical Occupations: Boring-Machine Operator; Drill-Press Operator; Reaming-Machine Tender; Countersinker; Driller.

054 SHEARING-SHAVING

Cutting, severing, slicing, and shaving materials, using keen-edged cutting tools. Includes cutting glass, plastics, and other materials with heated wires. Distinguish from Sawing (056), which involves use of serrated tools to cut materials by wearing out a kerf.

Clipping	Die Cutting	Snipping	Trimming

Typical Occupations: Hot-Wire Cutter; Die Cutter; Fabric Cutter; Fabric Trimmer; Slitting-Machine Operator; Shearing-Machine Operator; Cutting-Department Supervisor; Book Trimmer; Shoe-Parts Cutter; Plastic-Material Cutter; Skiving-Machine Operator.

055 MILLING-TURNING-PLANING

Shaping materials by the paring and smoothing action of rigid cutting tools (usually fed into rotating materials) and rotating cutting tools (usually fed into stationary materials). Distinguish from Chipping (052), in which the cutting away of flakes and fragments is accomplished by chisel-like tools actuated by a percussive power source.

Broaching	Grooving	Rabbeting	Shaving
Dadoing	Mortising	Routing	Tonguing
Gaining	Profiling	Scarfing	Undercutting

Typical Occupations: Lathe Operator; Milling-Machine Operator; Machine Setter; Wood-Carving-Machine Operator; Tooth Cutter; Gear Cutter; Screw-Machine Operator.

056 SAWING

Severing and shaping materials by the reciprocal or rotary cutting action of a blade which wears out a kerf. The blade may be serrated or be made of, or coated with, abrasives. Excluded from this work field is the felling of trees, which is covered by Logging (004). Distinguish from Shearing-Shaving (054), which includes a severing function but without wearing a kerf.

Crosscutting	Gaining	Mitering	Tenoning
Dadoing	Grooving	Ripsawing	

Typical Occupations: Cut-Off-Saw Operator; Band-Saw Operator; Gang Sawyer; Kerf-Machine Operator; Last Trimmer.

057 MACHINING

Shaping parts by any combination of the following work fields: Abrading (051), Boring (053), Chipping (052), Milling-Turning-Planing (055), Sawing (056), and Shearing-Shaving (054).

Forming

Typical Occupations: Shop Machinist; Tool-and-Die Maker; Shop Supervisor; Job Setter.

061 FITTING-FOLDING

Folding, joining, and fitting parts without the use of bolts, screws, nails, rivets, solder, welding equipment, and glue. This work field includes such job activities as interlacing and joining parts, such as boards and precut and fabricated wood or metal units; fitting together parts of shoes; putting coils and insulation into frames to form stators; assembling parts of mechanical pencils; pressing bushings into bearing housings; and putting together pins and buttons to form campaign badges. Distinguish from Fastening (062), which involves joining materials by fastening with staples, eyelets, grommets, and snaps.

Bending	Hanging	Packing	Springing
Bracing	Inlaying	Pulling	Squeezing
Clamping	Inserting	Pushing	Tapping
Clinching	Interweaving	Shoving	Threading
Creasing	Inverting	Sliding	Tightening
Crimping	Jamming	Slipping	Twisting
Hammering	Looping	Splicing	Wedging

Typical Occupations: Pen Assembler; Folder; Stringer; Basket Maker; Clock-and-Watch Parts Assembler; Pleater.

062 FASTENING

Joining lightweight material (such as paper, cardboard, and fabrics) with fasteners, such as staples, eyelets, grommets, and snaps. Assignment is not made when the joining of materials involves methods applicable to other work fields, such as Bolting-Screwing (071), Fitting-Folding (061), Gluing-Laminating (063), Nailing (072), Riveting (073), Soldering-Brazing (083), and Welding (081).

Clinching	Inserting	Shoving	Threading
Compressing	Inverting	Sliding	Tightening
Creasing	Jamming	Slipping	Twisting
Crimping	Looping	Splicing	Wedging
Hammering	Pressing	Springing	
Hanging	Pulling	Squeezing	
Inlaying	Pushing	Tapping	

Typical Occupations: Stitching-Machine Operator; Stapler; Eyelet-Machine Operator; Wreath Maker.

063 GLUING-LAMINATING

Fastening together parts with sticky substances, such as cement, glue, paste, gum, and other adhesive media. Includes bonding of parts by application of heat and pressure.

Brushing	Daubing	Pressing	Stretching
Clamping	Fusing	Rolling	Wetting
Compressing	Moistening	Spreading	

Typical Occupations: Cementer; Glue-Machine Operator; Combining-Machine Operator; Bonding-Machine Operator; Cloth Laminator; Hot-Press Worker; Heat-Sealing-Machine Operator.

071 BOLTING-SCREWING

Fastening together parts with threaded bolts and screws fitted through adjoining holes previously bored and threaded, or by forcing threaded screws through parts. In some instances, holes may be partially bored but not prethreaded to accommodate screws, or bolts may be secured in place by inserting them in threaded nuts. Distinguish from Riveting (073), which involves the use of nonthreaded bolts to fasten parts.

Tapping	Threading	Tightening	Twisting

Typical Occupations: Clock-and-Watch-Parts Assembler; Power-Tool Operator; Vehicle-Light Assembler; Screw Remover; Wooden-Heel Attacher; Spring Assembler.

072 NAILING

Fastening together parts with devices, such as nails, tacks, spikes, brads, and staples. Distinguish from Riveting (073), in which a nonthreaded fastening device is secured by hammering and pressing to spread protruding shank ends. Distinguish from Fastening (062), where light materials are joined.

Driving (nails)	Stapling	Tacking
Hammering	Striking	

Typical Occupations: Nailer; Shoe-Parts Assembler; Stapler; Tack Puller; Tacker.

073 RIVETING

Fastening parts with headed, malleable bolts, pins, and rods fitted through previously bored holes, and hammering and pressing shank ends. Distinguish from Fastening (062), which involves joining light materials.

Bucking	Dimpling	Hammering	Squeezing
Clinching	Driving	Peening	

Typical Occupations: Riveter; Riveting Inspector.

081 WELDING

Joining metal, glass, and plastic parts by heating surfaces to induce fusion with or without the application of filler materials and pressure. Forge-welding, which involves applying sharp blows, is covered by Pressing-Forging (134). Distinguish from Flame Cutting-Arc Cutting-Beam Cutting (082), in which similar equipment is used to sever parts, and from Soldering-Brazing (083), which involves joining parts by the adhesion of solder.

Burning	Melting	Stirring
Fusing	Puddling	

Typical Occupations: Welder; Welding Supervisor; Welding Inspector; Lead Burner.

082 FLAME CUTTING-ARC CUTTING-BEAM CUTTING

Severing materials by subjecting materials to intense heat, using equipment, such as oxyacetylene torches, electric-arc cutting equipment, and laser beams. Distinguish from Welding (081), which may use the same equipment but for the purpose of joining materials. Cutting by use of hot-wire is included in Shearing-Shaving (054).

Burning	Scarfing	Scraping

Typical Occupations: Flame Cutter; Scrap Burner; Scarfing Operator; Laser-Beam Cutter.

083 SOLDERING-BRAZING

Joining metal parts or filling depressions in metal with molten solder or brazing alloy. Distinguish from Welding (081), in which parts are joined by fusion under heat.

Dipping	Melting	Smoothing	Sweating
Heating	Rubbing	Spreading	

Typical Occupations: Brazer; Solderer; Furnace Operator; Brazing Assembler.

091 MASONING

Constructing structures of brick, stone, marble, and similar building materials, usually set in beds of mortar; and spreading and smoothing plaster, mortar, stucco, and similar materials to form and cover structural elements. Distinguish from Laying-Covering (092), in which materials are fastened to surfaces as finish and insulating coverings.

Bricking	Imbedding	Rubbing	Tamping
Brushing	Patching	Scraping	Tapping
Finishing	Pointing	Setting	Tearing Out
Floating	Pressing	Spattering	Wetting

Typical Occupations: Mason; Plasterer; Plastering Supervisor; Concrete Finisher.

092 LAYING-COVERING

Covering the surface of structural units, such as roofs, floors, pipes, duct work, tanks, boilers, and refrigeration and air-conditioning equipment, or objects with materials in the form of sheets, blocks, tile, and rolled goods (including insulation bats). Distinguish from Masoning (091), which involves constructing as well as covering structural units; from Gluing-Laminating (063), which involves fastening parts together to assemble rather than cover; and from Caulking (094), which includes filling spaces with loose insulating materials.

Cementing	Pasting	Rolling	Tamping
Gluing	Patching	Smoothing	Tapping
Inlaying	Pointing	Spreading	Tying
Matching	Pressing	Stapling	Wrapping

Typical Occupations: Floor Layer; Carpet Layer; Roofer; Insulation Worker; Pipe Coverer; Siding Installer.

094 CAULKING

Sealing and filling holes, crevices, cracks, joints, seams, depressions, and other spaces with a material (other than solder) for such purposes as making object or structure airtight, waterproof, and weatherproof. Includes the blowing of loose insulation materials into open spaces, but not the laying of insulation material as a cover, which is included in Laying-Covering (092).

Blowing (loose insulating materials)	Hammering	Ramming	Smoothing
	Puttying	Scraping	

Typical Occupations: Putty Spreader; Caulker; Hole Filler; Insulation Blower; Plywood-Panel Sealer; Barrel Liner.

095 PAVING

Covering surfaces with materials, such as asphalt, concrete, tar, oil, and gravel.

Compacting	Oiling	Scraping	Tamping
Filling	Patching	Smoothing	
Leveling	Rolling	Spreading	

Typical Occupations: Paving-Machine Operator; Spreader Operator; Curbing-Machine Operator; Paving Supervisor; Sprayer Operator.

101 UPHOLSTERING

Covering, padding, trimming, or renovating upholstered furniture, mattresses, car seats, automobile, train, or aircraft interiors, and the like by any combination of Bolting-Screwing, Gluing, Nailing, Sewing, and Shearing-Shaving. Jobs involved with only one of these work fields are listed thereunder.

Draping	Packing	Spreading	Tacking
Measuring	Padding	Stretching	Tufting
Molding	Smoothing	Stuffing	Tying

Typical Occupations: Automobile Upholsterer; Furniture Upholsterer; Upholstery Repairer; Upholsterer, Assembly Line.

102 STRUCTURAL FABRICATING-INSTALLING-REPAIRING

Fabricating, installing, and repairing structures and objects whose components are static and may require shaping to fit by any combination of the following work fields: Abrading (051), Bolting-Screwing (071), Boring (053), Brushing-Spraying (153), Caulking (094), Chipping (052), Fastening (062), Fitting-Folding (061), Flame Cutting-Arc Cutting-Beam Cutting (082), Gluing-Laminating (063), Immersing-Coating (151), Laying-Covering (092), Masoning (091), Milling-Turning-Planing (055), Molding (136), Nailing (072), Paving (095), Pressing-Forging (134), Riveting (073), Sawing (056), Sewing-Tailoring (171), Shearing-Shaving (054), Soldering-Brazing (083), and Welding (081).

Aligning	Clinching	Measuring	Sinking
Anchoring	Coupling	Padding	Splicing
Blocking Up	Glazing	Plumbing	Staying
Bracing	Knocking Down	Positioning	Truing
Cementing	Leveling	Prying	
Clamping	Lining Up	Rigging	

Typical Occupations: Construction Inspector; Carpenter; Boat Builder and Repairer; Boilermaker; Musical-Instrument Maker; Cabinetmaker; Cooper; Aircraft Assembler; Structural-Steel Erector; Pipefitter; Plumber; Propmaker.

111 ELECTRICAL-ELECTRONIC FABRICATING-INSTALLING-REPAIRING

Fabricating, installing, and repairing objects that have electrical and electronic functioning elements by any combination of the following work fields: Abrading (051), Bolting-Screwing (071), Boring (053), Fitting-Folding (061), Nailing (072), Riveting (073), Soldering-Brazing (083), Welding (081), and Winding (163). Distinguish from Structural Fabricating-Installing-Repairing (102) and Mechanical Fabricating-Installing-Repairing (121).

Calibrating	Plugging In	Testing	Twisting
Connecting	Stringing	Threading	Wiring
Hooking Up	Switching	Turning	

Typical Occupations: Electrician; Instrument Mechanic; Appliance Assembler; Electronics Tester; Electrical-Equipment Installer; Electrical-Systems Installer and Repairer; Telephone-and-Telegraph Equipment Installer and Repairer.

121 MECHANICAL FABRICATING-INSTALLING-REPAIRING

Fabricating, installing, and repairing objects that have moving parts of mechanically functioning elements by any combination of the following work fields: Abrading (051), Bolting-Screwing (071), Boring (053), Brushing-Spraying (153), Chipping (052), Fastening (062), Fitting-Folding (061), Flame Cutting-Arc Cutting-Beam Cutting (082), Gluing-Laminating (063), Immersing-Coating (151), Milling-Turning-Planing (055), Nailing (072), Pressing-Forging (134), Riveting (073), Sawing (056), Sewing-Tailoring (171), Shearing-Shaving (054), Soldering-Brazing (083), and Welding (081).

Aligning   Calibrating

Typical Occupations: Machinist; Tool-and-Die Maker; Automobile Mechanic; Air-Conditioning Mechanic; Gunsmith; Maintenance Mechanic; Watch Repairer.

131 MELTING

Changing materials from solid to liquid state (usually by heat) for such purposes as compounding with other materials, refining by separation (through accompanying chemical change), and making materials amenable to shaping and casting. Distinguish from Soldering-Brazing (083), and Welding (081), in which melting occurs incidental to joining parts together.

Agitating	Firing	Loading	Tapping
Charting	Fluxing	Pouring	Throwing
Drawing	Fueling	Shoveling	
Dumping	Heating	Skimming	
Filling	Kindling	Stirring	

Typical Occupations: Foundry Supervisor; Open-Hearth-Furnace Operator; Blast-Furnace Supervisor.

132 CASTING

Shaping materials by pouring, injecting, and pressing into a mold and permitting or causing to solidify. Distinguish from Die Sizing (135), in which shaping is effected by dies and rollers; Molding (136), in which shaping is dependent on worker; and Pressing-Forging (134), which involves application of force or sharp blows to accomplish shaping.

Blowing	Flooding	Placing (in mold)
Brushing	Inflating	Stretching
Filling	Kneading	Throwing (in mold)

Typical Occupations: Die-Casting-Machine Operator; Coremaker; Bowling-Ball Molder; Injection-Molding-Machine Tender.

133 HEAT CONDITIONING

Hardening, softening, and toughening materials by heating and cooling with or without accompanying chemical change. Materials may be subjected to heat alone to alter molecular structure of materials and induce special qualities, such as hardness, flexibility, and ductility; or material may be treated with heat aided by carbonizing materials and chemical baths to impart a hard "skin" to the material. Included also is the activity in which materials are heated to treat them for further processing (e.g., bringing metal bars to prescribed red-hot temperature).

Annealing	Freezing	Plunging
Bluing	Immersing	Quenching
Drawing	Packing	Refrigerating

Typical Occupations: Heat-Treat Supervisor; Annealer; Glass Bender; Rivet Heater.

134 PRESSING-FORGING

Shaping, severing, piercing, and forge-welding materials by a force pushed against or through materials, or by applying sharp blows (as in hammering). Distinguish from Casting (132), in which molds are used to shape material; Die Sizing (135), which utilizes dies and rollers in shaping; Surface Finishing (032), which is predominately fabric oriented; and Molding (136), which involves the cumulative addition of material to original mass (by worker) in accomplishing shaping of material.

Beating	Dimpling	Molding	Striking
Braking	Dishing	Pounding	Swaging
Clipping	Drawing	Rolling	Twisting
Coiling	Flaring	Shearing	
Compressing	Hitting	Spinning	
Crimping	Kneading	Stamping	

Typical Occupations: Blacksmith; Forge-Shop Supervisor; Punch-Press Operator; Hammersmith.

135 DIE SIZING

Shaping material by forcing it through dies, drawing it through dies, and reducing it between rollers. Distinguish from Casting (132), in which shaping is achieved by use of molds; Surface Finishing (032), which is fabric oriented; Molding (136), which involves a cumulative buildup (by worker) in shaping materials; and Pressing-Forging (134), in which force or sharp blows are applied.

Compressing	Pouring	Ramming	Squeezing
Extruding	Pressing	Rollforging	Stamping
Measuring	Pulling	Rolling	Straining

Typical Occupations: Chalk-Extruding-Machine Operator; Cold-Rolling Supervisor; Extrusion Supervisor.

136 MOLDING

Shaping material by cumulative addition of material (by worker) to build up original mass and pressing material into shape. Includes removing excess material to obtain finished product. Distinguish from Casting (132), in which shaping is primarily dependent on molds to shape material; Die Sizing (135), which utilizes dies or rollers to accomplish shaping; and Pressing-Forging (134), which involves applying a force or sharp blows to shape material.

Compacting	Laying	Rolling	Spreading
Forming	Moistening	Smearing	Stuffing
Jolting	Packing	Smoothing	Taping
Kneading	Padding	Softening	Vulcanizing

Typical Occupations: Concrete Sculptor; Cigarmaker; Candlemaker; Artificial-Plastic-Eye Maker; Vulcanizer.

141 BAKING-DRYING

Drying, solidifying, tenderizing, and otherwise subjecting materials to heat. Distinguish from Distilling (144), in which heating results in the refinement, concentration, and condensation of substances, gases, and vapors; and from Heat Conditioning (133), in which treatment of materials with heat induces special qualities, such as hardness, flexibility, and ductility.

Burning	Firing	Seasoning (lumber)
Curing	Fluffing	Smoking
Dehydrating	Roasting	Tumbling

Typical Occupations: Fish Smoker; Cocoa-Bean Roaster; Tobacco Curer; Veneer-Drier Supervisor; Kiln Firer.

142 CRUSHING-GRINDING

Reducing and separating materials into smaller particles, such as granules, grits, crumbs, chips, powder, paste, and pulp, by means of compressing, cutting, and smashing.

Beating	Dispersing	Milling (grain)	Rolling
Blowing	Kneading	Pulpifying	Tapping
Chopping	Mashing	Pulverizing	Tumbling

Typical Occupations: Miller Supervisor; Powdered-Sugar-Pulverizer Operator; Concrete-Patch-Plant Operator; Wood-Grinder Operator; Pulper.

143 MIXING

Combining and mingling liquid and solid materials to produce a single mass or compound.

Agitating	Dissolving	Scooping	Stirring
Blending	Homogenizing	Scraping	

Typical Occupations: Feed Blender; Paint Mixer; Fertilizer Mixer; Tobacco Blender; Clay-Preparation Supervisor.

144 DISTILLING

Refining and concentrating substances (following expulsion of gases and vapors) and recapturing and condensing gases and vapors driven off by heating liquids and solids in retorts, stills, and similar equipment.

Boiling Off	Compressing	Drawing Off	Melting
Breaking Down	Cooling	Evaporating	Percolating
Burning	Cracking	Firing	Refluxing
Charging	Dehydrogenating	Liquefying	Sweating (wax)

Typical Occupations: Fermentation Operator; Still Operator; Tomato-Paste Maker; Sugar Boiler.

145 SEPARATING

Separating substances and materials in mixtures from remainder of mixture components for purposes other than cleaning by means of filtering, sifting, straining, squeezing, centrifugal pressure, gravity, precipitation, and agitation.

Blowing	Drawing Off	Pressing	Sizing
Bolting (grain)	Gauging	Screening	Stirring
Draining	Heating	Shaking	Washing

Typical Occupations: Centrifugal Operator; Nut Sorter; Filter Tender; Brine-Tank-Separator Operator; Char-Filter Operator; Cocoa-Press Operator.

146 COOKING-FOOD PREPARING

Preparing food for human and animal consumption, by methods which may include those specific to other defined work fields. Distinguish from Butchering-Meat Cutting (034), which involves slaughtering domestic animals, poultry, and fish, and dressing and processing meats for marketing.

Basting	Flavoring	Pasteurizing	Seasoning
Boiling	Frying	Pickling	Spreading
Brewing	Heating	Rendering	Squeezing
Churning	Kneading	Roasting	
Curing	Measuring	Rolling	

Typical Occupations: Brewer; Chef; Cottage-Cheese Maker; Baker; Cook.

147 PROCESSING-COMPOUNDING

Processing materials other than food and photographs to attain desired results by any combination of the following work fields: Baking-Drying (141), Distilling (144), Heat Conditioning (133), Melting (131), Mixing (143), Saturating (152), and Separating (145). Distinguish from Cooking-Food Preparing (146), which involves food processing and from Developing-Printing (202), which involves reproducing records of data and designs by chemical means.

Amalgamating	Compounding	Oxidizing	Roasting
Boiling	Cooking	Percolating	Stirring
Carbonating	Heating	Polymerizing	Titrating
Charging	Neutralizing	Precipitating	

Typical Occupations: Chemical-Laboratory Technician; Pharmacist; Refinery Operator.

151 IMMERSING-COATING

Covering the surface of objects with a protective and decorative coating of liquid materials which dry and set by plunging, dipping, and otherwise submerging objects in the material. Distinguish from Brushing-Spraying (153), which does not involve the immersing method of coating; from Electroplating (154), in which immersing is a step in the electrolytic treatment of objects; and from Saturating (152), which involves impregnating materials rather than covering and coating objects.

Draining	Rolling	Suspending
Dumping	Squeezing	Wiping

Typical Occupations: Coating-Machine Operator; Dipper; Impregnating-Tank Operator; Roofing-Machine Operator; Wire-Coating Supervisor.

152 SATURATING

Impregnating materials with other substances (generally in solution) by dyeing, starching, shrinking, preserving, and softening to impart particular qualities. Distinguish from Brushing-Spraying (153), which involves coating without immersion; Electroplating (154), which involves electrolytic treatment of objects; and Immersing-Coating (151), which involves covering and coating materials.

Bleaching	Liming	Spraying	Stirring
Boiling	Moistening	Spreading	Submerging
Immersing	Rinsing	Steaming	

Typical Occupations: Rug Dyer; Shoe Dyer; Bleach-Range Operator; Cloth-Mercerizer Operator; Hide-and-Skin Colorer.

153 BRUSHING-SPRAYING

Covering the surfaces of objects with protective and decorative coating, such as waxes, paints, lacquers, and other compounds that dry and set. Equipment and tools used generally include brushes, rollers, and spray guns. Distinguish from Immersing-Coating (151), which involves submerging objects in solutions, and from Artistic Painting-Drawing (262), which involves producing designs or lettering.

Burning Off	Matching	Rubbing	Staining
Filling	Mixing	Scraping	Varnishing
Masking	Rolling	Spreading	Whitewashing

Typical Occupations: Jewelry Coater; Electrostatic Painter; House Painter; Spray Painter; Waterproofing Supervisor.

154 ELECTROPLATING

Covering the surface of objects with a coating of material by electrolysis. Distinguish from Immersing-Coating (151), in which coating is not accomplished by electrical action, although immersing the objects is a step in the process.

Brushing	Dusting	Immersing
Dipping	Electrodepositing	Rolling

Typical Occupations: Electrogalvanizing-Machine Operator; Production Plater; Optical-Glass Silverer; Zinc-Plating-Machine Operator.

161 COMBING-NAPPING

Cleaning, disentangling, and straightening material by forcing it through prongs of a comb and raising and producing a nap on materials. Includes such mechanical action as directing jets of air against yarn to change its physical structure and increase its bulk.

Fluffing	Shredding	Texturing
Pulling	Splitting	

Typical Occupations: Carding Supervisor; Comber Tender; Card Tender; Napper Tender; Mannequin-Wig Maker.

162 SPINNING

Combining, drawing out, and twisting material into strand-like form. Distinguish from Die-Sizing (135), in which material (usually metal and plastic) may be extruded and drawn into strand-like form, but without twisting.

Splicing	Threading	Tying

Typical Occupations: Drawing-Frame Tender; Winding-and-Twisting-Department Supervisor; Bow-String Maker; Frame Spinner.

163 WINDING

Coiling material about an object to form a spool or ball of the material or to cover the object.

Bunching	Lacing	Splitting	Threading
Coning	Reeling	Spooling	Tying

Typical Occupations: Yarn Winder; Cloth-Winding Supervisor; Wire-Winding-Machine Tender; Coil Winder; Mainspring Winder and Oiler.

164 WEAVING

Interlacing strands of yarns, wires, and other strand-like materials with other yarns, wires, and other strand-like materials to form textiles, wire, and similar products. Distinguish from Knitting (165), in which single strands are looped, and Tufting (166), in which interlacing is not present.

Braiding	Drawing	Picking
Doffing	Knotting	Tying

Typical Occupations: Endless-Belt-Weaving Supervisor; Carpet Weaver; Weaving Supervisor.

165 KNITTING

Interlacing strands of material in a series of connected loops to form textiles, wire, and similar products. Distinguish from Weaving (164), in which multiple strands are interlaced, and Tufting (166), in which no interlacing occurs.

Creeling	Hooking	Looping	Threading
Crocheting	Knotting	Stringing	Tying

Typical Occupations: Knitting-Machine Operator; Seamless-Hosiery Knitter; Knitting Supervisor; Trawl-Net Maker.

166 TUFTING

Inserting tufts and loops of yarn through material, by hand and machine, without interlacing or interlocking yarn. Distinguish from Weaving (164), which involves interlacing of strands; from Knitting (165), in which strands are looped; and from Sewing-Tailoring (171), which involves fastening materials principally with needle and thread.

Clustering	Drawing Through	Hooking

Typical Occupations: Tufting Supervisor; Rug-Frame Mounter; Tuft-Machine Operator; Rug Hooker; Burler.

171 SEWING-TAILORING

Joining, mending, and fastening materials with needle and thread by hand and machine. Includes simulated sewing by ultrasonic machines.

Basting	Gathering	Padding	Serging
Binding	Hemming	Patching	Stretching
Darning	Hemstitching	Puckering	Stuffing
Embroidering	Measuring	Ripping	Tucking

Typical Occupations: Luggage Repairer; Book-Sewing-Machine Operator; Quilting-Machine Operator; Upholstery Sewer; Ultrasonic-Seaming-Machine Operator; Sewing-Machine Operator.

182 ETCHING

Wearing away the surface of materials by the corrosive action of chemicals on exposed parts of material.

Corroding	Dusting	Scoring	Scribing
Desensitizing	Photoengraving	Scratching	

Typical Occupations: Etcher; Silk-Screen Etcher; Glass Etcher.

183 ENGRAVING

Inscribing the surface of material by incising.

Abrading	Chasing	Impressing	Shading
Carving	Graving	Intensifying	

Typical Occupations: Engraving Supervisor; Engraver; Pantographer.

191 PRINTING

Reproducing records of data and designs by transfer of ink and dye to surface of materials by use of type, plates, dies, silkscreens, and stencils. Includes typesetting, compositing, and reproducing printed matter by use of computerized typesetting and related printing equipment.

Coating	Embossing	Moistening	Stenciling
Composing (raised	Immersing	Registering	
printing)	Inking	Setting (type)	
Dampening	Measuring	Stamping	

Typical Occupations: Addressing-Machine Operator; Typesetting Supervisor; Silk-Screen Printer; Compositor; Web-Press Operator; Letter-Press Operator; Offset-Press Operator.

192 IMPRINTING

Indenting and perforating the surfaces of products to reproduce records of data by mechanical means. Distinguish from Pressing-Forging (134), which involves change of shape and form of products rather than indentation of surfaces.

Brushing	Heating	Pressing	Stamping
Embossing	Leveling	Spreading	

Typical Occupations: Embosser; Name-Plate Stamper; Leather Stamper.

201 PHOTOGRAPHING

Producing records (images) of things, people, places, and data by chemical changes on a sensitized surface (as a film) and by electronic means induced by light and similar waves.

Exposing	Framing	Posing
Focusing	Lighting	Zooming

Typical Occupations: Motion-Picture Photographer; Radiographer; Photocopying-Machine Operator; Audiovisual-Production Specialist; Lithographic-Plate Maker.

202 DEVELOPING-PRINTING

Reproducing records of data and designs by chemical means.

Coating	Enlarging	Opaquing	Soaking
Cropping	Immersing	Projecting	Spotting
Drying	Masking	Rubbing	Whirling

Typical Occupations: Film-Processing Supervisor; Film Developer; Film-Laboratory Technician; Developer; Film Printer.

211 APPRAISING

Evaluating and estimating the quality and value of data and things based on knowledge and judgment acquired through experience and training and by conducting performance tests. Includes interpretation of findings that may influence variations in machinery setups, formula modifications, and product processing. Whenever the techniques of Appraising require a technical background in another work field, assign that work field also. Distinguish from Inspecting-Measuring-Testing (212), which primarily involves comparison with predetermined standards.

Aligning	Feeling	Meshing	Timing
Breaking	Gauging	Sieving	Trying Out
Calibrating	Investigating	Smelling	Turning
Classifying	Magnetizing	Stretching	Twisting
Diluting	Magnifying	Tasting	Typing (blood)
Dissolving	Marking	Tearing	Validating
Driving	Measuring	Testing	Weighing

Typical Occupations: Metallurgical-and-Quality-Control-Testing Supervisor; Medical-Laboratory Technician; Real-Estate Appraiser; Fire Inspector.

212 INSPECTING-MEASURING-TESTING

Examining materials and products to verify conformance to predetermined standards and characteristics, such as size, weight, composition, and color. Distinguish from Appraising (211), which involves evaluating things and data based primarily on judgment and knowledge rather than on comparison with readily verifiable standards.

Bending	Feeling	Picking	Twisting
Breaking	Gauging	Shaking	Verifying
Comparing	Grading	Stretching	Weighing
Culling	Marking	Tearing	
Detecting	Matching	Turning	

Typical Occupations: Shipping-and-Receiving Weigher; Spring Tester; Bowling Ball Weigher and Packer; Production Weigher; Quality Control Inspector.

221 STOCK CHECKING

Receiving, storing, issuing, requisitioning, and accounting for stores of materials and materials in use; involves the physical handling of the materials. Representative job activities covered by this work field include processing records and keeping materials on hand in balance with operational needs; assigning locations and space to items according to size, quantity, and type; verifying quantity, identification, condition, and value of items and the physical handling of items, such as binning, picking, stacking, and counting; receiving, checking, and delivering items; verifying completeness of incoming and outgoing shipments; preparing and otherwise committing stocks for shipment; keeping and conducting inventory of merchandise, materials, stocks, and supplies; filling orders and requisitions; and issuing tools, equipment, and materials.

Cataloging	Posting	Routing	Tagging
Marking	Pricing	Securing	Transcribing
Matching	Punching	Selecting	Tying
Measuring	Replacing	Shelving	
Ordering	Replenishing	Sorting	

Typical Occupations: Stock Clerk; Distribution-Warehouse Manager; Librarian; Mail Clerk; Parts Clerk; Order Filler; Shipping-and-Receiving Clerk.

231 VERBAL RECORDING-RECORD KEEPING

Preparing, keeping, sorting, and distributing records and communications, primarily verbal in character but including symbol devices, to communicate and systematize information and data by methods not specifically defined elsewhere, as in Developing-Printing (202), Imprinting (192), Photographing (201), Printing (191), and Stock Checking (221). Distinguish from Numerical Recording-Record Keeping (232), where records are also involved but the primary activity is computation.

Addressing	Listing	Reading	Taking Dictation
Checking	Locating	Routing	Taking Minutes
Collating	Mailing	Searching	Typing
Counting	Marking	Segregating	Verifying
Editing	Posting	Selecting	Writing
Filing	Punching	Stamping	

Typical Occupations: Secretary; Stenographer; File Clerk; Typist.

232 NUMERICAL RECORDING-RECORD KEEPING

Systematizing information on transactions and activities into accounts and numerical records through the application of arithmetic, bookkeeping, statistics, and other quantitative procedures (including paying and receiving money). Distinguish from Verbal Recording-Record Keeping (231), in which the primary activity is the keeping of records without computation.

Adding	Disbursing	Making Change	Stamping
Auditing	Dividing	Matching	Subtracting
Balancing	Endorsing	Multiplying	Tabulating
Cashiering	Entering	Posting	Totaling
Checking	Grouping	Prorating	Typing
Coding	Itemizing	Recapitulating	Verifying
Counting	Listing	Sorting	Writing

Typical Occupations: Actuary; Accountant; Bookkeeper; Teller; Cashier; Posting Clerk.

233 DATA PROCESSING

Planning, developing, testing, evaluating, and executing a systematic sequence of activities or operations to process alphabetic, numeric, and symbolic data or to solve problems by means of computer systems. This work field applies only to jobs in which processing data and solving related problems are the purpose of the job, rather than the means by which the worker accomplishes a task. Distinguish from Verbal Recording-Record Keeping (231) which involves the keeping of records without computation; Numerical Recording-Record Keeping (232) which involves the keeping of records with computation; and from Printing (191) in which computerized equipment may be used in reproducing printed matter. Computer hardware engineering is included in Work Field 244-Engineering. Data entry is included in Work Field 231-Verbal Recording-Record Keeping.

Analyzing	Editing	Modifying	Scheduling
Correcting	Entering	Monitoring	Storing
Deleting	Explaining	Programming	Verifying
Documenting	Interpreting	Retrieving	

Typical Occupations: Systems Analyst; Computer Programmer; Computer Operator; User Support Specialist; Software Engineer; Data Communications Technician.

241 LAYING OUT

Plotting reference points or tracing working diagrams onto surfaces of materials as guides in the working and processing of the materials. Distinguish from Styling (264), which includes spacing and positioning of objects and parts, printed material, and artwork that is sometimes termed "layout" work.

Blocking	Draping	Pinning	Stamping
Chalking	Inscribing	Scoring	Tapping
Coating	Outlining	Scratching	Transferring
Dotting	Perforating	Scribing	

Typical Occupations: Tool-and-Die Maker; Patternmaker; Model Maker; Template Maker.

242 DRAFTING

Drawing plans, diagrams, graphs, tables, charts, and maps of things, places, and data to be used by others. Drawings are usually to scale and reflect aspects of the subject delineated, such as dimensions and weight.

Detailing	Lettering	Plotting	Tracing
Diagramming	Measuring	Sketching	

Typical Occupations: Drafter; Technical Illustrator; Map Editor.

243 SURVEYING

Taking linear and angular measurements to ascertain the contour, dimensions, and position of the earth's surface. Included are such survey specialties as cartography, construction, property, geodesy, hydrography, topography, mining, photogrammetry, land development, and mapping.

Calculating	Marking	Pacing	Staking
Locating	Measuring	Plotting	Taping

Typical Occupations: Surveyor; Geodesist; Navigator.

244 ENGINEERING

Planning and designing machinery, structures, and systems to develop and utilize the properties of matter, work capacities of people, and sources of power, on the basis of known facts, principles, and theories. Included are such engineering disciplines as ceramic, electrical, electronic, civil, mechanical, industrial, and chemical.

Calculating	Investigating	Testing
Formulating	Scheduling	Writing

Typical Occupations: Architect; Aerodynamicist; Mechanical Engineer; Chemical Engineer; Metallurgist; Industrial Engineer.

251 RESEARCHING

Inquiring into fundamental knowledge areas, such as social, physical, and allied sciences, industry, and commerce, for the purpose of discovering facts and making interpretations, and revising and verifying recognized conclusions, theories, laws, and procedures in the light of newly discovered facts. Additionally, this work field includes formulating and testing hypotheses on the basis of information obtained by using specialized apparatus and techniques, by making expeditions, and by reading or observing. When expertise in another work field is required, assign that work field also.

Analyzing	Dissecting	Inoculating	Reporting
Classifying	Documenting	Isolating	Synthesizing
Collecting	Examining	Locating	Writing
Defining	Experimenting	Measuring	

Typical Occupations: Research Engineer; Operations-Research Analyst; Physicist; Geologist; Botanist; Curator; Consultant.

261 WRITING

Reporting, editing, promoting, translating, creating, and interpreting ideas in written form. Excludes translation of spoken foreign passages and sign language of the deaf which is included in Information Giving (282).

Adapting	Depicting	Proofreading	Verifying
Analyzing	Describing	Reading	
Criticizing	Outlining	Summarizing	

Typical Occupations: Copywriter; Critic; Playwright; Newscaster; Reporter; Editor; Proofreader.

262 ARTISTIC PAINTING-DRAWING

Creating and reproducing designs of lettering and depicting ideas pictorially to achieve functional and aesthetic effects, using color media (oil paints, tempera, water colors, etc.) and devices, such as pencils, crayons, brushes, and spray guns. Distinguish from Brushing-Spraying (153) and Immersing-Coating (151), which involve covering objects but without producing designs or lettering.

Blanking Out	Inking	Spotting Out	Tracing
Blocking Out	Rubbing	Spraying	Wiping
Coloring	Shading	Tinting	
Copying	Sketching	Touching Up	

Typical Occupations: Painting Restorer; Cartoonist; Illustrator; Painter; Music Copyist.

263 COMPOSING-CHOREOGRAPHING

Originating and interpreting ideas in musical form. Includes creating dynamic body movements to express rhythmically various music forms.

Arranging	Orchestrating	Translating	Writing
Harmonizing	Scoring	Transposing	

Tyypical Occupations: Choreographer; Composer; Orchestrator; Arranger.

264 STYLING

Designing and arranging objects, products, and materials for functional and aesthetic purposes. Frequently involves preparing work sketches and drawings, making models and prototypes, and producing sample items.

Adapting	Displaying	Molding	Tracing
Cutting	Laying Out	Placing	
Decorating	Modifying	Sketching	

Typical Occupations: Landscape Architect; Art Director; Display Designer; Hair Stylist.

271 INVESTIGATING

Obtaining and evaluating data about persons, places, and incidents for purposes such as solving criminal cases; settling claims; estimating credit risks; determining the qualifications, integrity, and loyalty of people; assessing eligibility for social-service-assistance programs; and ensuring compliance with laws and regulations. Distinguish from Researching (251), which involves inquiry and examination into areas of fundamental knowledge.

Advising	Inspecting	Questioning
Enforcing	Interrogating	Scanning
Inquiring	Interviewing	Searching

Typical Occupations: Market-Research Analyst; Coroner; Caseworker; Claims Examiner; Detective.

272 LITIGATING

Carrying out legal procedures, such as prosecuting and defending by pleading case, presenting evidence, debating in court, drawing up legal papers, and interpreting statutes.

Adjudicating	Arbitrating	Probating	Trying (cases)
Advising (clients)	Cross-Examining	Questioning	

Typical Occupations: Lawyer; Judge; Patent Agent.

281 SYSTEM COMMUNICATING

Effecting the transmission of information through electrical and electronic systems. Distinguish from Information Giving (282), which involves direct contact with the public in receiving and obtaining information to be transmitted, and from Data Processing (233), which involves the establishment and testing of the means of the transmission of information rather than the continuous transmission of information.

Announcing	Entering	Retrieving	Transmitting
Calling	Receiving	Ringing	Tuning
Dispatching	Relaying	Sending	

Typical Occupations: Air-Traffic Coordinator; Recording Engineer; Telephone Operator; Dispatcher; Telegrapher; Motion-Picture Projectionist.

282 INFORMATION GIVING

Providing information to people regarding places, events, programs, and procedures. Distinguish from the giving of information, which is involved in accomplishing such objectives as those of Accommodating (291), Merchandising-Sales (292), Teaching (296), and System Communicating (281). Includes giving information over the phone in response to an inquiry.

Advising	Explaining	Lecturing	Receiving
Answering	Informing	Reading	Speaking

Typical Occupations: Guide; Home Economist; Announcer; Information Clerk; Receptionist.

291 ACCOMMODATING

Providing specialized personal convenience and physical services to people and animals. Distinguish from services provided in Health Caring-Medical (294).

Attending	Exercising	Manicuring	Tinting
Bathing	Feeding	Massaging	Ushering
Currying	Greeting	Paging	Waiting (on)
Cutting (hair)	Grooming	Posting	Watering (animals)
Dressing	Introducing	Running Errands	Waving (hair)
Escorting	Making Arrangements	Shampooing	

Typical Occupations: Undertaker; Waitress; Cosmetologist; Barber; Attendant; Animal Caretaker.

292 MERCHANDISING-SALES

Buying, selling, renting, and demonstrating materials, products, and services, usually in retail and wholesale establishments. Includes soliciting contributions of money and time for charitable and other causes. Distinguish from Information Giving (282).

Collecting	Fitting	Peddling	Supplying
Describing	Interviewing	Promoting	Taking Tickets
Displaying	Leasing	Purchasing	
Distributing	Negotiating	Showing	

Typical Occupations: Sales Engineer; Sales Manager; Sales Agent; Auctioneer; Dispensing Optician; Salesperson.

293 PROTECTING

Protecting human, animal, and plant life and property against loss from fire, pests, and other natural hazards, and from negligence, criminal acts, and unlawful practices. Includes work situations, such as maintaining peace and order, directing traffic, patrolling establishments and areas, and apprehending lawbreakers; extinguishing fires; and exterminating pests.

Burning	Demolishing	Firefighting	Policing
Cautioning	Draining	Fumigating	Spraying
Conserving	Dusting	Guarding	

Typical Occupations: Park Ranger; Security Guard; Firefighter; Police Officer; Exterminator; Dog Catcher; Ski Patroller.

294 HEALTH CARING-MEDICAL

Treating people and animals with physical and mental problems. Distinguish from Accommodating (291) and Advising-Counseling (298).

Bandaging	Exercising	Massaging	Taking Pulse
Bathing	Injecting	Monitoring	Treating
Diagnosing	Inoculating	Prescribing	
Disinfecting	Interviewing	Quarantining	
Examining	Investigating	Rubbing	

Typical Occupations: Anesthesiologist; General Practitioner; Psychiatrist; Dentist; Oral Surgeon; Nurse; Physical Therapist; Podiatrist; Veterinarian.

295 ADMINISTERING

Managing and directing people, organizations, programs, and activities above the first-line supervision level.

Analyzing	Coordinating	Negotiating
Authorizing	Formulating	Planning
Contracting	Hiring	Scheduling

Typical Occupations: Principal; Dean; Director; Manager; Superintendent.

296 TEACHING

Instructing and training people and animals. Distinguish from Information Giving (282).

Demonstrating	Grading	Planning	Testing
Directing	Lecturing	Reviewing	
Examining	Observing	Supervising	

Typical Occupations: Faculty Member; Instructor; Teacher; Dramatic Coach; Animal Trainer.

297 ENTERTAINING

Exhibiting specialized artistic, physical, or mental skills to amuse or divert audiences.

Acting	Demonstrating	Miming	Singing
Balancing	Impersonating	Performing	Staging
Conducting	Juggling	Portraying	
Dancing	Lecturing	Rehearsing	

Typical Occupations: Actor; Dancer; Musician; Orchestra Conductor; Automobile Racer; Professional Athlete; Clown.

298 ADVISING-COUNSELING

Effecting the adjustment of people with financial, vocational, spiritual, educational, and other problems according to established procedures. Distinguish from Accommodating (291), Health Caring-Medical (294), and Litigating (272).

Arbitrating	Explaining	Planning	Scheduling
Authorizing	Interviewing	Reporting	Suggesting
Consulting	Investigating	Researching	Testing
Evaluating	Monitoring	Reviewing	Visiting

Typical Occupations: Counselor; Clergy Member; Financial Planner; Caseworker.

CHAPTER 5

MATERIALS, PRODUCTS, SUBJECT MATTER, AND SERVICES

The Work Performed component of MPSMS includes:

Basic **Materials** processed, such as fabric, metal, or wood.

Final **Products** made, such as automobiles; cultivated, such as field crops; harvested, such as sponges; or captured, such as wild animals.

Subject Matter or data dealt with or applied, such as astronomy or journalism.

Services rendered, such as barbering or janitorial.

MPSMS is the final link in a chain describing (1) what the worker does (Worker Functions); (2) what gets done (Work Fields); (3) to what (MPSMS).

The determination and assignment of an appropriate MPSMS code and title for a specific job is essential (1) to place the job in its occupational group of the DOT and (2) to contribute to an understanding of the basic knowledge required of the worker. The assigned Work Field(s) and MPSMS together answer the question, "What does the worker need to know?"

MPSMS categories are closely related in organization and content to categories in the Standard Industrial Classification Manual (SIC) and to educational classifications of subject matter. Some categories of MPSMS are tangible and some are intangible. Categories of tangibles cover materials and products, such as Grains and Alcoholic Beverages. Categories of intangibles involve specialized knowledge or services, such as Dramatics and Air Transportation, and cannot be expressed by listing a material or product.

ORGANIZATION OF MPSMS

The MPSMS component contains 48 groups subdivided into 336 categories. The groups and categories have three-digit identification code numbers. The code numbers for groups end in "0". The code numbers for categories have the same first two digits as the group in which they are contained with two exceptions. The groups of 560 Machinery and Equipment, except Electrical and 700 Architecture and Engineering contain more than nine categories and require two sets of code numbers. Each group has a residual category with a code number ending in "9".

Assign the most appropriate MPSMS classification. If needed, as many as three separate classifications may be assigned. When a job's MPSMS corresponds to categories in different groups, assign the individual categories and their corresponding codes. When the job's MPSMS corresponds to three or more categories within the same group, assign the group code. When the job's MPSMS corresponds in general to the group but not to a specific category within it, assign the residual "not elsewhere classified" code.

Information contained in MPSMS groups and categories may be accessed through three indexes:

1. MPSMS Groups: This index provides an overview of the classification structure and lists the MPSMS Groups in numerical order according to Materials and Products, Subject Matter, and Services.

2. Classifications, Definitions, and Examples of MPSMS: This index provides a complete classification of the MPSMS groups and their categories. Following each group code and title is a brief explanatory statement defining the group's limits and broadly indicating the general occupations and industries included in that group. This is followed by a cross-reference statement that alerts the reader to related MPSMS found in other groups and indicates the distinction between the related MPSMS.

The codes and titles of the categories comprising the group are listed under each group definition. Additionally, many categories are illustrated by specific items in parentheses immediately following the category titles. These examples are not intended to be a complete representation of the individual categories but can be used as a guideline to determine whether a specific MPSMS is included in an individual category.

3. Alphabetical Listing of MPSMS: This listing of MPSMS and their corresponding codes is helpful in locating the appropriate group and category titles for MPSMS specifically named in the group or category titles, the group definitions, or the illustrative examples. Since the Alphabetical Listing does not always use the exact MPSMS title, the analyst must always use the code to locate the correct title as listed in the Classification Index.

PROCEDURE FOR ASSIGNING MPSMS

Select one or more categories that, together with the Work Field(s), best reflect the specific technology(ies) with which the worker is involved. If an appropriate category of MPSMS cannot be identified, locate the most appropriate **major group** and assign the "n.e.c." code that ends with "9". The codes ending with "0" should be used only to designate a generalized MPSMS or a combination of three or more categories in the group when the assigning of specific, i.e., not general, MPSMS is not appropriate.

Enter, in Item 8 of the JAR, the code(s) and title(s) of the MPSMS classification(s) selected.

When assigning MPSMS, apply the Sentence Analysis Technique (see Chapter 6) to avoid confusing MTEWA with MPSMS and to facilitate the assignment of a subject matter or service category.

The MPSMS classification for a given job is generally based on the overall purpose of the job, usually reflected by the primary knowledge required of the worker. In production jobs, the MPSMS classification can be a material or a final product; it is based on the end-product of the job and not the end-product of the establishment. For example, a fabric cutter in a furniture plant is assigned an MPSMS category in Group 420 Fabrics and Related, not in Group 460 Furniture and Fixtures. When the primary knowledge is in terms of a product being made, the product is rated. When the primary knowledge is in terms of a specific material being processed, the material is rated.

First-line supervisory jobs are usually assigned the basic MPSMS classification of the workers supervised. Repairer jobs are assigned only the Products classifications of the items repaired. Machine cleaning and lubricating jobs are assigned the Products classifications of the machines cleaned and lubricated. Teaching jobs that involve specific subject areas are assigned both the Subject Matter classifications of the specific subjects taught as well as 931-Educational Services; teachers who teach a range of subjects, such as elementary school teachers, are assigned only 931. When a Service classification is assigned, either a Subject Matter, a Material, or a Product classification should also be assigned, when possible, since it is the primary knowledge required of the worker that is depicted by MPSMS and not the environmental setting. Commodity-sales jobs are assigned the appropriate category under 880-Merchandising Services, as well as the Material or Product classification for the item sold; if a variety of commodities are sold, only 880 is assigned.

MATERIALS AND PRODUCTS

300 PLANT FARM CROPS

310 HORTICULTURAL SPECIALTIES, FOREST TREES, AND FOREST PRODUCTS

320 ANIMALS

330 MARINE LIFE

340 RAW FUELS AND NONMETALLIC MINERALS

350 RAW METALLIC MINERALS

360 STRUCTURES

370 ORDNANCE

380 FOOD STAPLES AND RELATED

390 FOOD SPECIALTIES

400 TOBACCO PRODUCTS

410 TEXTILE FIBERS AND RELATED

420 FABRICS AND RELATED

430 TEXTILE PRODUCTS

440 APPAREL

450 LUMBER AND WOOD PRODUCTS

460 FURNITURE AND FIXTURES

470 PAPER AND ALLIED PRODUCTS

480 PRINTED AND PUBLISHED PRODUCTS

490 CHEMICAL AND ALLIED PRODUCTS

500 PETROLEUM AND RELATED PRODUCTS

510 RUBBER AND MISCELLANEOUS PLASTIC PRODUCTS

520 LEATHER AND LEATHER PRODUCTS

530 STONE, CLAY, AND GLASS PRODUCTS

540 METAL, FERROUS AND NONFERROUS

550 FABRICATED METAL PRODUCTS, EXCEPT ORDNANCE, MACHINERY, AND TRANS-PORTATION EQUIPMENT

560 MACHINERY AND EQUIPMENT, EXCEPT ELECTRICAL

580 ELECTRICAL AND ELECTRONIC MACHINERY, EQUIPMENT, AND SUPPLIES

590 TRANSPORTATION EQUIPMENT

600 MEASURING, ANALYZING, AND CONTROLLING INSTRUMENTS: PHOTOGRAPHIC, MEDICAL, AND OPTICAL GOODS; AND WATCHES AND CLOCKS

610 MISCELLANEOUS FABRICATED PRODUCTS

SUBJECT MATTER

700 ARCHITECTURE AND ENGINEERING

720 MATHEMATICS AND PHYSICAL SCIENCES

730 LIFE SCIENCES

740   SOCIAL SCIENCES

750   ARTS AND LITERATURE

SERVICES

850   TRANSPORTATION SERVICES

860   COMMUNICATION SERVICES

870   ELECTRIC, GAS, AND SANITARY SERVICES

880   MERCHANDISING SERVICES

890   GENERAL BUSINESS, FINANCE, INSURANCE, AND REAL ESTATE SERVICES

900   DOMESTIC, BUILDING, AND PERSONAL SERVICES

910   AMUSEMENT AND RECREATION SERVICES

920   MEDICAL AND OTHER HEALTH SERVICES

930   EDUCATIONAL, LEGAL, MUSEUM, LIBRARY, AND ARCHIVAL SERVICES

940   SOCIAL, EMPLOYMENT, AND SPIRITUAL SERVICES

950   REGULATION, PROTECTION, AND RELATED GOVERNMENT SERVICES

960   MISCELLANEOUS SERVICES

MATERIALS AND PRODUCTS

300 PLANT FARM CROPS

This group includes field crops, vegetables, melons, fruits, and tree nuts in a nonprocessed state produced by farmers, harvesters, sorters, graders, packers, and related workers. Plant farm crop produce or products in a manufactured, preserved, or otherwise processed state are classified in Groups 380 or 390 or with those products or materials to which they are most closely related (confectionery products, cider, wines, yarn, etc.).

301 Grains

302 Field Crops, except Grain (cotton, tobacco, sugar crops, peanuts, hay, etc.)

303 Vegetables and Melons

304 Citrus Fruits

305 Fruits, except Citrus (including berries, grapes, olives, dates, etc.)

306 Tree Nuts

309 Plant Farm Crops, n.e.c.

310 HORTICULTURAL SPECIALTIES, FOREST TREES, AND FOREST PRODUCTS

This group includes nursery and forest products in a nonprocessed state produced by nursery and greenhouse workers, forest-product gatherers, and related workers. Logs, cut timber, and forest products in a processed state are classified in Group 450 or with those products or materials to which they are most closely related (furniture, musical instruments, caskets, etc.).

311 Floricultural and Related Nursery Products (bulbs, florists' greens, flowers, shrubbery, flower and vegetable seeds and plants, sod, etc.)

312 Ornamental Trees

313 Standing Timber (including Christmas trees)

314 Forest Nursery Products (reforestation, including tree seeds)

319 Horticultural Specialties, Forest Trees, and Forest Products, n.e.c. (balsam needles, barks, crude rubber, ginseng, gums, maple sap, mushrooms, Spanish moss, natural resins, teaberries, etc.)

320 ANIMALS

This group includes animals raised, bred, cared for, hunted, and trapped by farmers, ranchers, breeders, shearers, product gatherers, hunters, trappers, operators of game preserves, animal caretakers, and related workers. Animal products in a manufactured, preserved, or otherwise processed state are classified in Groups 380 and 520 or with those products to which they are most closely related (feathers, sporting goods, woolen fabrics, yarn, etc.). Animal trainers are classified in Group 910.

321 Cattle (including raw milk)

322 Hogs

323 Sheep and Goats

324 Poultry and Other Fowl (including eggs)

325 Captive Fur-Bearing Animals

326 Game and Wildlife

327 Horses and Other Equines

329 Animals, n.e.c. (bees, cats, dogs, laboratory animals, zoo animals, etc.)

330 MARINE LIFE

> This group includes finfish, shellfish, and other marine life caught, gathered, or cultivated and harvested by fishers, farmers, growers, and related workers. Seafoods in a canned, cured, or preserved state are classified in Group 380.

331 Finfish

332 Shellfish

339 Marine Life, n.e.c. (sea urchins, terrapins, turtles, whales, frogs, sponges, seaweeds, etc.)

340 RAW FUELS AND NONMETALLIC MINERALS

> This group includes fuel and nonmetallic minerals occurring in a natural state, extracted by miners, drillers, blasters, loaders, and related workers. Also included is the milling (crushing, grinding, screening, washing, etc.) of nonmetallic minerals at the mine site or elsewhere by millers, splitters, grinders, and related workers. Fuel or nonmetallic mineral products in a refined, manufactured, or otherwise processed state are classified in Groups 490, 500, and 530 or with those products or materials to which they are most closely related (paints, asphalt, gasoline, glassware, asbestos products, clay products, stone products, etc.).

341 Coal and Lignite

342 Crude Petroleum and Natural Gas

343 Stone, Dimension

344 Stone, Crushed and Broken

345 Sand and Gravel

346 Clay (bentonite, fire clay, fuller's earth, kaolin, etc.)

347 Chemical and Fertilizer Minerals (barite, fluorspar, potash, soda, borate, phosphate rock, rock salt, sulfur, etc.)

349 Raw Fuels and Nonmetallic Minerals, n.e.c. (gypsum, mica, native asphalt, pumice, asbestos, talc, graphite, etc.)

350 RAW METALLIC MINERALS

> This group includes metallic minerals occurring in a natural state, extracted by miners, drillers, blasters, loaders, and related workers. Also included is dressing (crushing, grinding, washing, drying, sintering, leaching, and separating) of metal ores by crushers, grinders, leachers, and related workers. Metallic mineral products in a refined, smelted, manufactured, or otherwise processed state are classified in Groups 540 and 550 or with those products or materials to which they are most closely related (ingots, metal castings, tinware, metal stampings, wire products, silverware, etc.).

351 Iron Ores

352 Copper Ores

353 Lead and Zinc Ores

354 Gold and Silver Ores

355 Bauxite and Other Aluminum Ores

356 Ferroalloy Ores, except Vanadium (including chromium, cobalt, etc.)

357 Mercury Ores

358 Uranium, Radium, and Vanadium Ores

359 Raw Metallic Minerals, n.e.c. (including ores such as antimony, beryllium, platinum, tin, titanium, etc.)

360 STRUCTURES

This group includes buildings and heavy construction (1) constructed, erected, installed, or razed by carpenters, bricklayers, plumbers, riggers, pavers, structural-steel workers, track layers, wreckers, and other construction industry workers; and (2) maintained or repaired by various maintenance and repair workers. This group includes special trade contractors engaged in specialized construction activities, such as plumbing, painting, carpentering, etc. (see SIC Major Group 17). Prefabricated wooden buildings and mobile homes are classified in Group 450 while prefabricated metal buildings are classified in Group 550. The utilization of structures to render a transportation, public utility, or other service is classified under Groups 850 and 870 while the extraction of raw materials from excavations or mines is classified in Groups 340 and 350.

361 Buildings, except Prefabricated (residential, farm, industrial, commercial, public, etc.)

362 Highways and Streets (including athletic fields, airports, bridle paths, parking areas, parkways, etc.)

363 Bridges, Tunnels, Viaducts, and Elevated Highways

364 Water, Gas, and Sewer Mains; Pipelines; and Communication Lines and Power Lines (cable lines, radio and television transmitting towers, sewage collection and disposal lines, pumping stations, telegraph and telephone lines, etc.)

365 Marine Construction (harbor and waterway construction, such as breakwaters, canals, channels, cofferdams, dams, dikes, harbors, levees, locks, piers, wharves, etc.)

366 Power Plant Projects (hydroelectric, nuclear, etc.)

367 Railroads and Subways

368 Oil Refineries

369 Structures, n.e.c. (drainage systems; industrial furnaces, incinerators, kilns, and ovens; irrigation systems; ski tows; water-treatment plants; etc.)

370 ORDNANCE

This group includes weapons, parts, and ammunition manufactured or repaired by gunsmiths, machine operators, assemblers, repairers, and related workers. Military tanks and space vehicles are classified in Group 590. Electronic sighting and fire control equipment is classified in Group 580, while optical sighting and fire control equipment is classified in Group 600.

371 Guns, Howitzers, Mortars, and Related Equipment (naval, aircraft, anti-aircraft, tank, coast, and field artillery having a bore over 30 mm. or 1.18 inch and components)

372 Ammunition, except Small Arms (ammunition over 30 mm. or 1.18 inch, including bombs, chemical warfare projectiles, depth charges, grenades, mines, missile warheads, torpedoes, etc.)

373 Small Arms (firearms having a bore of 30 mm. or 1.18 inch and below and parts)

374 Small Arms Ammunition (ammunition for small arms having a bore of 30 mm. or 1.18 inch and below)

375 Guided Missiles

379 Ordnance and Accessories, n.e.c. (bazookas, flamethrowers, smoke generators, etc.)

380 FOOD STAPLES AND RELATED

This group includes food staples and animal feeds cured, pickled, smoked, canned, frozen, milled, or otherwise processed by workers. Foods in a natural or unprocessed state are classified in Groups 300, 320, and 330. Food specialties, such as sugar, candy, beverages, and coffee, are classified in Group 390.

381 Grain Mill Products (including animal and fowl feeds)

382 Meat Products, Processed (including eggs)

383 Dairy Products

384   Bakery Products

385   Oils and Fats, Edible

386   Seafoods, Processed (canned, cured, and fresh or frozen packaged seafoods)

387   Fruits and Vegetables, Processed (canned, dried, dehydrated, frozen, and pickled fruits and vegetables, including preserves, jams, jellies, juices, sauces, seasonings, and salad dressings; and canned specialties, such as baby foods, health foods, and soups)

389   Food Staples and Related, n.e.c.

390   FOOD SPECIALTIES

This group includes coffee, sugar, confectionery products, beverages, flavoring extracts, and other food specialties. Food-staple products, such as meat, dairy, bakery, and grain-mill products and processed fruits, vegetables, and seafoods, are classified in Group 380.

391   Coffee, Tea, and Spices

392   Sugar and Syrup (cane and beet sugar, syrup, and molasses)

393   Confectionery and Related Products (candy, stuffed dates, salted nuts, chocolate, cocoa, chewing gum, etc.)

394   Flavoring Extracts and Flavoring Syrups

395   Beverages, Alcoholic (wines; malt beverages; and distilled, rectified, and blended liquors)

396   Soft Drinks and Carbonated Waters

397   Macaroni, Spaghetti, Vermicelli, Noodles

398   Vinegar and Cider

399   Food specialties, n.e.c. (baking powder, ice, yeast, peanut butter, potato chips, etc.)

400   TOBACCO PRODUCTS

This group includes cigarettes, cigars, smoking and chewing tobacco, snuff, and stemmed and redried tobacco processed by workers. Tobacco in a natural or unprocessed state is classified in Group 300.

401   Cigarettes

402   Cigars

403   Tobacco, Chewing, Smoking, and Snuff

404   Tobacco, Stemmed and Redried

409   Tobacco Products, n.e.c.

410   TEXTILE FIBERS AND RELATED

This group includes the preparation or finishing of natural, synthetic, glass, and silk fibers and the subsequent manufacture and finishing of yarn, thread, twine, and cordage by carders, cleaners, combers, drawers, dyers, mercerizers, pickers, spinners, sorters, texturers, twisters, winders, and related workers. The basic manufacture of synthetic and glass fibers is classified in Group 490 and 530, respectively. Fabrics are classified in Group 420.

411   Yarn

412   Thread

413   Cordage and Twine

414   Fiber Stock (including natural, synthetic, glass, and silk fibers)

419   Textile Fibers and Related, n.e.c. (waste and recovered fibers, etc.)

420 FABRICS AND RELATED

This group includes the manufacture of woven, nonwoven, and knit fabrics produced by weavers, knitters, needle-loom operators, dyers, and related workers. Rubberized fabrics are classified in Group 510 and coated fabrics in Group 430. Knitted garments, hosiery, blankets, bedsheets, pillowcases, and other textile products are classified in Groups 430 and 440, regardless of where manufactured.

421 Fabrics, Broad Woven Cotton, Synthetic Fiber, Glass Fiber, and Silk

422 Fabrics, Broad Woven Wool (including wool felt and haircloth)

423 Narrow Fabrics and Related Smallwares (ribbons, shoelaces, tapes, etc.)

424 Fabrics, Knitted

425 Fabrics, Nonwoven (except knitted)

429 Fabrics and Related, n.e.c. (linen, jute, hemp, ramie, etc.)

430 TEXTILE PRODUCTS

This group includes textile products, such as carpets and rugs, fancy textiles, paddings and upholstery filling, coated fabrics, house furnishings, and canvas products. Textile and rubberized fabrics are classified in Groups 420 and 510, respectively. Apparel is classified in Group 440.

431 Carpets and Rugs (woven, tufted, braided, etc.)

432 Textiles, Fancy (trimmings, hatters' fur, stamped art goods, art needlework, embroideries, lace goods, etc.)

433 Paddings and Upholstery Filling (batting, padding, wadding, and filling)

434 Impregnated and Coated Fabrics (artificial leather, oilcloth, etc. [except rubberized fabric])

435 Housefurnishings (blankets, bedspreads, comforters, curtains, dishcloths, draperies, mopheads, napkins, pillows, pillowcases, quilts, sheets, slipcovers, tablecloths, towels, washcloths, etc.)

436 Canvas and Related Products (textile bags, awnings, tents, tarpaulins, etc.)

439 Textile Products, n.e.c. (felt goods, fishing nets, flags, hammocks, handwoven and crocheted products, parachutes, sleeping bags, etc.)

440 APPAREL

This group includes apparel, except rubber or rubberized, produced by workers, such as cutters, sewers, tailors, pressers, and blockers. Rubber clothing and rubberized fabrics are classified in Group 510. Footwear is classified in Groups 510 and 520. Leather gloves and mittens and fur pelts are classified in Group 520.

441 Men's and Boys' Suits, Coats, and Overcoats (including vests, uniforms, and tuxedos)

442 Men's and Boys' Furnishings, Work Clothing, and Allied Products (shirts, nightwear, underwear, neckwear, trousers, athletic apparel, bathing suits, etc.)

443 Women's, Girls', and Infants' Outerwear (blouses, rompers, shirts, dresses, skirts, suits, coats, neckwear, athletic apparel, bathing suits, etc.)

444 Women's, Girls', and Infants' Undergarments (underwear, nightwear, brassieres, girdles, etc.)

445 Hats (except fur)

446 Hosiery

447 Fur Goods (coats, jackets, hats, neckpieces, and trimmings, etc.)

449 Apparel, n.e.c. (dress and work gloves [except rubber and all leather]; robes and dressing gowns; raincoats and other waterproof outer garments [except rubber or rubberized]; leather and sheepskin-lined clothing; apparel belts; and costumes, diapers, garters, handkerchiefs, suspenders, etc.)

450 LUMBER AND WOOD PRODUCTS

This group includes logs, veneer and plywood, prefabricated wood buildings, mobile homes, particleboard, and wood containers and other articles produced by fallers, loggers, splitters, sawyers, planers, shapers, sanders, jointers, gluers, assemblers, and related workers. Furniture is classified in Group 460. Prefabricated metal buildings are classified in Group 550. Structures fabricated at the construction site are classified in Group 360.

451 Logs and Hewn Timber Products, Untreated (wood bolts, pilings, poles, posts, fence rails, etc.)

452 Sawmill, Planing Mill, and Treated Wood Products (lumber, fuelwood, cooperage stock, hardwood dimension stock, flooring, shingles, etc.; and doors, moldings, shutters, stairways, window frames, and other millwork products)

453 Veneer and Plywood

454 Wood Containers (including pallets and skids)

455 Prefabricated Wood Buildings, Mobile Homes, and Structural Wood Members

456 Particleboard

457 Wood Articles (clothespins, dowels, gavels, ladders, mallets, marquetry, mirror and picture frames, oars, toilet seats, toothpicks, yardsticks, etc.)

459 Lumber and Wood Products, n.e.c. (cork, rattan, reed, straw, wicker, and willow products)

460 FURNITURE AND FIXTURES

This group includes furniture and fixtures produced by sawyers, shapers, planers, jointers, gluers, welders, riveters, assemblers, and related workers. Concrete and stone furniture are classified in Group 530.

461 Wood Household Furniture, except Upholstered (including television, radio, phonograph, and sewing machine cabinets)

462 Wood Household Furniture, Upholstered

463 Metal Household Furniture

464 Mattress, Bedsprings, and Sofa Beds (chair beds, spring cushions, etc.)

465 Wood Office, Public Building, and Related Furniture (chalkboards, bookcases, pews, desks, etc.)

466 Metal Office, Public Building, and Related Furniture (filing cabinets, bookcases, chairs, etc., including seats for aircraft, automobile, railroad, and other public conveyances)

467 Wood and Metal fixtures (partitions, shelving, lockers, display cabinets, kitchen cabinets, costumers, display cases, racks, stands, telephone booths, etc.)

468 Plastic, Glass, and Fiberglass Furniture and Fixtures

469 Furniture and Fixtures, n.e.c. (beauty and barber shop equipment; reed, rattan, wicker, and willow furniture and fixtures; and drapery hardware and window blinds and shades)

470 PAPER AND ALLIED PRODUCTS

This group includes pulp, paper, paperboard, building paper, building board, and converted paper products, such as paper bags, boxes, envelopes, and stationery. Books, business forms, greeting cards, newspapers, periodicals, and other printed materials produced in printing and publishing establishments are classified in Group 480.

471 Pulp

472 Nonconverted Paper and Paperboard, except Building (paper stock, newsprint, parchment paper, cardboard, etc.)

473 Nonconverted Building Paper and Building Board (asbestos, asphalt, construction, and insulating paper; asphalt board, fiberboard, roofing board, wallboard, etc.)

474 Converted Paper and Paperboard Products, except Containers and Boxes (coated, glazed, or varnished paper; envelopes; paper bags; die-cut paper, paperboard, and cardboard; pressed and molded pulp goods; sanitary paper products; stationery and tablets; corrugated and laminated paper, paper novelties, wallpaper, etc.)

475 Paperboard Containers and Boxes

479 Paper and Allied Products, n.e.c.

480 PRINTED AND PUBLISHED PRODUCTS

This group includes books, newspapers, magazines, trade journals, periodicals, greeting cards, business forms, directories, and related printed materials prepared by printing-press operators, bookbinders, and related workers. Printing types, plates, and rollers prepared (for use by printing-press operators) by lithographic-plate makers, photoengravers, compositors, stenotypists, pantographers, and related workers are classified in Group 560.

481 Newspapers

482 Periodicals (comics, magazines, trade journals, etc.)

483 Books and Pamphlets

484 Manifold Business Forms (office and business forms, fanfold forms, salesbooks, etc.)

485 Greeting Cards (except hand painted)

486 Blankbooks, Looseleaf Binders, and Related Products (account books, albums, checkbooks, ledgers and ledger sheets, receipt books, record albums, sample books, etc.)

489 Published and Printed Products, n.e.c. (atlases, catalogs, directories, maps, paper patterns, racetrack programs, sheet music, shopping news, technical papers, etc.)

490 CHEMICAL AND ALLIED PRODUCTS

This group includes the production of basic chemicals, chemical products to be used in further manufacture, and finished chemical products for ultimate consumption or as materials and supplies in other industries. The extraction of raw chemical materials from excavations and mines is classified in Groups 340 and 350. Synthetic fiber products, petroleum and related products, and synthetic rubber products are classified in Groups 410 and 420, 500, and 510, respectively. Glass fibers are classified in Group 530.

491 Chemicals, Inorganic (alkalies and chlorine; industrial gases; and inorganic pigments, salts, and compounds, etc.)

492 Plastics Materials and Synthetic Resins; Synthetic Rubber; and Synthetic Fibers, except Glass

493 Drugs (biological products, such as bacterial and virus vaccines, toxoids and analogous products, serums, plasmas, and other blood derivatives; medicinal chemicals and botanical products; and pharmaceutical preparations in form intended for final consumption, such as ampules, tablets, capsules, vials, ointments, medicinal powders, solutions, and suspensions)

494 Soap, Detergents, and Cleaning Preparations and Perfumes, Cosmetics, and Other Toilet Preparations

495 Paints, Varnishes, Lacquers, Enamels, and Allied Products (paint and varnish removers, putties, wood fillers and sealers, paintbrush cleaners, etc.)

496 Chemicals, Organic (gum and wood chemicals; cyclic [coal tar] crudes and intermediates and synthetic organic dyes and pigments; and noncyclic organic chemicals, organic solvents, polyhydric alcohols, synthetic perfume and flavoring materials, rubber-processing chemicals, plasticizers, synthetic tanning agents, chemical warfare gases, and acid and polyhydric alcohol esters, amines, etc.)

497 Agricultural Chemicals (fertilizers and pesticides)

499 Chemical and Allied Products, n.e.c. (adhesives and sealants, explosives, printing ink, carbon black, etc.)

500 PETROLEUM AND RELATED PRODUCTS

This group includes petroleum, paving and roofing materials, fuel briquettes, and coke refined, manufactured, and compounded by workers. Petroleum, coal, and asphalt occurring in a natural state are classified in Group 340. Petrochemical products are classified in Group 490 or with those products or materials to which they are most closely related.

501 Petroleum Products (fuel oils, gasoline, illuminating oils, jet fuels, lubricants, paraffin waxes, etc.)

502 Paving Materials (asphalt and tar-paving mixtures and blocks)

503 Roofing Materials (asphalt and other saturated roofing felts, and roofing cements and coatings)

504 Fuel Briquettes, Packaged Fuel, and Powdered Fuel

505 Coke (regardless of where produced)

509 Petroleum and Related Products, n.e.c.

510 RUBBER AND MISCELLANEOUS PLASTIC PRODUCTS

This group includes tires and tubes, rubber and plastic footwear, rubber and plastic hose and belting, fabricated rubber products, and miscellaneous plastic products as produced by blenders, casters, compounders, curers, driers, extruders, laminators, molders, press operators, and related workers. Rubber products made from synthetic rubber and reclaimed rubber are also included in this classification. Manufacture of plastic materials is classified in Group 490. Plastic furniture, fiberglass boats, and other similar products are classified in Groups 460 and 590 or with the products or materials to which they are most closely related. Leather footwear is classified in Group 520.

511 Tires and Tubes

512 Rubber and Plastic Footwear

513 Reclaimed Rubber

514 Rubber and Plastic Hose and Belting (air line hose, conveyor belts, plastic or rubber garden hose, heater hose, V-belts, etc.)

519 Rubber and Miscellaneous Plastic Products, n.e.c. (rubberized fabrics; rubber clothing, specialties, and sundries, such as aprons, bathing caps and suits, cloaks, gloves, wet suits, balloons, combs, erasers, life rafts and life jackets, teething rings, toys, and water bottles; and molded plastics and miscellaneous plastic products, such as awnings, bottles, clothespins, downspouts and gutters, ice chests and coolers, hardware, kitchenware, novelties, pipe and pipe fittings, shower stalls, and tableware)

520 LEATHER AND LEATHER PRODUCTS

This group includes hides, skins, and fur pelts, and leather footwear, gloves and mittens, luggage, personal goods, and other products produced by tanners, dyers, buffers, cutters, trimmers, cementers, assemblers, stitchers, and related workers. Fur goods and leather garments are classified in Group 440. Rubber footwear is classified in Group 510.

521 Hides, Skins, and Leather (includes fur pelts)

522 Footwear, except Rubber (boot and shoe cut stock and findings, slippers, sandals, moccasins, athletic shoes, canvas boots, etc.)

523 Leather Gloves and Mittens

524 Luggage of any Material (including attache, camera, musical instrument cases, etc.)

525 Handbags and Related Accessories of any Material (billfolds, jewelry cases, key cases, purses, tobacco pouches, etc.)

529 Leather and Leather Products, n.e.c. (belting, dog collars and leashes, desk sets, razor strops, saddlery, harness, whips, etc.)

530 STONE, CLAY, AND GLASS PRODUCTS

This group includes stone, clay, and glass products machined, processed, fabricated, and repaired by machine operators, processors, fabricators, and related workers. Crushing, grinding, screening, washing, etc., of nonmetallic minerals are classified in Group 340. Asbestos paper, electric light bulbs, and optical and ophthalmic lenses are classified in Groups 470, 580, and 600, respectively.

531 Flat, Pressed, or Blown Glass and Glassware (float or plate glass, window glass, pressed glass tableware, glass bottles, glass fibers, etc., produced from raw materials)

532 Glass Products Made of Purchased Glass (cut-glass tableware; leaded, stained, and art glass; mosaic glass; ground glass; mirrors; watch crystals; glass novelties; etc.)

533 Cement, Hydraulic (natural, Portland, masonry, etc.)

534 Structural Clay Products (brick and structural clay tile; ceramic wall and floor tile; clay firebrick and other heat resisting clay products; clay drain, roofing, and sewer tile, etc.)

535 Pottery and Related Products (china and earthenware plumbing fixtures and fittings; porcelain electrical supplies; and chinaware, earthenware, porcelain ware, and stoneware)

536 Concrete, Gypsum, and Plaster Products (concrete block, brick, pipe, furniture, etc.; ready-mixed concrete; quicklime and hydrated lime; and gypsum products, such as plaster and plasterboard)

537 Cut Stone and Stone Products (building and monumental stone, cut stone furniture, etc.)

538 Abrasive, Asbestos, and Related Products (abrasive products, such as grinding and buffing wheels, sandpaper, and steel wool; asbestos products, such as building and insulating materials and brake linings; and gaskets, packing, and sealing devices)

539 Stone, Clay, and Glass Products, n.e.c. (mineral wool, nonclay refractories and crucibles, plaster of paris and papier mache statuary and art goods, etc.)

540 METAL, FERROUS AND NONFERROUS

This group includes pigs and ingots; basic metal shapes, such as plates, sheets, strips, rods, bars, pipes, and tubing; and basic metal products, such as castings, wire, cable, nails, and spikes, smelted, refined, rolled, drawn, extruded, or similarly processed by furnace operators, hot and cold mill operators, casters, mold makers, drawers, extruders, and related workers. Fabricated metal products are classified according to the type of products to which they are most closely related.

541 Blast Furnace, Steelworks, and Rolling and Finishing Mill Products (pig iron; steel ingots; basic iron and steel shapes, such as plates, sheets, strips, rods, bars, pipes, and tubing; and steel wire, cable, nails, spikes, staples, etc.)

542 Metal Castings (ferrous and nonferrous)

543 Nonferrous Metals, Smelted and Refined (copper, lead, zinc, aluminum, and other nonferrous metal pigs, ingots, slabs, etc.)

544 Nonferrous Metals, Rolled, Drawn, and Extruded (basic nonferrous metal shapes, such as plates, sheets, strips, rods, bars, pipes, and tubing; and nonferrous wire and cable)

549 Metal, Ferrous and Nonferrous, n.e.c. (steel balls; powdered iron; nonferrous nails, spikes, and staples, etc.)

550 FABRICATED METAL PRODUCTS, EXCEPT ORDNANCE, MACHINERY, AND TRANSPORTATION EQUIPMENT

This group includes fabricated metal products, such as metal cans and containers; cutlery, handtools, and general hardware; nonelectric heating apparatus; fabricated structural metal products; forgings and stampings; and fabricated wire products. Ordnance is classified in Group 370. Machinery is classified in Groups 560 and 580. Transportation equipment is classified in Group 590. Other fabricated metal products are classified with those materials or products to which they are most closely related (professional, scientific, and controlling instruments; watches and clocks; jewelry and silverware; etc.)

551   Metal Cans and Containers (cans, barrels, drums, kegs, pails, etc.)

552   Cutlery, Handtools, and General Hardware (cutlery, such as cleavers, clippers, knives, razors, scissors, and shears; handtools, such as axes, bits, chisels, mechanics' and carpenters' handtools, garden tools, and handsaws and saw blades; and hardware, such as builders' hardware, furniture hardware, and motor-vehicle hardware)

553   Nonelectric Heating Equipment and Plumbing Fixtures (enameled iron and metal sanitary ware; plumbing-fixture fittings and trim [brass goods]; and nonelectric heating equipment [except warm-air furnaces], such as gas, oil, or wood burning heaters, steam or hot water domestic furnaces, radiators, and solar heaters)

554   Fabricated Structural Metal Products (fabricated structural metal; metal doors, sash, frames, molding, and trim; fabricated plate work [boiler-shops]; sheet metal work; architectural and ornamental metalwork, such as fire escapes, flagpoles, and lampposts; and prefabricated metal buildings and components)

555   Screw-Machine Products (including bolts, nuts, screws, rivets, and washers)

556   Metal Forgings and Stampings (ferrous and nonferrous forgings and metal stampings, such as automotive stampings, bottle and jar caps and tops, ashtrays, garbage cans, helmets, license tags, and radio and television chassis)

557   Fabricated Wire Products (barbed wire; paper clips; and wire springs, fencing, screening, garment hangers, etc.)

559   Fabricated Metal Products, except Ordnance, Machinery, and Transportation Equipment, n.e.c. (steel springs; valves and pipe fittings [except plumbers' brass goods]; metal foil and leaf; fabricated pipe; safes and vaults; etc.)

560   MACHINERY AND EQUIPMENT, EXCEPT ELECTRICAL

This group includes machinery, equipment, parts, attachments, and accessories, except electric, and portable electric- and pneumatic-powered tools manufactured or repaired by machine assemblers, installers, repairers, and related workers. It encompasses printing type, plate, and rollers prepared (for use by printing-press operators) by lithographic platemakers, photoengravers, compositors, stenotypists, and related workers. Refer to corresponding SIC Groups in SIC Major Group 35 Machinery, Except Electrical for a complete listing of machinery and equipment encompassed in the MPSMS categories listed below. Refer to SIC Group 355 Special Industry Machinery, Except Metalworking Machinery for a complete listing of machinery and equipment encompassed in MPSMS category 567 Special Industrial Machinery. Electrical machinery, household appliances, and electric warm-air furnaces are classified in Group 580. Laboratory scales and balances are classified in Group 600. Transportation equipment is classified in Group 590.

561   Engines and Turbines (steam, hydraulic, and gas [except aircraft] turbines, steam engines [except locomotive], and turbine-generator and other internal-combustion engines and parts [except aircraft and nondiesel automotive])

562   Farm and Garden Machinery and Equipment (including farm and garden wheel tractors and snow blowers and throwers)

563   Construction Machinery and Equipment (bulldozers, concrete mixers, nonindustrial plant cranes, dredging machinery, pavers, power shovels, etc.)

564   Mining and Oil Field Machinery and Equipment (coal breakers; mine cars; core drills; coal cutters; portable rock drills; mineral cleaning, concentration, and rock-crushing machinery; and gas, oil, and water-well machinery and equipment; etc.)

565 Materials-Handling Machinery and Equipment (elevators and moving stairways; conveyors and conveying equipment; hoists, industrial cranes, and monorail systems; industrial trucks, tractors, trailers, and stackers; etc.)

566 Metalworking Machinery and Equipment (metal cutting and forming machine tools; special dies and tools, die sets, jigs and fixtures, industrial molds and patterns; machine-tools accessories and measuring devices; power-driven handtools; rolling mill machinery and equipment; welding equipment; automotive maintenance equipment; etc.)

567 Special Industrial Machinery (food products, textile, woodworking, paper industries, and printing trades machinery and other special industry machinery, equipment, parts, attachments, and accessories not elsewhere classified)

568 General Industrial Machinery and Equipment (pumps and pumping equipment; ball and roller bearings; air and gas compressors; blowers and exhaust and ventilating fans; speed changers, industrial high-speed drives, and gears; industrial process furnaces and ovens; mechanical power transmission equipment; etc.)

571 Office, Computing, and Accounting Machines (typewriters; electronic computing equipment; calculating and accounting machines; scales and balances [except laboratory]; and dictating, duplicating, and shorthand machines; etc.)

572 Service-Industry Machinery (automatic merchandising machines; commercial laundry, dry cleaning, and pressing machines; measuring and dispensing pumps; and car-washing machinery, commercial food-warming equipment, floor sanding, washing, and polishing machines, industrial vacuum cleaners, etc.)

573 Refrigeration and Air-Conditioning Equipment (commercial and industrial refrigeration equipment and systems; air-conditioning units; warm-air furnaces [except electric]; soda fountain and beer-dispensing units; humidifiers and dehumidifiers [except room]; evaporative condensers [heat-transfer equipment]; etc.)

579 Machinery and Equipment, except Electrical, n.e.c. (carnival machines and equipment, sand riddles, catapults, etc.)

580 ELECTRICAL AND ELECTRONIC MACHINERY, EQUIPMENT, AND SUPPLIES

This group includes machinery, apparatus, and supplies for the generation, storage, transmission, transformation, and utilization of electrical energy and household appliances and lighting fixtures, as produced or repaired by workers. Electric measuring instruments and graphic-recording instruments are classified in Group 600.

581 Electric Transmission and Distribution Equipment (power, distribution, and specialty transformers, such as doorbell and rectifier transformers; lighting fixture ballasts; line-voltage regulators; and switchgear and switchboard apparatus, such as power switches, circuit breakers, power switching equipment, switchboards and cubicles, control and metering panels, and power fuse mountings)

582 Electrical Industrial Apparatus (motors, generators, and parts [except starting motors], such as motor generator sets and railway motors and control equipment; industrial controls, such as motor starters, rheostats, and solenoid switches; electric welding apparatus; carbon and graphite products, such as brush blocks and electrodes; and battery chargers, blasting machines, fixed and variable capacitors, condensers, and rectifiers, etc.)

583 Household Appliances (household electric and nonelectric cooking equipment, such as stoves, ovens, and ranges; household refrigerators and home and farm freezers; household laundry equipment, including coin-operated washers and driers; electric housewares and fans, such as electric blankets, space heaters, blenders, broilers, toasters, knives, razors, toothbrushes, and household fans [except attic]; household vacuum cleaners; domestic and industrial sewing machines; and household dishwashers, floor waxers and polishers, garbage-disposal units, trash compactors, and water heaters)

584 Electric Lighting and Wiring Equipment (electric lamps, such as incandescent filament, vapor and fluorescent, and photoflash and photoflood; current-carrying wiring devices, such as attachment plugs and caps, convenience outlets, fluorescent starters, lamp sockets and receptacles, lightning arrestors and coils, and overhead trolley-line material; noncurrent-carrying wiring devices, such as conduits and fittings, electrical insulators and insulation material [except glass and porcelain], and boxes for junctions, outlets, switches, and fuses; residential, commercial, industrial, and institutional electric lighting fixtures; vehicular-lighting equipment; and other lighting equipment, such as flashlights, searchlights, lanterns, and lamp fixtures, including ultraviolet and infrared lamp fixtures)

585 Home-Entertainment Electric Equipment (radio- and television-receiving sets [except communication types], auto radios and tape players, public address systems, phonographs, home recorders, phonograph records, prerecorded magnetic tape, etc.)

586 Communication and Related Equipment (telephone and telegraph apparatus and parts; radio- and television-transmitting and signaling equipment, such as broadcasting and communication equipment and parts; detection equipment and apparatus, such as electronic field detection apparatus, light- and heat-emission operating apparatus, object-detection apparatus [radar], navigational electronic equipment, electronic sighting and fire control equipment, and aircraft- and missile-control systems; and related equipment, such as laser systems and equipment, and railway, highway, and traffic signals)

587 Electronic Components and Accessories (radio- and television-receiving type electron tubes, including cathode-ray picture tubes; transmitting, industrial, and special-purpose electron tubes; semiconductors and related devices; electronic capacitors; resistors for electric applications; electronic coils, transformers, and other inductors; connectors for electronic applications; and other electronic components, such as receiving antennas, printed circuits, switches, and wave guides)

589 Electrical and Electronic Machinery, Equipment, and Supplies, n.e.c. (storage batteries; primary batteries, dry and wet; x-ray apparatus and tubes, and electromedical and electrotherapeutic apparatus; electrical equipment for internal combustion engines, including armatures, starting motors, alternators, and generators for automobile and aircraft, spark plugs, magnetos, coils, distributors, and high-frequency ignition systems; electron-beam metal-cutting, forming, and welding machines, ultrasonic cleaning and welding machines; and appliance and extension cords, Christmas-tree-lighting sets, electric bells and chimes, electric-fireplace logs, and electric warm-air furnaces)

590 TRANSPORTATION EQUIPMENT

This group includes motor vehicles, aircraft, space vehicles, ships, boats, railroad equipment, motorcycles, bicycles, and other transportation equipment as produced, maintained, and repaired by workers. Wheel tractors, tracklaying and off-highway contractors' tractors, and industrial materials handling machinery and equipment are classified in Group 560. Mobile homes are classified in Group 450. Tires and tubes and rubber boats are classified in Group 510. Diesel and semidiesel engines and electrical systems for internal-combustion engines are classified in Groups 560 and 580, respectively.

591 Motor Vehicles and Motor-Vehicle Equipment (motor vehicles; passenger car bodies; truck and bus bodies; motor-vehicle parts and accessories including engines and parts [except diesel]; truck trailers; and motor homes)

592 Aircraft and Parts (aircraft; aircraft engines and parts; and other aircraft parts and accessories, such as aircraft bodies, deicing equipment, landing gear, propellers, etc.)

593 Ships and Boats (barges, cargo vessels, combat vessels, hydrofoil vessels, lighters, tankers, tugboats, etc. and boat kits and boats [except rubber])

594 Railroad Equipment (locomotives and locomotive frames, engines, and parts; railroad, street, and rapid-transit cars and car equipment; and trackless trolleys)

595 Motorcycles, Bicycles, and Parts

596 Space Vehicles and Parts (including propulsion units)

597   Travel Trailers and Campers

598   Military Tanks and Tank Components

599   Transportation Equipment, n.e.c. (all terrain vehicles [ATV], golfcarts, pushcarts, snowmobiles, wheelbarrows, etc.)

600   MEASURING, ANALYZING, AND CONTROLLING INSTRUMENTS; PHOTOGRAPHIC, MEDICAL, AND OPTICAL GOODS; AND WATCHES AND CLOCKS

> This group includes measuring, testing, analyzing, and controlling instruments and associated sensors and accessories; optical instruments and lenses; surveying and drafting instruments; surgical, medical, and dental instruments, equipment, and supplies; ophthalmic goods; photographic equipment and supplies; and watches and clocks as manufactured and repaired by workers. Balances and scales, other than laboratory, and machinists' precision-measuring tools are classified in Group 560.

601   Engineering, Laboratory, Scientific, and Research Instruments and Equipment (nautical, navigational, aeronautical, surveying, and drafting instruments and instruments for laboratory work and scientific research [except optical instruments])

602   Measuring and Controlling Instruments (residential- and commercial-environment-regulating controls; household-appliance-regulating controls; measurement, display, and control instruments for industrial-process variables; totalizing-fluid-meters and counting devices, such as gas meters, water meters, speedometers, and taximeters; electricity and electrical-signal measuring and testing instruments, such as ammeters, voltmeters, and diode and transistor testers; and physical-property-testing-apparatus, nuclear instruments, aircraft-engine instruments, etc.)

603   Optical Instruments and Lenses (lenses, prisms, microscopes, telescopes, field and opera glasses, and optical sighting and fire control, measuring, and testing instruments and equipment, such as telescopic sights, wind and percentage correctors, refractometers, spectrometers, spectroscopes, colorimeters, polariscopes, etc.)

604   Surgical, Medical, and Dental Instruments and Supplies (medical, surgical, ophthalmic, and veterinary instruments and apparatus; orthopedic, prosthetic, and surgical appliances, arch supports, and other foot appliances; fracture appliances, elastic hosiery, and abdominal supporters, braces, and trusses; bandages; surgical gauze and dressings; sutures; adhesive tapes and medicated plasters; personal safety appliances and equipment; and dental equipment, supplies, and instruments, such as artificial teeth, dental metals, alloys and amalgams, and dental drills, forceps, pliers, etc.)

605   Ophthalmic Goods (ophthalmic frames, lenses, sunglass lenses, contact lenses, etc.)

606   Photographic Equipment and Supplies (still and motion picture cameras and projection apparatus; photocopy and microfilm equipment; blueprinting and diazotype [white printing] apparatus and equipment; sensitized film, paper, cloth, and plates; and prepared photographic chemicals)

607   Watches, Clocks, Clockwork-Operated Devices, and Parts (mechanical and electric clocks, watches, mechanisms for clockwork-operated devices, clock and watch parts, watchcases, appliance timers, etc.)

609   Measuring, Analyzing, and Controlling Instruments; Photographic, Medical and Optical Goods; and Watches and Clocks, n.e.c.

610   MISCELLANEOUS FABRICATED PRODUCTS

> This group includes jewelry; silverware, plated wire, and stainless steel ware; musical instruments; games and toys; sporting and athletic goods; pens, pencils, and other office and artists' materials; costume jewelry and novelties, buttons, and miscellaneous notions; brooms and brushes; caskets; and other miscellaneous products. Bicycles are classified in Group 590. Athletic apparel are classified in Group 440. Firearms are classified in Group 370. Drafting instruments are classified in Group 600. Glass novelties are classified in Group 530. Rubber floor coverings and cork floor and wall tile are classified in Group 510 and 450, respectively.

611 Jewelry, Precious Metal (precious metal jewelry [with or without stones], umbrella and cane trimmings, and jewel settings and mountings)

612 Silverware, Plated Ware, and Stainless Steel Ware (flatware, hollowware, ecclesiastical ware, trophies, etc.)

613 Jewelers' Findings and Materials and Lapidary Work (jewelers' findings and materials and cut and polished real and synthetic jewels for settings, bearings, phonograph-needle points, etc.)

614 Musical Instruments and Parts (pianos, violins, musical-instrument keys and strings, etc.)

615 Games and Toys (dolls; chess sets; toy air rifles; children's vehicles [except bicycles], including baby carriages and strollers; etc.)

616 Sporting and Athletic Goods, except Firearms and Apparel (fishing tackle; golf and tennis goods; baseball, football, basketball, and boxing equipment; billiard and pool tables and equipment; roller skates and ice skates; gymnasium and playground equipment; bowling-alley equipment and accessories; etc.)

617 Pens, Pencils, and Other Office and Artists' Materials (pens, soft-tipped markers, mechanical pencils, and parts; lead pencils, crayons, and artists' materials [except drafting instruments]; marking devices, such as inking pads, steel letters and figures, stencils, and hand stamps, dies, and seals; and carbon paper and inked ribbons)

618 Costume Jewelry and Novelties, Buttons, and Notions (costume jewelry, novelties, and ornaments; feathers, plumes, and artificial trees, flowers, fruits, and foliage [except glass]; buttons and button parts, blanks, and molds; and needles, pins, hooks and eyes, buckles, slide and snap fasteners, etc.)

619 Miscellaneous Fabricated Products, n.e.c. (brooms, brushes, and paint rollers; signs and advertising displays, including neon signs and advertising novelties; burial caskets, casket linings, and burial vaults [except concrete]; hard-surface floor covering [except rubber and cork]; and candles, cigarette holders and smoking pipes, coin-operated amusement machines, embroidery kits, fire extinguishers, globes, mannequins, matches, canes, umbrellas, etc.)

SUBJECT MATTER

700 ARCHITECTURE AND ENGINEERING

This group includes subject matter dealing with the practical application of physical laws and principles of engineering and architecture for the development and utilization of machines, materials, instruments, structures, processes, and services. It encompasses those professional and kindred occupations dealing with or applying engineering or architectural principles and techniques in specialized areas, such as research, design, construction, testing, procurement, production, operations, and sales.

701 Architectural Engineering (including floating structures)

702 Aeronautical Engineering

703 Electrical, Electronic Engineering

704 Civil Engineering (including sanitary and environmental health)

705 Ceramic Engineering

706 Mechanical Engineering (including heating, ventilating, air-conditioning, refrigerating, and automotive engineering)

707 Chemical Engineering

708 Mining and Petroleum Engineering

711 Metallurgical Engineering

712 Industrial Engineering (methods, production, and safety engineering; cost and quality control; time, motion, and incentive studies; plant layout; etc.)

713 Agricultural Engineering (machine and structure design and development; soil and water conservation; pest control; etc.)

714 Marine Engineering (design, development, and installation of ship machinery and related equipment)

715 Nuclear Engineering

716 Surveying, Cartographic Engineering (photogrammetry, topography, mapping, etc.)

719 Architecture and Engineering, n.e.c. (pollution control, ordnance, optical, biomedical, photographic, logistics, laser, and packaging engineering, etc.)

720 MATHEMATICS AND PHYSICAL SCIENCES

This group includes subject matter dealing with research pertaining to the physical universe, and the application of established mathematical and scientific laws and principles to specific problems and situations. It encompasses mathematicians, computer programmers, astronomers, chemists, physicists, geologists, geophysicists, geodesists, and related professional and kindred occupations.

721 Mathematics (actuarial, operations research, computer applications, etc.)

722 Astronomy

723 Chemistry (organic, inorganic, physical, analytical, etc. [excluding biochemistry])

724 Physics (excluding biophysics)

725 Geology and Geophysics (mineralogy, paleontology, petrology, meteorology, seismology, hydrology, oceanography, etc.)

729 Mathematics and Physical Sciences, n.e.c. (geography, pollution control, environmental research, etc.)

730 LIFE SCIENCES

This group includes subject matter dealing with research to increase basic knowledge of living organisms, including humans, and the practical application of biological and behavioral theories. It includes agronomists, horticulturists, anatomists, biologists, biochemists, biophysicists, botanists, psychologists, and related professional and kindred workers.

731 Agriculture, Horticulture, and Forestry (animal husbandry, agronomy, soil science, forestry and conservation, etc.)

732 Biological Sciences (anatomy, biology, genetics, pharmacology, physiology, bacteriology, pathology, biochemistry, biophysics, etc.)

733 Psychology (includes counseling)

739 Life Sciences, n.e.c.

740 SOCIAL SCIENCES

This group includes subject matter dealing with human society and its characteristic elements, such as origin, race, or state; and with economic and social relations and institutions involved in a human being's existence as a member of an organized community. It includes economists, political scientists, biographers, historians, sociologists, anthropologists, archeologists, philologists, linguists, and related professional and kindred workers. Social work is classified in Group 940.

741 Economics

742 Political Science

743 History

744 Sociology (includes criminology)

745 Anthropology (archeology, ethnology, and ethnography)

749   Social Sciences, n.e.c. (philology, linguistics, etc.)

750   ARTS AND LITERATURE

This group includes subject matter dealing with the integration of personal expression and artistic or literary concepts, techniques, or processes to create, perform, conduct, or edit artistic or literary works or activities which elicit an emotional or aesthetic response. It includes landscape painters, sculptors, illustrators, cartoonists, furniture designers, interior designers, motion-picture photographers, actors/actresses, dancers, musicians, composers, writers, editors, and related professional and kindred occupations. Commercial decorating, window trimming, and modeling services are classified in Group 880. Photofinishing services are classified in Group 890.

751   Fine Arts (creative art, such as designing, drawing, and illustrating)

752   Graphic Arts (commercial art, such as designing, drawing, and illustrating)

753   Photography (still and motion-picture photography)

754   Dramatics

755   Rhythmics (dancing)

756   Music

757   Literature and Journalism

759   Arts and Literature, n.e.c.

SERVICES

850   TRANSPORTATION SERVICES

This group includes railroad, motor-vehicle, water, air, and pipeline transportation services provided by locomotive engineers, conductors, bus and truck drivers, ship and airline pilots, stevedores, deckhands, transportation agents, pumpstation operators, pipeline laborers, and related workers. Maintenance and repair services are classified in Group 590. Automobile services other than maintenance and repair are classified in Group 960. Natural, liquefied-petroleum, manufactured, and mixed gas production and distribution services are classified in Group 870. Ambulance services are classified in Group 920.

851   Interurban Railroad Transportation (railroad line-haul, switching, and terminal, etc.)

852   Local and Suburban Transit and Interurban Highway Passenger Transportation (subway, trolley coach, street railway, and aerial tramway; bus line, charter, and terminal; taxicab; school bus; etc.)

853   Motor Freight Transportation and Warehousing (local and long-distance trucking; trucking terminal; public warehousing and storage)

854   Water Transportation (deep sea and inland waterway transportation; lighterage, towing, and tugboat; taxi, excursion, and sightseeing boat; marine-cargo handling; canal; etc.)

855   Air Transportation (air cargo and passenger transportation; airport terminal; etc.)

856   Pipeline Transportation (except natural gas)

859   Transportation Services, n.e.c. (freight forwarding; freight, travel, and tourist agency; highway bridge, toll bridge, toll road, and tunnel; stockyard; etc.)

860   COMMUNICATION SERVICES

This group includes aural or visual communication and broadcasting services provided by telephone and telegraph operators, radio and television broadcasters, radar-station operators, telephoto operators, and related workers. Newspapers, magazines, and related printed and published products are classified in Group 480. Telephone message services are classified in Group 890. Lecturing and public-speaking services are classified in Group 930. Installation, maintenance, and repair of communication structures and equipment are classified in Group 360 and 580, respectively.

861   Telephone Communication (wire or radio)

862   Telegraph Communication (wire or radio)

863   Radio Broadcasting

864   Television Broadcasting

869   Communication Services, n.e.c. (cablevision, missile tracking and radar, telephoto, ticker tape, etc.)

870   ELECTRIC, GAS, AND SANITARY SERVICES

This group includes electric, gas, and steam generation, transmission, and distribution services, and water supply, irrigation, and sanitary services, provided by substation operators, power plant operators, meter readers, gas-pumping station operators, watershed tenders, wastewater-treatment plant operators, sludge-control operators, and related workers. Installation, maintenance, and repair of electric, gas, and sanitary service structures and equipment are classified in Groups 360, 560, 580, and 600.

871   Electric Services (includes nuclear-generating)

872   Gas Production and Distribution (natural, manufactured, mixed, and liquefied-petroleum gas)

873   Water-Supply and Irrigation Services

874   Sanitary Services (sewerage, refuse, street cleaning)

875   Steam Supply (includes heated and cooled air)

879   Electric, Gas, and Sanitary Services, n.e.c.

880   MERCHANDISING SERVICES

This group includes retail and wholesale trade, route sales and delivery, auctioneering, vending, rental, sales promotion, merchandise displaying, and related merchandising services rendered by commodity-sales personnel, vendors, peddlers, newspaper carriers, sales-route drivers, auctioneers, rental clerks, cashiers, demonstrators, models, window dressers, commercial decorators, professional shoppers, buyers, and similar workers. Sales personnel engaged in selling finance, insurance, real estate, transportation, utilities, advertising, and related services are classified according to the services being sold.

881   Retail Trade

882   Wholesale Trade

883   Route Sales and Delivery Services (including coin-machine collecting)

884   Auctioneering, Vending, and Rental Services

885   Sales Promotion Services (demonstrating, modeling, etc.)

889   Merchandising Services, n.e.c. (commercial decorating, window trimming, professional shopping, etc.)

890   GENERAL BUSINESS, FINANCE, INSURANCE, AND REAL ESTATE SERVICES

This group includes insurance and real estate services and clerical, accounting, general administration, financial, advertising, photofinishing, and similar business services of a general nature rendered by various clerical workers, accountants, auditors, personnel officers, plant managers, bank officials, insurance and real estate agents, stockbrokers, public relations representatives, photofinishers, divers, sign painters, and related workers. Specialized business services, such as transportation, communication, public utility, merchandising, medical, legal, government, etc., are classified in their respective service groups.

891   Clerical Services, except Bookkeeping (stenographic, secretarial, typing, filing, duplicating, etc.)

892   Accounting, Auditing, and Bookkeeping Services

893   General Administration and Administrative Specialties (general management, personnel administration, job evaluation, consulting, computer programming, data processing, etc.)

894 Financial Services (banking, credit, collection, savings and loan, investment, trust, securities and commodities, etc.)

895 Insurance and Real Estate

896 Advertising and Public Relations Services

897 Blueprinting, Photocopying, Photofinishing, and Printing Services

898 Production Services (stock chasing, timekeeping, etc.)

899 General Business, Finance, Insurance, and Real Estate Services, n.e.c. (telephone message, news reporting, press clipping, trading stamp, commercial testing laboratory, bail bonding, commercial diving, messenger, sign painting and lettering, etc.)

900 DOMESTIC, BUILDING, AND PERSONAL SERVICES

> This group includes private household, lodging, meal, beauty and barber, janitorial, laundry, funeral, steam bath, and related services provided by bartenders, cooks, chauffeurs, hair stylists, janitors, bellhops, maids, morticians, spa operators, waitresses, and related workers. Babysitting services in private homes are also included. Apparel and furnishings alteration and repair services are classified according to the product altered or repaired. Non-domestic child and adult care services without accompanying medical care are classified in Group 940; medical care services are classified in Group 920.

901 Domestic Services (babysitting, maid, chauffeuring, gardening, etc.)

902 Lodging Services (hotel, rooming house, camp, trailer park, etc.)

903 Meal Services, except Domestic (food, beverage, and catering)

904 Beauty and Barbering Services

905 Janitorial and Portering Services (building cleaning, baggage handling, window cleaning, chimney cleaning, floor waxing, etc.)

906 Apparel and Furnishings Services (laundry, dry cleaning, pressing, dyeing, linen and diaper supply, shoeshine, garment storage, etc.)

907 Funeral and Crematory Services

909 Domestic, Building, and Personal Services, n.e.c. (clothing rental, dating and escort, health spa, massage, steam bath, etc.)

910 AMUSEMENT AND RECREATION SERVICES

> This group includes motion picture, theater, sports, and related entertainment services provided by movie producers, directors, projectionists, extras, propmakers, high riggers, athletes, athletic coaches and trainers, animal trainers, caddies, concession attendants, gambling-hall attendants, ushers, wardrobe attendants, ride operators, and related workers. Dramatics, dancing, and music instructors and professional performers are classified in Groups 930 and 750, respectively.

911 Motion Picture Services (production and distribution; casting and directing; film editing, developing, printing, and rental; ushering and ticket taking; etc.)

912 Theater Services (production; casting; booking; costume and scenery design; lighting; ticket agency; ushering and ticket taking; etc.)

913 Sports Services (sports participation and related sport support functions)

919 Amusement and Recreation Services, n.e.c. (theatrical and amusement performing, amusement ride and carnival services, game room services, park services, and related support functions)

920 MEDICAL AND OTHER HEALTH SERVICES

> This group includes medical and other health services provided to others by physicians, dentists, osteopaths, optometrists, podiatrists, nurses, therapists, dietitians, medical-laboratory technicians, dental hygienists, dental assistants, medical assistants, nurse aides, orderlies, and related workers. Ambulance and veterinary services are also included.

921 Physician Services, including Surgical

922 Dental Services, including Surgical

923 Optometric, Chiropractic, and Related Services

924 Nursing, Dietetic, and Therapeutic Services

925 Health Technological Services (clinical laboratory, dental hygiene, radiological, etc.)

926 Medical Assistant, Aide, and Attendant Services

929 Medical and Other Health Services, n.e.c. (ambulance, veterinary, etc.)

930 EDUCATIONAL, LEGAL, MUSEUM, LIBRARY, AND ARCHIVAL SERVICES

This group includes educational, legal, museum, library, and archival services provided by teachers, professors, instructors, home economists, lecturers, lawyers, judges, librarians, archivists, museum curators, and related workers. Animal trainers and coaches and trainers of professional athletes are classified in Group 910.

931 Educational Services (includes vocational training, farm and home advising, and lecturing services)

932 Legal Services

933 Museum, Library, and Archival Services

939 Educational, Legal, Museum, Library, and Archival Services, n.e.c.

940 SOCIAL, EMPLOYMENT, AND SPIRITUAL SERVICES

This group includes services rendered to individuals and groups with employment, spiritual, child- or adult-care needs, or social problems, such as poverty, family maladjustment, antisocial behavior, financial mismanagement, or inadequate housing. It encompasses employment interviewers and clerks, personnel recruiters, clergy members, nursery school attendants, companions, case workers, social workers, parole and probation officers, and related professional and social service occupations. Psychological and counseling services to provide social, behavioral, educational, or vocational guidance are classified in Group 730. Educational services are classified in Group 930. Domestic babysitting services are classified in Group 900.

941 Social and Welfare Services (adoption, disaster, family location, homemaking, old-age assistance, refugee, travelers' aid, etc.)

942 Child and Adult Residential and Day-Care Services (nursery school, foster home, orphanage, rest home, training school, etc.)

943 Employment Services (recruitment, interviewing, and placement)

944 Spiritual Services (ministerial)

949 Social, Employment, and Spiritual Services, n.e.c. (parole, probation, etc.)

950 REGULATION, PROTECTION, AND RELATED GOVERNMENT SERVICES

This group includes services concerned with regulation, protection, postal, government, and related activities, such as fire and police/security protection, military services, food and drug inspection, customs control, and tax collection, whether provided by the government or by the private sector. It encompasses police officers, security guards, fire chiefs, jailers, military occupations, customs inspectors, food and drug inspectors, immigration inspectors, postmasters, mail deliverers, and other related occupations.

951 Protective Services, except Military (property security, armored car services, crime prevention, fire and police protection, wildlife protection, etc.)

952 Military Services

953 Regulatory Law Investigation and Control Services (customs, immigration, internal revenue, food and drug, safety and health, environmental and housing, licensing, etc.)

954 Postal Services

959   Regulation, Protection, and Related Government Services, n.e.c.

960   MISCELLANEOUS SERVICES

> This group includes motor-vehicle, deodorizing, exterminating, decontaminating, elevator, taxidermy, and other miscellaneous services provided by parking-lot attendants, tow-truck operators, car-wash attendants, exterminators, fumigators, air-purifier servicers, decontaminators, elevator operators, taxidermists, and related workers. Motor-vehicle maintenance and repair services are classified in Group 590. Messenger and advertising services are classified in Group 890.

961   Motor-Vehicle Services, except Maintenance and Repair (parking, storage, towing, undercoating, washing, etc.)

962   Deodorizing, Exterminating, and Decontaminating Services

969   Miscellaneous Services, n.e.c. (elevator, gardening, groundskeeping, and landscaping; taxidermy; etc.)

604	Abdominal Braces, Supporters, and Trusses
538	Abrasive Products
486	Account Books
571	Accounting Machines
892	Accounting Services
721	Actuarial Mathematics
499	Adhesives
604	Adhesive Tapes
893	Administration and Administrative Specialty Services
941	Adoption Services
942	Adult Day- and Residential-Care Services
619	Advertising Displays and Novelties
896	Advertising Services
931	Advising Services, Farm and Home
852	Aerial Tramway Transportation Services
702	Aeronautical Engineering
601	Aeronautical Instruments
497	Agricultural Chemicals
713	Agricultural Engineering
731	Agriculture Sciences
731	Agronomy
855	Air-Cargo-Transportation Services
568	Air Compressors
706	Air-Conditioning Engineering
573	Air-Conditioning and Refrigeration Equipment
573	Air-Conditioning Units
592	Aircraft and Parts
592	Aircraft Accessories
586	Aircraft-Control Systems
592	Aircraft-Deicing Equipment
602	Aircraft-Engine Instruments
592	Aircraft Engines and Parts
589	Aircraft Generators
371	Aircraft Guns
602	Aircraft Instruments
592	Aircraft Propellers
466	Aircraft Seats
514	Air Line Hose
855	Air-Passenger-Transportation Services
362	Airports
855	Airport-Terminal Services
615	Air Rifles, Toy
855	Air-Transportation Services
486	Albums (Printed)
395	Alcoholic Beverages
496	Alcohols, Polyhydric
491	Alkalies
604	Alloys, Dental

599	All-Terrain Vehicles (ATV)
589	Alternators, Aircraft and Automobile
355	Aluminum Ores
543	Aluminum, Smelted and Refined
604	Amalgams, Dental
929	Ambulance Services
496	Amines, Acid and Polyhydric Alcohol
602	Ammeters
372	Ammunition, except Small Arms
374	Ammunition, Small Arms
493	Ampules
910	AMUSEMENT AND RECREATION SERVICES
919	Amusement-Arcade Services
619	Amusement Machines, Coin-Operated
919	Amusement-Park Services
723	Analytical Chemistry
600	ANALYZING INSTRUMENTS
732	Anatomy
381	Animal Feeds
731	Animal Husbandry
320	ANIMALS
325	Animals, Captive Fur-Bearing
329	Animals, Laboratory
329	Animals, Zoo
587	Antennas, Receiving
745	Anthropology
371	Anti-aircraft Guns
359	Antimony Ore
440	APPAREL
906	Apparel and Furnishing Services
442	Apparel, Men's and Boys' Athletic
443	Apparel, Women's, Girls', and Infants' Athletic
589	Appliance Cords
602	Appliance-Regulating Controls, Household
604	Appliances, Foot, Fracture, and Surgical
583	Appliances, Household
607	Appliance Timers
519	Aprons, Rubber
745	Archeology
701	Architectural Engineering
554	Architectural Metalwork
700	ARCHITECTURE AND ENGINEERING
933	Archival Services
604	Arch Supports
589	Armatures, Aircraft and Automobile
951	Armored-Car Services
532	Art Glass
539	Art Goods, Plaster of Paris and Papier Mache
432	Art Goods, Stamped
618	Artificial Flowers and Fruit
618	Artificial Foliage (except Glass)

434 Artificial Leather	474 Bags, Paper
604 Artificial Teeth	439 Bags, Sleeping
618 Artificial Trees	436 Bags, Textile
371 Artillery	899 Bail-Bonding Services
617 Artist Materials (except Drafting Instruments)	384 Bakery Products
	399 Baking Powder
432 Art Needlework	571 Balances (except Laboratory)
750 ARTS	581 Ballasts, Lighting Fixture
751 Arts, Fine	568 Ball Bearings
752 Arts, Graphic	519 Balloons, Rubber
473 Asbestos Building Paper	919 Ballroom Services
538 Asbestos Products	549 Balls, Steel
349 Asbestos (Raw Mineral)	319 Balsam Needles
556 Ash Trays, Stamped Metal	604 Bandages
473 Asphalt Board and Building Paper	894 Banking Services
349 Asphalt, Native	557 Barbed Wire
502 Asphalt-Paving Mixtures and Blocks	904 Barbering Services
503 Asphalt Roofing Felts	469 Barber-Shop Equipment
722 Astronomy	593 Barges
913 Athletes	347 Barite
442 Athletic Apparel, Men's and Boys'	319 Barks
443 Athletic Apparel, Women's, Girls', and Infants'	551 Barrels, Metal
	541 Bars and Rods, Iron and Steel
362 Athletic Fields	544 Bars and Rods, Nonferrous Metal
616 Athletic Goods (except Firearms and Apparel)	616 Baseball Equipment
	616 Basketball Equipment
522 Athletic Shoes	519 Bathing Caps, Rubber
489 Atlases	442 Bathing Suits, Men's and Boys' (non-rubber)
524 Attache Cases	519 Bathing Suits, Rubber
584 Attachment-Wiring Caps and Plugs	443 Bathing Suits, Womens', Girls', and Infants' (non-rubber)
884 Auctioneering Services	
892 Auditing Services	589 Batteries, Primary, Dry and Wet
572 Automatic Merchandising Machines	589 Batteries, Storage
589 Automobile Generators	582 Battery Chargers
961 Automobile-Parking and Storage Services	433 Batting
466 Automobile Seats	355 Bauxite Ore
961 Automobile Services, except Maintenance and Repair	379 Bazookas
	568 Bearings, Ball and Roller
556 Automobile Stampings	613 Bearings, Cut and Polished Jewel
961 Automobile-Towing Services	904 Beauty Services
961 Automobile-Undercoating Services	469 Beauty-Shop Equipment
961 Automobile-Washing Services	464 Beds, Sofa and Chair
706 Automotive Engineering	435 Bedspreads
566 Automotive-Maintenance Equipment	464 Bedsprings
585 Auto Radios and Tape Players	573 Beer-Dispensing Units
436 Awnings, Canvas	329 Bees
519 Awnings, Plastic	392 Beet Sugar
552 Axes	589 Bells, Electric
	529 Belting, Leather
	514 Belting, Rubber and Plastic
	449 Belts, Apparel
615 Baby Carriages and Strollers	514 Belts, Conveyor
387 Baby Foods, Canned	346 Bentonite
901 Babysitting Services	305 Berries
493 Bacterial Vaccines	359 Beryllium Ore
732 Bacteriology	395 Beverages, Alcoholic
905 Baggage-Handling Services	903 Beverage Services

395	Beverages, Malt	604	Braces, Abdominal
595	Bicycles and Parts	538	Brake Linings (Asbestos)
525	Billfolds	553	Brass Goods, Plumbing
913	Billiard-Parlor Services	444	Brassieres
616	Billiard Tables and Equipment	564	Breakers, Coal
486	Binders, Looseleaf	365	Breakwaters
732	Biochemistry	534	Brick, Clay
493	Biological Products	536	Brick, Concrete
732	Biological Sciences	363	Bridges
732	Biology	859	Bridge Services, Highway
719	Biomedical Engineering	362	Bridle Paths
732	Biophysics	504	Briquettes, Fuel
552	Bits	586	Broadcasting Equipment and Parts
486	Blankbooks	863	Broadcasting Services, Radio
583	Blankets, Electric	864	Broadcasting Services, Television
435	Blankets (except Electric)	421	Broad Woven Cotton Fabrics
541	Blast-Furnace Products	422	Broad Woven Wool Fabrics
582	Blasting Machines	583	Broilers (Household)
395	Blended Liquors	344	Broken and Crushed Stone
583	Blenders (Household)	619	Brooms
469	Blinds, Window	582	Brush Blocks (Carbon and Graphite)
536	Block, Concrete	619	Brushes
493	Blood Derivatives	618	Buckles
443	Blouses	538	Buffing Wheels
568	Blower Fans	552	Builders' Hardware
562	Blowers, Snow	905	Building-Cleaning Services
531	Blown Glass and Glassware	538	Building Materials (Asbestos)
606	Blueprinting Apparatus and Equipment	473	Building Paper and Building Board, Nonconverted
897	Blueprinting Services	900	BUILDING SERVICES
593	Boat Kits	361	Buildings, except Prefabricated
854	Boat Services, Excursion, Sightseeing, and Taxi	554	Buildings, Prefabricated Metal
		455	Buildings, Prefabricated Wood
593	Boats, except Rubber	537	Building Stone
519	Boats, Rubber	584	Bulbs, Electric Light
592	Bodies, Aircraft	311	Bulbs, Plant
591	Bodies, Truck	563	Bulldozers
555	Bolts, Metal	619	Burial Caskets
451	Bolts, Wood	619	Burial Vaults, except Concrete
372	Bombs	890	BUSINESS SERVICES, GENERAL
466	Bookcases, Metal	484	Business Forms
465	Bookcases, Wood	852	Bus-Line Services, Charter
912	Booking Services, Theater	852	Bus-Line Services, Terminal
892	Bookkeeping Services	618	Button Blanks and Molds
483	Books and Pamphlets	618	Buttons and Parts
486	Books, Account, Receipt, and Sample		
522	Boot and Shoe Cut Stock and Findings		
467	Booth, Telephone		
522	Boots, Canvas		
347	Borate	467	Cabinets, Display
493	Botanical Products	466	Cabinets, Filing (Metal)
556	Bottle and Jar Caps and Tops	467	Cabinets, Kitchen
531	Bottles, Glass	461	Cabinets, Phonograph, Radio, Sewing Machine, and Television
519	Bottles, Plastic		
616	Bowling-Alley Equipment and Accessories	364	Cable Lines
913	Bowling-Alley Services	544	Cable, Nonferrous Metal
475	Boxes and Containers, Paperboard	541	Cable, Steel
616	Boxing Equipment	869	Cablevision Services

571 Calculating Machines	321 Cattle
524 Camera Cases	533 Cement, Hydraulic (Natural, Portland, Masonry)
606 Cameras, Motion Picture	503 Cements, Roofing
606 Cameras, Still	705 Ceramic Engineering
597 Campers	534 Ceramic Wall and Floor Tile
902 Camp Services	464 Chair Beds
365 Canals	466 Chairs, Metal
854 Canal Services	465 Chalkboards, Wood
619 Candles	365 Channels
393 Candy	852 Charter-Bus-Line Services
619 Canes	556 Chassis, Radio and Television (Metal Stamped)
392 Cane Sugar	901 Chauffeuring Services
611 Cane Trimmings	486 Checkbooks
387 Canned Food Specialties	490 CHEMICAL AND ALLIED PRODUCTS
551 Cans, Metal	347 Chemical and Fertilizer Minerals
556 Cans, Stamped Metal	707 Chemical Engineering
522 Canvas Boots	497 Chemicals, Agricultural
436 Canvas Products	496 Chemicals, Gum and Wood
582 Capacitors, Electrical (Fixed and Variable)	491 Chemicals, Inorganic
587 Capacitors, Electronic	493 Chemicals, Medicinal
584 Caps, Attachment Wiring	496 Chemicals, Organic
556 Caps, Bottle and Jar	606 Chemicals, Photographic
519 Caps, Rubber Bathing	496 Chemicals, Rubber-Processing
493 Capsules (Pharmaceutical Preparations)	496 Chemicals, Wood
591 Car Bodies, Passenger	496 Chemical Warfare Gases
396 Carbonated Waters	372 Chemical Warfare Projectiles
499 Carbon Black	723 Chemistry
617 Carbon Paper	723 Chemistry, Analytical
582 Carbon Products	723 Chemistry, Inorganic
472 Cardboard (Except Die Cut)	723 Chemistry, Organic
474 Cardboard, Die Cut	723 Chemistry, Physical
485 Cards, Greeting (except Hand Painted)	615 Chess Sets
579 Carnival Machines and Equipment	393 Chewing Gum
919 Carnival Services	403 Chewing Tobacco
552 Carpenters' Handtools	942 Child Day-Care and Residential-Care Services
431 Carpets	615 Children's Vehicles (except Bicycles)
615 Carriages, Baby	589 Chimes, Electric
594 Cars and Equipment, Railroad	905 Chimney-Cleaning Services
594 Cars and Equipment, Rapid Transit	535 China Plumbing Fixtures
564 Cars, Mining	535 Chinaware
716 Cartographic Engineering	923 Chiropractic Services
572 Car-Washing Machinery	552 Chisels
524 Cases, Attache, Camera, Musical Instrument	491 Chlorine
467 Cases, Display	393 Chocolate
525 Cases, Jewelry and Key	589 Christmas Tree-Lighting Sets
619 Casket Linings	313 Christmas Trees (Standing Timber)
619 Caskets, Burial	356 Chromium Ore
911 Casting Services, Motion Picture	398 Cider
912 Casting Services, Theater	619 Cigarette Holders
542 Castings, Ferrous and Nonferrous Metal	401 Cigarettes
542 Castings, Metal	402 Cigars
489 Catalogs	581 Circuit Breakers
579 Catapults	304 Citrus Fruits
903 Catering Services	704 Civil Engineering
587 Cathode-Ray Picture Tubes	346 Clay
329 Cats	534 Clay, Brick
	346 Clay, Fire

413	Cordage	854	Deep-Sea Transportation Services
589	Cords, Appliance	573	Dehumidifiers (except Room)
589	Cords, Extension	592	Deicing Equipment, Aircraft
564	Core Drills	883	Delivery Services
459	Cork Products	885	Demonstrating Services (Sales Promotions)
474	Corrugated and Laminated Paper	604	Dental Equipment
494	Cosmetics	925	Dental-Hygiene Services
712	Cost-Control Engineering	604	Dental Instruments
912	Costume-Design Services	604	Dental Metals, Alloys and Amalgams
618	Costume Jewelry	922	Dental Services
467	Costumers	604	Dental Supplies
449	Costumes	922	Dental Surgical Services
302	Cotton Crops	962	Deodorizing Services
421	Cotton Fabrics	372	Depth Charges
733	Counseling	912	Design, Costume
602	Counting Devices	529	Desk Sets, Leather
565	Cranes, Industrial	466	Desks, Metal
563	Cranes, Nonindustrial Plant	465	Desks, Wood
617	Crayons	586	Detection Equipment and Apparatus
751	Creative Arts	494	Detergents
894	Credit Services	897	Developing Services, Film (Photofinishing)
907	Crematory Services	911	Developing Services, Motion Picture Film
951	Crime-Correction Services	449	Diapers
744	Criminology	906	Diaper-Supply Services
439	Crocheted Products	606	Diazotype (white printing) Apparatus and Equipment
539	Crucibles, Nonclay	571	Dictating Machines
342	Crude Petroleum	474	Die-Cut Paper, Paperboard, and Cardboard
319	Crude Rubber	561	Diesel Engines and Parts (except Aircraft)
344	Crushed and Broken Stone	566	Die Sets
564	Crushing Machinery, Rock	617	Dies, Hand
581	Cubicles and Switchboards	566	Dies, Special
435	Curtains	924	Dietetic Services
464	Cushions, Spring	365	Dikes
953	Customs Services	452	Dimension Stock, Hardwood
532	Cut-Glass Tableware	343	Dimension Stone
552	Cutlery	602	Diode Testers
522	Cut Stock and Findings, Boot and Shoe	911	Directing Services, Motion Picture
537	Cut Stone	489	Directories
537	Cut Stone Furniture	941	Disaster Services
564	Cutters, Coal	435	Dishcloths
496	Cyclic (Coal Tar) Crudes	583	Dishwashers, Household
496	Cyclic Organic Intermediates	572	Dispensing Pumps
		573	Dispensing Units, Beer
		573	Dispensing Units, Soda Fountain
		467	Display Cabinets and Cases
		602	Display Instruments, Industrial Process Variables
383	Dairy Products	619	Displays, Advertising
365	Dams	583	Disposal Units, Garbage
919	Dancehall Services	395	Distilled Liquors
755	Dancing	581	Distribution Equipment, Electric
893	Data Processing Services	872	Distribution Services, Gas
305	Dates	911	Distribution Services, Motion Picture
393	Dates, Stuffed	581	Distribution Transformers
909	Dating Services	589	Distributors
942	Day-Care Services, Child and Adult	899	Diving Services, Commercial
962	Decontaminating Services	529	Dog Collars and Leashes
889	Decorating Services, Commercial	329	Dogs

587	Electron Tubes, Transmitting	421	Fabrics, Broad Woven Cotton
589	Electrotherapeutic Apparatus	422	Fabrics, Broad Woven Wool
363	Elevated Highways	434	Fabrics, Coated (except Rubberized)
565	Elevators	421	Fabrics, Glass Fiber
969	Elevator Services	434	Fabrics, Impregnated (except Rubberized)
432	Embroideries	424	Fabrics, Knitted
619	Embroidery Kits	425	Fabrics, Nonwoven (except Knitted)
943	Employment Services	519	Fabrics, Rubberized
553	Enameled Iron and Metal Sanitary Ware	421	Fabrics, Silk
495	Enamels	421	Fabrics, Synthetic Fiber
700	ENGINEERING AND ARCHITECTURE	941	Family Location Services
601	Engineering Instruments and Equipment	432	Fancy Textiles
592	Engines, Aircraft	484	Fanfold Forms
561	Engines and Parts, Diesel and Semidiesel	568	Fans, Industrial Blower
561	Engines and Parts, Internal Combustion (except Aircraft and Non-Diesel Automotive)	568	Fans, Industrial Exhaust and Ventilating
		583	Fans, Household (except Attic)
		931	Farm-Advising Services
561	Engines and Turbines (except Aircraft and Non-Diesel Automotive)	361	Farm Buildings
		300	FARM CROPS, PLANT
591	Engines, Motor Vehicles (except Diesel)	583	Farm Freezers
561	Engines, Steam (except Locomotive)	562	Farm Machinery and Equipment
594	Engines, Steam Locomotive	562	Farm Wheel Tractors
474	Envelopes	618	Fasteners, Slide and Snap
704	Environmental Health Engineering	385	Fats and Oils, Edible
602	Environmental Regulating Controls, Commercial and Residential	618	Feathers
		381	Feeds, Animal and Fowl
953	Environmental Regulatory Law Investigation and Control Services	439	Felt Goods
		503	Felts, Asphalt Roofing
729	Environmental Research	422	Felt, Wool
327	Equines	451	Fence Rails
899	Equipment Rental-and-Leasing Services	557	Fencing, Wire
519	Erasers, Rubber	356	Ferroalloy Ores
909	Escort Services	540	FERROUS METAL
496	Esters, Acid and Polyhydric Alcohol	542	Ferrous Metal Castings
745	Ethnography	347	Fertilizer and Chemical Minerals
745	Ethnology	497	Fertilizers
573	Evaporative Condensers (Heat-Transfer Equipment)	473	Fiberboard
		468	Fiberglass Furniture and Fixtures
854	Excursion-Boat Services	414	Fibers, Glass (Finishing)
568	Exhaust Fans	531	Fibers, Glass (Production)
499	Explosives	414	Fibers, Natural and Silk
589	Extension Cords	414	Fiber Stock
962	Exterminating Services	414	Fibers, Synthetic (Finishing)
394	Extracts, Flavoring	492	Fibers, Synthetic (Production)
618	Eyes and Hooks	410	FIBERS, TEXTILE
		419	Fibers, Waste and Recovered
		371	Field Artillery
		302	Field Crops (except Grain)
		603	Field Glasses
550	FABRICATED METAL PRODUCTS, EXCEPT ORDNANCE, MACHINERY AND TRANSPORTATION EQUIPMENT	466	Filing Cabinets, Metal
		891	Filing Services
		495	Fillers, Wood
559	Fabricated Pipe, Metal	433	Filling, Upholstery
554	Fabricated Plate Work (Boiler Shops)	911	Film-Editing Services
554	Fabricated Structural Metal	606	Film Sensitized
557	Fabricated Wire Products	894	Financial Services
420	FABRICS AND RELATED	522	Findings and Cut Stock, Boot and Shoe

613	Findings, Jewelers'	602	Fluid Meters, Totalizing
751	Fine Arts	584	Fluorescent Lamps
331	Finfish	584	Fluorescent Starters
541	Finishing Mill Products	347	Fluorspar
534	Firebrick, Clay	559	Foil and Leaf, Metal
346	Fire Clay	618	Foliage, Artificial (except Glass)
586	Fire Control Equipment, Electronic	953	Food Control Services
603	Fire Control Equipment, Optical	567	Food Products Machinery and Equipment
554	Fire Escapes, Metal	903	Food Services
619	Fire Extinguishers	390	FOOD SPECIALTIES
589	Fireplace Logs, Electric	380	FOOD STAPLES AND RELATED
951	Fire Protection Services	572	Food-Warming Equipment, Commercial
331	Fish (Finfish)	604	Foot Appliances
439	Fishing Nets	616	Football Equipment
616	Fishing Tackle	522	Footwear (except Rubber)
332	Fish (Shellfish)	512	Footwear, Rubber and Plastic
584	Fittings, Electric	604	Forceps, Dental
559	Fittings, Metal Pipe (except Plumbers')	314	Forest Nursery Products
519	Fittings, Plastic Pipe	310	FOREST PRODUCTS
553	Fixture Fittings and Trim, Plumbing (Brass Goods)	731	Forestry
		310	FOREST TREES
535	Fixtures and Fittings, China and Earthenware Plumbing	556	Forgings, Metal
		484	Forms, Business, Fanfold, and Office
460	FIXTURES AND FURNITURE	942	Foster Home Services
469	Fixtures and Furniture, Barber and Beauty Shop	324	Fowl
		381	Fowl Feeds
468	Fixtures and Furniture, Plastic, Glass, and Fiberglass	604	Fracture Appliances
		457	Frames, Mirror and Picture
469	Fixtures and Furniture, Rattan, Reed, Wicker, and Willow	605	Frames, Ophthalmic
		554	Frames, Metal Window and Door
584	Fixtures, Electric Lighting	452	Frames, Wooden Window
467	Fixtures, Wood and Metal	583	Freezers, Home and Farm
554	Flagpoles, Metal	859	Freight Agency Services
439	Flags	859	Freight Forwarding Services
379	Flame Throwers	339	Frogs
584	Flashlights	618	Fruit, Artificial (except Glass)
531	Flat Glass or Glassware	387	Fruits and Vegetables, Processed
612	Flatware	304	Fruits, Citrus
394	Flavoring Extracts	305	Fruits (except Citrus)
496	Flavoring Materials, Synthetic	504	Fuel Briquettes
394	Flavoring Syrups	501	Fuel, Jet
531	Float Glass	501	Fuel Oils
619	Floor Coverings, Hard-Surface (except Rubber and Cork)	504	Fuel, Packaged and Powdered
		340	FUELS, RAW
452	Flooring	452	Fuelwood
583	Floor Polishers (Household)	346	Fuller's Earth
572	Floor-Polishing Machines (Commercial)	907	Funeral Services
572	Floor-Sanding Machines (Commercial)	325	Fur-Bearing Animals, Captive
534	Floor Tile, Ceramic	447	Fur Coats and Jackets
572	Floor-Washing Machinery (Commercial)	447	Fur Goods
583	Floor Waxers	447	Fur Hats
905	Floor-Waxing Services	589	Furnaces, Electric Warm-Air
311	Floricultural Nursery Products	369	Furnaces, Industrial (Constructed)
311	Florists' Greens	568	Furnaces, Industrial Process
311	Flowers	553	Furnaces, Steam or Hot Water (Domestic)
618	Flowers, Artificial (except Glass)	573	Furnaces, Warm-Air (except Electric)
311	Flower Seeds and Plants	447	Fur Neckpieces

349	Graphite (Raw Mineral)
345	Gravel and Sand
485	Greeting Cards (except Hand Painted)
372	Grenades
538	Grinding Wheels
532	Ground Glass
969	Groundskeeping Services
375	Guided Missiles
919	Guide Services, Tourist
496	Gum and Wood Chemicals
319	Gums (including Pine)
371	Guns, Howitzers, Mortars, and Related Equipment
519	Gutters and Downspouts, Plastic
616	Gymnasium Equipment
349	Gypsum
536	Gypsum Products

422	Haircloth
439	Hammocks
525	Handbags
617	Hand Dies
449	Handkerchiefs
552	Handsaws
617	Hand Seals
617	Hand Stamps
552	Handtools, Nonpower
566	Handtools, Power
439	Handwoven Products
557	Hangers, Wire Garment
365	Harbor Construction
552	Hardware, Builders'
469	Hardware, Drapery
552	Hardware, Furniture
552	Hardware, General
552	Hardware, Motor Vehicle
519	Hardware, Plastic
452	Hardwood Dimension Stock
529	Harness
445	Hats (except Fur)
447	Hats, Fur
432	Hatters' Fur
302	Hay (Crops)
953	Health-Control Services
387	Health Foods, Canned
920	HEALTH SERVICES
909	Health-Spa Services
925	Health-Technological Services
875	Heated-Air Services
586	Heat-Emission Operating Apparatus
514	Heater Hose
553	Heaters, Nonelectric
583	Heaters, Space and Water (Household)

706	Heating Engineering
553	Heating Equipment, Nonelectric
573	Heat-Transfer Equipment
556	Helmets, Metal
429	Hemp Fabrics
521	Hides
589	High-Frequency Ignition Systems
568	High-Speed Drives, Industrial
859	Highway Bridge Services
852	Highway PassengerTransportation Services, Interurban
362	Highways and Streets
586	Highway Traffic Signals
743	History
322	Hogs
565	Hoists
612	Hollowware
931	Home Advising Services
583	Home Freezers
941	Homemaking Services
585	Home Recorders
618	Hooks and Eyes
327	Horses
731	Horticulture
310	HORTICULTURAL SPECIALTIES, FOREST TREES, AND FOREST PRODUCTS
514	Hose, Air Line
514	Hose, Garden
514	Hose, Heater
514	Hose, Rubber and Plastic
446	Hosiery
604	Hosiery, Elastic
902	Hotel Services
553	Hot Water or Steam Domestic Furnaces
435	House Furnishings
602	Household-Appliance-Regulating Controls
583	Household Appliances
583	Household Dishwashers
583	Household Fans (except Attic)
463	Household Furniture, Metal
462	Household Furniture, Upholstered Wood
461	Household Furniture, Wood (except Upholstered)
583	Household Laundry Equipment
583	Household Ovens, Ranges, and Stoves
583	Household Refrigerators
583	Household Vacuum Cleaners
583	Household Water Heaters
583	Housewares, Electric
953	Housing-Control Services
371	Howitzers
536	Hydrated Lime
533	Hydraulic Cement
561	Hydraulic Turbines
366	Hydroelectric Power Plants
725	Hydrology
573	Humidifiers (except Room)

457	Mallets
395	Malt Beverages
893	Management Services, General
484	Manifold Business Forms
619	Mannequins
872	Manufactured Gas Services
319	Maple Sap
716	Mapping
489	Maps
854	Marine Cargo-Handling Services
365	Marine Construction
714	Marine Engineering
330	MARINE LIFE
617	Marking Devices
457	Marquetry
909	Massage Services
619	Matches
565	Materials-Handling Machinery and Equipment
720	MATHEMATICS
721	Mathematics, Actuarial
464	Mattresses
903	Meal Services, except Domestic
602	Measurement Instruments, Industrial Process Variables
602	Measuring and Controlling Instruments
602	Measuring and Testing Instruments, Electricity and Electrical Signals
600	MEASURING INSTRUMENTS
603	Measuring Instruments, Fire Control
603	Measuring Instruments, Optical
572	Measuring Pumps
382	Meat Products, Processed
706	Mechanical Engineering
552	Mechanics' Handtools
607	Mechanisms, Clockwork-Operated
926	Medical Aid Services
926	Medical Assistant Services
926	Medical Attendant Services
600	MEDICAL GOODS
604	Medical Instruments and Apparatus
920	MEDICAL SERVICES
604	Medicated Plasters
493	Medicinal Chemicals
493	Medicinal Powders, Solutions, and Suspensions
303	Melon Crops
880	MERCHANDISING SERVICES
357	Mercury Ores
899	Message Services, Telephone
899	Messenger Services
467	Metal and Wood Fixtures
554	Metal Buildings, Prefabricated
551	Metal Cans and Containers
542	Metal Castings, Ferrous and Nonferrous
589	Metal-Cutting-and-Forming Machines, Electron Beam

566	Metal-Cutting Machine Tools
540	METAL, FERROUS AND NONFERROUS
467	Metal Fixtures
559	Metal Foil and Leaf
556	Metal Forgings and Stampings
566	Metal-Forming Machine Tools
463	Metal Household Furniture
350	METALLIC MINERALS, RAW
711	Metallurgical Engineering
466	Metal Office Furniture
466	Metal Public-Building Furniture
604	Metals, Dental
611	Metals, Precious
554	Metalwork, Architectural and Ornamental
566	Metalworking Machinery and Equipment
725	Meteorology
581	Metering Panels
602	Meters, Totalizing-Fluid and Counting Services
712	Methods Engineering
349	Mica
606	Microfilm Equipment
603	Microscopes
952	Military Services
598	Military Tanks and Tank Components
321	Milk, Raw
452	Millwork Products
564	Mine Cars
564	Mineral-Cleaning Machinery
725	Mineralogy
347	Mineral, Chemical and Fertilizer
340	MINERALS, NONMETALLIC
539	Mineral Wool
708	Mining Engineering
564	Mining Machinery and Equipment
372	Mines (Military)
944	Ministerial Services
457	Mirror and Picture Frames
532	Mirrors
610	MISCELLANEOUS FABRICATED PRODUCTS
960	MISCELLANEOUS SERVICES
586	Missile-Control Systems
375	Missiles, Guided
869	Missile-Tracking Services
372	Missile Warheads
523	Mittens, Leather
872	Mixed Gas Services
455	Mobile Homes
522	Moccasins
885	Modeling Services
392	Molasses
474	Molded and Pressed Pulp Goods
519	Molded Plastics
554	Molding and Trim, Metal
452	Moldings, Wood
566	Molds, Industrial
565	Monorail Systems

537	Monumental Stone	619	Neon Signs
435	Mopheads	481	Newspapers
371	Mortars	472	Newsprint
532	Mosaic Glass	899	News-Reporting Services
319	Moss, Spanish	442	Nightwear, Men's and Boys'
606	Motion-Picture Cameras	444	Nightwear, Women's, Girls', and Infants'
911	Motion-Picture Casting and Directing Services	539	Nonclay Refractories and Crucibles
911	Motion-Picture Developing and Printing Services	473	Nonconverted Building Paper and Board
		472	Nonconverted Paper and Paperboard (except Building)
911	Motion-Picture Film Editing Services	496	Noncyclic Organic Chemicals
753	Motion-Picture Photography	540	NONFERROUS METAL
911	Motion-Picture Production and Distribution Services	542	Nonferrous Metal Castings
		544	Nonferrous Metals, Rolled, Drawn, and Extruded
606	Motion-Picture Projection Equipment	543	Nonferrous Metals, Smelted and Refined
911	Motion-Picture Rental Services	340	NONMETALLIC MINERALS
712	Motion Study Engineering	425	Nonwoven Fabrics (except Knitted)
595	Motorcycles and Parts	397	Noodles
853	Motor-Freight Transportation Services	618	Notions
853	Motor-Freight Warehousing Services	618	Novelties, Costume
582	Motor Generator Sets	619	Novelties, Advertising
591	Motor Homes	532	Novelties, Glass
582	Motors, except Starting Motors	519	Novelties, Plastic
582	Motors, Railway	871	Nuclear Electricity Generating Services
589	Motors, Starting	715	Nuclear Engineering
582	Motor Starters (Industrial Controls)	602	Nuclear Instruments
591	Motor-Vehicle Accessories	366	Nuclear Power Plants
591	Motor-Vehicle Engines (except Diesel)	311	Nursery Products, Floricultural
552	Motor-Vehicle Hardware	314	Nursery Products, Forest
591	Motor Vehicles and Parts	942	Nursery School Services
611	Mountings, Jewel	924	Nursing Services
565	Moving Stairways	555	Nuts and Bolts
933	Museum Services	393	Nuts, Salted
319	Mushrooms	306	Nuts, Tree
756	Music		
524	Musical Instrument Cases		
614	Musical Instruments and Parts		
		457	Oars, Wood
		586	Object-Detection Apparatus
		725	Oceanography
549	Nails, Nonferrous Metal	484	Office Forms
541	Nails, Steel	466	Office Furniture, Metal
435	Napkins	465	Office Furniture, Wood
423	Narrow Fabrics	571	Office Machines
414	Natural Fibers	617	Office Materials
342	Natural Gas	553	Oil Burning Heaters
872	Natural Gas Services	434	Oilcloth
601	Nautical Instruments	564	Oil Field Machinery and Equipment
371	Naval Guns	368	Oil Refineries
586	Navigational Electronic Equipment	385	Oils and Fats, Edible
601	Navigational Instruments	501	Oils, Illuminating
447	Neckpieces, Fur	564	Oil Well Machinery and Equipment
442	Neckwear, Men's and Boys'	493	Ointments
443	Neckwear, Women's, Girls', and Infants'	941	Old-Age-Assistance Services
618	Needles	305	Olives
319	Needles, Balsam	603	Opera Glasses

606	Photographic Chemicals	584	Plugs, Attachment-Wiring
719	Photographic Engineering	553	Plumbing-Fixture Fittings and Trim (Brass Goods)
606	Photographic Equipment and Supplies		
600	PHOTOGRAPHIC GOODS	535	Plumbing Fixtures and Fittings, China and Earthenware
753	Photography		
753	Photography, Movie and Still	553	Plumbing Fixtures, Enameled Metal
723	Physical Chemistry	618	Plumes
602	Physical-Property Testing Apparatus	453	Plywood
720	PHYSICAL SCIENCES	603	Polariscopes
921	Physician Services	451	Poles, Wood
921	Physician Surgical Services	951	Police Protection Services
724	Physics	583	Polishers, Floor (Household)
732	Physiology	572	Polishing Machines, Floor (Commercial)
614	Pianos	742	Political Science
457	Picture and Mirror Frames	719	Pollution Control (Engineering)
365	Piers	729	Pollution Control (Technical)
541	Pig Iron	496	Polyhydric Alcohols
491	Pigments, Inorganic	616	Pool Tables and Equipment
496	Pigments, Synthetic Organic	535	Porcelain Electrical Supplies
543	Pigs, Nonferrous Metal	535	Porcelain Ware
451	Pilings	564	Portable Rock Drills
435	Pillowcases	905	Portering Services
435	Pillows	954	Postal Services
319	Pine Gums	451	Posts, Wood
618	Pins	347	Potash
519	Pipe and Pipe Fittings, Plastic	399	Potato Chips
536	Pipe, Concrete	535	Pottery Products
559	Pipe, Fabricated	525	Pouches, Tobacco
559	Pipe Fittings and Valves, Metal (except Plumbers')	324	Poultry
		504	Powdered Fuel
364	Pipelines (Construction)	549	Powdered Iron
856	Pipeline Transportation Services	493	Powders, Medicinal
541	Pipes and Tubing, Iron and Steel	364	Power and Communication Lines
544	Pipes and Tubing, Nonferrous Metal	566	Power-Driven Handtools
943	Placement Services	581	Power Fuse Devices
452	Planing-Mill Products	581	Power Fuse Mountings
300	PLANT FARM CROPS	366	Power Plant Projects
712	Plant-Layout Engineering	563	Power Shovels
493	Plasmas	581	Power Switches
536	Plaster	581	Power Switching Equipment
536	Plasterboard	581	Power Transformers
539	Plaster of Paris, Statuary and Art Goods	568	Power Transmission Equipment, Mechanical
512	Plastic Footwear	611	Precious Metal Jewelry
468	Plastic Furniture and Fixtures	611	Precious Metals
514	Plastic Hose and Belting	554	Prefabricated Metal Buildings
496	Plasticizers	455	Prefabricated Wood Buildings
510	PLASTIC PRODUCTS	899	Press Clipping Services
492	Plastics Materials	474	Pressed and Molded Pulp Goods
612	Plated Ware	531	Pressed Glass and Glassware
531	Plate Glass	531	Pressed-Glass Tableware
541	Plates, Iron and Steel	572	Pressing Machines
544	Plates, Nonferrous Metal	906	Pressing Services
606	Plates, Sensitized	589	Primary Batteries, Dry and Wet
554	Plate Work, Fabricated (Boiler Shops)	480	PRINTED AND PUBLISHED PRODUCTS
359	Platinum Ore	587	Printed Circuits
616	Playground Equipment	499	Printing Ink
604	Pliers, Dental	911	Printing Services, Motion Picture

874	Refuse Services
953	Regulatory Law Control Services
953	Regulatory Law Investigation Services
899	Rental and Leasing Equipment Services
884	Rental Services
911	Rental Services, Motion Picture
913	Rental Services, Sports Equipment
899	Reporting Service, News
361	Residential Buildings
942	Residential-Care Services, Adult and Child
602	Residential Environmental-Regulating Controls
319	Resins, Natural
492	Resins, Synthetic
587	Resistors, Electronic Applications
942	Rest Home Services
881	Retail Trade Services
953	Revenue Services
582	Rheostats
755	Rhythmics
423	Ribbons
617	Ribbons, Inked
555	Rivets
449	Robes
564	Rock-Crushing Machinery
564	Rock Drills, Portable
347	Rock Salt
541	Rods and Bars, Iron and Steel
544	Rods and Bars, Nonferrous Metal
568	Roller Bearings
616	Roller Skates
566	Rolling-Mill Machinery and Equipment
541	Rolling-Mill Products
443	Rompers
473	Roofing Board
503	Roofing Coatings and Cements
503	Roofing Felts
503	Roofing Materials
534	Roofing Tile
902	Rooming-House Services
883	Route Sales Services
510	RUBBER AND MISCELLANEOUS PLASTIC PRODUCTS
519	Rubber Clothing
319	Rubber, Crude
512	Rubber Footwear
514	Rubber Hose and Belting
519	Rubberized Fabrics
496	Rubber-Processing Chemicals
513	Rubber, Reclaimed
519	Rubber Specialties and Sundries
492	Rubber, Synthetic
431	Rugs

529	Saddlery
559	Safes
604	Safety Appliances and Equipment
953	Safety Control and Investigation Services
712	Safety Engineering
387	Salad Dressings
484	Salesbooks
885	Sales-Promotion Services
883	Sales-Route Services
393	Salted Nuts
347	Salt, Rock
491	Salts, Inorganic
486	Sample Books
522	Sandals
345	Sand and Gravel
572	Sanding Machine, Floor
538	Sandpaper
579	Sand Riddles
704	Sanitary Engineering
474	Sanitary Paper Products
874	Sanitary Services
554	Sash, Metal
503	Saturated Roofing Felts
387	Sauces
894	Savings and Loan Services
552	Saw Blades
452	Sawmill Products
552	Saws, Hand
571	Scales (except Laboratory)
912	Scenery-Design Services
912	Scenery-Lighting Services
852	School-Bus Services
942	School Services, Nursery
942	School Services, Training
601	Scientific Research Instruments (except Optical Instruments)
552	Scissors
557	Screening, Wire
555	Screw-Machine Products
555	Screws
751	Sculpturing
386	Seafood, Fresh or Frozen Packaged
386	Seafoods, Processed
499	Sealants
495	Sealers, Wood
538	Sealing Devices, Asbestos
617	Seals, Hand
584	Searchlights
464	Seats, Aircraft, Automobile, Railroad, and Public Conveyances
387	Seasonings
339	Sea Urchins
339	Seaweed
891	Secretarial Services
894	Securities and Commodities Services
951	Security Property Services
311	Seeds, Flower and Vegetable

314	Seeds, Tree
725	Seismology
587	Semiconductors
561	Semidiesel Engines and Parts
606	Sensitized Cloth, Film, Paper, and Plates
493	Serums
572	Service-Industry Machinery
613	Settings, Cut and Polished Jewel
611	Settings, Jewel
364	Sewage-Collection and Disposal Lines
874	Sewerage Services
364	Sewer Mains
534	Sewer Tile
461	Sewing-Machine Cabinets, Wood
583	Sewing Machines, Domestic
583	Sewing Machines, Industrial
469	Shades, Window
552	Shears
323	Sheep
449	Sheepskin-Lined Clothing
554	Sheet Metal Work
489	Sheet Music
435	Sheets
541	Sheets and Strips, Iron and Steel
544	Sheets and Strips, Nonferrous Metal
332	Shellfish
467	Shelving
452	Shingles, Wood
714	Ship-Machinery Design and Development
593	Ships
593	Ships, Cargo Vessel and Tankers
593	Ships, Combat Vessel
593	Ships, Hydrofoil
442	Shirts, Men's and Boys'
443	Shirts, Women's, Girls', and Infants'
423	Shoelaces
522	Shoes, Athletic
906	Shoeshine Services
489	Shopping News
889	Shopping Services, Professional
571	Shorthand Machines
563	Shovels, Power
519	Shower Stalls, Plastic
311	Shrubbery
452	Shutters, Wood
586	Sighting Equipment, Electronic
603	Sighting Equipment, Optical
854	Sightseeing Boat Service
603	Sights, Telescopic
586	Signals, Railway
586	Signals, Traffic
899	Sign Painting-and-Lettering Services
619	Signs
619	Signs, Neon
421	Silk Fabrics
414	Silk Fibers
354	Silver and Gold Ore

612	Silverware
616	Skates, Roller and Ice
454	Skids, Wood
521	Skins
443	Skirts
369	Ski-Tow Erection
543	Slabs, Nonferrous Metal
439	Sleeping Bags
618	Slide Fasteners
435	Slipcovers
522	Slippers
373	Small Arms
374	Small-Arms Ammunition (30 mm or 1.18 inch and below)
541	Smelted and Refined Ferrous Metals
543	Smelted and Refined Nonferrous Metals
379	Smoke Generators
619	Smoking Pipes
403	Smoking Tobacco
618	Snap Fasteners
562	Snow Blowers and Throwers
599	Snowmobiles
403	Snuff
494	Soap
940	SOCIAL, EMPLOYMENT, AND SPIRITUAL SERVICES
740	SOCIAL SCIENCES
941	Social Services
744	Sociology
584	Sockets and Receptacles, Lamps
311	Sod
347	Soda
573	Soda-Fountain-Dispensing Units
464	Sofa Beds
396	Soft Drinks
617	Soft-Tipped Markers
713	Soil-Conservation Engineering
731	Soil Science
553	Solar Heaters
582	Solenoid Switches
493	Solutions, Medicinal
496	Solvents, Organic
387	Soups
583	Space Heaters
596	Space Vehicles and Parts
397	Spaghetti
319	Spanish Moss
589	Spark Plugs
909	Spa Services, Health
581	Specialty Transformers
603	Spectrometers
603	Spectroscopes
568	Speed Changers
602	Speedometers
391	Spices
549	Spikes, Nonferrous Metal
541	Spikes, Steel

944	Spiritual Services
339	Sponges
616	Sporting Goods (except Firearms and Apparel)
913	Sports Equipment, Rental Services
913	Sports-Participants Services
913	Sports Services
464	Spring Cushions
559	Springs, Steel
557	Springs, Wire
565	Stackers
532	Stained Glass
612	Stainless-Steel Ware
565	Stairways, Moving
452	Stairways, Wood
432	Stamped Art Goods, Textile
556	Stampings, Automobile
556	Stampings, Metal
617	Stamps, Hand
467	Stands (Wood and Metal)
549	Staples, Nonferrous Metal
541	Staples, Steel
584	Starters, Fluorescent
582	Starters, Motor
589	Starting Motors
474	Stationary
539	Statuary, Plaster of Paris and Papier Mache
909	Steam-Bath Services
561	Steam Engines (except Locomotive)
553	Steam or Hot-Water Domestic Furnace
875	Steam-Supply Services
561	Steam Turbines
541	Steel and Iron Pipes and Tubing
541	Steel and Iron Plates, Sheets, Strips, Rods, and Bars
549	Steel Balls
541	Steel Cable
541	Steel Ingots
617	Steel Letters and Figures
541	Steel Nails, Spikes, Staples
541	Steel Wire
538	Steel Wool
541	Steelworks Products
617	Stencils
891	Stenographic Services
606	Still Cameras
753	Still Photography
898	Stock-Chasing Services
859	Stockyard Services
537	Stone, Building and Monumental
530	STONE, CLAY, AND GLASS PRODUCTS
344	Stone, Crushed and Broken
537	Stone, Cut
343	Stone, Dimension
537	Stone Products

535	Stoneware
589	Storage Batteries
961	Storage Services, Automobile
906	Storage Services, Garment
853	Storage Services, Public
583	Stoves, Household
459	Straw Products
594	Street Cars and Equipment
874	Street-Cleaning Services
852	Street-Railway Services
362	Streets and Highways
615	Strollers, Baby
534	Structural Clay Products
534	Structural Clay Tile
554	Structural Metal, Fabricated
455	Structural Wood Members
713	Structure and Machine Design and Development, Agricultural
360	STRUCTURES
393	Stuffed Dates
852	Suburban-Transit Passenger-Transportation Services
367	Subways
852	Subway-Transportation Services
392	Sugar, Cane and Beet
302	Sugar Crops
441	Suits, Men's and Boys'
443	Suits, Women's, Girls', and Infants'
347	Sulfur
605	Sunglass Lenses
604	Supporters, Abdominal
604	Surgical Appliances
604	Surgical Dressings
604	Surgical Gauze
604	Surgical, Medical, and Dental Instruments and Apparatus
922	Surgical Services, Dental
921	Surgical Services, Physician
716	Surveying
601	Surveying Instruments
449	Suspenders
493	Suspensions, Medicinal
604	Sutures
581	Switchboards and Apparatus, Electrical
584	Switches, Electrical
587	Switches, Electronic
581	Switches, Power
581	Switchgear Apparatus, Electrical
581	Switching Equipment, Power
421	Synthetic-Fiber Fabrics
414	Synthetic Fibers
492	Synthetic Fibers (except Glass)
496	Synthetic Flavoring
496	Synthetic Organic Dyes
496	Synthetic Organic Pigments
496	Synthetic Perfume
492	Synthetic Resins

482	Trade Journals	587	Tubes, Industrial Electron
899	Trading-Stamp Services	587	Tubes, Radio and Television Receiving, Electron
586	Traffic Signals	587	Tubes, Special-Purpose, Electron
586	Traffic Signals, Highway and Railway	587	Tubes, Transmitting Electron
902	Trailer-Park Services	589	Tubes, X-ray
565	Trailers	541	Tubing and Pipes, Iron and Steel
597	Trailers, Travel	544	Tubing and Pipes, Nonferrous Metal
591	Trailers, Truck	593	Tugboats
913	Trainers, Athletic	854	Tugboat Services
942	Training-School Services	363	Tunnels
931	Training Services, Vocational	859	Tunnel Services
587	Transformers	561	Turbine-Generator-Engines and Parts (except Aircraft and Non-Diesel Automotive)
581	Transformers, Distribution	561	Turbines
581	Transformers, Doorbell	561	Turbines, Hydraulic, Steam, and Gas (except Aircraft)
581	Transformers, Power		
581	Transformers, Rectifiers		
581	Transformers, Specialty	339	Turtles
602	Transistor Testers	441	Tuxedos
581	Transmission Equipment, Electric	413	Twine
587	Transmitting Electron Tubes	571	Typewriters
590	TRANSPORTATION EQUIPMENT	891	Typing Services
850	TRANSPORTATION SERVICES		
855	Transportation Services, Air		
855	Transportation Services, Air-Cargo and Passenger		
854	Transportation Services, Deep Sea	589	Ultrasonic Cleaning Machines
852	Transportation Services, Local Passenger	589	Ultrasonic Welding Machines
853	Transportation Services, Motor Freight	584	Ultraviolet-Lamp Fixtures
856	Transportation Services, Pipeline	619	Umbrellas
854	Transportation Services, Water	611	Umbrella Trimmings
583	Trash Compactors, Household	961	Undercoating Services, Automobile
859	Travel-Agency Services	441	Uniforms
941	Travelers'-Aid Services	444	Undergarments, Women's, Girls', and Infants'
597	Travel Trailers	442	Underwear, Men's and Boys'
306	Tree Nuts	444	Underwear, Women's, Girls', and Infants'
618	Trees, Artificial	433	Upholstery Filling
314	Tree Seeds	358	Uranium Ore
312	Trees, Ornamental	911	Ushering Services, Motion Picture
554	Trim and Molding, Metal	912	Ushering Services, Theater
889	Trimming Services, Window		
447	Trimmings, Fur		
432	Trimmings, Textile		
432	Trimmings, Umbrella		
852	Trolley-Coach Services	493	Vaccines, Bacterial and Virus
584	Trolley-Line Material, Overhead	583	Vacuum Cleaners, Household
594	Trolleys, Trackless	572	Vacuum Cleaners, Industrial
612	Trophies	559	Valves and Pipe Fittings, Metal (except Plumbers')
442	Trousers		
591	Truck Bodies	358	Vanadium Ores
853	Trucking Services, Local and Long-Distance	584	Vapor Lamps
		582	Variable Capacitors
853	Trucking-Terminal Services	474	Varnished Paper
565	Trucks, Industrial	495	Varnishes
591	Truck Trailers	495	Varnish Remover
604	Trusses, Abdominal	559	Vaults
894	Trust Services	619	Vaults, Burial
511	Tubes and Tires	514	V-Belts

303	Vegetable Crops
387	Vegetables and Fruits, Processed
311	Vegetable Seeds and Plants
615	Vehicles, Children's (except Bicycles)
584	Vehicular-Lighting Equipment
884	Vending Services
453	Veneer
706	Ventilation Engineering
568	Ventilator Fans
397	Vermicelli
441	Vests
604	Veterinary Instruments and Apparatus
929	Veterinary Services
363	Viaducts
493	Vials, Pharmaceutical Preparations
398	Vinegar
614	Violins
493	Virus Vaccines
931	Vocational-Training Services
581	Voltage Regulators, Line
602	Voltmeters

433	Wadding
473	Wallboard
474	Wallpaper
534	Wall Tile, Ceramic
853	Warehousing Services, Motor Freight
853	Warehousing Services, Public
589	Warm-Air Furnaces, Electric
573	Warm-Air Furnaces, (except Electric)
435	Washcloths
555	Washers, Metal
572	Washing Machinery, Car
572	Washing Machines, Floor
583	Washing Machines, Household and Coin-Operated
961	Washing Services, Automobile
419	Waste Fibers
607	Watchcases
532	Watch Crystals
600	WATCHES AND CLOCKS
607	Watches and Parts
519	Water Bottles, Rubber
713	Water-Conservation Engineering
583	Water Heaters, Household
364	Water Mains
602	Water Meters
449	Waterproof Outer Garments (except Rubber or Rubberized)
873	Water-Supply Services
854	Water-Transportation Services
369	Water-Treatment Plants
365	Waterway Construction
854	Waterway-Transportation Services, Inland

564	Water-Well Machinery and Equipment
587	Wave Guides, Electronic
583	Waxers, Floor
941	Welfare Services
905	Waxing Services, Floor
582	Welding Apparatus, Electric
566	Welding Equipment
589	Welding Machines, Ultrasonic or Electron-Beam
941	Welfare Services
564	Well Machinery and Equipment
589	Wet Primary Batteries
519	Wet Suits, Rubber
339	Whales
365	Wharves
599	Wheelbarrows
562	Wheel Tractors, Farm and Garden
529	Whips, Leather
882	Wholesale Trade Services
469	Wicker Furniture and Fixtures
459	Wicker Products
326	Wildlife and Game
951	Wildlife-Protection Services
469	Willow Furniture and Fixtures
459	Willow Products
603	Wind and Percentage Correctors
554	Window and Door Frames, Metal
469	Window Blinds and Shades
905	Window-Cleaning Services
452	Window Frames, Wood
531	Window Glass
889	Window-Trimming Services
395	Wines
544	Wire, Nonferrous Metal
557	Wire Products
862	Wire Services, Telegraph Communications
861	Wire Services, Telephone Communications
557	Wire Springs
541	Wire, Steel
584	Wiring Equipment, Electric
496	Wood and Gum Chemicals
467	Wood and Metal Fixtures
457	Wood Articles
451	Wood Bolts
455	Wood Buildings, Prefabricated
553	Wood Burning Heaters
454	Wood Containers
495	Wood Filler
467	Wood Fixtures
461	Wood Household Furniture (except Upholstered)
462	Wood Household Furniture, Upholstered
465	Wood Office Furniture
452	Wood Products, Treated
465	Wood Public-Building Furniture
495	Wood Sealers
567	Woodworking Industrial Machinery and Equipment
422	Wool Fabrics

CHAPTER 6

SENTENCE ANALYSIS TECHNIQUE

Sentence Analysis is the technique used by the analyst to determine, in all job-worker situations, the appropriate components of Work Performed: Worker Functions; Work Fields; and Materials, Products, Subject Matter, and Services. The technique permits even the most complex job-worker situation to be stated in a simple, brief, declarative sentence. However, the technique should not be confused with style conventions used to describe tasks in a JAR.

The technique that has been developed uses the answers to three basic questions about the work setting to build a sentence that has three standard parts and which describes Work Performed.

The three basic questions are as follows:

1.   What does the worker do?

2.   What gets done? or what is the purpose of the worker's action?

3.   What is the final result?

The answers to these questions provide the framework of Sentence Analysis. (The subject of the basic sentence is the worker and is implied but not stated.) The following list shows how the Work Performed components are used as parts of a sentence to present the information obtained from the answers to the above questions:

1.   The Worker Function is used as the verb (in the third person, singular, present tense).

2.   MTEWA, people, or information is used as the direct object of the verb.

3.   Work Fields and MPSMS are used in an infinitive phrase. The infinitive reflects the Work Field(s), and MPSMS is the object of the infinitive.

For jobs in which the worker's significant involvement is with a Data Worker Function, the object of the verb is information in some form. For jobs in which the worker's significant involvement is with a People Worker Function, the object of the verb is usually the people to whom a service is being rendered. For jobs in which the worker's significant involvement is with a Things Worker Function, the object of the verb is a machine, tool, equipment, or work aid through which the action of the verb is performed.

Several examples of job-worker situations, which have been summarized using the sentence analysis technique, are presented in the following charts with an accompanying example of the information reworded for use in a Job Summary statement. The three numbers in parentheses in the analysis sentence represent the specific Worker Function, Work Field, and MPSMS, respectively. This information is presented as an additional aid to show the analyst how to create a Job Summary statement that accurately reflects the information obtained about a job-worker situation.

Question:	What Does the Worker Do?		What Gets Done?	What is the Final Result?
Work Performed Component:	Worker Function	MTEWA, People, or Information	Work Field	MPSMS
Sentence Part:	Verb	Direct Object	Infinitive Phrase	
			Infinitive	Objective of the Infinitive

SIGNIFICANT INVOLVEMENT WITH DATA

Sentence Analysis: Synthesizes (0) ideas and information   to research (251)   mathematics (721).

Job Summary Statement: Conducts research in fundamental mathematics and in application of mathematical techniques to science, management, and other fields, and solves or directs solutions to problems in various fields by mathematical methods.

SIGNIFICANT INVOLVEMENT WITH PEOPLE

Sentence Analysis: Serves (7) patrons   to accommodate (291)   patrons (910).

Job Summary Statement: Assists patrons to find seats at entertainment events.

SIGNIFICANT INVOLVEMENT WITH THINGS

Sentence Analysis: Handles (7) handtruck   to move (011)   tobacco (404).

Job Summary Statement: Distributes tobacco within or near cigarette manufacturing facility, using handtruck.

SIGNIFICANT INVOLVEMENT WITH DATA AND PEOPLE

Sentence Analysis: (data) Analyzes (2) textbooks, test results, and other data   to teach (296)   academic subject (931).

(people) Instructs (2) students   to teach (296)   academic subject (931).

Job Summary Statement: Teaches English in public secondary school.

Question:	What Does the Worker Do?		What Gets Done?	What is the Final Result?
Work Performed Component:	Worker Function	MTEWA, People, or Information	Work Field	MPSMS
Sentence Part:	Verb	Direct Object	Infinitive Phrase	
			Infinitive	Objective of the Infinitive

SIGNIFICANT INVOLVEMENT WITH DATA AND THINGS

Sentence Analysis:	(data) Analyzes (2) designs and other data	to machine (057)	jewelry articles (611 & 613).
	(things) Precision works (1) machines and handtools	to machine (057)	jewelry articles (611 & 613).

Job Summary Statement: Fabricates and repairs jewelry articles, such as rings, brooches, pendants, bracelets, and lockets.

SIGNIFICANT INVOLVEMENT WITH PEOPLE AND THINGS

Sentence Analysis:	(people) Informs (6) patrons	to entertain (297)	patrons (919).
	(things) Operates (3) mechanical riding equipment	to entertain (297)	patrons (919).

Job Summary Statement: Operates or informs patrons how to operate mechanical riding devices at amusement park.

SIGNIFICANT INVOLVEMENT WITH DATA, PEOPLE, AND THINGS

Sentence Analysis:	(data) Coordinates (1) treatment procedures of patients	to treat (294)	dental problems (922).
	(people) Advises (0) dental patients	to treat (294)	dental problems (922).
	(things) Precision works (1) dental instruments	to treat (294)	dental problems (922).

Job Summary Statement: Diagnoses and treats diseases, injuries, and malformations of teeth and gums, and related oral structures.

When using the Work Performed components, do not confuse MTEWA and MPSMS. Machines and equipment are listed in MPSMS categories when they constitute materials or products for certain jobs, and should be used for MPSMS only where they apply as materials or products. These same machines or equipment, when used to complete a function (immediate object of a things verb through which the action of the verb or Work Function is performed) are not considered materials or products, but as MTEWA. A job in which the worker builds or repairs a machine is assigned the MPSMS code for that machine. A job in which the worker operates or sets up a machine is assigned the MPSMS of what the machine processes or produces. Finally, note that in some instances for a machine-related things job, the statement derived through the sentence analysis technique may approximate the Job Summary statement.

CHAPTER 7

GENERAL EDUCATIONAL DEVELOPMENT

General Educational Development (GED), a component of Worker Characteristics, embraces those aspects of education (formal and informal) which contribute to the worker's (a) reasoning development and ability to follow instructions, and (b) acquisition of "tool" knowledge such as language and mathematical skills. This is education of a general nature which does not have a recognized, fairly specific occupational objective. Ordinarily, such education is obtained in elementary school, high school, or college. However, it may be obtained from experience and self-study.

DIVISIONS OF GED SCALE

The GED Scale is composed of three divisions: Reasoning Development, Mathematical Development, and Language Development. Each should be considered and rated independently of the others in evaluating the levels required for a job. In theory Mathematics and Language are components of Reasoning; therefore, Reasoning should have at least as high a rating as the higher one assigned for Mathematics or Language.

RATIONALE FOR GED SCALE DEFINITIONS

The description of the various levels of language and mathematical development are based on the curriculum taught in schools throughout the United States. An analysis of mathematics courses in school curriculums reveals distinct levels of progression in the primary and secondary grades and in college. These levels of progression facilitated the selection and assignment of six levels of GED for the mathematical development scale.

However, though language courses follow a similar pattern of progression in primary and secondary school, particularly in learning and applying the principles of grammar, this pattern changes at the college level. The diversity of language courses offered at the college level precludes the establishment of distinct levels of language progression for these four years. Consequently, language development is limited to five defined levels of GED.

A sample of job-worker situations for each GED level has been placed on a scale. These situation descriptions do not include all work devices that may be used by the worker. However, they have been written to make the GED level of each as explicit as possible. These situations have been written to make their level value as explicit as possible. Since the discrimination by level is dependent on a verbal expression, it is not precise. Familiarity with the total range of illustrative situations should contribute, however, to the use and application of the scales.

Scale of General Education Development (GED)

LEVEL	REASONING DEVELOPMENT	MATHEMATICAL DEVELOPMENT	LANGUAGE DEVELOPMENT
6	Apply principles of logical or scientific thinking to a wide range of intellectual and practical problems. Deal with nonverbal symbolism (formulas, scientific equations, graphs, musical notes, etc.) in its most difficult phases. Deal with a variety of abstract and concrete variables. Apprehend the most abstruse classes of concepts.	Advanced calculus: Work with limits, continuity, real number systems, mean value theorems, and implicit function theorems. Modern Algebra: Apply fundamental concepts of theories of groups, rings, and fields. Work with differential equations, linear algebra, infinite series, advanced operations methods, and functions of real and complex variables. Statistics: Work with mathematical statistics, mathematical probability and applications, experimental design, statistical inference, and econometrics.	Same as Level 5.
5	Apply principles of logical or scientific thinking to define problems, collect data, establish facts, and draw valid conclusions. Interpret an extensive variety of technical instructions in mathematical or diagrammatic form. Deal with several abstract and concrete variables.	Algebra: Work with exponents and logarithms, linear equations, quadratic equations, mathematical induction and binomial theorem, and permutations. Calculus: Apply concepts of analytic geometry, differentiations, and integration of algebraic functions with applications. Statistics: Apply mathematical operations to frequency distributions, reliability and validity of tests, normal curve, analysis of variance, correlation techniques, chi-square application and sampling theory, and factor analysis.	Reading: Read literature, book and play reviews, scientific and technical journals, abstracts, financial reports, and legal documents. Writing: Write novels, plays, editorials, journals, speeches, manuals, critiques, poetry, and songs. Speaking: Coversant in the theory, principles, and methods of effective and persuasive speaking, voice and diction, phonetics, and discussion and debate.
4	Apply principles of rational systems to solve practical problems and deal with a variety of concrete variables in situations where only limited standardization exists. Interpret a variety of instructions furnished in written, oral, diagrammatic, or schedule form. (Examples of rational systems include: bookkeeping, internal combustion engines, electric wiring systems, house building, farm management, and navigation.)	Algebra: Deal with system of real numbers; linear, quadratic, rational, exponential, logarithmic, angle and circular functions, and inverse functions; related algebraic solution of equations and inequalities; limits and continuity; and probability and statistical inference. Geometry: Deductive axiomatic geometry, plane and solid, and rectangular coordinates. Shop Math: Practical application of fractions, percentages, ratio and proportion, measurement, logarithms, practical algebra, geometric construction, and essentials of trigonometry.	Reading: Read novels, poems, newspapers, periodicals, journals, manuals, dictionaries, thesauruses, and encyclopedias. Writing: Prepare business letters, expositions, summaries, and reports, using prescribed format and conforming to all rules of punctuation, grammar, diction, and style. Speaking: Participate in panel discussions, dramatizations, and debates. Speak extemporaneously on a variety of subjects.

LEVEL	REASONING DEVELOPMENT	MATHEMATICAL DEVELOPMENT	LANGUAGE DEVELOPMENT
3	Apply commonsense understanding to carry out instructions furnished in written, oral, or diagrammatic form. Deal with problems involving several concrete variables in or from standardized situations.	Compute discount, interest, profit and loss; commission, markup, and selling price; ratio and proportion; and percentage. Calculate surfaces, volumes, weights, and measures. Algebra: Calculate variables and formulas; monomials and polynomials; ratio and proportion variables; and square roots and radicals. Geometry: Calculate plane and solid figures, circumference, area, and volume. Understand kinds of angles and properties of pairs of angles.	Reading: Read a variety of novels, magazines, atlases, and encyclopedias. Read safety rules, instructions in the use and maintenance of shop tools and equipment, and methods and procedures in mechanical drawing and layout work. Writing: Write reports and essays with proper format, punctuation, spelling, and grammar, using all parts of speech. Speaking: Speak before an audience with poise, voice control, and confidence, using correct English and well-modulated voice.
2	Apply commonsense understanding to carry out detailed but uninvolved written or oral instructions. Deal with problems involving a few concrete variables in or from standardized situations.	Add, subtract, multiply, and divide all units of measure. Perform the four operations with like common and decimal fractions. Compute ratio, rate, and percent. Draw and interpret bar graphs. Perform arithmetic operations involving all American monetary units.	Reading: Passive vocabulary of 5,000-6,000 words. Read at rate of 190-215 words per minute. Read adventure stories and comic books, looking up unfamiliar words in dictionary for meaning, spelling, and pronunciation. Read instructions for assembling model cars and airplanes. Writing: Write compound and complex sentences, using cursive style, proper end punctuation, and employing adjectives and adverbs. Speaking: Speak clearly and distinctly with appropriate pauses and emphasis, correct pronunciation, variations in word order, using present, perfect, and future tenses.
1	Apply commonsense understanding to carry out simple one- or two-step instructions. Deal with standardized situations with occasional or no variables in or from these situations encountered on the job.	Add and subtract two-digit numbers. Multiply and divide 10's and 100's by 2, 3, 4, 5. Perform the four basic arithmetic operations with coins as part of a dollar. Perform operations with units such as cup, pint, and quart; inch, foot, and yard; and ounce and pound.	Reading: Recognize meaning of 2,500 (two- or three-syllable) words. Read at rate of 95-120 words per minute. Compare similarities and differences between words and between series of numbers. Writing: Print simple sentences containing subject, verb, and object, and series of numbers, names, and addresses. Speaking: Speak simple sentences, using normal word order, and present and past tenses.

REASONING DEVELOPMENT

Level 1

Apply commonsense understanding to carry out simple one- or two-step instructions. Deal with standardized situations with occasional or no variables in or from these situations encountered on the job.

R-1:1   Mark size, lot number, contents, or other identifying information or symbols on containers or directly on articles by placing stencil on object and rubbing ink or paint brush across open lettering.

R-1:2   Covers drycleaned clothing and household articles with plastic bags, and sorts articles for route delivery. Hangs drycleaned articles on rail according to route number or color of drycleaning ticket.

R-1:3   Scans rags for hardware such as buttons and snaps, and holds rags against rotating blade that cuts hardware from rags and cuts rags into specified size. Sorts rags into bins according to color and fabric.

R-1:4   Tends bandsaw that cuts wooden stock for toys and games. Stacks number of pieces of stock on cutting table against preset ripping fence. Pushes cutting table against saw until stock is severed. Drops cut pieces into tote box.

R-1:5   Feeds eggs into machine that removes earth, straw, and other residue from egg surface prior to shipment. Places eggs in holder that carries them into machine where rotating brushes or water sprays remove residue.

R-1:6   Removes cleaned eggs from discharge trough and packs them in cases for shipment.

Level 2

Apply commonsense understanding to carry out detailed but uninvolved written or oral instructions. Deal with problems involving a few concrete variables in or from standardized situations.

R-2:1   Guards street crossing during school hours when children are going to and from school. Directs actions of children and traffic at street intersections to ensure safe crossing. Records license numbers of vehicles disregarding traffic signals and reports them to police.

R-2:2   Delivers messages, documents, packages, and other items to offices or departments within establishments or to other business concerns by walking, using bicycle or motor cycle, or riding public conveyances.

R-2:3   Screws watch balance and balance bridge assembly to pillar plate. Places pillar plate in holding fixture and positions balance and bridge assembly on plate, securing it with screws. Tests balance for vertical play by gently moving it up and down with tweezers, determining from experience if shake is within acceptable limits. Touches oil-filled hypodermic needle to jewel to oil lower balance jewel prior to assembling. Observes minute parts with aid of loupe and handles parts with tweezers.

R-2:4   Assists customer to launder or dryclean clothes, using self-service equipment. Gives instructions to customer in clothes preparations, such as weighing, sorting, fog-spraying spots, and removing perishable buttons. Assigns machine and points out posted instructions regarding equipment operation.

Level 3

Apply commonsense understanding to carry out instructions furnished in written, oral, or diagrammatic form. Deal with problems involving several concrete variables in or from standardized situations.

R-3:1 Operates cord or cordless switchboard to provide answering service for clients. Greets caller and announces name or phone number of client. Records and delivers messages, furnishes information, accepts orders, and relays calls. Places telephone calls at request of client or to locate client in emergencies. Files messages.

R-3:2 Requisitions transportation from motor, railroad, and airline companies to ship plant products. Reads shipping orders to determine quantity and type of transportation needed. Contacts company to make arrangements and to issue instructions for loading products. Annotates shipping orders to inform shipping department of loading locations and time of arrival of transportation.

R-3:3 Installs and adjusts television receivers and antennas, using handtools. Selects antenna according to type of set and location of transmitting station. Secures antenna in place with bracket and guy wire, observing insurance codes and local ordinances to protect installation from lightning and other hazards. Tunes receiver on all channels and adjusts screws to obtain desired density, linearity, focus, and size of picture.

R-3:4 Sets up and adjusts compression, injection, or transfer machines used to mold plastic materials to specified shape. Adjusts stroke of ram, using handtools. Connects steam, oil, or water lines to mold or regulates controls to regulate mold temperature. Sets machine controls to regulate forming pressure of machine and curing time of plastic in mold.

Level 4

Apply principles of rational systems to solve practical problems and deal with a variety of concrete variables in situations where only limited standardization exists. Interpret a variety of instructions furnished in written, oral, diagrammatic, or schedule form.

R-4:1 Plans layout and installs and repairs wiring, electrical fixtures, apparatus, and control equipment. Plans new or modified installations according to specifications and electrical code. Prepares sketches showing locations of all wiring and equipment or follows diagrams or blueprints prepared by others. Tests continuity of circuit to ensure electrical compatibility and safety of all components, using standard instruments such as ohmmeter, battery, and oscilloscope.

R-4:2 Inspects internal combustion engine for conformance to blueprints and specifications, using measuring instruments and handtools. Reviews test data to locate assemblies and parts not functioning according to specifications. Measures dimensions of disassembled parts and assemblies, such as pistons, valves, bearings, and injectors, using scale, micrometers, special tools, and gauging setups. Compares measurements against specifications to locate faulty parts.

R-4:3 Draws and letters charts, schedules, and graphs to illustrate specified data, such as wage trends, absenteeism, labor turnover, and employment needs, using drafting instruments, such as ruling and lettering pens, T-squares, and straightedge or using drafting software and computer terminal.

R-4:4 Schedules appointments, gives information to callers, takes dictation, and relieves officials of minor administrative and business details. Reads and routes incoming mail. Composes and types routine correspondence. Greets visitors, ascertains nature of business, and conducts visitors to appropriate person.

R-4:5 Cares for patients and children in private homes, hospitals, sanitariums, and similar institutions. Takes and records temperature, pulse, and respiration rate. Gives standard medications as directed by physician or nurse. Sterilizes equipment and supplies, using germicides, sterilizer, or autoclave. Prepares food trays, feeds patients, and records food and liquid intake and output.

Level 5

Apply principles of logical or scientific thinking to define problems, collect data, establish facts, and draw valid conclusions. Interpret an extensive variety of technical instructions in mathematical or diagrammatic form. Deal with several abstract and concrete variables.

R-5:1   Interviews persons with problems, such as personal and family maladjustment, lack of finances, unemployment, and physical and mental impairment, to determine nature and degree of problems. Obtains and evaluates patient data, such as physical, psychological, and social factors. Counsels patients individually or in groups and assists them to plan for solution of problems.

R-5:2   Studies clerical and statistical methods in commercial or industrial establishments to develop improved and standardized procedures. Consults supervisors and clerical workers to ascertain functions of offices or sections, methods used, and personnel requirements. Prepares reports on procedures and tasks of individual workers.

R-5:3   Interviews property holders and adjusts damage claims resulting from activities connected with prospecting, drilling, and production of oil and gas, and laying of pipelines on private property. Examines property titles to determine their validity and acts as company agent in transactions with property owners. Investigates and assesses damage to crops, fences, and other properties and negotiates claim settlements with property owners. Collects and prepares evidence to support contested damage in court.

R-5:4   Studies traffic conditions on urban or rural arteries from fixed position, vehicle, or helicopter to detect unsafe or congested conditions and to observe locations of alternative routes. Evaluates statistical and physical data supplied by engineering department regarding such considerations as vehicle count per mile, load capacity of pavement, feasibility of widening pavement, and projected traffic load in future.

R-5:5   Prepares and conducts inservice training for company personnel. Evaluates training needs in order to develop educational materials for improving performance standards. Performs research relating to course preparation and presentation. Compiles data for use in writing manuals, handbooks, and other training aids. Develops teaching outlines and lesson plans, determines content and duration of courses, and selects appropriate instructional procedures based on analysis of training requirements for company personnel.

R-5:6   Renders general nursing care to patients in hospital, infirmary, sanitarium, or similar institution. Administers prescribed medications and treatments in accordance with approved techniques. Prepares equipment, and aids physician during treatments and examinations of patients. Observes, records, and reports to supervisor or physician patients' conditions, reactions to drugs, treatments, and significant incidents.

Level 6

Apply principles of logical or scientific thinking to a wide range of intellectual and practical problems. Deal with nonverbal symbolism (formulas, scientific equations, graphs, musical notes, etc.) in its most difficult phases. Deal with a variety of abstract and concrete variables. Comprehend the most abstruse classes of concepts.

R-6:1   Designs and conducts experiments to study problems in human and animal behavior. Formulates hypotheses and experimental designs to investigate problems of growth, intelligence, learning, personality, and sensory processes. Selects, controls, and modifies variables in laboratory experiments with humans and animals. Analyzes data and evaluates its significance in relation to original hypotheses.

R-6:2   Reconstructs records of extinct cultures, especially preliterate cultures. Studies, classifies, and interprets artifacts, architectural features, and types of structures to determine their age and cultural identity. Establishes chronological sequence of development of each culture from simpler to more advanced levels.

R-6:3 Arbitrates, advises, and administers justice in a court of law. Establishes rules of procedures on questions for which standard procedures have not been established by law or by a superior court. Examines evidence in criminal cases to determine if charges are true or to determine if evidence will support charge. Instructs jury on application of facts to questions of law.

R-6:4 Interprets results of experiments in physics, formulates theories consistent with data obtained, and predicts results of experiments designed to detect and measure previously unobserved physical phenomena. Applies mathematical methods to solution of physical problems.

R-6:5 Plans, organizes, and conducts research for use in understanding social problems and for planning and carrying out social welfare programs. Develops research designs on basis of existing knowledge and evolving theory. Constructs and tests methods of collecting data. Collects information and makes judgments through observation and interviews, and review of documents. Analyzes and evaluates data. Interprets methods employed and findings to individuals within agency and community.

MATHEMATICAL DEVELOPMENT

Level 1

Add and subtract two-digit numbers. Multiply and divide 10's and 100's by 2, 3, 4, 5. Perform the four basic arithmetic operations with coins as part of a dollar. Perform operations with units such as cup, pint, and quart; inch, foot, and yard; ounce and pound.

M-1:1 Weighs items as a part of the packing process, using balance scales. Places container on scale and adds to or removes portion of contents from container until scale registers specified weight.

M-1:2 Dips sheets of muslin in shellac, tacks sheets in layers on stretcher frame to dry, and measures and cuts dried fabric into squares of specified size, using tape measure and shears.

M-1:3 Transfers hog-back skins from vat to grading table and measures size and length of skin on graduated board. Separates skins according to size.

M-1:4 Counts novelty case parts to verify amount specified on work ticket and stacks and bundles parts prior to spraying.

M-1:5 Tends battery of automatic machines equipped with circular knives that cut paper tubing into containers for shotgun shells. Fills hopper with tubes and starts machine. Verifies length of containers for conformance to standards, using fixed gauge.

Level 2

Add, subtract, multiply, and divide all units of measure. Perform the four operations with like common and decimal fractions. Compute ratio, rate, and percent. Draw and interpret bar graphs. Perform arithmetic operations involving all American monetary units.

M-2:1 Measures, marks, and cuts carpeting and linoleum with knife to get maximum number of usable pieces from standard size rolls, following floor dimensions or diagrams.

M-2:2 Measures width of pleats in women's garments, using yardstick. Counts number of pleats in garment and multiplies the number by the price per pleat to determine service charge for cleaning garment.

M-2:3 Weighs and measures specified quantities of ingredients of infant formulas, using scales, graduated measures, and spoons. Computes number of calories per fluid ounce of formula.

M-2:4 Sells cigars, cigarettes, corsages, and novelties to patrons in hotels, nightclubs, and restaurants. Collects cash for items sold and makes change.

M-2:5   Drives truck to transport materials to specified destinations such as railroad stations, plants, or residences. Calculates amount of bill and delivery charge, collects payment for goods delivered, making change as necessary.

Level 3

Compute discount, interest, profit, and loss; commission, markup, and selling price; ratio and proportion; and percentage. Calculate surfaces, volume, weights, and measures.

ALGEBRA: Calculate variables and formulas; monomials and polynomials; ratio and proportion variables; and square roots and radicals.

GEOMETRY: Calculate plane and solid figures, circumference, area, and volume. Understand kinds of angles and properties of pairs of angles.

M-3:1   Computes wages and posts wage data to payroll records. Computes earnings from timesheets and work tickets, using calculator. Operates posting machine to compute and subtract deductions, such as income tax withholdings, social security payments, and insurance.

M-3:2   Rents automobiles to customers at hotels and transportation stations. Computes cost of rental, based on per-day and per-mile rates.

M-3:3   Receives cash from customers in payment for goods or services and records amounts received. Computes bill, itemized lists, and tickets showing amount due, using adding machine or cash register. Makes change and cashes checks.

M-3:4   Measures tensile strength, hardness, ductility, or other physical properties of metal specimens on various types of testing machines. Calculates values, such as unit tensile strength and percentage elongation.

M-3:5   Controls purification unit to remove impurities such as moisture and oxygen from helium gas used in balloons. Calculates amount of gas transferred, using slide rule.

Level 4

ALGEBRA: Deal with system of real numbers; linear, quadratic, rational, exponential, logarithmic, angle and circular functions, and inverse functions; related algebraic solution of equations and inequalities; limits and continuity and probability and statistical inference.

GEOMETRY: Deductive axiomatic geometry, plane and solid, and rectangular coordinates.

SHOP MATH: Practical application of fractions, percentages, ratio and proportion, measurement, logarithms, practical algebra, geometric constructions, and essentials of trigonometry.

M-4:1   Inspects flat glass and compiles defect data based on samples to determine variances from acceptable quality limits. Calculates standard control tolerances for flat glass, using algebraic formulas, plotting curves, and drawing graphs.

M-4:2   Keeps records of financial transactions of establishment. Balances books and compiles reports to show statistics, such as cash receipts and expenditures, accounts payable and receivable, profit and loss, and other items pertinent to operation of business.

M-4:3   Calculates tonnage and prepares tonnage report of ship's cargo for assessment of port traffic. Converts metric measurements of foreign manifests into pounds and cubic feet, using formulas and calculating machine.

M-4:4   Lays out and cuts plastic patterns used for pantograph engraving according to sketches or blueprints, using drafting instruments and engraving tools. Establishes reference points on plastic sheet and computes layout dimensions, following blueprints.

M-4:5   Surveys earth's surface, using surveying instruments, and oversees engineering survey party engaged in determining exact location and measurements of points, elevations, lines, areas, and contours of earth's surface to secure data used for construction, mapmaking, land valuation, mining, or other purposes. Verifies by calculations accuracy of survey data secured.

Level 5

ALGEBRA: Work with exponents and logarithms, linear equations, quadratic equations, mathematical induction and binomial theorem, and permutations.

CALCULUS: Apply concepts of analytic geometry, differentiations, and integration of algebraic functions with applications.

STATISTICS: Apply mathematical operations to frequency distributions, reliability and validity of tests, normal curve, analysis of variance, correlation techniques, chi-square application and sampling theory, and factor analysis.

M-5:1   Plans survey and collects, organizes, interprets, summarizes, and analyzes numerical data on sampling or complete enumeration bases. Evaluates reliability of sources of data, adjusts and weighs raw data, and organizes and summarizes data into tabular forms amenable to analysis of variance and principles of statistical inference.

M-5:2   Develops, fabricates, assembles, calibrates, and tests electronic systems and components used in aircraft and missile production and testing operations. Establishes circuit layout dimensions by mathematical calculations and principles.

M-5:3   Applies knowledge of mathematics, probability, statistics, principles of finance and business to problems in life and health insurance, annuities, and pensions. Constructs probability tables regarding fire, natural disasters, and unemployment, based on analysis of statistical data and other pertinent information.

M-5:4   Applies principles of accounting to install and maintain general accounting system. Designs new system or modifies existing system to provide records of assets, liabilities, and financial transactions of establishment.

M-5:5   Plans, designs, conducts, and analyzes results of experiments to study problems in human and animal behavior. Analyzes test results, using statistical techniques, and evaluates significance of data in relation to original hypothesis.

Level 6

ADVANCED CALCULUS: Work with limits, continuity, real number systems, mean value theorems, and implicit function theorems.

MODERN ALGEBRA: Apply fundamental concepts of theories of groups, rings, and fields. Work with differential equations, linear algebra, infinite series, advanced operational methods, and functions of real and complex variables.

STATISTICS: Work with mathematical statistics, mathematical probability and application, experimental design, statistical inference, and econometrics.

M-6:1   Conducts and oversees analyses of aerodynamic and thermodynamic systems and aerophysics problems to determine suitability of design for aircraft and missiles. Establishes computational procedures for and methods of analyzing problems.

M-6:2   Analyzes physical systems, formulates mathematical models of systems, and sets up and operates analog computer to solve scientific and engineering problems. Prepares mathematical model of problem, applying principles of advanced calculus and differential equations.

M-6:3   Observes and interprets celestial phenomena and relates research to basic scientific knowledge or to practical problems such as navigation. Determines mathematically sizes, shapes, brightness, spectra, motions, and positions of sun, moon, planets, stars, nebulas, and galaxies.

M-6:4   Conducts research in fundamental mathematics and solves or directs solutions to problems in research, development, production, and other activities by mathematical methods. Conceives and develops ideas for application of mathematics such as algebra, geometry, number theory, logic, and topology.

M-6:5   Conducts research into phases of physical phenomena, develops theories and laws on basis of observation and experiments, and devises methods to apply laws and theory of physics to industry, medicine, and other fields. Describes and expresses observations and conclusions in mathematical terms.

LANGUAGE DEVELOPMENT

Level 1

READING: Recognize meaning of 2,500 (two- or three-syllable) words. Read at rate of 95-120 words per minute. Compare similarities and differences between words and between series of numbers.

WRITING: Print simple sentences containing subject, verb, and object, series of numbers, names, and addresses.

SPEAKING: Speak simple sentences, using normal word order and present and past tenses.

L-1:1   Delivers telephone directories to residence and business establishments, following oral instructions or address list.

L-1:2   Obtains reels of motion picture film from stock as specified on shipping order. Wraps paper band bearing film identification around each reel, ties reels with string, and sets them aside for shipment.

L-1:3   Pastes labels and tax stamps on filled whiskey bottles passing on conveyor. Looks at bottles to ascertain that labels and stamps have been correctly applied. Packs whiskey bottles in cartons. Pastes identification labels onto cartons.

L-1:4   Packs small arms ammunition in bandoleer belt pockets. Compares ammunition identification data stenciled on belt with work order to ensure packing of correct caliber cartridges. Places cardboard separator between two filled ammunition clips and slides them into cardboard packet.

Level 2

READING: Passive vocabulary of 5,000-6,000 words. Read at rate of 190-215 words per minute. Read adventure stories and comic books, looking up unfamiliar words in dictionary for meaning, spelling, and pronunciation. Read instructions for assembling model cars and airplanes.

WRITING: Write compound and complex sentences, using proper end punctuation and employing adjectives and adverbs.

SPEAKING: Speak clearly and distinctly with appropriate pauses and emphasis, correct pronunciation, variations in word order, using present, perfect, and future tenses.

L-2:1   Announces availability of seats and starting time of show. Answers such questions as length of performances, coming attractions, and locations of telephones or rest rooms.

L-2:2   Delivers messages, documents, packages, and other items to offices or departments within establishment.

L-2:3   Tends machines and equipment that grind, mix, form, and cook raw fish to make fishcakes. Places paste in mixing machine and adds specified amounts of flour, water, and spices.

L-2:4   Fills requisitions, work orders, or requests for materials, tools, or other stock items. Prepares and attaches shipping tags to containers. Keeps records of materials or items received or distributed.

L-2:5   Serves food to patrons at counters and tables of coffee shops, lunchrooms, and other dining establishments. Presents menu, answers questions, and makes suggestions regarding food and services.

Level 3

READING: Read a variety of novels, magazines, atlases, and encyclopedias. Read safety rules, instructions in the use and maintenance of shop tools and equipment, and methods and procedures in mechanical drawing and layout work.

WRITING: Write reports and essays with proper format, punctuation, spelling, and grammar, using all parts of speech.

SPEAKING: Speak before audience with poise, voice control, and confidence, using correct English and well-modulated voice.

L-3:1   Types letters, reports, stencils, forms, addresses, or straight-copy materials from rough draft or corrected copy. Files correspondence, cards, invoices, receipts, and other records in alphabetical or numerical order or according to subject matter, phonetic spelling, or some other system.

L-3:2   Renders personal service to railroad passengers to make their trip pleasant and comfortable. Greets passengers and answers questions about train schedules, travel routes, and railway services.

L-3:3   Keeps records of products returned to manufacturer to credit customer's account, to replace damaged merchandise, or to file damage claims. Verifies incoming items against bills of lading. Prepares routing and shipping forms on outgoing items.

L-3:4   Drives truck over established route to deliver, sell, and display products or render services. Calls on prospective customers to solicit new business. Writes delivery orders.

L-3:5   Services automobiles, buses, trucks, and other automotive vehicles with fuel, lubricants, and accessories. Prepares daily report of fuel, oil, and accessories sold. Answers customers' questions regarding location of streets and highways, points of interest, and recreational areas.

Level 4

READING: Read novels, poems, newspapers, periodicals, journals, manuals, dictionaries, thesauruses, and encyclopedias.

WRITING: Prepare business letters, expositions, summaries, and reports, using prescribed format and conforming to all rules of punctuation, grammar, diction, and style.

SPEAKING: Participate in panel discussions, dramatizations, and debates. Speak extemporaneously on a variety of subjects.

L-4:1   Composes letters in reply to correspondence concerning such items as request for merchandise, damage claims, credit information, delinquent accounts, or to request information. Reads incoming correspondence, types or dictates reply, or selects and completes form letters.

L-4:2   Interviews applicants to obtain such information as age, marital status, work experience, education, training, and occupational interest.

L-4:3   Compiles lists of prospective customers to provide leads to sell insurance. Contacts prospective customers, explains features of policies, and recommends amount and type of coverage based on analyses of prospects' circumstances.

L-4:4   Inspects and tests storage batteries in process of manufacture to verify conformity with specifications. Records inspection and test results, compares them with specifications, and writes reports for use in correcting manufacturing defects.

L-4:5   Repairs and overhauls automobiles, buses, trucks, and other automotive vehicles. Reads technical manuals and other instructional materials.

Level 5

READING: Read literature, book and play reviews, scientific and technical journals, abstracts, financial reports, and legal documents.

WRITING: Write novels, plays, editorials, journals, speeches, manuals, critiques, poetry, and songs.

SPEAKING: Conversant in the theory, principles, and methods of effective and persuasive speaking, voice and diction, phonetics, and discussion and debate.

L-5:1   Introduces various types of radio and television programs, interviews guests, and acts as master of ceremonies. Describes public events, such as parades and conventions, and reads news flashes and advertising copies during broadcasts.

L-5:2   Instructs students in techniques of public speaking and oral reading to develop effective speech and delivery in them. Teaches enunciation of words, intonation, gestures, and other disciplines of voice and delivery.

L-5:3   Collects and analyzes facts about newsworthy events by interview, investigation, or observation, and writes newspaper stories that conform to prescribed editorial techniques and format. Interviews persons and observes events and writes story, referring to reference books, newspaper files, or other authoritative sources to secure additional relevant facts.

L-5:4   Writes service manuals and related technical publications concerned with installation, operation, and maintenance of electronic, electrical, mechanical, and other equipment. Interviews workers to acquire or verify technical knowledge of subject. Rewrites articles, bulletins, manuals, or similar publications.

L-5:5   Assists legal representatives in preparation of written contracts covering other than standardized agreements. Reviews agreement for conformity to company rates, rules, and regulations. Writes agreement in contractual form and obtains necessary legal department approval.

Level 6

(Same as Level 5)[1]

L-6:1   Directs editorial activities of newspaper and negotiates with production, advertising, and circulation department heads. Confers with editorial policy committee and negotiates with department heads to establish policies and reach decisions affecting publications. Writes leading or policy editorials on specific public issues.

L-6:2   Plans, organizes, and conducts research for use in understanding social problems and for planning and carrying out social welfare programs. Constructs and tests methods of data collection. Collects, analyzes, and evaluates data. Writes reports containing descriptive, analytical, and evaluative content; interprets methods employed; and submits findings to individuals within agency and community.

L-6:3   Conducts and oversees analyses of aerodynamic and thermodynamic systems and aerophysics problems to determine suitability of design for aircraft and missiles. Evaluates test data and interprets established data to others. Prepares reports covering such subjects as power plant installation, thermal ice protection, air-conditioning, pressurization, and heat transfer.

---

[1]The diversity of language courses offered at the college level precludes distinguishing the two top levels of language development from each other by specific definitions. Instead, the college levels are characterized as a continuum, during which time language content remains the same but is progressively refined or specialized. Therefore, Levels 5 and 6 of language development share the same definition. Level 6 represents more advanced development of the definition content.

L-6:4   Advises corporations concerning legal rights, obligations, and privileges. Studies Constitution, statutes, decisions, and ordinances. Examines legal data to determine advisability of defending or prosecuting lawsuit.

L-6:5   Teaches one or more subjects, such as economics, chemistry, law, or medicine, within a prescribed curriculum. Prepares and delivers lectures to students. Reviews current literature in field of study. Writes articles for publication in professional journals.

PROCEDURE FOR EVALUATING AND RECORDING GED REQUIREMENTS

Determine the level of General Educational Development required for a worker to acquire the background knowledge and follow the instructions in the specific job-worker situation. Evaluate the job tasks in terms of the three categories of the GED scale. After determining the level required for Reasoning, Math, and Language, based on comparison of job duties with definitions and benchmarks in the HAJ, enter the level number for each category in Item 9 of the JAR.

CHAPTER 8

SPECIFIC VOCATIONAL PREPARATION

Specific Vocational Preparation (SVP), a component of Worker Characteristics, is defined as the amount of lapsed time required by a typical worker to learn the techniques, acquire the information, and develop the facility needed for average performance in a specific job-worker situation. Lapsed time is not the same as work time. For example, 30 days is approximately 1 month of lapsed time and not six 5-day work weeks, and 3 months refers to 3 calendar months and not 90 work days.

This training may be acquired in a school, work, military, institutional, or vocational environment. It does not include the orientation time required of a fully qualified worker to become accustomed to the special conditions of any new job. Nor does it include that amount of time that a worker spends to learn the reasoning, language, and mathematical skills which are often learned in school and which are also necessary for a person to be able to function in society. Within job analysis, a difficulty factor is assigned to this latter component (General Educational Development); a time factor is not. Specific vocational training includes:

a. vocational education (high school; commercial or shop training; technical school; art school; and that part of college training which is organized around a specific vocational objective);

b. apprenticeship training (for apprenticeable jobs only);

c. inplant training (organized classroom study provided by an employer);

d. on-the-job training (serving as learner or trainee on the job under the instruction of a qualified worker);

e. essential experience in other jobs (serving in less responsible jobs which lead to the higher grade job or serving in other jobs which qualify).

SCALE OF SPECIFIC VOCATIONAL PREPARATION

Level	Time[1]
1	Short demonstration only
2	Anything beyond short demonstration up to and including 1 month
3	Over 1 month up to and including 3 months
4	Over 3 months up to and including 6 months
5	Over 6 months up to and including 1 year
6	Over 1 year up to and including 2 years
7	Over 2 years up to and including 4 years
8	Over 4 years up to and including 10 years
9	Over 10 years

NOTE: The levels of this scale are mutually exclusive and do not overlap.

---

[1]Time that applies to General Educational Development is not considered in estimating Specific Vocational Preparation.

A sample of job-worker situations for each SVP level has been placed on a scale. These situations have been provided to aid the analyst in rating the specific vocational preparation level for each job.

DEFINITIONS AND EXAMPLES OF SVP LEVELS

Level 1   Short demonstration only

1:1   Inserts corrected, typed word in copy prior to photostating. Cuts out misspelled words, using razor. Fastens corrected word to tape and inserts in cutout area.

1:2   Feeds eggs into machine that removes earth, straw, and other residue from egg surface prior to shipment. Places eggs in holder that carries them into machine for washing. Removes cleaned eggs from discharge trough and packs them in cases.

1:3   Plants seedling in predetermined forest areas. Carries plants wrapped in wet moss and digs holes of prescribed size, using mattock. Places seedling in hole and tamps dirt around plant with foot. Paces off specified distance to next site and repeats planting process.

1:4   Feeds cylindrical stock into one or more threading machines. Shovels, dumps, or inserts material in hopper of machine that automatically threads stock. Carries or wheels filled and empty containers to and from machine.

1:5   Examines paper winding on reel for defects, such as spots, holes, and wrinkles, and inserts strip of paper in roll to flag defects for removal at cutting and rewinding machine.

1:6   Assists operator in winding unfinished cloth into skeins by feeding and off bearing reeling machine. Lifts end of cloth roll and mounts roll in box or bar of reeling machine. Observes cloth being wound and guides it into even skeins on reel.

1:7   Fills glasses with tap beer and hands them to waiters who serve patrons. Inserts taps in unopened barrels.

1:8   Sets up pins in bowling alley and returns thrown balls to customer. Spots pins on pegs in floor or places them in rack which lowers pins into position. Returns balls to players by rolling them along inclined runway.

1:9   Feeds farm products, such as stripped hop vines, hay, and corn stalks, into machine that chops them and blows them into storage bin or silo. Pitches material onto feed conveyors. Rakes up spilled material.

1:10   Weighs and records weight of materials, such as cotton, sugarcane, paper, and tobacco, to keep production, receiving, or other records. Reads dial to ascertain weight of object and records weight on ticket or material or inserts ticket into automatic recorder that prints weight on ticket.

Level 2   Anything beyond short demonstration up to and including 30 days

2:1   Obtains credit information, such as status of installment accounts, on individuals from credit departments of business and service establishments, using telephone, facsimile, or written correspondence. Copies information onto form to provide current information for credit record on file.

2:2   Selects talking books for mailing to blind library patrons. Compares borrower's written request with list of available titles. Selects books, following borrower's request, or selects substitute titles, following such criteria as age, education, and interest of borrower.

2:3   Changes bills or coins of large denomination into smaller units for convenience of patrons at places of amusement, such as penny arcades, carnivals, and gambling establishments. Cashes checks that are endorsed and approved by management.

2:4   Lifts green-clay products, such as brick, roofing tile, or quarry floor tile, from press-conveyor belt and stacks them in specified pattern on kiln car, drier rack, or pallet.

2:5 Trims fat, skin, tendons, tissues, and ragged edges from meat cuts, such as loins, hams, sirloins, and chops, using meathook and knife. Trims fatback from hog bellies and cuts bellies into specified shapes, using knife. Trims meat and fat from bones and places trimmings and bones in separate containers.

2:6 Assists patrons at entertainment events in finding seats, searching for lost articles, and locating such facilities as rest rooms and telephones. Distributes programs to patrons.

2:7 Drives cars between parking lot and entrance to restaurant, department store, or other establishment rendering parking service to patrons.

2:8 Tests blood of poultry to ascertain presence of pullorum disease. Pricks vein in bird's wing, using needle. Collects blood on wire loop and drops blood into pullorum reactor. Examines blood for specks that indicate presence of pullorum disease.

2:9 Dips metal parts into molten solder to bond them together using any combination of following methods: (1) twists, crimps, or holds parts together and dips them in solder for specified time; (2) dips parts separately and solders them together, using soldering iron; (3) clamps workpiece onto fixture and depresses lever to lower workpiece into solder pot.

Level 3   Over 30 days up to and including 3 months

3:1 Attaches tickets to cut garment parts to identify parts cut from same layer of cloth and to identify parts that match in shade for assembly into one garment. Staples tickets to parts, using hand stapler. Positions ticket and garment part under head of stapling machine and depresses pedal of machine that staples ticket to part.

3:2 Drives truck over established route to collect coins and refill vending machines. Loads truck with supplies according to written or verbal instructions. Drives truck to establishment, collects coins, refills machine, and records amount of money collected. Reports malfunctioning machines to maintenance department for repairs.

3:3 Cares for animals under treatment for disease, injury, or for production of serums in animal hospital. Sterilizes surgical instruments and other equipment, such as rubber gloves and syringes, using germicides and autoclave. Administers anesthetics and medications under direction of veterinarian. Bathes and brushes animals and clips their hair and nails.

3:4 Attends to personal needs of handicapped children in school to receive specialized academic and physical training. Wheels handicapped children to classes, lunchrooms, and treatment rooms. Prepares children for physical therapy treatment, secures them in equipment, and lowers them into baths or pools, using hoists. Helps children to walk, board buses, put on braces, eat, dress, and perform other physical activities.

3:5 Receives articles, such as shoes and clothing, to be repaired or cleaned in personal service establishment. Quotes prices and prepares work ticket. Sends articles to work department. Returns finished articles to customer and collects amount due.

3:6 Tends variety of machine tools, such as lathes, drill presses, or milling machines, to machine metal workpieces according to production specifications. Positions workpiece in fixture or loads automatic feeding device. Starts machine, engages feed, and observes operation. Verifies conformance of machined workpieces to specifications, using fixed gauges, calipers, or micrometer.

3:7 Examines hairsprings for flatness and concentricity, using tweezers and loupe. Stretches spring to be sure it lies in one plane, spacing is uniform between coils, and spring is free from blemishes.

3:8 Plants, cultivates, and harvests trees, shrubs, and ornamental flowering plants in nursery. Mixes soil with other materials, such as sand and peat moss, to prepare plant beds and plants specified seeds, seedlings, or bulbs. Fumigates plants to kill insect pests. Grafts buds onto trees of different varieties as directed.

3:9 Interviews applicants for employment and processes application forms. Interviews applicants to obtain information, such as age, work experience, education, and occupational interest. Refers qualified applicants to employing official. Writes letters to references indicated on application or telephones agencies, such as credit bureaus and finance companies.

3:10 Types letters, reports, stencils, forms, addresses, or other straight copy materials from rough draft or corrected copy.

Level 4   Over 3 months up to and including 6 months

4:1 Verifies accuracy of loan applications and prepares file for each loan transaction. Compares original application with credit report. Prepares loan worksheet, insurance record, credit report, and application copy for each loan.

4:2 Operates machine to reproduce data or ruled forms on paper from type in flat impression bed or plates on revolving cylinder. Selects type or embossed plate and sets it up on cylinder of flat bed of machine. Loads paper in feed tray and makes adjustments to parts, such as inking rolls or ribbon and feeding mechanism. Starts machine which automatically pushes sheets under revolving cylinder or against flat impression bed of type where paper is printed.

4:3 Assists in care of hospital patients, under direction of nursing and medical staff. Bathes, dresses, and undresses patients. Transports patients to treatment units, using wheelchair, or assists them to walk. Drapes patients for examinations and treatments and performs such duties as holding instruments and adjusting lights. Takes and records temperature, pulse and respiration rates, and food and liquid intake and output as directed.

4:4 Tends one or more machines that wash commercial, industrial, or household articles, such as garments, blankets, curtains, draperies, fine linens, and rags. Loads or directs workers in loading machine with articles requiring identical treatment. Starts machine and turns valves to admit specified amounts of water, soap, detergent, bluing, and bleach.

4:5 Guards inmates in penal institution in accordance with established policies, regulations, and procedures. Observes conduct and behavior of inmates to prevent disturbances and escapes. Inspects locks, window bars, grilles, doors, and gates for signs of tampering. Guards and directs inmates during work assignments.

4:6 Controls furnace to relieve internal stresses in metal objects and to soften and refine grain structure. Charges objects directly onto furnace bed or packs them into boxes or tubes sealed with clay to prevent oxidation. Reduces heat and allows objects to cool in furnace or removes objects from furnace and allows them to cool in open air.

4:7 Drives gasoline- or diesel-powered tractor-trailer combination, usually over long distances, to transport and deliver goods, livestock, or materials in liquid, loose, or packaged form. Inspects truck and prepares report on truck condition before and after trips.

4:8 Installs circuit wiring in automobiles, truck trailers, and mobile homes for lights, ignition, and other electrical apparatus, following diagrams and color code. Cuts and locates openings in walls and ceiling for wire, light fixtures, outlet boxes, and fuse holders, using electric drill and router. Threads wires or cables through holes and secures them to frame. Installs fixtures and boxes. Connects terminals to power source to test operation of fixtures.

4:9 Pours liquid candy into chilled molds to form solid candy figures. Dumps or pours candy into warming pan and turns dial to heat product to pouring temperature. Stirs candy to facilitate melting and pours it into chilled mold.

4:10 Patrols assigned beat on foot, using motorcycle or patrol car, or on horseback to control traffic, prevent crime or disturbance of peace, and arrest violators. Disperses unruly crowds at public gatherings. Reports to scene of accidents, renders first aid to injured, and investigates causes and results of accident. Inspects public establishments requiring licenses to ensure compliance with rules and regulations. Issues tickets to traffic violators. Directs and routes traffic.

Level 5   Over 6 months up to and including 1 year

5:1 Performs routine tests in medical laboratory for use in treatment and diagnosis of disease. Prepares tissue samples for pathologist, takes blood samples, and prepares vaccines. Carries out such laboratory tests as urinalyses and blood counts, using microscopes, micrometers, and similar instruments. Makes quantitative and qualitative chemical and biological analyses of body specimens under supervision of medical technologist or pathologist.

5:2 Performs assigned duties in business organization, depending on nature of business, to gain knowledge and experience for promotion to management positions. Participates in work of such departments of business as credit, sales, engineering, advertising, accounting, traffic, warehousing, or personnel, performing various duties under close supervision. Observes techniques utilized by experienced workers, learns line and staff functions of each department, and becomes familiar with management policies and viewpoints as they affect each phase of business operations.

5:3 Takes dictation in shorthand of correspondence, reports, and other matters and transcribes dictated material, using typewriter. Performs a variety of clerical duties, such as tabulating and posting data in record books and preparing, issuing, and sending out receipts, bills, invoices, and checks, or works in a stenographic pool transcribing material from sound recordings.

5:4 Receives, stores, and issues supplies and equipment and compiles records of supply transactions aboard ship. Verifies that supplies received are listed on requisitions and invoices. Stores, issues, and inventories supplies and equipment. Compiles report of expenditures.

5:5 Sells men's furnishings, such as neckties, shirts, belts, hats, and accessories. Advises customer on coordination of accessories.

5:6 Operates barrel plating equipment to coat metal objects electrically with metal to build up, protect, or decorate surfaces. Places metal objects in mesh container and immerses them in cleaning solution. Places objects in perforated barrel, turns handle to lower barrel into plating solution and to close electrical contacts. Starts flow of electric current through plating solution, causing plating metal at anode to decompose and be deposited on objects in barrel.

5:7 Controls equipment to bleach pulp. Starts pump and adjusts controls to regulate flow of pulp to absorption towers, bleaching and soaking tanks, and pulp washers according to specified bleaching sequence. Opens valves to allow metered flow of such chemicals as liquid and gaseous chlorine, caustic soda, and peroxide into pulp. Starts agitators to mix pulp and chemicals. Adjusts controls to ensure that pulp bleaching meets specifications, following laboratory test reports.

5:8 Assembles and adjusts typewriters and office machines or subassemblies, using handtools and holding devices. Screws and bolts parts together, using screwdrivers, wrenches, and other handtools. Tests operation of machines and typewriters to detect loose and binding parts and to determine synchronization of related parts. Verifies tensions and clearances of parts, using tension scales and space and feeler gauges.

5:9 Performs any combination of the following duties on construction projects, usually working in utility capacity, transferring from one task where demands require worker with varied experience and ability to work without close supervision: Measures distances from grade stakes and drives stakes, stretches tight line, and positions blocks up under forms. Mixes concrete, using portable concrete mixer. Gives direction to workers engaged in dumping concrete into forms. Erects shoring and braces. Aids construction equipment operators to align and move equipment, such as cranes, power shovels, and backhoes, by verifying grades and signaling operators to adjust machines to conform to grade specifications.

5:10 Coats, decorates, glazes, retouches, or tints articles, such as fishing lures, toys, dolls, pottery, artificial flowers, greeting cards, and household appliances, using airbrush. Stirs or shakes coating liquid and thinner to mix them to specified consistency. Pours liquid into airbrush container, couples spray gun to airhose, and starts compressor. Turns adjusting sleeve on nozzle of spray gun to regulate spray pattern and presses button on airbrush to spray coating over workpiece or to spray specified designs and decorations on workpiece.

Level 6   Over 1 year up to and including 2 years

6:1   Performs dental prophylactic treatments and instructs group and individuals in care of teeth and mouth. Removes calcareous deposits, accretions, and stains from teeth by scraping accumulation of tartar from teeth and beneath margins of gums, by using rotating brush, rubber cup, and cleaning compounds. Charts conditions of decay and disease for diagnosis and treatment by dentist. Lectures community organizations and other interested groups regarding oral hygiene, using motion pictures, charts, and other visual aids.

6:2   Keeps records of financial transactions of establishment. Verifies and enters details of transactions in account and cash journals from items, such as sales slips, invoices, check stubs, inventory records, and requisitions. Balances books and compiles reports to show statistics, such as cash receipts and expenditures, accounts payable and receivable, profit and loss, and other items. Calculates employee wages from plant records or timecards and makes up checks or withdraws cash from bank for payment of wages.

6:3   Sells insurance to new and present clients, recommending amount and type of coverage based on analysis of prospect's circumstances. Compiles lists of prospective clients to provide leads most likely to produce additional business. Explains features of policies offered. Calculates rates to be applied to policy for each prospect, using rate books.

6:4   Identifies stains in wool, synthetic, and silk garments and household fabrics and applies chemical solutions to remove them, determining spotting procedures on basis of type of fabric and nature of stain. Sprinkles chemical solvents over stain and pats area with brush or sponge until stain is removed. Sprays steam, water, or air over spot to flush out chemicals and dry garment.

6:5   Controls still, from central control board, to distill brandy, gin, or whiskey. Adjusts valves to control temperature and rate of flow of distilling materials through still and auxiliary equipment, such as stripping column, rectifier, condenser, and tribox. Observes gauges, dials, and charts to ensure that temperature and rate of flow of distillants are maintained according to formula. Determines proof of distilled liquor by ascertaining temperature and specific gravity of liquor, using thermometer and hydrometer.

6:6   Inspects wool to sort and grade it according to length of fiber, color, and degree of fineness, utilizing sight, touch, experience, and established specifications. Shakes fleece over screen-topped table to remove dust. Picks out foreign matter, such as burrs, sticks, strings, and cinders. Breaks fleece into pieces and inspects and sorts them according to quality.

6:7   Sets up and operates two or more types of machine tools, such as lathes, milling machines, boring machines, and grinders, to machine metal workpieces according to specifications, tooling instructions, standard charts, applying knowledge of machining methods. Reads blueprint or job order for product specifications, such as dimensions and tolerances, and tooling instructions, such as fixtures, feed rates, cutting speeds, depth of cut, and cutting tools to be used. Positions tool in toolholder. Moves controls to position tool and workpiece and to set specified feeds, speeds, and depth of cut. Starts machine. Observes operation and verifies conformance of machined workpiece to specifications, using measuring instruments, such as fixed gauges, calipers, and micrometers.

6:8   Arranges layout of work stations on assembly line, following written specifications and oral instructions, to prepare line for production of electronic components, such as printed circuit boards, transformer assemblies, and wiring harness and cables. Reads specifications including lists of materials and wiring diagrams to requisition equipment, such as piece parts, tools, test instruments, jigs, and fixtures for work stations. Positions equipment in specified arrangement at work stations.

6:9   Cuts, shapes, and polishes precious and synthetic gems. Positions rough stone in holder and holds stone against edge of revolving saw or lapidary slitter impregnated with diamond dust to cut and slit stone. Selects shaping wheel and applies abrasive compound. Holds lapidary stick against revolving shaping wheel and lapidary disk to shape stone and grind facets.

6:10   Alters women's ready-to-wear garments as instructed. Rips stitches from darts and seams of section to be altered. Operates sewing machine to sew ripped sections to customer's measurements. Sews sections of garment, such as hem, sleeve, or lining, using needle and thread.

Level 7   Over 2 years up to and including 4 years

7:1   Plans artistic, architectural, and structural features of any class of buildings and like structures. Sketches designs and details, using drawing instruments. Makes engineering computations to determine the strength of materials, beams, and trusses. Estimates quantities needed for project and computes cost.

7:2   Applies electronic theory, principles of electrical circuits, electrical testing procedures, engineering mathematics, physics, and related subjects to lay out, build, test, troubleshoot, repair, and modify developmental production and production electronic equipment, such as computers, missile-control instrumentation, and machine tool numerical controls. Assembles experimental circuitry or complete prototype model according to engineering instructions, technical manuals, and knowledge of electronic systems and components and their function. Writes technical reports and develops charts, graphs, and schematics for use by engineers in evaluating system.

7:3   Supervises and coordinates activities of clerical staff of an establishment. Prepares work schedules and expedites workflow. Reviews work performed, prepares employee ratings, and conducts employee benefit and insurance programs. Computes and compiles data and prepares records and reports. Studies and standardizes procedures to improve efficiency of department. Coordinates work operations of other departments. Estimates budget needs.

7:4   Commands ship to transport passengers, freight, and other cargo across oceans, bays, lakes, and in coastal waters. Sets course of ship, using navigational aids, such as charts, area plotting sheets, compass, and sextant. Determines geographical position of ship by use of loran or azimuths of celestial bodies. Calculates landfall by use of electronic sounding devices and by following contour lines on chart. Coordinates activities of crewmembers.

7:5   Supervises and coordinates activities of pantry, storeroom, and noncooking kitchen workers, and purchases or requisitions foodstuffs, kitchen supplies, and equipment. Inspects kitchens and storerooms to ensure that premises and equipment are clean and in order and that sufficient foodstuffs and supplies are on hand to ensure efficient service. Examines incoming purchases for quality. Coordinates activities of cleaning personnel and storage and supply workers.

7:6   Operates control panel to regulate temperature, pressure, rate of flow, and tank level in petroleum refining, processing, and treating units and petro-chemical units according to process schedules. Observes instruments and meters to verify specified conditions and records reading. Moves and adjusts dials, switches, valves, and levers on control panel to regulate and coordinate process variable, such as flow, temperature, pressures, and chemicals as specified. Records results of laboratory analysis.

7:7   Installs and repairs gas meters, regulators, ranges, heaters, and refrigerators in customer's establishment, using manometers, voltmeter, handtools, and pipe-threading tools. Measures, cuts, and threads pipe and connects it to feeder line and equipment or appliance. Tests and examines pipelines and equipment to locate leaks and faulty pipe connections and to determine pressure and flow of gas. Dismantles meters and regulators, and replaces defective pipes, thermocouples, thermostats, valves, and indicator spindles, using handtools.

7:8   Repairs or replaces upholstery in automobiles, buses, and trucks. Removes old upholstery from seats and door panels of vehicle. Measures new padding and covering materials, and cuts them to required dimensions. Adjusts or replaces seat springs and ties them in place. Sews covering material together, using sewing machine. Fits covering to seat frame. Repairs or replaces convertible tops.

7:9   Assembles, plants, and detonates charges of industrial explosives to loosen earth, rock, stumps, or to demolish structures facilitating removal. Examines mass, composition, structure, and location of object to be blasted; estimates amount and determines kind of explosive to be used. Assembles primer and places it with main charge in hole or near object to be blasted. Gives signal to clear area and detonates charge.

7:10 Develops exposed photographic film or sensitized paper in series of chemical and water baths to produce negative or positive prints. Mixes developing and fixing solutions, following formula. Immerses exposed film or photographic paper in developer solution to bring out latent image. Immerses negative or paper in stop-bath to arrest developer action, in hypo-solution to fix image, and in water to remove chemicals.

Level 8   Over 4 years up to and including 10 years

8:1 Conducts experiments on substances to develop and improve materials and products and to discover scientific facts. Combines organic compounds to make new substances or to duplicate substances found in nature. Carries out and participates in experiments designed to develop and improve, by chemical means, color, texture and strength, and lasting qualities of paint, rubber, wood, dye, petroleum, and other organic compounds and by-products. Develops new uses for chemical by-products and devises new procedures for preparing organic compounds.

8:2 Directs, coordinates, and participates in motion picture art work production concerned with design of sets, scenic effects, and costumes. Plans costuming of cast. Refers to technical literature to ensure that scenes and costumes depict accurate representation of given period or location. Coordinates efforts of departments to achieve harmonious color effects in production of color films.

8:3 Manages farm concerned with raising, harvesting, packing, and marketing farm products for corporations, cooperatives, and other owners. Analyzes market conditions to determine acreage allocations. Negotiates with bank officials to obtain credit from bank. Purchases farm machinery and equipment. Prepares financial and other management reports. Confers with purchasers and determines when and under what conditions to sell products.

8:4 Supervises and coordinates activities of cooks engaged in the preparation of desserts, pastries, confections, and ice cream. Plans production for pastry department according to menu or special requirements. Supplies recipes for and suggests methods and procedures to pastry workers. Fashions table and pastry decorations, such as statuaries and ornaments, from sugar paste and icings.

8:5 Supervises and coordinates activities of workers engaged in operation of blast furnace to produce molten pig iron. Directs workers in charging furnace with specified amounts of raw materials, such as iron ore, coke, and limestone. Observes color of molten metal through tuyeres or reads pyrometer and orders changes in furnace temperature and pressure. Estimates amounts of ferro-silicon, manganese, and phosphorous to add to molten metal to obtain specified type of pig iron.

8:6 Inspects, tests, and adjusts new and reworked tools, dies, gauges, jigs, and fixtures for conformance to specifications, such as dimensions, tolerances, and hardness. Computes angles, radii, and other dimensions, using algebra, geometry, and trigonometry. Lays out center lines and reference points on parts. Measures angular dimensions, radii contours, clearances, thread lead, and other specifications, using precision measuring instruments.

8:7 Constructs and repairs dental appliances according to dentist's prescription. Fabricates full and partial dentures, using wax and plaster models, surveyors, tooth-color scales, articulators, and electric grinders and polishers. Constructs crowns, inlays, and wire frames by forming gold and platinum wire or by casting in mold in centrifugal casting furnace. Constructs porcelain teeth from impression, using powdered porcelain and water, electric furnaces, grinding wheels, and tooth-color scales.

8:8 Repairs and maintains electrical equipment in generating station or powerhouse. Tests defective equipment to determine cause of malfunction or failure, using voltmeters, ammeters, and related electrical testing apparatus. Repairs and replaces equipment, such as relays, switches, supervisory controls, and indicating and recording instruments. Tests and repairs switchboard and equipment circuitry, interpreting wiring diagrams to trace and connect numerous wires carrying current for independent functions.

8:9 Prepares flight schedules for airline. Reviews schedules and travel loads and determines need for schedule revision. Prepares advance schedules in accordance with known and estimated passenger travel patterns between designated points and availability of equipment. Studies company and inter-line schedules to coordinate flights and devise schedule patterns. Prepares request for route use, as directed by Schedule Committee, and assembles supporting material based on analysis of passenger loads and travel patterns.

8:10 Manages industrial organization. Determines and executes administrative policies through subordinate managers. Coordinates activities of departments, such as production, distribution, engineering, maintenance, personnel, and selling. Plans and directs marketing of product to develop new markets and maintain sales volume and competitive position in industry.

Level 9   Over 10 years

9:1 Supervises and coordinates activities of workers engaged in installation, maintenance, repair, servicing, enlargement, and relocation of water distribution and sewage facilities. Analyzes trends, such as population and industrial growth of area serviced, to determine adequacy of current facilities and to forecast future community demands for water and sewage facilities. Designs plans to meet and serve expanding community needs. Confers with administrative and technical personnel to coordinate departmental activities with organizational demands.

9:2 Provides leadership for professional staff and participates in development of academic policy and programs of college or university. Supervises department or division heads or deans of individual colleges. Determines scheduling of courses and recommends implementation of additional courses. Advises students on choice of major academic area and coordinates academic advising efforts of deans of colleges and faculty. Participates in activities of faculty committees, such as curriculum committee and faculty personnel committee.

9:3 Administers affairs of museum and conducts scientific research programs. Directs activities concerned with instructional, research, and public service objectives of institutions. Obtains, develops, and organizes new collections to build up and improve educational and research facilities. Organizes and conducts field parties engaged in scientific research, performing duties such as gathering scientific papers, selecting personnel, and securing financial support for expeditions.

9:4 Directs editorial activities of newspaper and negotiates with production, advertising, and circulation department heads. Appoints editorial heads and supervises work of their department in accordance with newspaper policy. Writes leading or policy editorials. Confers with editorial policy committee and negotiates with production, circulation, and advertising department heads to establish policies and reach decisions affecting publication.

9:5 Creates and writes musical compositions. Invents melodic, harmonic, and rhythmic structures to express ideas musically within circumscribed musical form, such as symphony, sonata, or opera. Translates melodies, harmonies, and rhythms into musical notes and records notes on scored music paper.

9:6 Directs engineering departments of petroleum production or pipeline company and advises management on engineering problems. Reviews engineering designs for neatness and accuracy. Directs engineering personnel in formulating plans, designs, costs estimates, and specifications for oil field or pipeline construction, maintenance, and modernization programs. Supervises engineering office workers computing budgets, compiling reports, and conducting special investigations and studies to evaluate efficiency of engineering programs.

9:7 Administers private, corporate, and probate trusts. Examines or drafts trust agreement to ensure compliance with legal requirements and terms creating trust. Locates, inventories, and evaluates assets of probated accounts. Directs realization of assets, liquidation of liabilities, payment of bills, preparation of Federal and State tax returns, and collection of earnings.

9:8 Directs and coordinates activities of municipal police department in accordance with authority delegated by board of police. Promulgates rules and regulations for department. Coordinates and administers daily police activities through subordinates. Directs activities of personnel engaged in preparing budget proposals, maintaining police records, and recruiting employees.

9:9   Plans, administers, and directs intercollegiate athletic activities in college or university. Interprets and participates in formulating extramural athletic policies. Directs athletic coaches and members of coaching staff. Prepares budget estimates. Assumes immediate responsibilities for receipts and expenditures of department and for production of income, such as scheduling sports events and controlling and managing ticket sales.

9:10 Develops and administers policies of organization in accordance with corporation character. Establishes operating objectives and policies for firm. Reviews progress and makes necessary changes in company plans. Directs preparation of major financial programs, such as pricing policies and salary and wage schedules, to ensure operating efficiency and adequate investment and dividend returns.

PROCEDURE FOR EVALUATING AND RECORDING SVP REQUIREMENTS

SVP is the amount of time required for a typical worker, taking the usual training available, to perform the duties of the job in a way to be accepted as a fully qualified worker. SVP is estimated by the analyst based upon an evaluation of the job. In making this evaluation, the analyst considers the employer's requirements shown in Item 11 of the JAR and the examples for the various levels of SVP. However, the entries in Item 11, Employer Requirements, are not to be used as a worktable for computing SVP. They are two separate and distinct entries which can complement each other, but are not intended to provide the same information. The information in Item 11 must be considered and may be the basis for SVP, provided it is reasonable.

NOTE: In calculating SVP for Item 9 of the JAR, count the average four-year college curriculum as equivalent to two years of specific vocational preparation, and count each year of graduate school as a year of specific vocational preparation. At the secondary level of vocational education, count two classroom hours as an hour of SVP. However, at the post-secondary level of vocational education, count each classroom hour as an hour of SVP.

If there is disagreement with the employer's training requirement, the analyst should follow the employer's requirement in Item 11 of the JAR with an asterisk and explain the disagreement in Item 18 (General Comments). The final SVP rating represents the analyst's judgment based on an assessment and evaluation of all pertinent data gathered.

Enter in Item 9 of the JAR, the SVP level that applies to the job.

CHAPTER 9

APTITUDES

Aptitudes, a component of Worker Characteristics, are the capacities or specific abilities which an individual must have in order to learn to perform a given work activity. There are 11 Aptitudes used by USES for job analysis. Nine Aptitudes are measured by the United States Employment Service's General Aptitude Test Battery (GATB). Two others, Eye-Hand-Foot Coordination and Color Discrimination, have been added to these for job analysis because they are considered to be occupationally significant. Measurements for these Aptitudes have not been developed for the GATB. The 11 Aptitudes are:

G - General Learning Ability

V - Verbal Aptitude

N - Numerical Aptitude

S - Spatial Aptitude

P - Form Perception

Q - Clerical Perception

K - Motor Coordination

F - Finger Dexterity

M - Manual Dexterity

E - Eye-Hand-Foot Coordination

C - Color Discrimination

Decades of research have established the validity of the GATB in measuring the aptitudes of individuals. The USES job analysis technique of estimating the aptitude requirements of jobs has its basis not only in the GATB Aptitude definitions but in USES test development standards as well. In test validation procedures using the GATB, Test Research Analysts apply precise statistical and other quantitative as well as qualitative standards to determine validated test requirements for use as job selection criteria and counseling).

LEVELS OF APTITUDES

In job analysis, aptitude estimates are useful as analytical and descriptive tools and can be expressed in terms of the following levels which reflect the amount of the aptitudes possessed by segments of the working population:

1. The top 10 percent of the population. This segment of the population possesses an extremely high degree of the aptitude.

2. The highest third exclusive of the top 10 percent of the population. This segment of the population possesses an above average or high degree of the aptitude.

3. The middle third of the population. This segment of the population possesses a medium degree of the aptitude ranging from slightly below to slightly above average.

4. The lowest third exclusive of the bottom 10 percent of the population. This segment of the population possesses a below average or low degree of the aptitude.

5. The lowest 10 percent of the population. This segment of the population possesses a negligible degree of the aptitude.

Aptitude Levels				
1	2	3	4	5
Extremely High Aptitude Ability	High Degree of Aptitude Ability	Medium Degree of Aptitude Ability	Lower Degree of Aptitude Ability	Markedly Low Aptitude Ability
Top 10%	Highest Third Excluding Top 10%	Middle Third	Lowest Third Excluding Top 10%	Bottom 10%
Percent of Working Population				

PROCEDURE FOR RATING APTITUDES

Every aptitude factor must be considered independently in the rating process for each job. The analyst estimates the level of each aptitude required of the worker for average, satisfactory performance based on a careful evaluation of the work activities of the job and the specific worker abilities which can be identified in terms of the aptitudes. Then the appropriate aptitude level number is assigned. Certain of the aptitudes can be identified through study of the physical actions which the worker performs, such as Motor Coordination, Finger Dexterity, and Eye-Hand-Foot Coordination; other Aptitudes, such as Spatial, Numerical, and General Learning Ability, are identified by considering worker judgments and other mental processes involved in performing the job satisfactorily. Aptitude levels are determined by comparing the tasks of the job with the aptitude definitions, interpretive information, and the examples of work activities shown for each level which appear in the next section of this chapter.

Note that for each of the eleven aptitudes there are not any examples of job duties for level 5. Level 5 is used to indicate that for the job under study the amount of aptitude required is negligible or the aptitude is not required at all. Since level 5 represents an aptitude level that is not required or is required only in negligible amounts and which, according to the table above, represents job duties which 90 to 100 percent of the working population could perform satisfactorily, examples of job duties for this level are not provided. If there is a doubt as to which of two levels should be assigned, select the lower level. Enter in the box immediately below each Aptitude letter in Item 9 of the JAR a number, one through five, to indicate the estimated Aptitude level required in the job.

The definition of each Aptitude is followed by interpretive information for analysts which provides supplementary information relating the definition to specific work activities and examples of job or task summaries illustrating each of the five levels of the Aptitude. The definitions reflect the Aptitudes as seen in people. The interpretive information reflects the Aptitudes as observed in jobs. Most of the examples are based on qualitative analyses contained in the technical reports of the SATB's. Although there are no illustrations for Aptitude factors K and M at level 1, this does not preclude assignment of level 1 when the analysis of a job warrants it.

G — GENERAL LEARNING ABILITY: The ability to "catch on" or understand instructions and underlying principles; the ability to reason and make judgments. Closely related to doing well in school.

Interpretive Information for Analysts: Consider such factors as: work requiring the ability to define problems, collect information, establish facts, and draw valid conclusions; work requiring the use of logic or scientific thinking to solve a variety of problems; work requiring the use of measurable and verifiable information for making decisions or judgments; understanding detailed work procedures; planning, organizing, coordinating, and directing own work and that of others; coping with a variety of duties; following written or oral instructions; or selecting appropriate work aids and materials to perform a set of tasks.

LEVEL 1

G-1:1   Conducts research in fundamental mathematics and in application of mathematical techniques to science, management, and other fields and solves or directs solutions to problems in various fields by mathematical methods:

General learning ability is required to understand meanings and relationships of mathematical symbols, formulas, and concepts; to assimilate background information required to understand problems from various fields; to develop or apply appropriate methods and procedures for solving problems; and to present solutions or methodologies for solutions in logical and systematic forms and sequences.

G-1:2   Diagnoses and treats diseases, injuries, and malformations of teeth, gums, and related oral structures:

General learning ability is required to understand and apply principles of dental anatomy, bacteriology, and physiology for diagnosis and treatment and to use techniques of dental restoration and prosthetics. Must understand the operation and function of dental tools and equipment and the uses of dental metals, alloys, and amalgams.

G-1:3   Converts symbolic statements of administrative data or business problems to detailed logical flow charts for coding into computer language:

General learning ability is required to understand and apply work statement instructions, recommended procedural routines, and related informational data; to identify and organize elements of a problem into logical sequence for computer operation by means of preparing block diagrams and flow charts; to make analytical and logical analyses in planning procedural routines; to have a working knowledge of the company business organization and management and with modern office methods and procedures; and to have a complete familiarity with programming principles and techniques in order to discuss programming methods, requirements, and approaches with line and staff personnel.

G-1:4   Writes original plays, such as tragedies, comedies, or dramas, or adapts themes from fictional, historical, or narrative sources for dramatic presentation:

General learning ability is required to utilize basic principles of play writing, including basic research of characters, dress, and furnishings of the time-setting of the play, and to show depth of understanding in the development of situations and roles.

G-1:5   Receives individual applications for insurance to evaluate degree of risk involved and accepts applications following company's underwriting policies:

General learning ability is required to understand and apply principles of insurance, finance, and economics. Must be able to understand application of information, such as medical reports, occupational hazards, financial reports, fire inspection reports, and insurance maps. Must work with actuarial formulas, study and relate all phases of an insurance risk problem, and come to a decision beneficial to the needs of the applicant and to the interests of the company.

G-1:6   Studies origin, relationship, development, anatomy, functions, and basic principles of plant and animal life:

General learning ability is required to study scientific facts and concepts which are needed for an understanding of the structure, function, development, and relationship of living organisms and to draw conclusions or generalizations from accumulated facts.

G-1:7   Coordinates activities of radio and television studio and control-room personnel to ensure technical quality of pictures and sound for programs originating in studio or from remote pickup points:

General learning ability is required to plan and arrange for all audio, visual, and special effects equipment and technical personnel needed for programs; to use judgment to determine number of cameras, etc., necessary to achieve specified effects; and to give work assignments to technicians who control and maintain lights, audio and visual controlling equipment, microphones, and cameras. Must understand functions and capabilities of equipment to give directions.

LEVEL 2

G-2:1   Renders general nursing care to patients in hospital, infirmary, sanitarium, or similar institution (Registered Nurses):

General learning ability is required to learn and apply principles of anatomy, physiology, microbiology, nutrition, psychology, and patient care used in nursing; to recognize and interpret symptoms and reactions; to make independent judgments in the absence of doctor; and to determine methods and treatments to use when caring for patients with varying illnesses or injuries.

G-2:2   Applies principles of accounting to devise and implement system for general accounting:

General learning ability is required to learn, understand, and apply accounting principles and procedures; to evaluate accounting and record-keeping systems; to analyze current and regulatory problems and develop system which provides needed records for internal operation and to meet requirements of government agencies; and to prepare analyses and interpretation of data for company officials.

G-2:3   Plans layout, installs, and repairs wiring, electrical fixtures, apparatus, and control equipment:

General learning ability is required to learn and understand principles of electricity; to read and interpret blueprints and specifications; to plan new or modified installations; and to diagnose problems and select the most feasible methods of repair.

G-2:4   Rents, buys, and sells property for clients on commission basis:

General learning ability is required to learn and make proper interpretation and application of law, legislation, and qualification requirements; and to keep informed of marketing conditions and property values.

G-2:5 Analyzes a variety of specifications, lays out metal stock, sets up and operates machine tools, and fits and assembles parts to make and repair metalworking dies, cutting tools, jigs, fixtures, gauges, and machinists' handtools, applying knowledge of tool and die design and construction, shop mathematics, metal properties, and layout, machining, and assembly procedures:

General learning ability is required to understand blueprints and other specifications; to plan sequence of operations and layout and setup procedures; to determine type of machine and tools to use and machine settings based on type of operations to be performed, type of material being processed, and dimensions and other specifications to be achieved.

G-2:6 Draws and corrects topographical maps from source data, such as surveying notes, aerial photographs, or other maps:

General learning ability is required to learn and apply drafting principles, procedures, and symbols and the geometry and mathematics peculiar to topography and to translate aerial photographs and other data into accurate maps.

G-2:7 Prepares bodies for interment, in conformity with legal requirements:

General learning ability is required to learn and apply basic principles and techniques related to mortuary science including chemistry, anatomy, physiology, principles of preservation, disinfection, circulatory embalming, cavity treatment, hygiene, microbiology, restoration, and cosmetics; and to learn the laws and regulations relating to embalming.

LEVEL 3

G-3:1 Takes dictation, in shorthand, of correspondence, reports, and other matters and transcribes dictated material, using typewriter:

General learning ability is required to learn meaning and usage of shorthand symbols; to learn typewriter operation and memorize keyboard; to learn rules for format of business letters and reports and rules of spelling, punctuation, and grammar.

G-3:2 Repairs, maintains, and installs electrical systems and equipment, such as motors, transformers, wiring, switches, and alarm systems:

General learning ability is required to learn basic electrical theory and circuitry, blueprint reading, local building codes, and safety practices; and to use reason and judgment in diagnosing faults and choosing most feasible method of repair.

G-3:3 Prepares and compiles records in hospital nursing unit, such as obstetrics, pediatrics, or surgery:

General learning ability is required to make independent judgments regarding task priorities; to integrate and interpret informational and situational data; and to respond quickly to data input.

G-3:4 Drives truck over established route to deliver, sell, and display products or render services:

General learning ability is required to acquire and use knowledge of company products or services, unit cost, and policies; to discuss customer's needs and promote sales; to apply company policies and own judgment regarding delivery procedures, credit extension, discounts, etc., in a manner to maintain good customer relations; to maintain accounts and records; and to determine best driving routes to reach customers.

G-3:5 Assembles and loads a variety of solid-propellant rocket motors:

General learning ability is required to learn the various steps in preparing and loading solid-propellant fuels for rockets; to understand specifications and follow them explicitly when mixing liquid and dry ingredients to form propellant; to use judgment when handling and processing propellant to avoid explosions; to determine when chemicals are properly mixed and cured from instrument readings on control panel, and using charts and direct observation via TV monitors.

G-3:6   Cares for ill, injured, convalescent, and handicapped persons in hospitals, clinics, private homes, sanitariums, and similar institutions (Licensed Practical Nurse):

General learning ability is required to learn and apply principles and techniques of basic nursing skills, body structure and functions, personal hygiene, nutrition, and first aid; and to use judgment in patient care, moving patients, and giving prescribed medicines and injections.

G-3:7   Provides beauty service for customers:

General learning ability is required to learn the various phases of cosmetology including hair cutting, styling, setting, and facial treatment, and the various methods used; to use reason and judgment to suggest various treatments to customers and assist them in deciding on hair style according to their individual features and taste.

LEVEL 4

G-4:1   Assists in care of hospital patients, under direction of nursing and medical staff:

General learning ability is required to learn patient care and handling and hospital routine; to understand and carry out orders correctly; to use reason and judgment in handling patients, noting patient's condition and reporting symptoms or reactions which may indicate a change in condition.

G-4:2   Makes women's garments, such as dresses, coats, and suits, according to customer specifications and measurements:

General learning ability is required to understand basic principles of garment construction and pattern alteration; to understand instructions from customers and patterns; and to reason when altering patterns to customers' measurements.

G-4:3   Sorts agricultural produce, such as bulbs, fruits, nuts, and vegetables, according to grade, color, and size, discards cull items and foreign matter, and places produce in containers:

Recognizes indications of defects, such as spots or softness, and learns grading characteristics for a variety of produce. Uses judgment in sorting out partially defective produce.

G-4:4   Feeds or removes metal stock from automatic fabricating machines:

Learns work routine, acceptable tolerances, and difference between acceptable imperfections and those to be rejected. Uses judgment to determine, from observing parts processed or machine operation, when machine should be stopped because of some malfunction.

G-4:5   Operates alphabetic and numeric keypunch machine, similar in operation to electric typewriter, to transcribe data from source material onto punchcards, paper or magnetic tape, or magnetic cards, and to record accounting or statistical data for subsequent processing by automatic or electronic data processing equipment:

General learning ability is required to follow instructions to ensure that correct format is followed in preparing program cards and reading the data.

G-4:6   Assists workers engaged in preparing foods for hotels, restaurants, or institutions, by washing, peeling, cutting or grinding meats, vegetables, or fruits, preparing salads, mixing ingredients for desserts, portioning foods on plates or serving trays, loading serving trays on delivery carts, carrying pans and kettles to and from work station, and cleaning work area, equipment, and utensils:

General learning ability is required to learn routine of kitchen, location of materials, equipment, and utensils, and various tasks to be performed. Must understand instructions pertaining to mixing of ingredients for salads, gelatin, and pudding-mix desserts; and for portioning food.

LEVEL 5 NO ILLUSTRATIONS (see page 9-2)

V — VERBAL APTITUDE: The ability to understand the meaning of words and to use them effectively. Ability to comprehend language, to understand relationships between words, and to understand the meanings of whole sentences and paragraphs.

Interpretive Information for Analysts: Consider reading comprehension required to use or understand oral or written instructions or specifications, texts used in training, and reference materials used in work or mastery of required technical terminology.

LEVEL 1

V-1:1   Conducts research in fundamental mathematics and in application of mathematical techniques to science, management, and other fields, and solves or directs solutions to problems in various fields by mathematical methods:

Verbal aptitude is required to understand meanings and relationships of mathematical symbols, formulas, and concepts; to develop methods and procedures of problem solving through reasoning; to understand terminology from such fields as engineering, data processing, or management in order to discuss problems with others whose background is in such fields and explain to them how mathematical concepts can be adapted to the solution of their problems; and to present solutions in logical and systematic forms and sequences.

V-1:2   Attends to variety of medical cases in general practice, diagnosing, prescribing medicine for, and otherwise treating diseases and disorders of the human body, and performing surgery:

Verbal aptitude is required for reading comprehension of complex technical materials in such areas as anatomy, biochemistry, physiology, pharmacology, pathology, bacteriology, and radiology; and for facility of expression to explain illness, treatment, or preventive measures to patients, or to discuss diagnosis and symptoms with colleagues.

V-1:3   Designs chemical plant equipment and devises processes for manufacturing chemicals and products, such as gasoline, synthetic rubber, plastics, detergent, cement, and paper and pulp, applying principles and technology of chemistry, physics, mechanical and electrical engineering, and related areas:

Verbal aptitude is required to acquire the technical vocabulary of chemistry and engineering; to read and understand reference materials; and to write technical reports and design or production specifications.

V-1:4   Directs editorial activities of newspaper and negotiates with production, advertising, and circulation department heads as owner's representative:

Verbal aptitude is required to write lead or policy editorials explaining complex political, social, or other issues in language which will be understood by most readers; to interpret the editorial policy of the firm on specific issues to other editorial writers; and to speak at professional and community functions as a representative of the publisher.

V-1:5   Conducts criminal and civil lawsuits, draws up legal documents, advises clients as to legal rights, and practices other phases of law; and represents client in court, and before quasi-judicial or administrative agencies of government:

Verbal aptitude is required to comprehend and interpret legal terminology for use in preparing legal documents, and in presenting oral or written arguments.

V-1:6   Selects, catalogs, and maintains library collection of books, periodicals, documents, films, recordings, and other materials, and assists groups and individuals to locate and obtain materials:

Verbal aptitude is required to review materials preparatory to purchase to see that they do not duplicate others and are consistent with the subject matter collection policy of the library; to accurately determine subject matter of books in order to properly code them and prepare cross-references; and to prepare and give talks to groups of patrons.

V-1:7 Collects, analyzes, and develops occupational data concerning jobs, job qualifications, and worker characteristics to facilitate personnel, administrative, or information functions in private or public organizations:

Verbal aptitude is required to read, understand, and interpret various kinds of technical data; to write reports, letters, and job descriptions concisely and clearly; and to conduct information gathering interviews.

V-1:8 Draws cartoons for publication to illustrate highlights of news topics in satirical or humorous manner:

Verbal aptitude is required to read news items to obtain subject for cartoons; discuss policy and method of presentation with editor; translate ideas from verbal to pictorial form; and to select most significant wording for caption to bring out meaning of cartoon.

LEVEL 2

V-2:1 Converts symbolic statement of business problem to detailed logical flow charts for coding into computer language and solution by means of automatic data processing equipment:

Verbal aptitude is required to read and understand statements of operations and procedural routines from various departments; to discuss program objectives and output requirements with supervisor and department heads; to explain programming techniques and principles while attending briefings, meetings, and interviews; and to write a documentation of each program's development.

V-2:2 Instructs students in one or more subjects, such as English, mathematics, or social studies, in private, religious, or public secondary school (high school):

Verbal aptitude is required to read and understand textbooks or other literature related to the subject matter taught; to lecture on, discuss, and explain subject matter to convey information to the students; to write lesson plans and outlines; and to read students' papers and write critiques.

V-2:3 Edits motion picture film and sound track:

Verbal aptitude is required to listen critically to the dialogue and to determine if it is understandable and maintains the story continuity.

V-2:4 Interviews job applicants in employment agency and refers them to prospective employers for consideration:

Verbal aptitude is required to speak and understand the applicants' language in order to learn their background, qualifications, and goals and to explain the employment service to employers and obtain requirements data for job orders.

V-2:5 Reads books or scripts of radio and television programs to detect and recommend deletion of vulgar, immoral, libelous, or misleading statements:

Verbal aptitude is required to understand the expressed and implied meanings and possible connotations of words in script and statements in the context used.

V-2:6 Schedules and assigns motor vehicles and drivers for the conveyance of freight according to company and government regulations and policies:

Verbal aptitude is required to read and understand the rules, laws, regulations, and policies of the company, union, and Interstate Commerce Commission; to effectively communicate instructions to drivers; and to write reports.

V-2:7 Sells automotive parts and equipment and advises customers on substitution or modification of parts when replacement is not available:

Verbal aptitude is required to ask pertinent questions to determine merchandise desired by customer; to answer technical questions and explain use of parts; and to provide other information requested.

V-2:8 Takes dictation, in shorthand, of correspondence, reports, and other matters, and transcribes material, using typewriter:

Verbal aptitude is required to comprehend meaning of words to record and transcribe dictation accurately.

LEVEL 3

V-3:1 Operates switchboard to provide answering service for clients:

Verbal aptitude is required to greet caller and announce name and phone number of client; to record and deliver messages; to furnish information; to accept orders; and to relay calls.

V-3:2 Types letters, reports, stencils, forms, addresses, or other straight copy material from rough draft or corrected copy:

Verbal aptitude is required to understand the meaning of words, sentences, and whole paragraphs well enough so that, in copying from a rough draft, insertions which are out of context or incorrectly placed can be noted.

V-3:3 Supervises and coordinates activities of workers engaged in assembly of electronic equipment such as radar and sonar units, missile control systems, computers, cables and harnesses, and test equipment:

Explains wiring and soldering procedures to new employees. Reads test reports to determine cause of equipment failures and explains procedures to workers to correct practices that result in defects. Explains company policies and discusses grievances with workers or their representative.

V-3:4 Questions patients to obtain their medical history, personal data, and to determine if they are allergic to dental drugs or have any complicating illnesses:

Converses with patient in reassuring manner; explains post-operative care, oral hygiene, and importance of preventive dentistry to patients. Greets patients, answers telephone, and schedules appointments.

V-3:5 Sells variety of commodities in sales establishment:

Describes salient features to customer and advises customer in making selection by explaining use of particular article or suggesting other articles.

V-3:6 Sets up and operates machine tools, and fits and assembles parts to make or repair metal parts, mechanisms, tools, or machines, applying knowledge of machines, shop mathematics, metal properties, and layout machining procedures:

Verbal aptitude is required to read text materials while attending classes during training or apprenticeship; and to understand language in shop orders, specifications, and other written or oral instructions.

V-3:7 Provides beauty service for customers; suggests coiffure according to physical features of patron and current styles, or determines coiffure from instructions of patron; suggests cosmetics for conditions, such as dry or oily skin:

Verbal aptitude is required to greet patrons, ascertain services desired, and explain beauty treatments, hair styles, and other services.

V-3:8 Repairs and overhauls automobiles, buses, trucks, and other automotive vehicles:

Reads and interprets technical manuals, charts, and parts manuals to plan work procedures and select replacement parts; discusses nature and extent of damage and repairs needed with customer and service manager.

V-3:9   Constructs, erects, installs, and repairs structures and fixtures of wood, plywood, and wallboard, using carpenter's handtools and power tools, and conforming to local building codes:

Verbal aptitude is required to read blueprints for information pertaining to materials and dimensions; and to understand building codes and company safety practice rules.

LEVEL 4

V-4:1   Records brand marks used to identify cattle, produce, or other commodities to facilitate identification:

Reads applications for new brands and official brand record; records assignment or reassignment of brands; reads to file reports of field inspectors.

V-4:2   Mixes and bakes ingredients according to recipes and production order to produce breads, pastries, and other baked goods:

Must read recipes and production orders to determine number and kind of bakery products to make, ingredients to use, and mixing and baking instructions.

V-4:3   Welds metal parts together, as specified by layout, diagram, work order, or oral instructions, using equipment which introduces a shield of inert or noncombustible gas around the electric arc to prevent oxidation:

Verbal aptitude is required to read work order or receive oral instructions indicating type of material and number of units to be welded, type and size of electrode material to use, type of gas shield to use, settings for gas pressure, electric current amperage, and speed of electrode wire feed.

V-4:4   Tends any of a variety of machine tools, such as lathes, drill presses, milling machines, grinders, and special purpose machines, to machine metal workpieces to specifications on a production basis:

Reads written instructions or work orders to determine number and kind of parts to be machined and kind of metal stock or castings to use. Requests stock and cutting tools from stock room, specifying sizes, types, and amounts.

V-4:5   Cares for children in private home:

Must read directions for preparation of formulas, and possess sufficient vocabulary to understand instructions regarding care of children.

V-4:6   Services automobiles, buses, trucks, and other automotive vehicles with fuel, lubricants, and accessories as requested by customer:

Verbal aptitude is required to understand specific instructions from station manager and to communicate with customers.

V-4:7   Assembles metal toys on assembly line, changing tasks as directed according to work load of department; tends drill press or punch press; fits parts together; and joins parts using resistance welder, fold-over tabs, or nuts and bolts:

Verbal aptitude is required to understand oral instructions specifying parts to assemble, position of parts, sequence of assembly, and methods of fastening parts for several types and models of toys and stages of assembly.

LEVEL 5 NO ILLUSTRATIONS (see page 9-2)

N — NUMERICAL APTITUDE: The ability to perform arithmetic operations quickly and accurately.

Interpretive Information for Analysts: Consider activities, such as making change from currency of one denomination to another, keeping time or production records, using math or geometry to lay out geometric patterns, making accurate numerical measurements, and making or checking numerical entries. Consider the complexity of numerical operations as well as speed required and volume of arithmetic activity.

LEVEL 1

N-1:1   Conducts research in fundamental mathematics and in application of mathematical techniques to science, management, and other fields, and solves or directs solutions to problems in various fields by mathematical methods:

Numerical aptitude is required to understand mathematical symbols, formulas, and concepts; to develop methods and procedures of problem solving; and to test hypotheses and alternate theories.

N-1:2   Performs variety of engineering work in designing, planning, or overseeing the manufacture, construction, installation, or maintenance of electric or electronic systems, equipment, or machinery used in the generation, transmission, or utilization of electrical energy for domestic, commercial, or industrial consumption:

Numerical aptitude is required for the understanding and application of algebra, trigonometry, analytical geometry, calculus, and differential equations to engineering problems.

N-1:3   Converts engineering, scientific, and other technical problem formulations into format processible by computer:

Numerical aptitude is required to identify mathematical formulas, equations, and assumptions presented in support of problem; to analyze problem using mathematical formulas, tables, and reference materials; and to make computations involving the use of linear algebra, vector analysis, differential equations, and calculus to identify each mathematical element in the solution of the problem.

N-1:4   Collects, analyzes, and interprets data on problems of public finance:

Computes or formulates problems for solution by others to determine government income and expenditures by source and function, using such data as tax tables and rates, income and population projections, and proposed budget and expenditure projections. Determines impact of tax and fiscal policies on level of income and business activities. Computes initial and final distribution of tax burden and its effects from analysis of shifting and incidence patterns for various types of taxes. Computes probable revenues and effects of new taxes or tax rates. Computations and formulation of problems require the use of statistical methods, algebra, and some calculus.

N-1:5   Researches market conditions in local, regional, or national area to determine potential sales of a product or service:

Computes and analyzes statistical data on past sales of firm and general wholesale and retail sales trends to forecast future sales trends. Makes statistical projections based on population, income, sales data, and consumer surveys.

N-1:6   Reviews applications for casualty insurance to evaluate degree of risk involved, following company's underwriting policies:

Determines amount of risk company will insure, based on value of property and risks involved, and the premium thereon. Determines the value of each factor affecting the degree of risk and applies the applicable premium to each using rate tables or computes the weighted value of each factor to arrive at a final composite weight used to compute the premium; computes amount of insurance in force in the particular class of risk or in the same area to assure that the company is spreading its risks sufficiently according to probability tables.

N-1:7   Prepares cost and work completion estimates for engineering contract bids:

Numerical aptitude is required to compute and list total quantity of each type of material needed from blueprints and specifications; to compute quantity of standard sizes or lots needed for
each segment of structure or part; to estimate cost of raw materials, purchased equipment, or
subcontracted work, and labor, using price lists, standard or estimated time/cost figures, and
materials lists; and to set delivery or completion dates.

LEVEL 2

N-2:1   Applies principles of accounting to install and maintain accounting system:

Applies numerical reasoning to design or modify systems to provide records of assets, liabilities, and financial transactions; applying arithmetic principles to prepare accounts, records, and
reports based on them; auditing contracts, orders, and vouchers; and preparing tax returns and
other reports to government agencies.

N-2:2   Draws and corrects topographical maps from source data, such as surveying notes, aerial photographs, or other maps:

Numerical aptitude is required to make arithmetic computations to lay out scale representations
of mountains, cities, and other geographic features so that correct proportions and distances are
achieved.

N-2:3   Applies electronic theory, principles of electrical circuits, electrical testing procedures, mathematics, physics, and related subjects to lay out, build, test, troubleshoot, repair, and modify developmental and production electronic equipment, such as computers, missile-control instrumentation, and machine tool numerical controls:

Numerical aptitude is required to calculate value and sizes of circuitry components needed,
when not specified; to compute output values or potential of units; and to prepare graphs showing operating characteristics of system, using mathematical tables and formulas.

N-2:4   Develops resistance welding and brazing machine setup data for work orders to ensure that
parts conform to blueprints and engineering specifications, applying knowledge of machine
function, electronics, properties of metals, effects of heat, and shop mathematics:

Computes combination of pressure, current, holding time, and impact required to obtain specified weld, interpolating from tables and charts, and multiplying and dividing fractions and deci-
mals to arrive at machine settings. Measures and makes arithmetic computations to determine
dimensional setup for workpiece and electrodes and size of jigs or fixtures needed.

N-2:5   Schedules and assigns motor vehicles and drivers for availability, length of trip, freight requirements, vehicle capacities and licenses, and user preferences:

Numerical aptitude is required to compute truck capacities for various products; to estimate delivery time; to compute delivery charges; and to prepare statistical reports and studies on operations, equipment, and personnel.

N-2:6   Repairs electronic equipment, such as computers, industrial controls, radar systems, telemetering
and missile control systems, following blueprints and manufacturers' specifications using
handtools and test instruments:

Numerical aptitude is required to calculate dimensions; to determine output measurements of
components; to compute ratios when calibrating instruments; and to apply principles of geometry and trigonometry to compute angles and coordinates.

N-2:7   Directs operation of retail, self-service food store according to overall organizational policies:

Numerical aptitude is necessary to determine amounts of merchandise needed based on stock
and past sales; to prepare requisitions or orders; to adjust prices based on amount, condition
and salability of item; and to prepare financial reports, such as sales reports, time and payroll
reports, bank deposits, or inventories.

LEVEL 3

N-3:1 Supervises and coordinates activities of workers engaged in extracting alumina from bauxite:

Numerical aptitude is required to calculate feed rates of raw materials, using standard formulas and chemical analysis reports to compute rate of inputs; to study production schedules and estimate staff hour requirements for completion of job assignment; and to adjust work schedules or staffing to meet production requirements, using knowledge of capacities of machines and equipment; and to maintain time and production records.

N-3:2 Sells tickets for transportation agencies, such as airlines, bus companies, railroads, and steamship lines:

Numerical aptitude is required to compute ticket cost and taxes, using schedules and rate books; to check and weigh baggage; to compute travel time and fares for different types of accommodations; to prepare daily sales record showing number and class of tickets sold and amount of fare and taxes; and to count and balance cash with sales record.

N-3:3 Grows shrubs, rootstocks, cut flowers, or flowering bulbs:

Computes acreage to be planted according to estimated demand for species, availability and cost of seed, bulbs, or scion stock and space requirements for each variety. Maintains record of wages and hours of workers.

N-3:4 Constructs, erects, installs, and repairs structures and fixtures of wood, plywood, and wallboard, using carpenter's handtools and power tools:

Measures and computes unspecified dimensions to prepare layouts, mark cutting and assembly lines on materials, shape materials to prescribed measurements, and fit and install window and door frames, trim cabinet work, and hardware.

N-3:5 Acts as intermediary between importers, steamship companies, or airlines and Bureau of Customs by preparing and compiling documents required by Federal Government for a ship or airplane of foreign origin to discharge its cargo at a domestic port:

Computes and quotes duty rates and amounts of commodities, using excise and tariff rate tables applicable to commodity.

N-3:6 Designs and prepares decorated foods and artistic food arrangements for buffets in formal restaurants:

Reviews advance menus to determine amount and type of food to be served; prepares food according to recipe; computes amount of food needed, based on number of persons to be served and standard amounts per person; and adjusts standard recipes to obtain required quantities. Measures and weighs ingredients.

N-3:7 Receives cash from customers or from other employees in payment for goods or services in retail or service establishment, and records amount received:

Computes bill and itemizes list or ticket showing amount due, using adding machine or cash register; makes change, cashes checks, and issues receipts; records amount received and prepares reports of transactions; and reads and records totals on cash register verifying against cash on hand.

LEVEL 4

N-4:1 Makes women's garments, such as dresses, coats, and suits, according to customer specifications and measurements:

Measures customer to determine dimensions of garment; and adds and subtracts to adjust pattern to customer's dimensions.

N-4:2 Inspects loaded freight cars:

Measures height and width of loads to ensure that they will pass over bridges and through tunnels on scheduled route.

N-4:3   Coordinates and expedites flow of material, parts, and assemblies within or between departments in accordance with production and shipping schedules or department supervisors' priorities:

Numerical aptitude is required to determine quantities of material, adding and subtracting to determine items of total order which are in various stages of manufacturing sequence.

N-4:4   Sets up knitting machines to knit hose, garments, and cloth according to specifications and adjusts and repairs machines, using knowledge of machine function:

Must measure, add, and subtract to determine number and size of cams and links for setup, to synchronize machine, and to make repairs.

N-4:5   Mixes and bakes ingredients according to recipes to produce bread, pastries, and other baked goods:

Numerical aptitude is required to calculate quantities and proportions of ingredients based on master recipes and for the measurement of temperatures, time, and weights.

N-4:6   Records business transactions in journals, ledgers, and on special forms and transfers entries from one accounting record to another:

Adds totals of entries after posting and compares totals with original records to detect errors.

LEVEL 5 NO ILLUSTRATIONS (see page 9-2)

S — SPATIAL APTITUDE: The ability to think visually of geometric forms and to comprehend the two-dimensional representation of three-dimensional objects. The ability to recognize the relationships resulting from the movement of objects in space.

Interpretive Information for Analysts: Frequently described as the ability to "visualize" objects of two- or three-dimensions or to think visually of geometric forms. Work examples are such activities as laying out, positioning, and aligning objects; observing movements of objects, such as vehicles in traffic or machines in operation, and comprehending how the movements affect their spatial position concurrently; achieving balanced design; and understanding and anticipating the effects of physical stresses in structural situations.

LEVEL 1

S-1:1   Diagnoses and treats disease, injuries, and malformations of teeth, gum, and related oral structures:

Spatial aptitude is required to read x rays; to comprehend relation between teeth, tooth functions, tooth forms, stresses, and all phases of occlusion.

S-1:2   Conducts research in fundamental mathematics and in application of mathematical techniques to science, management, and other fields, and solves or directs solutions to problems by mathematical methods:

Spatial aptitude is required to visualize and understand the special relationships of objects and forces involved in a situation and their resultant effects on each other.

S-1:3   Plans and designs private residences, office buildings, theatres, public buildings, factories, and other structures; and organizes services necessary for their construction:

Plans layout of project, using visual imagination to integrate structural, mechanical, and ornamental elements into a unified design. Prepares sketches and elevation view of project for client. Prepares scale and full-size drawings for use by building contractors and craft workers.

S-1:4   Performs variety of engineering work in designing, planning, and overseeing manufacture, construction, installation, and operation of electric or electronic equipment, and systems, used in generation and utilization of electrical energy for industrial and domestic consumption:

Spatial aptitude is required in the design and construction of electrical systems and equipment to visualize the spatial relationships of static and dynamic components and the spatial characteristics of energy flow.

S-1:5   Draws and paints illustrations for advertisements, books, magazines, posters, billboards, and catalogs:

Renders details from memory, live models, manufactured products, or reference materials to execute design.

LEVEL 2

S-2:1   Prepares working plans and detail drawings from rough or detailed sketches or notes, for engineering or manufacturing purposes according to specified dimensions:

Spatial aptitude is required in interpreting blueprints, sketches, and specifications, and in preparing detailed, scale drawings of three-dimensional parts or mechanisms from sketches, layout, and oral instructions.

S-2:2   Performs dances alone, with partner, or in groups to entertain audience:

Spatial aptitude is required to interpret diagrams and instructions for proposed choreography; to visualize relative position of self with others; and to imagine how dance routines will appear to public.

S-2:3   Repairs and adjusts radios and television receivers, using handtools and electronic testing instruments:

Spatial aptitude is required to read circuit diagrams in order to assemble and repair radio and television set components; to visualize power flow and spatial relationship of components and circuits as they relate to various functions, to isolate them for testing, and to test each circuit serially; and to visualize the source of trouble from observation of picture or from sound.

S-2:4   Creates designs and prepares patterns for new types and styles of men's, women's, and children's wearing apparel or knitted garments:

Spatial aptitude is required to visualize the garment to be created and to sketch designs of it; to construct original patterns; and to use patterns to make garments.

S-2:5   Controls air traffic on and within vicinity of airport according to established procedures and policies to prevent collisions and to minimize delays arising from traffic congestion:

Spatial aptitude is required to observe the spatial relationships of aircraft within the immediate vicinity of the airport; and to visualize the relative positions of other aircraft from radar, time, distance, speed, and altitude information.

S-2:6   Sets up and operates machine tools, and fits and assembles parts to make or repair metal parts, mechanisms, tools, or machines, applying knowledge of mechanics, shop mathematics, metal properties, and layout machining procedures:

Spatial aptitude is required to interpret blueprints and sketches, make layouts, set up workpiece in chuck or on face plate, and to inspect completed work for compliance with shop orders and drawings.

S-2:7   Constructs, erects, installs, and repairs structures and fixtures of wood, plywood, and wallboard, using carpenter's handtools and power tools, and conforming to local building codes:

Spatial aptitude is required to interpret blueprints and visualize the three dimensional form of the structure from prints; to lay out workpieces from blueprints; to shape and fit parts; and to construct forms for pouring concrete.

S-2:8   Assists driller in operating machinery to drill oil or gas wells, using handtools or power tongs and wrenches:

Spatial aptitude is required to visualize spatial relationships rapidly while placing tools and guiding lower end of drill-pipe sections to rack and unrack them; and to constantly be aware of the location of other workers, tools, and materials as they move about work area in order to prevent accidents.

LEVEL 3

S-3:1   Operates bridge or gantry crane, consisting of hoist and operator's cab mounted on bridge which runs along track to lift, move, and load machinery, equipment, and variety of loose materials:

Spatial aptitude is required to observe the relationship between the moving load and fixed items, such as machines, trucks, posts, etc., in order to avoid bumping load, and to position load in trucks or on stacks, or dump it into machines or equipment.

S-3:2   Installs, adjusts, and maintains electrical wiring, switches, and fixtures in airplanes according to blueprints and wiring diagrams:

Spatial aptitude is required to determine sizes and types of control boxes, relays, instruments, and accessories to install, and the location from blueprints and wiring diagrams.

S-3:3   Forms sand molds for the production of metal castings, using handtools, power tools, patterns, and flasks, and applying knowledge of variables, such as metal characteristics, molding sand, contours of patterns, and pouring procedures:

Spatial aptitude is required to visualize mold shape from part print or pattern; to visualize flow of metal during pouring process and gas formation to determine location and size of runner and sprue holes; to visualize points of stress on mold during pouring; and to determine location for reinforcing material.

S-3:4   Constructs and repairs dental appliances according to prescription:

Spatial aptitude is required to visualize and sketch outline of prosthetic dental appliance on stone model of upper and lower jaws, using impressions as guides; and to check movement and fit of upper and lower jaw models to determine proper alignment, and to approximate position and function of appliance being made.

S-3:5   Supervises and coordinates activities of workers engaged in loading and unloading of ships' cargoes:

Visualizes available cargo space, spatial dimensions of individual shipments and how they can be rearranged, and order of removal at various ports to determine the sequence and arrangement of the load.

S-3:6   Makes women's garments, such as dresses, coats, and suits, according to customer's specifications and measurements:

Spatial aptitude is required to use patterns visualizing the relationship between pattern pieces and finished garment and following pattern instructions; and to alter basic patterns proportionally to adapt them to customer's measurements.

S-3:7   Sets up and operates machines that measure, print, cut, fold, glue, or seal plain or waxed papers, polyethylene film, or cellophane to form bags:

Spatial aptitude is required to adjust cutters, feeders, printing rollers, and other mechanisms according to specifications for type and size of bag being produced.

LEVEL 4

S-4:1   Inspects electronic units and subassemblies, such as radio transmitters, computer circuits, and cables, for conformance to specifications:

Spatial aptitude is required to examine completed assemblies relating them to configuration sheet to determine that components are in specified positions.

S-4:2   Tends film cutter and mounting press to mount color-film transparencies:

Aligns cutting blade of film-cutting machine with frame separating line between transparencies on film strips.

S-4:3   Smooths and finishes surfaces of poured concrete floors, walls, sidewalks, or curbs to specified textures, using handtools, including floats, trowels, and screeds:

Determines grade and contours from construction drawings and selects screeds needed to form or guide forming of work to specified shape.

S-4:4   Drives gasoline- or electric-powered industrial truck or tractor, equipped with forklift, elevating platform, or trailer hitch, to push, pull, lift, stack, or tier merchandise, equipment, or bulk materials in warehouse, storage yard, or factory:

Observes changing position of fork in relation to objects or materials to maneuver fork under load; observes position of load relative to other objects to move load about and to position or stack load.

S-4:5   Tends units of fresh-work cigar machine that cuts wrapper leaf and wraps leaf around bunch:

Spreads wrapper leaf over die of machine in such a manner as to obtain maximum cuts per leaf.

S-4:6   Joins and reinforces parts of articles, such as garments, curtains, parachutes, stuffed toys, hats, and caps; sews buttonholes and attaches fasteners, such as buttons, snaps, and hooks, to articles; or sews decorative trimmings to articles, using needle and thread:

Aligns parts, fasteners, or trimming, working with two dimensions in a single plane, to obtain desired appearance when item is in use.

LEVEL 5 NO ILLUSTRATIONS (see page 9-2)

P — FORM PERCEPTION: The ability to perceive pertinent detail in objects or in pictorial or graphic material. Ability to make visual comparisons and discriminations and see slight differences in shapes and shadings of figures and widths and lengths of lines.

Interpretive Information for Analysts: Consider such activities as inspecting surfaces for consistency in coloring, scratches, flaws, grain, texture, and the like; observing lint, dust, etc., on surfaces; determining if patterns are correct or match; and recognizing small parts.

NOTE: Spatial deals with visualization of the shape of objects as well as comprehension of forms in space. Form perception, on the other hand, pertains to the perception of surface details.

LEVEL 1

P-1:1   Conducts studies of all nonmetallic minerals used in horological industry:

Is able to perceive detail of grain size, pattern, and crystalline orientation in diamonds and abrasives and see differences in the features and size of grain angles using optical, x-ray, and other precision instruments.

P-1:2   Performs chemical, microscopic, and bacteriologic tests to provide data for use in treatment and diagnosis of disease:

Form perception is required to perceive pertinent details of shape, shade, and other characteristics when examining or comparing specimens or cultures under microscope.

LEVEL 2

P-2:1   Diagnoses and treats diseases, injuries, and malformations of teeth, gums, and related oral structures:

Is able to perceive details of tooth and tissue structure and condition, tooth form, shadings of teeth (when preparing dentures), shape and shading of teeth when examining x rays, and parallelism and fit of dentures and inlays.

P-2:2   Draws and corrects topographical maps from source data, such as surveying notes, aerial photographs, or other maps:

Is able to perceive details of land contours or other physical features in stereoscopic aerial photographs and other topographical maps; draw different widths and types of lines, each with specific meanings in topography; and assure that scale is maintained throughout drawing.

P-2:3   Develops specifications for and blows and shapes glass laboratory apparatus, such as test tubes, retorts, and flasks, and glass components for such apparatus as condensers, vacuum pumps, barometer, and thermometers:

Form perception is required to see details in customer's sketches and work plans; to observe when specified shape and angles are obtained in glass; to inspect glass visually for flaws and pin holes; and to read measuring instruments such as micrometers and calipers.

P-2:4   Changes undesirable details of illustrations which are to be reproduced by lithographic process:

Observes differences in shading (contrast) when comparing positives and negatives with original copy of illustration layout, and when applying dyes and etching solution. Must perceive details of object or fixture to apply opaque solution and halftone dots by hand; to pencil in highlights and retouch flaws; and to scrape areas to reduce density.

P-2:5   Analyzes variety of specifications, lays out metal stock, sets up and operates machine tools, and fits and assembles parts to make and repair metalworking dies, cutting tools, jigs, fixtures, gauges, and machinists' handtools, applying knowledge of tool and die design and construction, ship mathematics, metal properties, and layout, machining, and assembly procedures:

Form perception is required to read dial indicators and machine settings; to observe cut as it is made by tool to be sure surface of part is not scored; to inspect workpiece visually and with precision gauges to detect surface and dimensional defects; and to check fit of dies and parts.

P-2:6   Repairs radio receivers, phonographs, recorders, and other electronic-audio equipment, using circuit diagrams and test meters:

Form perception is required to inspect visually all circuits and connections for breaks or looseness; to detect defects in components by visual examinations; and to recognize components by their size, shape, and position.

P-2:7   Reads typescript or galley proof to detect and mark for correction any grammatical, typographical, or compositional errors:

Is able to perceive pertinent detail in proof, such as blurs, misshapen letters, margin alignment, and spacing.

LEVEL 3

P-3:1   Grades cured tobacco leaves preparatory to marketing or processing into tobacco products:

Visually inspects and feels leaves to determine their grade according to size and texture, and to detect damage to leaf.

P-3:2 Forms sand molds for production of metal castings, using handtools, power tools, patterns, and flasks, applying knowledge of variables, such as metal characteristics, molding sand, contours of patterns, and pouring procedures:

Form perception is required to determine appropriate length, width, and position of runners and sprue holes to be cut in mold; and to detect and repair damage to interior surfaces of mold.

P-3:3 Repairs and services office machines, such as adding, accounting, and calculating machines, and typewriters, using handtools, power tools, micrometers, and welding equipment:

Form perception is required to identify machine parts, and to detect defects in parts by their shape and alignment with other parts, when determining type and extent of repairs or service needed.

P-3:4 Inspects and assembles machined bomb-fuse parts, using handtools and power tools:

Examines machined parts prior to assembly for burrs and excess metal, using magnifying glass for small parts, and files and grinds off burrs and excess metal.

P-3:5 Cuts and trims meat to size for display or as ordered by customer, using handtools and power equipment, such as grinder, cubing machine, and power saw:

Form perception is required to align carcass with blade of saw in order to break down large sections into smaller standard cuts; to examine shape, marbling, fat, and bone to determine most economical means of preparing cuts; to trim fat, and bone and to examine shape and grain to determine cutting line to follow to make standard cuts, such as loin roasts, steaks, etc.

P-3:6 Prepares wire-wound coils for assembly in electronic or electrical equipment:

Inspects materials and coils for defects; locates tap wires in wound coils and pulls them out with tweezers and picks; bends wires to specified shape; and solders minute wires together or to terminal lugs.

P-3:7 Inspects glass bottles and glass containers from bottlemaking machine, rejects defective ware, and packs selected ware into cartons:

Form perception is required to inspect bottles and detect flaws in glass, such as cracks, checks, and splits, and irregularities of shape and size.

P-3:8 Operates battery of looms to weave yarn into cloth:

Form perception is required to make visual inspections of looms prior to and during operation to be sure shuttles are in position and no yarn strands are broken; and to detect mispicks, imperfections in weave, and breaks in warp fibers.

LEVEL 4

P-4:1 Operates cylinder press to score and cut paperboard sheets into box or container blanks:

Observes alignment of paperboard to adjust feeding and stacking mechanism. Inspects cutting and scoring lines to detect defects.

P-4:2 Performs one or more repetitive bench or line assembly operations to mass produce products, such as automobile or tractor radiators, blower wheels, refrigerators, or gas stoves:

Form perception is required when buffing parts to see when burrs are buffed from ends of tubing and taper with specified angle is attained; and to see small bubbles rise to surface of test tank denoting leak in coil, and to locate their source.

P-4:3 Receives, stores, and issues equipment, materials, supplies, merchandise, foodstuffs, or tools, and compiles stock records in stockroom, warehouse, or storage yard:

Examines stock to identify item according to size, shape or other characteristics in order to verify conformance to requisitions or invoice specifications.

P-4:4 Packs agricultural produce, such as bulbs, fruit, nuts, eggs, and vegetables, for storage or shipment:

Form perception is required to recognize differences in size, shape, and condition of produce; to pack produce in prescribed pattern according to sizes and shapes; to inspect produce visually for imperfections; and to identify and remove foreign matter.

P-4:5 Installs control cables to door, window, engine, and flight-control surfaces of airplanes according to specifications, using wrenches, screwdrivers, pliers, and drills:

Form perception is required to measure and locate positions for pulleys, guides, and brackets; to thread cable from control levers, through pulleys and guides to mechanism according to specified pattern; and to observe during functional checks to determine necessary adjustments.

P-4:6 Operates pressing machine to smooth surfaces, flatten seams, or shape articles, such as garments, drapes, slipcovers, and hose in manufacturing or dry cleaning establishments:

Form perception is required to position articles on press buck (padded table of machine) to ensure a smooth press; to shape articles when positioning; and to inspect garments for wrinkles and shape after pressing.

P-4:7 Welds metal parts together, as specified by layout, diagram, work order, or oral instructions, using equipment which introduces shield of inert gas between electrode and workpiece to prevent oxidation:

Form perception is required to see details in work diagrams, to align workpiece according to layout markings; to follow line to be welded; to guide torch; and to inspect weld bead for consistent size, straightness, and complete fill of joint.

LEVEL 5 NO ILLUSTRATIONS (see page 9-2)

Q — CLERICAL PERCEPTION: The ability to perceive pertinent detail in verbal or tabular material. Ability to observe differences in copy, to proofread words and numbers, and to avoid perceptual errors in arithmetic computation. A measure of speed of perception is required in many industrial jobs even when the job does not have verbal or numerical content.

Interpretive Information for Analysts: In trade and craft jobs consider the work orders, specifications, dials, gauges, and measuring devices which must be read. Consider whether perceptual errors in reading words and numbers or in rapidly comparing similar forms or shapes would result in defective work.

LEVEL 1

Q-1:1 Conducts research in fundamental mathematics and in application of mathematical techniques to science, management, and other fields; and solves or directs solutions to problems in various fields by mathematical methods:

Accurately perceives numbers when performing computations, applying methods of numerical analysis, and operating calculators, plotters, or other electrical computation machines in solving problems in support of mathematical, scientific, or industrial research activity, and in analyzing tabular material produced as part of such research.

Q-1:2 Reads and corrects proof while original copy is read aloud:

Clerical perception is required to see details in proof pages such as the way words are spelled, capitalized, hyphenated, and abbreviated; and to detect typographical errors, such as misspelling, wrong punctuation, skips, or repeats.

Q-1:3   Converts symbolic statement of business problems to detailed logical flow charts for coding into computer language and solution by means of automatic data processing equipment:

Clerical perception is required to perceive pertinent detail in program documentation, assembled data, and recommended program routines; to prepare input, output, and nomenclature lists; to translate step-by-step instructions from flow charts for console operator; to recognize and detect errors in program instructions; to correct errors by altering sequence of steps; and to avoid computation errors.

LEVEL 2

Q-2:1   Performs variety of clerical duties, such as filing correspondence, records, and reports; typing letters and reports; preparing bills; computing payrolls; compiling reports; addressing, sorting, and distributing mail; taking dictation; tabulating and posting data in record books; keeping inventory records; and giving information:

Clerical perception is required to read, record, and type numbers and names quickly and accurately, to file letters, prepare records and reports, and to post data.

Q-2:2   Reviews individual applications for insurance, evaluates the degree of risk involved, and accepts applications, following company's underwriting policies:

Clerical perception is required to compute accurately the value of property and risk involved; to figure premiums using tables and weighted values for risk factors; to note pertinent details in insurance applications and investigation reports; and to read accurately tables and insurance maps, indicating amount and type of insurance used in specific areas.

Q-2:3   Operates machine to perforate paper tape used to control casting type:

Clerical perception is required to read copy and strike keys accurately on keyboard to punch tape; to read tables to determine number of justification keys to punch to justify lines of type; and to read tables to avoid perceptual errors in arithmetic when converting line measures from one unit of measure to another.

Q-2:4   Answers inquiries regarding schedules; describes routes, services, and accommodations available; reserves space; and sells tickets for transportation agencies, such as airlines, bus companies, railroads, and steamship lines:

Clerical perception is required to read accurately schedules and manuals with route and accommodation information; to make out tickets and passenger lists and to record reservation information; to avoid perceptual errors when reading rate schedules, and computing fares and baggage charges; and to keep records of tickets sold, type of accommodations, fares, taxes, and payment.

Q-2:5   Performs chemical, microscopic, and bacteriologic tests to provide data for use in treatment and diagnosis of disease:

Clerical perception is required to read laboratory test request slips, to determine patient for whom tests are to be made, type of test, quantities and types of specimens to be taken, and special test instructions; to read words and chemical symbols on laboratory supplies for selection of exact chemical to use in tests; to read reference materials determining type and quantities of reagents to use in analysis; to perceive numbers accurately when performing arithmetic computations for quantitative analyses; and to perceive words and numbers accurately when filing test reports, specimens, and other records according to alphabetical and numerical systems.

Q-2:6   Determines conformance of cloth to weight standards by computing weight per yard of cloth and comparing computations with information on style card:

Clerical perception is required to read identification tag on bolt of cloth, to determine style number, weight, and length; to perceive accurately numbers and markings on slide rule in order to compute weight per yard; to compare computation with standard listed on style card; and to record accurately weight, yardage, weight per yard, and style number for each bolt on production sheet.

Q-2:7   Renders general nursing care to patients in hospital, infirmary, sanitarium, or similar institution:

Notes pertinent detail in written instructions, especially amounts and strengths of medications to administer; accurately perceives numbers when reading instruments, preparing medications, and filling syringes for injections; accurately records data on patients' charts, such as temperature, respiration, pulse count, blood pressure, medications, and dosage administered.

LEVEL 3

Q-3:1   Prepares and compiles records in hospital nursing unit, such as obstetrics, pediatrics, or surgery:

Clerical perception is required to post information to patients' charts from doctors' and nurses' notes and laboratory reports; to file charts in chart racks; to make up daily diet sheet for unit; and to maintain inventory of drugs and supplies.

Q-3:2   Drives truck over established route to deliver, sell, and display products or render services:

Clerical perception is required to fill out requisitions for merchandise and to check amounts received against requisition; to prepare sales slips for amounts sold, entering proper amount beside item listed on sales slip; and to avoid perceptual errors when computing total of sales and preparing reports of daily sales and collections.

Q-3:3   Marks or affixes trademark or other identifying information, such as size, color, grade, or process code on merchandise, material, or product:

Clerical perception is required to check specification to determine label and other information to be stamped on product; to select appropriate type and other symbols and place them in type box in order; and to compare sample to specification.

Q-3:4   Operates cash register to compute and record total sale and wraps merchandise for customers in department, variety, and specialty stores:

Clerical perception is required to record accurately amount of sale on cash register; to compare sales slip with price tickets on merchandise; and to copy cash register totals onto daily sales and receipt records.

Q-3:5   Assists in care of hospital patients, under direction of nursing and medical staff:

Clerical perception is required to read and record such data as temperature, pulse rate, and respiration rate; to record patient's food and fluid intake and output; and to read charts and instructions accurately.

Q-3:6   Performs combination of duties involved in binding books, magazines, pamphlets, directories, and catalogs:

Clerical perception is required to lay signatures on gathering table in correct page order for assembly; to gather up signatures in numerical order to form complete book body; and to inspect bound book bodies for proper pagination.

LEVEL 4

Q-4:1   Coordinates and expedites flow of materials, parts, and assemblies within or between departments in accordance with production and shipping schedules or department supervisors' priorities:

Clerical perception is required to compare identification number of parts, materials, or assemblies to identical numbers on shop order when locating items; and to take physical inventories of stock, tool, or equipment storage rooms, comparing inventory number or other identifying number to inventory list.

Q-4:2   Inspects finished glassware or flat glass for conformance to quality standards:

Clerical perception is required to read micrometers and gauges accurately to determine if dimensions are within specified tolerances; and to record number and type of defects.

Q-4:3 Drives gasoline- or electric-powered industrial truck or tractor, equipped with forklift, elevating platform, or trailer hitch to push, pull, lift, stack, or tier merchandise, equipment, or bulk materials in warehouse, storage yard, or factory:

Accurately perceives identification numbers and weights marked on materials, packing cases, or tote boxes to identify materials to be moved and to assure that weight of items lifted does not exceed vehicle capacity.

Q-4:4 Marks, sorts, and records number and type of soiled garments, linens, and other articles received for cleaning and laundering:

Clerical perception is required to enter number of each type of garment or article on laundry list; to write or stamp identification number or code on article or tag; and to accurately record identification number on laundry slip.

Q-4:5 Assists workers in business office by sorting, distributing, and collecting mail and interoffice correspondence and delivering office supplies to workers:

Avoids perceptual errors in reading names and addresses on mail in order to deliver it to proper destination.

Q-4:6 Sets up and operates coil winding machine to wind coils used in manufacture of electrical and electronic components, such as transformers, solenoids, chokes, and filters:

Clerical perception is required to observe counter and to stop machine after specified number of turns; and to read ohmmeter attached to resistance coil, winding or unwinding wire until specified resistance reading is obtained.

Q-4:7 Sells furniture, beds, and mattresses in department store or furniture store:

Clerical perception is required to avoid perceptual errors when making up bills of sales; when reading and recording identification numbers to make up inventory of stock; and when requisitioning stock from warehouse or checking on its availability.

LEVEL 5 NO ILLUSTRATIONS (see page 9-2)

K — MOTOR COORDINATION: The ability to coordinate eyes and hands or fingers rapidly and accurately in making precise movements with speed. Ability to make a movement response accurately and swiftly.

Interpretive Information for Analysts: Motor coordination involves hand movements guided by concentrated visual attention. It is present when objects are guided into position or parts are assembled. Typing and operating adding machines, calculators, and similar keyboards are examples of motor coordination in clerical occupations.

LEVEL 1 NO ILLUSTRATIONS

LEVEL 2

K-2:1 Types letters, reports, stencils, forms, addresses, or other straight copy material from rough draft or corrected copy:

Eye-finger coordination is required to type by "touch" with fingers striking the appropriate keys as the eyes follow the copy.

K-2:2 Itemizes and totals cost of customer's purchases of groceries, meat, and produce on a combination adding machine-cash register:

Motor coordination is required to coordinate finger, eye, and hand with speed.

K-2:3 Diagnoses and treats diseases, injuries, and malformations of the teeth, gums, and related oral structures:

Motor coordination is essential in using drills and other dental tools to extract, fill, or cap teeth; in positioning novocaine needle in gums; and in fitting artificial teeth, plates, and bridges.

K-2:4 Operates pantograph machine to transfer design in reduced form from zinc plate to varnished printing rollers:

Coordination between eyes and fingers is required in guiding needle point through line of design cut on plate to trace pattern on printing roll; and for moving stylet to follow colored lines in etched pattern.

K-2:5 Measures heel to toe length of stocking, using measuring lines on pairing table, and stacks stockings of comparable length, color, and grade for matching into pairs:

Motor coordination is required to coordinate eyes, hands, and fingers during measuring, color matching, and sorting, working at production pace.

K-2:6 Installs, repairs, adjusts, and calibrates pneumatic, electrical, and electronic instruments:

Motor coordination is required in using handtools to adjust or repair component parts of electronic instruments; to test and calibrate reassembled equipment with electrical testing devices; and to rewire and modify equipment in accordance to blueprints and schematics.

K-2:7 Works at discharge end of conveyor belt to inspect and box bakery products:

Motor coordination is required to remove products quickly from belt and place them in cartons according to specified arrangement.

LEVEL 3

K-3:1 Operates telephone switchboard to establish or assist customer in establishing local or long distance telephone connections:

Motor coordination is required to press proper keys or plug jacks into holes or slots on switchboard quickly in response to visual stimuli or lights on board, and often with several calls coming in and going out simultaneously.

K-3:2 Assembles electrical equipment, such as ammeters, galvanometers, and voltage meters:

Close correspondence is required between eyes and hands in using tools to position, adjust and tighten parts, such as screws, indicator arms, springs, and lugs.

K-3:3 Performs beauty services for patrons of beauty shop:

Coordination of eyes, hands, and fingers is required to cut, style, and tint hair, give facials, arch eyebrows, and manicure nails.

K-3:4 Drives gasoline-powered forklift truck to haul or stock materials and objects in or about establishment:

Coordinates eyes and hands or fingers in making precise movements with speed (pushing and pulling hand levers, gear shifts, and hand brakes) to drive truck and to raise, lower, or otherwise position forklift under objects to be moved.

K-3:5 Removes defective nuts and foreign matter from bulk nut meats:

Coordinates eye, hand, and finger movements to pick up and discard defective nut meats and foreign matter from conveyor belt, working at production rate.

K-3:6 Cuts, trims, and bones meats to prepare them for cooking, using knives, saw, and cleaver:

Motor coordination is required in adjusting saw blades; in cutting, boning, and trimming meats into desired portions with knives; and placing meats in grinders and cubing machines.

K-3:7 Assembles metal products, such as vacuum cleaners, valves, or hydraulic cylinders, working at bench or on shop floor:

Motor coordination is required in operating drill presses, punch presses, riveting machines, and various handtools in assembly operations; and in positioning, placing, and fitting of parts in each sub-assembly and main assembly.

K-3:8   Applies coats of plaster to interior walls, ceilings, and partitions of buildings to produce finished surface:

Motor coordination is essential in erecting scaffolding, mixing plaster to desired consistency, spreading plaster to attain uniform thickness, and creating decorative textures in finished coat by marking with brush or trowel.

K-3:9   Forms wire grids used in electron tubes, using winding, shaping, and cutting machines:

Motor coordination is required to coordinate eyes and fingers or hands to insert grid into chucks, to trim grids, and to thread wires through lathe.

LEVEL 4

K-4:1   Repairs defects, such as tears and holes in garments, linens, curtains, and draperies, and rebinds cleaned blankets by hand or by operating a sewing machine:

Eye and finger coordination is required in sewing, darning, or reweaving holes or tears in garments, curtains, or linens.

K-4:2   Performs tasks to finish and press household linens:

Motor coordination is required in placing garments into machine, making sure garments are properly aligned so that no wrinkles will be ironed into garments.

K-4:3   Sets up and operates machine tools, and fits and assembles parts to make or repair metal parts, mechanisms, tools, or machines:

Motor coordination is required to align workpiece and cutting tool in relation to one another; to move levers when operating machines; and in using handtools to perform such functions as chipping, filing, and scraping.

K-4:4   Assembles various aluminum or steel components of trailers:

Motor coordination is required to align and position trailer components to fit rivets, bolts, and screws into position, using riveting gun and handtools, and to fit trailer parts in prescribed position for correct assembly.

K-4:5   Receives, stores, and issues equipment, material, supplies, merchandise, foodstuff, or tools, and compiles records in stockroom, warehouse, or storage yard:

Coordinates eye, hand, and finger movements to wrap or box items and label packaged parts.

K-4:6   Harvests fruit, working as crewmember:

Coordinates hands and eyes to make necessary movements in selecting, picking, and depositing fruit into picking sack.

K-4:7   Operates traveling and stationary tables to feed steel blooms, billets, and slabs to rolls for successive passes through roll stands:

Eye-hand coordination is required to position tables and align rollers preparatory to feeding steel into rollers.

LEVEL 5 NO ILLUSTRATIONS (see page 9-2)

F — FINGER DEXTERITY: The ability to move the fingers and manipulate small objects with the fingers rapidly or accurately.

Interpretive Information for Analysts: Finger dexterity is present when bolts and screws are handled; small tools, machine controls, and the like are manipulated; musical instruments are played; and fine adjustments and alignments are made to instruments and machines. It may or may not be accompanied by visual stimuli.

LEVEL 1

F-1:1   Plays organ in recital, as accompanist, or as member of orchestra, band, or other musical group:

All ten fingers must be positioned in rapid integrated movements to depress specified keys at varying tempos on one or more keyboards of organ.

F-1:2   Performs surgical operations upon human body:

Finger movements of one hand are required to locate broken or cut blood vessel, to position vessel and place ligature about it, and to tie one of several types of knots in ligature to stem flow of blood from vessel.

LEVEL 2

F-2:1   Sets up and operates coil-winding machine to wind multiple coils used in manufacture of electrical and electronic components:

Positions and moves very small parts and thin wires with fingers and fits coil forms on winding arbor of machine; threads wire through guide mechanism of machine; and tapes wire to coil forms.

F-2:2   Adjusts watch movements to comply with mechanical and timing specifications:

Controls placement and movement of watchmaker tools and watch components with fingers in disassembling and cleaning watch movements; in adjusting lock, drop, and slide of escapement; in truing wheel and hairspring assembly; and in reassembling watch movements.

F-2:3   Installs optical elements, such as lenses, prisms, and mirrors in mechanical portion of such instruments as telescopes, cameras, and gunsights:

Finger dexterity is required to guide and move tools and to position component parts in performing such tasks as scraping, filing, and lapping instrument mounts to align optical elements; adjusting optical elements to calibrations; and inserting retaining rings into housings and securing them to posts or threads.

F-2:4   Assembles modules (units) of microelectronic equipment, such as satellite communications devices and hearing aids, using handtools, magnifying lens, and spotwelder:

Finger dexterity is required to insert lead wires of components, such as microdiodes, resistors, capacitors, and microtransistors, into mounting holes of plastic plate; and to attach color-coded wires between specified component leads to make circuit connections.

F-2:5   Engraves lettering and ornamental designs on silverware, trophies, eyeglass frames, and jewelry, using engraving tools:

Finger dexterity is required to position and control movements of engraving tools in cutting complicated designs on objects, such as pins, rings, and bracelets.

F-2:6   Packages pharmaceutical products by hand, working at production pace:

Finger dexterity is required in performing such tasks as inserting cotton in mouths of bottles, placing caps on bottles, pasting labels on bottles, inserting bottles into nested cartons, placing printed material in filled cartons, and packing individual cartons into larger cartons.

F-2:7   Makes women's garments, such as dresses, coats, and suits, according to customer specifications and measurements:

Finger dexterity is required in performing such tasks as positioning and pinning pattern sections and fabric; pinning or basting together fabric parts in preparation for sewing; and threading needle and sewing parts together by hand.

F-2:8   Diagnoses and treats diseases, injuries, and malformations of teeth, gums, and related oral structures:

Finger dexterity is required to position and guide dental picks and mirrors; position x-ray film in patient's mouth; suture extraction wounds; and trim and carve bite blocks with spatulas and carving instruments.

LEVEL 3

F-3:1   Feeds tungsten filament wire coils into machine that mounts them to stems in electric light bulb:

Finger dexterity is required to grasp coils with tweezers and insert them into slotted plate of mounting machine; and to pick up and examine finished mounts as they emerge from machine.

F-3:2   Takes dictation in shorthand and transcribes dictated materials, using typewriter:

Finger dexterity is required in forming shorthand symbols with pencil or pen and in depressing keys of typewriter.

F-3:3   Installs, maintains, and services sound and communication systems:

Finger movements are required in performing such tasks as picking up and installing tubes, transistors, and component parts; wiring units of system together; and turning dials to obtain required performance level.

F-3:4   Cuts and styles hair, using clippers, comb, and scissors, and performs other personal services for patrons of barber shop:

Controlled movement of fingers is required to use clippers, scissors, and other barber tools when cutting and shaping hair.

F-3:5   Operates battery of looms to weave yarn into cloth:

Finger dexterity is required to repair breaks in warp fiber by tying piece of yarn to broken end of warp and threading yarn through drop wires, needle eyes, and reed dents, using reed hooks.

F-3:6   Constructs and repairs dental appliances:

Finger dexterity is required in performing such tasks as sketching outline of appliance on stone model, aligning model on articulator and securing it to frame with plaster, and building wax impressions of metal frames, crowns, partials, and full dentures.

F-3:7   Packs agricultural produce, such as bulbs, fruits, nuts, eggs, and vegetables, for storage or shipment:

Finger dexterity is required in performing such tasks as lining containers with padding, inserting separators in containers, sorting produce according to size and color, wrapping material around produce, and placing produce in containers.

F-3:8   Welds metal parts together, using electric and oxyacetylene welding equipment:

Finger movements are required to connect pressure regulators to nozzles of oxygen and acetylene supply tanks; connect hoses to regulators and welding torch to hose; screw welding tip into torch; and to open regulator valves and light torch.

LEVEL 4

F-4:1   Mixes and bakes ingredients according to recipes to produce breads, pastries, and other baked goods:

Finger dexterity is required to work with ingredients and utensils and to perform such tasks as arranging strips of dough across tops of pies, and placing cut or formed dough in pans or on baking boards or trays.

F-4:2   Prepares, seasons, and cooks soups, meats, vegetables, desserts, and other foodstuffs for consumption in medical institutions:

Finger dexterity is required in using knives, brushes, scrapers, and other tools to clean, trim, slice, and dice vegetables, fruits, and meats; in portioning foods; in turning dials and valves on kitchen equipment; in removing dishes, napkins, and waste materials from food carts; in sorting and stacking dishes; and in lining pans and shelves with paper.

F-4:3   Sews fasteners and decorative trimmings to articles, sews buttonholes, and joins articles, using needle and thread:

Finger dexterity is required to thread needle, align articles, and hold articles in place while sewing.

F-4:4   Controls continuous operations of petroleum refining and processing units:

Finger dexterity is required to move knobs, buttons, and switches on control panels; to place charts; tapes, and graphs in recording part of instruments; and to set control arms and needle points in proper recording positions.

F-4:5   Repairs and maintains physical structures of commercial and industrial establishments, using handtools and power tools:

Finger dexterity is required to perform such tasks as making electrical repairs that involve splicing broken lines; installing switches, receptacles, and junction boxes; and replacing fuses.

LEVEL 5 NO ILLUSTRATIONS (see page 9-2)

M — MANUAL DEXTERITY: The ability to move the hands easily and skillfully. Ability to work with the hands in placing and turning motions.

Interpretive Information for Analysts: Manual dexterity involves working with the arms and hands. It is present when objects are moved or stacked by hand or in other situations in which wrists and hands are used in turning and placing movements.

NOTE: Finger movements (Finger Dexterity) may or may not accompany the exercise of manual dexterity.

LEVEL 1 NO ILLUSTRATIONS

LEVEL 2

M-2:1   Entertains audience by juggling and balancing objects:

Manual dexterity is required to throw, catch, handle, and balance three to five objects, such as balls, knives, tenpins, and chinaware.

M-2:2   Installs, repairs, maintains, and adjusts indicating, recording, telemetering, and controlling instruments used to measure and control variables, such as pressure, flow, temperature, motion, force, and chemical composition, using handtools and precision instruments:

Assembly, disassembly, and calibration of instruments require placing and turning movements of the hands. Works with handtools, such as screwdrivers, wrenches, and pliers, and bench tools, such as jeweler's lathe, pin vises, small buffer grinders, and ultrasonic cleaners, in repairing instruments.

M-2:3   Inspects eggs to ascertain quality and fitness for consumption or incubation according to prescribed standards:

Manual dexterity is required to pick up eggs from cardboard cases, roll and shift eggs within palm while inspecting them, and place acceptable eggs on shuffler rack while working at production-line pace.

M-2:4   Fabricates, assembles, installs, and repairs sheet metal products and equipment, such as control boxes, drainpipes, ventilators, and furnace castings, according to work orders or blueprints:

Manual dexterity is required to manipulate such tools as outline cutting torches, power hacksaw, slitting shear, and various hand drills to accomplish general work processes as cutting, forming, folding, grooving, bending, punching, and drilling holes; and to place workpiece in holding fixture, operate tool, and remove workpiece from machine.

M-2:5   Constructs and repairs metal-forming tools, dies, jigs, fixtures, and gauges, shaping parts with various metalworking machines and fitting them together, using handtools:

Manual dexterity is required in setting up machines; in building tool-holding devices; in fitting and assembling tools, gauges, and other mechanical equipment; and in performing such tasks as chipping, filing, scraping, and polishing surfaces of mechanical parts.

M-2:6   Sets up and operates drum-type machine to build pneumatic automobile tires according to specifications:

Manual dexterity is required in handling, placing, and guiding product components and tools in the process of tire building; in applying cement stick to drum; in tearing the measured length of ply stock from roll and wrapping ply around drum; in guiding stock while drum is rotated; in lapping ends of ply; and in smoothing tight splice.

M-2:7   Diagnoses and treats disease, injuries, and malformations of teeth, gums, and related oral structures:

Accurate and flexible wrist movements are required when using drills and other dental tools to extract, fill, or cap teeth; positioning novocaine needle in gums; and fitting artificial teeth, plates, and bridges.

M-2:8   Works at conveyor belt to package previously filled bottles, tubes, and boxes of pharmaceuticals by hand in individual or nested cardboard boxes:

Uses placing and turning hand movements in putting empty containers on conveyor belt; removing filled packages from conveyor; and packaging smaller containers in larger packages while maintaining a continuous production pace in all operations.

LEVEL 3

M-3:1   Repairs and rebuilds upholstered furniture, using handtools and knowledge of fabrics and upholstery methods:

Manual dexterity is required in using handtools; in handling and assembling spring units; in building up and securing padding; and in handling, positioning, and securing covered material.

M-3:2   Sets up, inspects, and repairs looms to weave cloth:

A variety of hand and wrist movements are required to adjust screws and levers, install gears, tighten bolts, and to repair and replace various mechanical parts of machine.

M-3:3   Drives gasoline- or electric-powered industrial truck, equipped with forklift, to push, pull, lift, stack, or tier material in warehouse, storage yard, or factory:

Manual dexterity is required to push and pull levers on truck, turn steering wheel, and stack materials on truck.

M-3:4   Tends machine that coats continuous rolls of wire, strips, or sheets with wax, paint, rubber, asphalt, or other coating material:

Manual dexterity is required in handling control levers; guiding strips into machine and onto rewind coils; repairing broken splices by hand; and in using small handtools to change degreasing pads and squeeze rollers.

M-3:5   Assembles, analyzes defects in, and repairs boilers, pressure vessels, tanks, and vats in the field, following blueprints and using handtools and power tools:

Uses placing and turning hand movements in aligning and fitting structures or plate sections in assembling boiler frames; in handling plumb bobs, levels, wedges, dogs, and turn buckles; and in riveting, welding, and caulking.

M-3:6   Sorts and segregates fruit, working as a crewmember:

Manual dexterity is required to place liners in boxes; grasp fruit and paper, and wrap fruit; and pack wrapped fruit in proper position in container.

M-3:7   Lays building materials to construct or repair walls, partitions, arches, sewers, and other structures:

Manual dexterity is required to manipulate equipment and tools; place and stack material; erect scaffold; mix and spread mortar; cut bricks; and embed iron rods in mortar.

M-3:8   Operates machine to press face of composed type and plates into wood fiber mats to form stereotype casting mold for printing:

Manual dexterity is required to manipulate tools to trim, plane, level, saw, and shave plates for printing.

LEVEL 4

M-4:1   Harvests fruit, working as crewmember:

Manual dexterity is required to position sizing loop around lemons; to clip lemons from stem; and to deposit lemons in boxes.

M-4:2   Repairs and maintains physical structures of commercial and industrial establishments, using handtools and power tools:

Manual dexterity is required in repairing and maintaining woodwork and furniture; making electrical repairs; patching and repairing cement, and making minor plumbing and pipe repairs.

M-4:3   Removes stems from tobacco leaves to prepare tobacco for use as filler, binder, or wrapper for cigars, plugs, or twist chewing tobacco:

Manual dexterity is required in the hand operation of picking up handful of tobacco, selecting single leaf, spreading it open and holding leaf with one hand while pulling out stem with other hand.

M-4:4   Finishes household linens, such as sheets, pillowcases, tablecloths, and napkins:

Manual dexterity is required to shake, sort, fold, and stack laundry; to tie bundles of laundry together; and to feed and guide material into ironer.

M-4:5   Controls the operation of battery of stills to distill crude oil:

Manual dexterity is required to turn knobs and switches on control panel; to position charts, tapes, and graphs in recording part of instruments; and to turn wheels and valves on the still and auxiliary equipment.

M-4:6   Tends circular knitting machine with automatic pattern controls that knits seamless hose:

Manual dexterity is required to pull hose over hands during operation; separate hose; stack yarns; thread yarn through proper channels when thread breaks; and to clean grease, lint, oil, etc., from machine.

M-4:7   Sorts rags and old clothing:

Manual dexterity is required to rip off buttons, pockets, hooks and eyes, snaps, and other foreign matter.

LEVEL 5 NO ILLUSTRATIONS (see page 9-2)

E — EYE-HAND-FOOT COORDINATION: The ability to move the hand and foot coordinately with each other in accordance with visual stimuli.

Interpretive Information for Analysts: This factor involves using eyes, hands, and feet coordinately. Unless there is definite coordination of hand and foot movements with what the eye sees, this factor is not present.

LEVEL 1

E-1:1   Performs gymnastic feats of skill and balance while swinging on a trapeze, turning somersaults, or executing flying stunts alone or as member of team:

Coordinates hand and foot motions with visual stimuli, in order to reach for and grasp approaching bar or other aerialist while standing on or hanging from another swinging bar.

E-1:2   Performs ballet dances alone, with partner, or in group to entertain audience:

Coordinates feet and hands with vision in order to interpret dance role and to move in specified relationship with other members of cast; in positioning arms and hands in coordination with other movements to achieve desired interpretive effect or expression, to maintain balance, or to lift, carry, or support other dancer.

E-1:3   Plays professional baseball:

Coordinates movements of hands and feet with what eye sees when catching, hitting, and throwing ball.

E-1:4   Instructs groups at playgrounds and schools in fundamentals and rules of competitive sports:

Coordination of hand and foot movements with visual stimuli is required to demonstrate, by example, techniques of play for various sports and movements and body positions which result in best execution of a particular "play" or maneuver.

E-1:5   Creates or interprets music on drum, as member of orchestra, band, or other musical group, to entertain audiences:

Eye-hand-foot coordination is required to hit or stroke drum heads with drum sticks or brushes and depresses pedals to activate other drums and cymbals simultaneously, while following musical score and conductor's baton.

LEVEL 2

E-2:1   Pilots airplane to transport passengers, mail, freight, or for other commercial purposes:

Coordinated movements of hand and foot controls in accordance with observed conditions of aircraft or external factors or conditions indicated by instrument readings is required to take over control of airplane in emergency or override programmed control in case of malfunction to taxi, take off, land, and control aircraft in flight.

E-2:2   Operates several types of powered construction equipment, such as compressors, pumps, hoists, derricks, cranes, shovels, tractors, scrapers, or graders, to excavate and grade earth, erect structural and reinforcing steel, and pour concrete:

Moves hand and foot controls in coordination with vision and each other to drive and steer machines and move materials into position.

E-2:3   Prunes and treats ornamental and shade trees and shrubs in yards and parks to improve their appearance, health, and value:

Eye-hand-foot coordination is required to climb trees or ladders and balance self while topping trees to control growth, sawing off dead, diseased, or undesirable limbs; scraping and filling cavities in trees with cement; and painting cut surfaces to seal them against insects and disease.

E-2:4   Raises, positions, and joins girders, columns, and other structural steel members to form completed structures or frameworks, working as member of crew:

Eye-hand-foot coordination is required to work above ground level while balancing on ladders, scaffolding, or structural members while raising, positioning, fitting, and joining structural pieces.

LEVEL 3

E-3:1   Attends to beef cattle on stock ranch:

Coordinates arm-hand and leg-foot motions with vision when riding horse to round up strays or to rope cattle; and to pin and tie down calves for branding.

E-3:2   Drives gasoline- or diesel-powered tractor-trailer truck combination, usually over long distances on highways, to transport and deliver goods, livestock, or materials in liquid, loose, or packaged form:

Eye-hand-foot coordination is required to operate clutch, brake, and accelerator pedals, gearshift lever, and steering wheel to guide tractor-trailer on highways and streets, turn corners, negotiate narrow passageways, and backing up to warehouse, terminal, or other loading docks.

E-3:3   Maintains and repairs mercury-vapor, electric-arc, fluorescent, or incandescent street lights or traffic signals:

Coordinates hand and foot movements with vision to climb ladder to reach lamp, or stand in tower-truck bucket moving levers to position bucket near lamp; to maintain balance while using hands and vision to test circuits, locate broken wires, and replace fuses, bulbs, and transformers.

E-3:4   Renders variety of personal services conducive to safety and comfort of airline passengers during flight:

Coordinates hand and foot movements with vision to serve food and beverages without spilling them; and to walk in aisle, when airplane encounters rough weather, carrying trays or other items.

E-3:5   Loads and unloads ships' cargoes:

Coordinates hand and foot motions with vision when guiding slings used to lift cargo to avoid tripping and to keep load from swinging and bumping into other objects; when standing on ladders, platforms, or other objects to stack and arrange cargo high in hold; and to store cargo in ship's hold to prevent shifting during voyage.

LEVEL 4

E-4:1   Tends machine that crimps eyelets, grommets, snaps, buttons, or similar fasteners to materials such as cloth, canvas, paper, plastic, leather, or rubber to reinforce holes and attach fasteners or parts:

Coordinates hand and foot motions with vision when positioning material, fasteners, and ram of machine, while depressing foot pedal to activate ram which crimps fastener to material.

E-4:2   Parachutes from airplane into forests to suppress forest fires:

Coordinates hand and leg movements with vision to pull shroud lines and collapse chute while landing in manner to reduce impact and to prevent being dragged by chute.

E-4:3   Operates pressing machine to smooth surfaces, flatten seams, or shape articles, such as garments, drapes, slipcovers, and hose, in manufacturing or dry cleaning establishment:

Simultaneous eye-hand-foot coordination is required to step on foot pedal, pull down on pressing head while observing garment to see that it does not slip out of position on press buck; to hold pedal down with foot to keep press head against garment; to press lever with fingers to emit steam from press head; and to keep pressure on press head handle to raise counterbalanced head gently, while stepping on second pedal to exhaust steam to cool and dry garment.

C — COLOR DISCRIMINATION: The ability to match or discriminate between colors in terms of hue, saturation, and brilliance. Ability to identify a particular color or color combination from memory and to perceive contrasting color combinations.

Saturation: Refers to the purity of color. Some colors have greater purity or amount of a certain color than others; that is, they have a more pronounced hue. For example, deep red is more "reddish" than light red.

Hue: Refers to the color itself and the various tints, shades, and attributes of a color which permit classification as reds, yellows, greens, or blues.

Brilliance: Refers to the brightness of a color. It is the amount of light reflected from a surface and can range from high to low, as when comparing a white snowflake with a mark made by a lead pencil.

Color Matching: Varying the components of a color mixture until it does not differ visually from a given sample.

Color Memory: The ability to retain an accurate visual image of a color and to be able to use it as a basis for matching and discriminating.

Interpretive Information for Analysts: Color discrimination may rely on one or a combination of the following: Identification of differences and similarities in colors from memory; using a visual standard against which colors can be matched or identified; or reproduction of colors using knowledge of color combinations.

LEVEL 1

C-1:1 Develops color formulas for printing textile and plastic materials and plans and directs activities of color shop:

Color discrimination is required to select and combine appropriate dyestuffs and pigments to achieve desired colors, distinguish minute differences in shades, and visualize the hue and brilliance which will result from mixing the primary colors in various proportions.

C-1:2 Paints portrait of person, usually in oil, on canvas, using living subject:

Color discrimination is required to combine paints and oils to develop colors which accurately reproduce coloring of subject; and to apply these colors on canvas in combinations of light and shade which give lifelike effect.

C-1:3 Studies production requirements, such as character, period, setting, and situation, and applies makeup to performers to alter their appearances in accordance with their roles:

Examines sketches, photographs, and plaster molds to form color image of characters to be depicted, selecting prostheses, cosmetics, and makeup materials, such as wigs, beards, rouge, powder, and grease paint, and applies these to change such physical characteristics of performers as facial features, skin texture, and coloring to produce effect appropriate to depict character and situation.

C-1:4 Reweaves damaged areas of oriental or other expensive rugs, following color, pattern, and weave of rug:

Color discrimination is required to perceive color scheme of rug so that proper alterations can be made which are consonant with rug's total color configuration, and to select yarn which is equivalent in color to that in rug.

LEVEL 2

C-2:1 Mixes stains, paints, and other coatings for use in painting according to formulas:

Color discrimination is required to detect any differences in color between mixture and sample and to rectify the color differences by adding pigment until exact shade is produced.

C-2:2   Investigates properties and treatment of metals to develop new alloys, new uses for metal and alloys, and methods of producing them commercially:

Spectroscopic study of metals and alloys requires ability to discriminate between various colors and shades of same color as they are refracted onto screen, and to judge dispersion of alloy particles and their relative purity by means of color emission.

C-2:3   Plans and designs artistic interiors for homes, hotels, ships, commercial and institutional structures, and other establishments:

Is well informed on outcome of blending various colors in interior decorating and capable of choosing color schemes which are harmonious with each other and particular setting.

C-2:4   Changes undesirable details of illustration copy which is to be reproduced by lithographic process:

Compares negative or positive with original copy to determine color correction, silhouetting, or opaquing requirements; prepares dye or other chemicals; and intensifies or reduces unsatisfactory tone values in film or glass by adding color to lithographic plates to achieve required hue.

C-2:5   Studies effects of drugs, gases, dusts, and other materials on tissues and physiological processes of animals and human beings:

Color shades and hues are used as basis for drawing valid conclusions about effect of drug or stain; and color matching is required when preparing two solutions of equal concentration or proportion.

C-2:6   Prepares, stuffs, and mounts skins of birds or animals in lifelike form:

Color memory is required in painting eyes, teeth, claws, and feathers to enhance lifelike appearance of specimen, and in dressing-out, embalming, or otherwise preparing animal carcasses.

C-2:7   Molds pulverized marble, metallic oxides or pigment, cement, and water in specific pattern to form terrazzo tile:

Color discrimination is essential in apprehending color values of pattern to be depicted; and color matching is required in mixing pigment, cement, and water, so that finished tile is equivalent in terms of color to that of standard.

LEVEL 3

C-3:1   Examines and grades pieces of leather to make articles, such as garments, gloves, and mittens, according to specifications:

Color discrimination is required to match color of leather in each grade so that it is equal in terms of hue, saturation, and brilliance.

C-3:2   Examines pearl buttons and sorts them according to grade:

Color discrimination is required to observe buttons on conveyor belt or worktable, at production-line pace; and to sort them into containers according to shade and purity of color and degree of iridescence.

C-3:3   Tests temperature of glass melting furnaces and regulates gas and air supply to maintain specified temperature:

Observes color of flame through opening of optical pyrometer and turns dial on pyrometer until color of wire filament matches luminosity of flame. This color matching technique requires the worker to be able to make discrimination in color between the flame and wire filament.

CHAPTER 10

TEMPERAMENTS

Temperaments, a component of Worker Characteristics, are the adaptability requirements made on the worker by specific types of jobs. The 11 Temperament factors identified for use in job analysis are:

D — **DIRECTING**, controlling, or planning activities of others.

R — Performing **REPETITIVE** or short-cycle work.

I — **INFLUENCING** people in their opinions, attitudes, and judgments.

V — Performing a **VARIETY** of duties.

E — **EXPRESSING** personal feelings.

A — Working **ALONE** or apart in physical isolation from others.

S — Performing effectively under **STRESS**.

T — Attaining precise set limits, **TOLERANCES**, and standards.

U — Working **UNDER** specific instructions.

P — Dealing with **PEOPLE**.

J — Making **JUDGMENTS** and decisions.

The category Temperaments is one of the components of job analysis because different job situations call for different personality traits on the part of the worker. Experience in placing individuals in jobs indicates that the degree to which the worker can adapt to work situations is often a determining factor for success. A person's dissatisfaction or failure to perform adequately can sometimes be attributed to an inability to adapt to a work situation rather than to an inability to learn and carry out job duties.

DEFINITIONS AND EXAMPLES OF THE TEMPERAMENT FACTORS

The 11 Temperament factors are defined below. Following each definition are examples of worker activities which illustrate the Temperament.

D   **DIRECTING**, Controlling, or Planning Activities of Others: Involves accepting responsibility for formulating plans, designs, practices, policies, methods, regulations, and procedures for operations or projects; negotiating with individuals or groups for agreements or contracts; and supervising subordinate workers to implement plans and control activities.

D:1   Teaches elementary school pupils academic, social, and manipulative skills.

D:2   Plans, implements, and coordinates program to reduce or eliminate occupational injuries, illnesses, deaths, and financial losses.

D:3   Commands ship to transport passengers, freight, and other cargo across oceans and coastal waters, coordinating activities of crewmembers.

D:4   Conducts prosecution in court proceedings on behalf of city, county, State, or Federal Government.

D:5   Supervises and coordinates activities of personnel engaged in operation of air-traffic control tower.

R   Performing **REPETITIVE** or Short-Cycle Work: Involves performing a few routine and uninvolved tasks over and over again according to set procedures, sequence, or pace with little opportunity for diversion or interruption. Interaction with people is included when it is routine, continual, or prescribed.

R:1   Addresses envelopes, cards, and similar items for mailing, by hand or using typewriter.

R:2   Feeds flat strips of hoop steel, in which rivet holes have been punched, into rollers of machine to form barrel hoops.

R:3   Packs layer of crushed ice on fresh food products packed in barrels, boxes, or crates to refrigerate them during shipment.

R:4   Loads and unloads materials from trucks at shipping and receiving platform.

R:5   Sorts incoming or outgoing mail into mail-rack pigeonholes or into mail sacks according to destination.

I   **INFLUENCING** People in their Opinions, Attitudes, and Judgments: Involves writing, demonstrating, or speaking to persuade and motivate people to change their attitudes or opinions, participate in a particular activity, or purchase a specific commodity or service.

I:1   Writes advertising copy for use by publication or for broadcast to promote sales of goods or services.

I:2   Persuades producers and announcers of radio and television musical shows to broadcast recordings produced by record manufacturer.

I:3   Introduces new fashions and coordinates promotional activities, such as fashion shows, to induce consumer acceptance.

I:4   Demonstrates products to customers to promote sales, displaying product and explaining features to customers.

I:5   Conducts safety meeting to acquaint plant personnel with potential hazards and need to comply with all safety regulations.

V   Performing a **VARIETY** of Duties: Involves frequent changes of tasks involving different aptitudes, technologies, techniques, procedures, working conditions, physical demands, or degrees of attentiveness without loss of efficiency or composure. The involvement of the worker in two or more work fields may be a clue that this temperament is required.

V:1   Schedules appointments, gives information to callers, takes dictation, and otherwise relieves officials of clerical work and minor administrative and business details.

V:2   Consults with management; observes jobs; interviews workers; compiles and analyzes occupational data; compiles reports; and transmits occupational information to facilitate personnel, administrative, and management functions of organization.

V:3   Assists physician in formulation of prescription for prosthesis; examines and evaluates patient's prosthetic needs; formulates design of prosthesis; selects material; makes casts, measurements, and model modifications; performs fitting; evaluates prosthesis on patient; instructs patient in use of prosthesis; and maintains patient records.

V:4   Plans itinerary for hunting and fishing trips; arranges for transporting individuals, equipment, and supplies; explains hunting and fishing laws; prepares meals; and provides first aid to injured.

V:5   Accommodates hotel patrons by registering and assigning guests to rooms; issuing room keys and escort instructions to bellhop; date-stamping, sorting, and racking mail; transmitting and receiving messages, using telephone; answering inquiries pertaining to hotel services and local shopping and dining facilities; keeping records of room availability and guests' accounts; computing bills; and collecting payments.

E **EXPRESSING** Personal Feelings: Involves creativity and self expression in interpreting feelings, ideas, or facts in terms of a personal viewpoint; treating a subject imaginatively rather than literally; reflecting original ideas or feelings in writing, painting, composing, sculpting, decorating, or inventing; or interpreting works of others by arranging, conducting, playing musical instruments, choreographing, acting, directing, critiquing, or editorializing.

E:1   Writes humorous material for publication or performance, selecting topic according to personal preference.

E:2   Paints variety of original subject material, conceiving and developing ideas for painting.

E:3   Creates and teaches original dances for ballet, musical, or revue.

E:4   Writes syndicated column on topics of reader interest to stimulate or mold public opinion.

E:5   Designs and sculpts three-dimensional artwork.

A Working **ALONE** or Apart in Physical Isolation from Others: Involves working in an environment that regularly precludes face-to-face interpersonal relationships for extended periods of time due to physical barriers or distances involved.

A:1   Locates and reports forest fires and weather phenomena from remote fire-lookout station; reports findings to base camp by radio or telephone.

A:2   Works below surface of water, using scuba gear or in diving suit, with air line extending to surface.

A:3   Explores likely regions to discover valuable mineral deposits, using topographical maps, surveys, reports, and knowledge of geology and mineralogy. Stakes claim according to Federal or State legal requirements.

A:4   Traps animals for pelts, live sale, bounty, or to relocate them to other areas. Sets traps, patrols trapline to remove catch, and resets or relocates traps.

A:5   Drives gasoline- or diesel-powered tractor-trailer combination long distances to transport and deliver products.

S Performing Effectively Under **STRESS**: Involves coping with circumstances dangerous to the worker or others.

S:1   Controls and extinguishes fires to protect life and property; positions and climbs ladder to gain access to upper level of buildings or to assist individuals from burning building.

S:2   Patrols assigned beat on foot, horseback, motorcycle, or in patrol car to control traffic, prevent crime or disturbance of peace, and arrest violators.

S:3   Performs surgery to correct deformities, repair injuries, prevent diseases, and improve function in patients, using a variety of surgical instruments and employing established surgical techniques.

S:4   Controls air traffic on and within vicinity of airport to prevent collisions; alerts support emergency crew and other designated personnel by radio or telephone when airplanes are having flight difficulties.

S:5   Repairs and replaces transmission and distribution power lines between generating stations, requiring use of precautionary work methods and safety equipment due to electrical hazards present when working on or near energized conduction and electrical accessories.

S:6   Pilots new, prototype, experimental, modified, and production aircraft to determine its airworthiness; puts aircraft through maneuvers, such as stalls, dives, glides, and speed runs to test and evaluate stability, control characteristics, and aerodynamic design.

T Attaining Precise Set Limits, **TOLERANCES**, and Standards: Involves adhering to and achieving exact levels of performance, using precision measuring instruments, tools, and machines to attain precise dimensions; preparing exact verbal and numerical records; and complying with precise instruments and specifications for materials, methods, procedures, and techniques to attain specified standards.

T:1 Weighs, measures, and mixes drugs and other medicinal compounds and fills bottles or capsules with correct quantity and composition of preparation, following prescriptions issued by physician or dentist.

T:2 Sets up and operates engine lathes to perform machining operations on metal or nonmetallic workpieces according to specifications, tooling instructions, standard charts, and knowledge of machinery procedures.

T:3 Moves precisely in combination with other dancers and coordinates body movements with music to perform chorus dances.

T:4 Establishes position of airplane, using navigation instruments and charts, celestial observation, or dead reckoning.

T:5 Examines parachute and lines to detect deviations from specifications and flaws in materials and work, using glass-topped table or fluorescent light, and marks defective areas.

T:6 Verifies and balances entries and records of financial transactions.

U Working **UNDER** Specific Instructions: Performing tasks only under specific instructions, allowing little or no room for independent action or judgment in working out job problems.

U:1 Installs plastic molding strips into slotted edges of metal tabletops, using mallet and bandsaw.

U:2 Mixes pharmaceuticals; issues medicines, labels, and stores supplies; and cleans equipment and work areas under direction of licensed, professional worker in hospital pharmacy.

U:3 Weighs or measures, grinds, chops, and mixes specified quantities of ingredients to prepare animal food.

U:4 Inspects materials and products for conformance to specifications, using fixed or preset measuring instruments.

U:5 Bends and adjusts plastic or metal eyeglass frames according to prescription specifications, using jewelers' handtools.

P Dealing with **PEOPLE**: Involves interpersonal relationships in job situations beyond receiving work instructions.

P:1 Counsels parolees having difficulty in readjusting to the community following release from prison.

P:2 Consults medical, nursing, and social service staffs concerning problems affecting patients' food habits and needs in order to formulate therapeutic diet menus compatible with each condition and treatment sequence.

P:3 Guides hunters and fishers to game areas, explains hunting and fishing laws, and recommends suitable firearms or fishing tackle to take specific game or fish.

P:4 Interviews job applicants to select persons meeting employee qualifications and informs applicants about job duties.

P:5 Receives callers at establishment, determines nature of business, and directs callers to destination.

J   Making **JUDGMENTS** and Decisions: Involves solving problems, making evaluations, or reaching conclusions based on subjective or objective criteria, such as the five senses, knowledge, past experiences, or quantifiable or factual data.

J:1   Examines paintings for color values, style of brushstroke, and aesthetic qualities to establish art period or to identify artist.

J:2   Tests and inspects products at various stages of production process and compiles and evaluates statistical data to determine and maintain quality and reliability of products.

J:3   Plans layout of newspaper edition determining placement of stories based on relative significance, available space, and knowledge of layout principles.

J:4   Evaluates individual applications for insurance for degree of risk involved and accepts applications following company's underwriting policies.

J:5   Examines food samples to determine sales appeal in restaurants; tastes prepared dishes to ascertain palatability and customer appeal.

J:6   Appraises real property to determine value for purchase, sales, investment, mortgage, or loan purposes considering location and trends or impending changes that could influence future value of property.

J:7   Examines and measures industrial diamonds to determine their quality, shape, and size, using classification standards and gauges.

PROCEDURE FOR RATING TEMPERAMENTS

Evaluate the work activities of the job for applicability of the Temperament factors by referring to the definitions of the factors. Select those factors considered to be important in relation to the kinds of adjustments which the worker must make for successful job performance. Do not assign Temperaments based on incidental work activities. Some simple jobs may require the worker to adjust to only one Temperament factor while other jobs may require adjustment to several. In Item 9 of the JAR enter the letter designation(s) of Temperament factor(s) considered to be important in relation to the kinds of adjustments which the worker must make for successful job performance.

CHAPTER 11

GUIDE FOR OCCUPATIONAL EXPLORATION

The *Guide for Occupational Exploration* (GOE) provides users with information about the interests, aptitudes, adaptabilities, and other requisites of occupational groups. The GOE is designed for use in self-assessment and counselor-assisted settings to help people understand themselves realistically in regard to their ability to meet job requirements.

The assignment of a GOE code to a JAR, and eventually a definition, provides a linkage from the GOE arrangement of occupations with similar interests, aptitudes, adaptability requirements, and other requisites to occupational definitions published in the DOT.

The GOE classification structure has three levels. The first level contains twelve interest areas that correspond to interest factors identified through research conducted by the Division of Testing in the U.S. Employment Service. The interest factors, identified by a two-digit code, are defined in terms of broad interest requirements of occupations as well as vocational interests of individuals. The twelve Interest Areas are:

01 Artistic	04 Protective	07 Business Detail	10 Humanitarian
02 Scientific	05 Mechanical	08 Selling	11 Leading-Influencing
03 Plants and Animals	06 Industrial	09 Accommodating	12 Physical Performing

The interest areas are subdivided into work groups. Each work group contains occupations that require similar adaptabilities and capabilities of the worker in similar work settings. The GOE contains descriptive information for each work group and identifies each occupation in the group with a four-digit code and title. In many interest areas, occupations that require the most education, training, and experience are in the first group while those requiring little formal education or experience are listed in the last group.

Work groups are subdivided into subgroups of occupations with even more homogeneous interests, aptitudes, and adaptability requirements. Each subgroup is identified with a unique six-digit code and title. Individual occupations are listed alphabetically within subgroups. Some subgroups contain occupations from more than one industry. When this occurs, occupations are listed within alphabetized industries.

Additional instructions for accessing the GOE and using the GOE, in conjunction with the U.S. Employment Service's GATB, for self-assessment or counselor-directed career exploration may be found in the GOE, section II. "Use of the Guide in Career Exploration".

PROCEDURE FOR ASSIGNING GOE CODE AND TITLE

Evaluate the interests, aptitudes, adaptability requirements, and other requisites of the job and compare them to the definitions and descriptive information provided in the GOE for Interest Areas and Work Groups. Compare the job to occupations clustered within individual subgroups. Select the six-digit code and corresponding GOE subgroup title into which the job best fits. Record the subgroup code and title in Item 6 of the JAR.

DEFINITIONS AND WORK GROUPS OF GOE INTEREST AREAS

The following pages contain descriptive information published in the GOE for the 12 Interest Areas and a list of the Work Groups within each Interest Area.

01 Artistic: An interest in creative expression of feelings or ideas.

You can satisfy this interest in several of the creative or performing arts fields. You may enjoy literature. Perhaps writing or editing would appeal to you. You may prefer to work in the performing arts. You could direct or perform in drama, music, or dance. You may enjoy the visual arts. You could become a critic in painting, use your hands to create or decorate products. Or you may prefer to model clothes or develop acts for entertainment.

01.01 Literary Arts	01.05 Performing Arts: Dance
01.02 Visual Arts	01.06 Craft Arts
01.03 Performing Arts: Drama	01.07 Elemental Arts
01.04 Performing Arts: Music	01.08 Modeling

02 Scientific: An interest in discovering, collecting, and analyzing information about the natural world and applying scientific research findings to problems in medicine, the life sciences, and the natural sciences.

You can satisfy this interest by working with the knowledge and processes of the sciences. You may enjoy researching and developing new knowledge in mathematics. Perhaps solving problems in the physical or life sciences would appeal to you. You may wish to study medicine and help humans or animals. You could work as a practitioner in the health field. You may want to work with scientific equipment and procedures. You could seek a job in research or testing laboratories.

02.01 Physical Sciences	02.03 Medical Sciences
02.02 Life Sciences	02.04 Laboratory Technology

03 Plants and Animals: An interest in activities to do with plants and animals, usually in an outdoor setting.

You can satisfy this interest by working in farming, forestry, fishing, and related fields. You may like doing physical work outdoors, such as working on a farm. You may enjoy animals. Perhaps training or taking care of animals would appeal to you. You may have management ability. You could own, operate, or manage farms or related businesses or services.

03.01 Managerial Work: Plants and Animals	03.03 Animal Training and Service
03.02 General Supervision: Plants and Animals	03.04 Elemental Work: Plants and Animals

04 Protective: An interest in using authority to protect people and property.

You can satisfy this interest by working in law enforcement, fire fighting, and related fields. You may enjoy mental challenge and intrigue. You could investigate crimes or fires. You may prefer to fight fires and respond to other emergencies. Or may want more routine work. Perhaps a job in guarding or patrolling would appeal to you. You may have management ability. You could seek a leadership position in law enforcement and the protective services.

04.01 Safety and Law Enforcement	04.02 Security Services

05 Mechanical: An interest in applying mechanical principles to practical situations using machines, handtools, or techniques.

You can satisfy this interest in a variety of jobs ranging from routine to complex professional positions. You may enjoy working with ideas about things (objects). You could seek a job in engineering or in a related technical field. You may prefer to deal directly with things. You could find a job in the crafts or trades, building, making or repairing objects. You may like to drive or to operate vehicles and special equipment. You may prefer routine or physical work in settings other than factories. Perhaps work in mining or construction would appeal to you.

05.01 Engineering
05.02 Managerial Work: Mechanical
05.03 Engineering Technology
05.04 Air and Water Vehicle Operation
05.05 Craft Technology
05.06 Systems Operation

05.07 Quality Control
05.08 Land and Water Vehicle Operation
05.09 Materials Control
05.10 Crafts
05.11 Equipment Operation
05.12 Elemental Work: Mechanical

06 Industrial: An interest in repetitive, concrete, organized activities in a factory setting.

You can satisfy this interest by working in one of many industries that manufacture goods on a mass production basis. You may enjoy manual work, using your hands or handtools. Perhaps you prefer to operate or take care of machines. You may like to inspect, sort, count, or weigh products, Using your training and experience to set up machines or supervise other workers may appeal to you.

06.01 Production Technology
06.02 Production Work

06.03 Quality Control
06.04 Elemental Work: Industrial

07 Business Detail: An interest in organized, clearly defined activities requiring accuracy and attention to details, primarily in an office setting.

You can satisfy this interest in a variety of jobs in which you can attend to the details of a business operation. You may enjoy using your math skills. Perhaps a job in billing, computing, or financial record keeping would satisfy you. You may prefer to deal with people. You may want a job in which you meet the public, talk on the telephone, or supervise other workers. You may like to operate computer terminals, typewriters, or bookkeeping machines. Perhaps a job in record keeping, filing, or recording would satisfy you. You may wish to use your training and experience to manage offices and supervise other workers.

07.01 Administrative Detail
07.02 Mathematical Detail
07.03 Financial Detail
07.04 Oral Communications

07.05 Records Processing
07.06 Clerical Machine Operation
07.07 Clerical Handling

08 Selling: An interest in bringing others to a point of view by personal persuasion, using sales and promotional techniques.

You can satisfy this interest in a variety of sales jobs. You may enjoy selling technical products or services. Perhaps you prefer a selling job requiring less background knowledge. You may work in stores, sales offices, or in customers' homes. You may wish to buy and sell products to make a profit. You can also satisfy this interest in legal work, business negotiations, advertising, and related fields found under other categories in the GOE.

08.01 Sales Technology
08.02 General Sales

08.03 Vending

09 Accommodating: An interest in catering to the wishes and needs of others, usually on a one-to-one basis.

You can satisfy this interest by providing services for the convenience of others, such as hospitality services in hotels, restaurants, airplanes, etc. You may enjoy improving the appearance of others. Perhaps working in the hair and beauty care field would satisfy you. You may wish to provide personal services, such as taking tickets, carrying baggage, or ushering.

09.01 Hospitality Services
09.02 Barber and Beauty Services
09.03 Passenger Services

09.04 Customer Services
09.05 Attendant Services

10 Humanitarian: An interest in helping individuals with their mental, spiritual, social, physical, or vocational concerns.

You can satisfy this interest by work in which caring for the welfare of others is important. Perhaps the spiritual or mental well-being of others concerns you. You could prepare for a job in religion or counseling. You may wish to help others with physical problems. You could work in the nursing, therapy, or rehabilitation fields. You may like to provide needed but less difficult care by working as an aide, orderly, or technician.

10.01 Social Services
10.02 Nursing, Therapy, and Specialized Teaching

10.03 Child and Adult Care

11 Leading-Influencing: An interest in leading and influencing others by using high-level verbal or numerical abilities.

You can satisfy this interest through study and work in a variety of professional fields. You may enjoy the challenge and responsibility of leadership. You could seek work in administration or management. You may prefer working with technical details. You could find a job in finance, law, social research, or public relations. You may like to help others learn. Perhaps working in education would appeal to you.

11.01 Mathematics and Statistics
11.02 Educational and Library
11.03 Social Research
11.04 Law
11.05 Business Administration
11.06 Finance

11.07 Services Administration
11.08 Communications
11.09 Promotion
11.10 Regulations Enforcement
11.11 Business Management Services
11.12 Contracts and Claims

12 Physical Performing: An interest in physical activities performed before an audience.

You can satisfy this interest through jobs in athletics, sports, and the performance of physical feats. Perhaps a job as a professional player or official would appeal to you. You may wish to develop and perform special acts such as acrobatics or wire walking.

12.01 Sports

12.02 Physical Feats

CHAPTER 12

PHYSICAL DEMANDS AND ENVIRONMENTAL CONDITIONS

Physical Demands and Environmental Conditions are components of Worker Characteristics. Physical Demands analysis is a systematic way of describing the physical activities that a job requires. It is concerned only with the physical demands of the job; it is not concerned with the physical capacity of the worker. Environmental Conditions are the surroundings in which a job is performed. To be considered present an Environmental Condition must be specific and related to the job.

These concepts provide two of the important criteria for collecting and classifying information about jobs. The resulting data have a significant role in exposing workers to a maximum number of job opportunities.

The Physical Demands of a job are defined in terms of twenty factors. In addition, fourteen factors are used to express the important Environmental Conditions under which a job is performed. Illustrative job-worker situations for these factors are provided below to assist the analyst in collecting these data.

The USES method of job analysis provides the means to describe and evaluate a job as it exists. This method permits the matching of workers and jobs based upon the workers' capabilities. The method also permits the modification of the physical demands of a job to fit the capabilities of disabled workers. The extent to which any job is suitable for modification is an area that may be pursued as a special application of job analysis.

PHYSICAL DEMAND FACTORS, DEFINITIONS, AND EXAMPLES

1. STRENGTH

This factor is expressed by one of five terms: Sedentary, Light, Medium, Heavy, and Very Heavy. In order to determine the overall rating, an evaluation is made of the worker's involvement in the following activities:

Position

Standing: Remaining on one's feet in an upright position at a work station without moving about.

Walking: Moving about on foot.

Sitting: Remaining in a seated position.

Weight/Force

Lifting: Raising or lowering an object from one level to another (includes upward pulling).

Carrying: Transporting an object, usually holding it in the hands or arms or on the shoulder.

Pushing: Exerting force upon an object so that the object moves away from the force (includes slapping, striking, kicking, and treadle actions).

Pulling: Exerting force upon an object so that the object moves toward the force (includes jerking).

Lifting, pushing, and pulling are expressed in terms of both intensity and duration. Judgments regarding intensity involve consideration of the weight handled, position of the worker's body or the part of the worker's body used in handling weights, and the aid given by helpers or by mechanical equipment. Duration is the total time spent by the worker in carrying out these activities. Carrying most often is expressed in terms of duration, weight carried, and distance carried.

Care must be exercised in evaluating jobs in the strength categories, particularly in interpreting the force and the physical effort a person must exert. For instance, a worker in an awkward crouching position may experience as much difficulty exerting five pounds of force as when exerting thirty pounds at waist height while standing. Also, if one is required continuously to lift, push, and pull objects weighing 15 pounds or to carry these objects long distances, a worker may exert as much physical effort as would be exerted in occasionally or even frequently lifting, pushing, and pulling objects twice as heavy, or in occasionally carrying these objects over short distances.

Controls: Hand-Arm and Foot-Leg

Controls entail use of one or both arms or hands (hand-arm) or one or both feet or legs (foot-leg) to move controls on machinery or equipment. In this sub-item, the analyst must consider whether the worker moves controls on the machine or equipment by using either right-side body members, left-side body members, or members of either or both sides. In addition, the use of hand-arm controls is distinguished from the use of foot-leg controls. Controls include but are not limited to buttons, knobs, pedals, levers, and cranks.

Sedentary Work

Exerting up to 10 pounds of force occasionally or a negligible amount of force frequently to lift, carry, push, pull, or otherwise move objects, including the human body. Sedentary work involves sitting most of the time, but may involve walking or standing for brief periods of time. Jobs are Sedentary if walking and standing are required only occasionally and all other Sedentary criteria are met.

S:1   Takes dictation and transcribes from notebook, using typewriter, while sitting at desk. Occasionally walks to various parts of department when called upon to take dictation.

S:2   Repairs defects in hosiery, using needle, thread, scissors, and mending cup while sitting at bench.

S:3   Examines watch jewels for defects, using microscope, while sitting at glass table.

S:4   Writes news stories for publication or broadcast from written notes supplied by reporting staff while sitting at desk. Occasionally walks to reference library to obtain supplemental material.

S:5   Drafts detailed drawings while sitting at drawing board. Occasionally walks to obtain items of negligible weight, such as paper, T-square, and other drafting supplies.

S:6   Telephones dealers to determine availability of type and model of automobile desired by customer and prepares papers for transfer of automobiles while sitting at desk.

S:7   Dispatches taxicabs in response to telephone requests for service while sitting at desk.

Light Work

Exerting up to 20 pounds of force occasionally, or up to 10 pounds of force frequently, or a negligible amount of force constantly to move objects. Physical demand requirements are in excess of those for Sedentary Work. Even though the weight lifted may be only a negligible amount, a job should be rated Light Work: (1) when it requires walking or standing to a significant degree; or (2) when it requires sitting most of the time but entails pushing or pulling of arm or leg controls; or (3) when the job requires working at a production rate pace entailing the constant pushing or pulling of materials even though the weight of those materials is negligible. NOTE: The constant stress and strain of maintaining a production rate pace, especially in an industrial setting, can be and is physically demanding of a worker even though the amount of force exerted is negligible.

L:1   Starts, stops, and controls speed of sewing machine, using pedal or knee lever, while sitting at table.

L:2   Pulls control lever of arbor press downward, exerting about five pounds of force to fit metal parts together, while sitting at bench.

L:3   Arranges records in file cabinets, drawers, and boxes. Walks to obtain records and stands while arranging them.

L:4   Wraps and bags articles for customers, standing and walking behind counter of variety store.

L:5   Lifts cans, jars, or bottles from cardboard box and places items on conveyor. Removes filled or capped containers, which weigh approximately 2 to 3 pounds, from one conveyor and places containers on another.

L:6   Serves food and refreshments to patrons in railroad car, walking from car to kitchen to obtain and relay orders and carrying food trays weighing up to 10 pounds.

Medium Work

Exerting 20 to 50 pounds of force occasionally, or 10 to 25 pounds of force frequently, or greater than negligible up to 10 pounds of force constantly to move objects. Physical demand requirements are in excess of those for Light Work.

M:1   Locates and moves materials and parts between work areas of plant to expedite processing of foods, lifting material usually weighing 15-20 pounds and occasionally weighing up to 50 pounds to place in car or handtruck.

M:2   Fastens metal objects to plating racks, carries filled racks weighing up to 20 pounds to cleaning, plating, and rinsing tanks, and immerses them in tanks.

M:3   Fabricates sheet metal articles, occasionally carrying tools and sheet metal weighing 50 pounds maximum to workbench. Lifts sheet metal to workbench and machine and pushes and pulls it into proper positions.

M:4   Carries lumber weighing occasionally up to 50 pounds from supply room to workbench, a distance of approximately 20 feet. Stands and bends most of time to lift lumber and pushes and pulls lumber to position on workbench or machine.

M:5   Lifts, pushes, and pulls tools to raise automobile, to remove tire from wheel, and to remount tire. Rolls tires, usually weighing approximately 20 pounds and occasionally weighing up to 50 pounds, to repair work area.

M:6   Dismantles, tests, adjusts, repairs, and installs engine parts of aircraft, walking and standing continuously. Frequently lifts and carries parts weighing up to 25 pounds for inspection and repair and pushes and pulls components into position on workbench.

Heavy Work

Exerting 50 to 100 pounds of force occasionally, or 25 to 50 pounds of force frequently, or 10 to 20 pounds of force constantly to move objects. Physical demand requirements are in excess of those for Medium Work.

H:1   Digs trench to specified depth and width, constantly pushing shovel into earth and lifting, carrying, and throwing shovelfuls of earth onto pile. Shovel often is raised to shoulder height and weight lifted is concentrated at its end. Shovel and earth weigh approximately 20 pounds, but the continuous effort involved requires strength comparable to that required by frequent lifting up to 50 pounds and occasional lifting up to 100 pounds.

H:2   Charges furnaces, lifting and carrying metal weighing 35-50 pounds. Frequently pushes and pulls from awkward crouching position to turn metal in furnace with tongs. Periodically withdraws metal from furnace and carries it, with assistance, to forge.

H:3   Fits pipe assemblies into place, frequently lifting and carrying pipe and pipe connections weighing 50 pounds and occasionally up to 100 pounds, with aid of helpers. Stands, stoops, and crouches while reaching above and below shoulder height to pull pipes into position.

H:4   Mixes pastry, standing almost continuously. Occasionally lifts and carries 100-pound bags of flour about 20 feet from stack to mixing bowl. Frequently turns and stoops to lift bags of sugar and shortening, each weighing 50 pounds.

H:5   Pushes handtruck up and down warehouse aisles, lifts cartons of items weighing an average of 65 pounds from storage shelves, and places cartons on handtruck to fill orders. Lifts cartons from handtruck in order to complete packing, wrapping, sealing, and labeling for shipping. Lifts and carries cartons to skids for shipping.

Very Heavy Work

Exerting in excess of 100 pounds of force occasionally, or in excess of 50 pounds of force frequently, or in excess of 20 pounds of force constantly to move objects. Physical demand requirements are in excess of those for Heavy Work.

V:1   Lifts lumber and other material weighing 50 pounds or more and carries to handtruck.

V:2   Transfers adult patients between bed and conveyance, frequently lifting them without assistance, and pushes wheelchair or wheeled stretcher to transport patients to hospital areas.

V:3   Loads and unloads truck when transporting or delivering articles, such as furniture, refrigerators, and machinery, many of which weigh in excess of 100 pounds.

V:4   Loads and unloads trailers and semitrailers with crates of produce weighing from 80 to 110 pounds.

V:5   Performs machine and hand operations necessary to fabricate and assemble boilers, tanks, vats, and other vessels made of heavy steel plates weighing up to 120 pounds.

V:6   Installs ship's steam, diesel, or electric propelling and auxiliary machinery and equipment, such as pumps, cargo-handling machinery, anchor-handling gear, ventilating and fire-fighting equipment, steering gear, and armament.

2.   CLIMBING

Ascending or descending ladders, stairs, scaffolding, ramps, poles, and the like, using feet and legs or hands and arms. Body agility is emphasized. Describe in Physical Demands comments section in terms of height, steepness, duration, and type of structure climbed.

C:1   Climbs ladder to attach advertising posters on elevated billboards.

C:2   Ascends poles to install, maintain, and repair telephone, telegraph, and electrical power lines.

C:3   Climbs fire escapes and ladders to gain access to upper levels of buildings or to assist individuals from burning structures.

C:4   Climbs trees to reach and trim branches interfering with transmission wires.

C:5   Climbs ladder to plaster ceilings.

3.   BALANCING

Maintaining body equilibrium to prevent falling when walking, standing, crouching, or running on narrow, slippery, or erratically moving surfaces; or maintaining body equilibrium when performing gymnastic feats. Describe in Physical Demands comments section in terms of type or condition of surface and activities during which balance must be maintained.

B:1   Balances to avoid falling or spilling food when serving passengers on airplane in flight.

B:2   Balances on slippery, erratically moving, floating barrier (boom) of logs while sorting logs according to species, size, and owners' markings.

B:3   Maintains equilibrium while dancing and performing difficult gymnastic feats.

B:4   Balances on narrow steel girders of building under construction while catching hot rivets tossed by Rivet Heater in bucket and inserting rivets in holes, using tongs.

B:5   Balances on scaffolding when installing glass on upper stories of building front.

4.   STOOPING

Bending body downward and forward by bending spine at the waist, requiring full use of the lower extremities and back muscles. Describe in Physical Demands comments section in terms of duration.

S:1   Stoops between plant rows to reach for and pull, twist, or cut harvestable crops.

S:2   Stoops while shoveling snow into truck.

S:3   Stoops while cleaning, waxing, and polishing floors, using waxing machine.

S:4   Stoops to gather worms in grassy areas for use as fish bait.

S:5   Stoops to refinish bodies of automobiles, to remove and replace damaged fenders, and to straighten and realign automobile frames.

5.   KNEELING

Bending legs at knees to come to rest on knee or knees. Describe in Physical Demands comments section in terms of duration.

K:1   Kneels while pressing carpet firmly in place over tackless strips, using handtools.

K:2   Operates concrete-wall grinder to remove bumps and rough spots from exposed concrete surface, working in kneeling position for sustained periods.

K:3   Kneels to connect wiring to fixtures and power equipment located in cramped places.

K:4   Kneels while examining rocks, minerals, and fossils to identify and determine sequence of processes affecting development of earth.

K:5   Kneels to adjust and repair electrically powered, automatic pinsetting bowling machines.

6.   CROUCHING

Bending body downward and forward by bending legs and spine. Describe in Physical Demands comments section in terms of duration.

C:1   Crouches over rows of rose plants to reach and cut plant rootstock.

C:2   Crouches to secure post and attach lead-in wire to antenna.

C:3   Crouches to spread mortar and position bricks on lower parts of walls.

C:4   Crouches to remove catch from and reset traps.

C:5   Crouches when filing correspondence in lower drawers of filing cabinets.

7.   CRAWLING

Moving about on hands and knees or hands and feet. Describe in Physical Demands comments section in terms of distance and duration.

C:1   Crawls underneath building to remove debris prior to spraying insecticide.

C:2   Crawls while smoothing and finishing surface of poured concrete sidewalks, using straightedge.

C:3   Crawls while cleaning, waxing, and polishing floors, using rags and brushes.

C:4   Crawls through narrow spaces to reach all parts of furnace when cleaning or repairing furnace.

C:5   Crawls into low attics and under buildings to inspect buildings for presence of vermin.

8. REACHING

Extending hand(s) and arm(s) in any direction.

R:1   Reaches for ledgers, tax tables, and writing instruments.

R:2   Reaches for drawings, chemically treated paper, and controls on machine to make blueprints.

R:3   Reaches for individual wires and winds them around pegs on harness board.

R:4   Reaches for knives, tubes, and other equipment while preparing body for burial.

R:5   Reaches for high branches to pick fruit.

9. HANDLING

Seizing, holding, grasping, turning, or otherwise working with hand or hands. Fingers are involved only to the extent that they are an extension of the hand, such as to turn a switch or shift automobile gears.

H:1   Handles tools, parts, and test instruments used to service and repair aircraft engines.

H:2   Grasps handtools and powered handtools when fitting and fastening automobile and truck components.

H:3   Handles and grasps combs, scissors, razors, and lotions while providing barbering services.

H:4   Uses arms and hands to turn steering wheel, operate gearshift, and handle baggage.

H:5   Holds parts and handles tools and lumber when building and repairing wooden articles.

10. FINGERING

Picking, pinching, or otherwise working primarily with fingers rather than with the whole hand or arm as in handling.

F:1   Fingers keys accurately when using adding and calculating machines.

F:2   Uses fingers constantly to count and sort coins and paper money and operate keys on cash register.

F:3   Squeezes and stretches sample of curd with fingers to determine firmness or texture of cheese.

F:4   Uses fingers to cut, pin, and sew sample garments.

F:5   Picks up and places rivets into holes of metal cabinets.

F:6   Positions pinion in machine holder, using tweezers.

11. FEELING

Perceiving attributes of objects, such as size, shape, temperature, or texture, by touching with skin, particularly that of fingertips.

F:1   Slides fingers over braille characters to feel discrepancies in proof.

F:2   Strokes fur to feel density of pelts in order to select pelts that have same thickness and length of fur.

F:3   Feels upholstery padding to determine conformance to specified degree of firmness.

F:4   Feels dough in dough-mixing machine for desired consistency before ending mixing cycle.

F:5   Feels poultry for presence of bruises, deformities, and pinfeathers and grades accordingly for quality.

F:6 Turns dial of micrometer until contact points touch surface of part to be measured, working to tolerances of .001 inch, and compares measurement with specifications.

12. TALKING

Expressing or exchanging ideas by means of the spoken word to impart oral information to clients or to the public and to convey detailed spoken instructions to other workers accurately, loudly, or quickly.

T:1 Speaks clearly and distinctly to instruct pilots.

T:2 Exhorts passing public to attend show.

T:3 Speaks in pleasant, well-controlled voice to present radio and television programs to audience.

T:4 Answers inquiries regarding departures, arrivals, stops, and destinations of scheduled buses or trains.

T:5 Interprets specifications, blueprints, and job orders to workers.

13. HEARING

Perceiving the nature of sounds by ear.

H:1 Test-drives vehicle and listens for rattles, squeaks, or other noises reported by customer, indicating malfunctioning or loose components.

H:2 Listens intently to sounds of safe locks while turning dial to open safe.

H:3 Listens attentively to take dictation and answer telephone.

H:4 Listens to sounds of running engine to detect possible faulty operation.

14. TASTING/SMELLING

Distinguishing, with a degree of accuracy, differences or similarities in intensity or quality of flavors or odors, or recognizing particular flavors or odors, using tongue or nose.

TS:1 Tastes and smells food being cooked to determine if it is cooked sufficiently.

TS:2 Determines, by smell, odor qualities of prepared materials used in the production of perfume.

TS:3 Tastes samples of food or beverages to determine palatability of product or to prepare blending formulas.

TS:4 Tastes baked pretzels and adjusts speed of conveyor or temperature of cooler, oven, or kiln to ensure pretzels conform to taste standards.

TS:5 Walks along pipelines to detect gas odor indicating leaks and notifies maintenance department of location of leaks.

15. NEAR ACUITY

Clarity of vision at 20 inches or less.

NA:1 Enters numerical data in bookkeeping ledgers.

NA:2 Sketches and paints, in minute detail, illustrations of anatomical and pathological specimens.

NA:3 Reads, compiles, computes, and records numerical and statistical data.

NA:4 Guides material under needle and continuously checks alignment and accuracy of stitching.

NA:5 Examines components for scratches, chips, and other defects, using magnifier.

16. FAR ACUITY

Clarity of vision at 20 feet or more.

FA:1   Watches for landmarks when taking off and landing airplane.

FA:2   Reads traffic signs at distances up to 200 feet while driving taxi.

FA:3   Identifies machine jams at distances of 20 to 35 feet.

FA:4   Observes forests from remote fire-lookout station to locate forest fires, and reports fires, using radio or telephone.

17. DEPTH PERCEPTION

Three-dimensional vision. Ability to judge distances and spatial relationships so as to see objects where and as they actually are.

DP:1   Observes farm machinery in operation to detect malfunctioning or defective units.

DP:2   Judges distances and space relationships of stationary and moving objects to avoid accidents while driving bus.

DP:3   Dismantles and reassembles engines, using handtools.

DP:4   Operates power derrick to load and unload loose materials from railroad cars, moving controls to raise, lower, and rotate boom and to raise and lower load line in response to signals.

DP:5   Observes products moving on conveyors to monitor flow and operation of automated conveyor system.

18. ACCOMMODATION

Adjustment of lens of eye to bring an object into sharp focus. This factor is required when doing near point work at varying distances from the eye.

A:1   Guides electric cutter through layers of fabric, continually keeping cutting lines in sharp focus.

A:2   Shifts gaze from viewing screen several feet distant to compare with data on correspondence and forms at near distance.

A:3   Inspects and adjusts minute parts, using unaided vision as well as magnifiers and precision gauges.

A:4   Reads typescript or proof of type setup to detect and mark for correction.

A:5   Examines tissue samples under microscope for atypical characteristics and records findings on data sheet.

19. COLOR VISION

Ability to identify and distinguish colors.

CV:1   Performs pH titration test to ascertain if material is within specified limits, requiring ability to observe subtle color changes.

CV:2   Makes discriminating comparison of color hue and color brightness in lipsticks.

CV:3   Identifies resistors by color code and connects colored wires to specific terminals.

CV:4   Assists customers in color-coordinating selection of wall coverings.

CV:5   Mixes inks to obtain proper color and shade, comparing results with sample.

20. FIELD OF VISION

Observing an area that can be seen up and down or to right or left while eyes are fixed on a given point.

FV:1   Rides racehorse at racetrack, relying on peripheral vision to observe relative positions of nearby horses during race.

FV:2   Monitors control-board panels and TV monitors from desk and notifies supervisor when machine maintenance is required.

FV:3   Observes actions of participants of sporting event to detect infractions of rules.

FV:4   Drives taxicab in city traffic.

FV:5   Observes racing cars passing start-finish line of track to obtain count of laps completed by each competitor.

ENVIRONMENTAL CONDITION FACTORS, DEFINITIONS, AND EXAMPLES

1.   EXPOSURE TO WEATHER

Exposure to outside atmospheric conditions.

W:1   Erects and repairs electric power lines and is exposed to hot, cold, wet, or windy conditions.

W:2   Delivers mail to residential areas, spending 75 percent of working time outdoors.

W:3   Picks field crops, frequently in heat of sun, continuing during periods of light rain.

W:4   Directs actions of school children and traffic at street intersections to ensure safe crossing.

W:5   Patrols assigned areas to prevent game law violations, investigates reports of damage to crops and property by wildlife, and gathers biological information. Works outdoors in all kinds of weather and travels by car, boat, airplane, horse, and on foot.

2.   EXTREME COLD

Exposure to nonweather-related cold temperatures.

EC:1   Stores ice in cold-storage room.

EC:2   Works in cooler room, usually kept at approximately 40' F., while cutting beef carcasses into standard cuts.

EC:3   Stores ice cream in hardening room to solidify and keep ice cream in good condition. Enters and leaves room constantly.

EC:4   Packs dressed fish in ice. Shovels layer of ice in box and fills body cavity of each fish with ice. Places fish in box and fills remainder of box with ice. Room temperature must be below freezing to prevent ice from melting.

EC:5   Tends freeze tunnel to quick-freeze food products. Patrols tunnel to observe progress of food product to ensure freezing. Scrapes conveyor to remove excess ice or frost.

3.   EXTREME HEAT

Exposure to nonweather-related hot temperatures.

EH:1   Works close to hot stove during cooking operations while performing various activities, such as agitating, testing, and draining cooking mixture.

EH:2   Charges furnace, turns billets in furnace, and withdraws heated billets.

EH:3   Works constantly around hot tumblers in laundry room, reaching in and removing partially cooled articles.

EH:4   Controls movement of machine that spreads hot asphalt on streets and roads and is subject to intense heat produced by heating mechanism of machine.

EH:5   Controls furnace to relieve internal stresses in metal objects and to soften and refine grain structure. Places metal objects directly into furnace. Reduces heat and allows objects to cool in furnace.

EH:6   Tends battery of preset final-drying chambers that automatically dry macaroni long goods. Pushes rack of macaroni into drying chambers and starts drying cycle. Removes rack of dried macaroni after completion of drying cycle.

4.   WET AND/OR HUMID

Contact with water or other liquids or exposure to nonweather-related humid conditions.

WH:1   Presses garment, using pressing machine, and is constantly exposed to oppressive humidity resulting from steam emitted by pressing machine and by damp garments which are being ironed.

WH:2   Feeds food products into washing machine preparatory to cooking and canning. Handles wet food and works in wet area.

WH:3   Maintains kitchen work area and restaurant equipment and utensils in clean condition. Washes worktables, hoses out garbage cans, and washes pots, pans, trays, and dishes by hand. Hands are in constant contact with water.

WH:4   Dumps containers of fish into fresh water tank for cleaning; removes wet fish from tank and trims fins and tails, removes skin, and cuts fish into pieces of specified size. Constantly handles wet fish and works in wet area.

WH:5   Loads damp articles into tumblers and removes hot, dried articles from tumblers, working in humid atmosphere.

5.   NOISE INTENSITY LEVEL

The noise intensity level to which the worker is exposed in the job environment. This factor is expressed by one of five levels. Consider all the benchmarks within a level as providing an insight into the nature of the specific levels.

Code	Level	Illustrative Examples
1	Very Quiet	isolation booth for hearing test; deep sea diving; forest trail
2	Quiet	library; many private offices; funeral reception; golf course; art museum
3	Moderate	business office where typewriters are used; department store; grocery store; light traffic; fast food restaurant at off-hours
4	Loud	can manufacturing department; large earth-moving equipment; heavy traffic
5	Very Loud	rock concert - front row; jackhammer work; rocket engine testing area during test

6.   VIBRATION

Exposure to a shaking object or surface.

V:1   Operates compressed air, rock-drilling machine. Worker is exposed to continuous vibrations.

V:2   Operates tractor to scoop earth. Worker is subject to intense vibration while scraper is forced into ground and while tractor is driven forward to fill scraper with dirt.

V:3   Operates cylinder-type printing press. Worker is subject to continuous vibration when printing press is in operation.

V:4   Operates drilling equipment to drill holes in walls or slabs of concrete to facilitate installation and repair of utility systems and equipment. Continuous vibration is felt by worker.

V:5   Positions metal workpiece in lower die and presses pedal, causing ram to strike metal repeatedly, forcing it to shape of die impression. Vibration is caused by the repeated striking of the ram against the metal.

7.   ATMOSPHERIC CONDITIONS

Exposure to conditions such as fumes, noxious odors, dusts, mists, gases, and poor ventilation, that affect the respiratory system, eyes, or the skin.

AC:1   Pours pigments, paint paste, and thinner into can and stirs mixture with paddle, working in metal-finishing plant. Worker breathes fumes and odors of paint ingredients.

AC:2   Stacks grain by hand or with pitchfork during harvesting and threshing and is exposed to heavy concentration of dust from movement of grain.

AC:3   Takes care of animals, such as dogs, mice, and monkeys, which are being used for medical tests. Cleans and sterilizes cages, pens, and surrounding areas, such as walls, windows, and floors, using steam or germ-killing solutions. Sprays or spreads insect-killing solutions or powders. Worker is subject to disagreeable odors and skin irritants from solutions.

AC:4   Repairs and overhauls automobiles. Worker is exposed to fumes and odors of grease, oil, gas, and engine exhaust.

AC:5   Shampoos hair and scalp with various ingredients and rinses. Applies bleach, dye, or tint to color customer's hair. Worker is exposed to strong odors and skin irritants from various hair preparations and lotions.

8.   PROXIMITY TO MOVING MECHANICAL PARTS

Exposure to possible bodily injury from moving mechanical parts of equipment, tools, or machinery.

MP:1   Sets up and operates variety of woodworking machines to surface, cut, and shape lumber, and to fabricate parts for wood products. Worker is subject to possible cuts, abrasions, injury to eyes, and loss of extremities.

MP:2   Tends fabricating machines, such as shears, brakes, straightening presses, and punches to shape and bend metal plates, sheets, and structural shapes. Worker is subject to possible injury, such as cuts, fractures, crushed hands or feet, hernia, and eye injury from metalworking machinery.

MP:3   Constructs, erects, installs, and repairs structures and fixtures of wood, plywood, and wallboard. Worker is subject to possible bodily injury from power saws and other power tools.

MP:4   Inspects and adjusts automatic pinsetters. Worker is subject to possible bodily injury from machinery.

9.   EXPOSURE TO ELECTRICAL SHOCK

Exposure to possible bodily injury from electrical shock.

ES:1   Repairs energized electric power lines. Worker is subject to possible severe burns or electrocution.

ES:2   Operates high voltage equipment and works with high voltage circuits while operating substation. Worker is subject to possible electrical shock and electrocution.

ES:3   Repairs and maintains electrical equipment in generating station or powerhouse. Worker is subject to possible electrical shock and electrocution.

ES:4   Plans, lays out, installs, and repairs wiring, electrical fixtures, apparatus, and control equipment. Worker is subject to possible electrical shock and electrocution.

10.   WORKING IN HIGH, EXPOSED PLACES

Exposure to possible bodily injury from falling.

HP:1   Repairs energized electric power lines, working from bucket of cherry picker or after climbing pole. Worker is subject to possible bodily injury from falls.

HP:2   Climbs poles, ladders, or scaffolding to install rigging to raise, lower, or support equipment, such as scenery and lighting equipment for theatrical productions. Worker is subject to possible bodily injury from falls.

HP:3   Applies coats of paint, varnish, stain, or lacquer to exterior and interior surfaces, working from ladder or scaffolding. Worker is subject to possible bodily injury from falls.

HP:4   Constructs, maintains, and demolishes elevated structures, such as smokestacks, water tanks, and steeples. Worker is subject to possible bodily injury from falls.

11.   EXPOSURE TO RADIATION

Exposure to possible bodily injury from radiation.

RE:1   Prepares, administers, and measures radioactive isotopes in therapeutic, diagnostic, and tracer studies, utilizing variety of radioisotope equipment. Worker is subject to possible bodily injury from exposure to radiation.

RE:2   Operates x-ray equipment. Worker is subject to possible bodily injury from exposure to radiation.

RE:3   Operates and maintains nuclear reactor. Worker is subject to possible bodily injury from exposure to gamma and neutron radiation.

RE:4   Monitors radiation in work environment where radioactive material is used. Worker is subject to possible bodily injury from exposure to radiation.

12.   WORKING WITH EXPLOSIVES

Exposure to possible injury from explosions.

E:1   Maintains and repairs gas lines, equipment, and appliances. Worker is subject to possible bodily injury from gas fume ignition and explosions.

E:2   Maintains, repairs, and overhauls machinery that uses nitroglycerine. Worker is subject to possible bodily injury from nitroglycerine explosions.

E:3   Tests ammunition in ammunition manufacturing plant. Worker is subject to possible bodily injury from exploding ammunition.

E:4   Determines most effective and economical methods of extracting underground coal deposits. Worker is subject to possible bodily injury from gas explosions during the time worker is in underground mining areas.

13. EXPOSURE TO TOXIC OR CAUSTIC CHEMICALS

Exposure to possible bodily injury from toxic or caustic chemicals.

TC:1   Tends equipment that mixes chemicals for use in bleaching, cleaning, desizing, latexing, mercerizing, and finishing canvas goods, carpets, and rugs, felt goods, and textile yarns and fabrics. Worker is subject to possible chemical burns from strong acids or anhydrous ammonia.

TC:2   Studies effects of toxic substances on physiological functions of human beings, animals, and plants to develop data for use in consumer protection and industrial safety programs. Worker is subject to possible bodily injury from toxic substances.

TC:3   Loads conveyor of battery-crushing machine. Worker is exposed to possible bodily injury from acid in batteries.

TC:4   Tends equipment that chemically cleans semiconductor wafers used in manufacture of semiconductor components, such as transistors, diodes, and integrated circuits. Worker is exposed to possible bodily injury from cleaning solutions used, such as hydrogen peroxide, sulfuric acid, and hydrochloric acid.

14. OTHER ENVIRONMENTAL CONDITIONS

Explain other Environmental Conditions, not defined above, in Environmental Conditions Comments.

OC:1   Demolishes parts of buildings to reach and combat fires and rescue persons endangered by fire and smoke. Is exposed to burns, fumes, smoke, and falling objects.

OC:2   Mines ore or coal in underground mine. Cuts channel under working face to facilitate blasting; charges and sets off explosives to blast down material; and installs timbering to support walls and roof. Exposed to danger of mine collapse, explosion of natural gas, and suffocation.

OC:3   Patrols assigned beat to prevent crime or disturbance of peace. Worker is subjected to bodily injury or death from law violators.

OC:4   Dives in ocean to maximum depth of three hundred feet. Worker is subject to bends and other conditions associated with high water pressure and oxygen deprivation.

OC:5   Patrols ski slopes prior to allowing public use. Worker is exposed to danger of avalanches.

PROCEDURE FOR PREPARING
PHYSICAL DEMANDS AND ENVIRONMENTAL CONDITIONS
SECTION OF THE JAR
(Refer to Sample at End of Chapter)

ID Number

Enter the same number that appears on the front page of the JAR which this section accompanies.

PHYSICAL DEMAND AND ENVIRNOMENTAL CONDITION SYMBOLS

The following symbols are used to indicate the presence or absence of a Physical Demand or Environmental Condition. Enter the appropriate one for each activity.

Code	Frequency	Definition
N	Not Present	Activity or condition does not exist.
O	Occasionally	Activity or condition exists up to 1/3 of the time.
F	Frequently	Activity or condition exists from 1/3 to 2/3 of the time.
C	Constantly	Activity or condition exists 2/3 or more of the time.

STRENGTH

Position

Enter beside each activity, Standing, Walking, and Sitting, the percentage of time the worker spends in each activity rounded to 5% intervals of time. The percentages entered should add to 100%. When they do not, provide an explanation in the Physical Demands comments section. Also enter in the comments section information to substantiate and explain entries made for each of the three activities.

Weight/Force

Record in the appropriate frequency column for each activity the range of pounds the worker lifts or carries or the pounds of force the worker exerts to push or pull objects. When the activity is not present, record an "X" under N (Not Present). When the weight of incidental objects lifted or carried infrequently (paper, pens, pencils) or the force exerted to push or pull objects (switches, heat- or touch-sensitive buttons or keys) is negligible, record an "X" in the N column next to the activity. In this instance an entry of "X" in the N column can indicate negligible weights lifted/carried or force exerted for pushing/pulling an object as well as that the activity is not present. When objects of negligible weight are lifted/carried or a negligible pushing/pulling force is exerted and, in the analyst's opinion, the Strength factor is influenced by the frequency of this pushing/pulling or lifting/carrying of negligible weights, record "0-1" in the appropriate O, F, or C column. Enter in the Physical Demands comments section information to substantiate and explain entries in the frequency columns of the Weight/Force section. Also, Physical Demands 9-Handling, or 10-Fingering, and possibly 8-Reaching, must have positive entries (O, F, or C) to be in agreement with the positive entries in this section.

Controls

Record in the space beside "Hand-Arm" an "N" (Not Present) when the job does not require the use of arms or hands to move controls, or one of the following letters "R", "L", "B", or "E" to indicate the use of **R**ight or **L**eft hand or arm, **B**oth right and left hands or arms, or **E**ither right or left hand or arm, when it does. Follow the same procedure for supplying information regarding the use of "Foot-Leg" controls. When any activity is too complex to be noted in this way, explain them in the Physical Demands comments section. Also, record in the comments section information to substantiate positive entries (R, L, B, E) in the Controls section and to explain how the use of controls affects the Strength Level rating. Positive entries for Hand-Arm in the Controls section usually require positive entries for Pushing/Pulling in the Weight/Force section and frequently require entries for Physical Demands Factor 10, Fingering, since all three are interrelated.

1. Strength Level

Evaluate the percentages of time spent standing, walking, and sitting (Position Section), the amount of weights lifted/carried, the force exerted for pushing/pulling (Weight/Force Section), and the use of controls (Controls Section) to determine the Strength Level rating for the job, according to the definitions for the Strength Levels listed above. Generally, the analyst will be able to determine the Strength Level rating from the frequency and weight/force matrix in the table below. There are, however, two other considerations which may affect the final rating. The weights recorded in the Weight/Force Section, considered alone, may suggest that the job is S, Sedentary, but when the worker performs tasks in an awkward position, job performance is more difficult; this causes the worker to expend more energy than when working in a less awkward posture. A second consideration for rating Strength Level occurs when the worker lifts, carries, pushes, or pulls objects of negligible weight at a rapid and prolonged pace, such as in production work. Even though the weights and forces are negligible, a Strength Level rating of L, Light instead of S, Sedentary is justified. In both cases, record information in the Physical Demands comments section to substantiate the rating. After determining the overall strength requirements of the job, select and enter a capital S, L, M, H, or V in the space beside 1. Strength Level.

The following table is provided as an aid in the determination of Strength Levels:

LIMITS OF WEIGHTS LIFTED/CARRIED OR FORCE EXERTED

RATING	Occasionally (O)	Frequently (F)	Constantly (C)
SEDENTARY	* - 10	*	-
LIGHT	* - 20	* - 10	*
MEDIUM	20 - 50	10 - 25	* - 10
HEAVY	50 - 100	25 - 50	10 - 20
VERY HEAVY	100 +	50 +	20 +

* negligible weight

The range excludes the lower number and includes the higher number, i.e, the range 10 - 25 excludes 10 (begins at 10 +) and includes 25. Overlapping ranges of * - 10 in the Occasionally (O) column for Sedentary and Light jobs are differentiated on the basis of the worker's posture and whether work is performed at a production rate. For example, all Sedentary jobs involve constantly sitting. However, in some jobs workers sit constantly but exert force of an amount or at a frequency rate that exceeds the limits for Sedentary. Such jobs are, therefore, rated at least Light.

2-20. All Other Physical Demands

Record the appropriate frequency symbol in the space provided opposite each activity. Record in the Physical Demands Comments section for each activity marked present, supplemental or clarifying information pertinent to each activity, such as apparatus used; dimensions of workspace, tools, and materials used; speed, distance, duration, and frequency of actions; sensory requirements; and complexity of communications. In each instance identify the comments with the numbered factor and the activity to which it pertains.

NOTE: Physical Demands factors other than those cited may affect the Strength Level rating for a job. In instances when such Physical Demands are of a degree that the Strength Level rating is affected, assign the rating that accurately reflects the strength requirement of the job. Enter in the Physical Demands Comments section the justification for the rating.

Environmental Conditions

Record opposite each condition the appropriate frequency symbol (N, O, F, C), except for factor 5, Noise Intensity Level. For factor 5, consider: 1) the various levels of noise in the job, 2) how often each particular level of noise occurs in the job, and 3) how long each particular noise level lasts. Record the number that represents the noise intensity level which most closely describes the general background noise, or sound, present in the job environment. When there are varying levels, explain in the Environmental Conditions Comments section the levels, their frequencies, and sources. Record in the comments section for each Environmental Condition marked present, supplemental or clarifying information, such as temperature, duration, length of time, and source of condition.

NOTE: When the employer has installed protective devices which effectively eliminate the condition and the worker has no choice regarding their use, the condition is considered to be eliminated and is not present. The analyst should note this fact in the Environmental Conditions Comments section. However, when a protective device is subject to the worker's discretionary use, the condition is not considered to be eliminated and is reported as present.

Protective Clothing and Personal Devices

When present, list any clothing or devices, such as earplugs, masks, goggles, steel-tipped shoes, insulated gloves, and hard hats, which the worker is required to wear in order to protect the worker or the product against injury, disease, or contamination. Describe any item that is unusual or special and with which the reader will not be familiar.

ID Block

Enter the name of the analyst who prepared the report, the date the written analysis was completed, the name of the Field Center analyst who reviewed it, and the date the review was made.

If the JAR is reviewed by an official of the establishment, an officer of a trade or professional association or union, or another informed person, enter the name of the person, the organization, and the person's title but do not enter the name of the establishment in which the job was analyzed.

The following two pages contain sample Physical Demands and Environmental Conditions Forms.

PHYSICAL DEMANDS

ID NO. _____

Physical Demands	Comments

Strength

    Position

        Standing   _____ %

        Walking   _____ %

        Sitting   _____ %

    Weight/Force

	N	O	F	C
Lifting				
Carrying				
Pushing				
Pulling				

    Controls: Hand-Arm _____ Foot-Leg _____

1. Strength Level: _____

2. Climbing _____
3. Balancing _____
4. Stooping _____
5. Kneeling _____
6. Crouching _____
7. Crawling _____
8. Reaching _____
9. Handling _____
10. Fingering _____
11. Feeling _____
12. Talking _____
13. Hearing _____
14. Tasting/Smelling _____
15. Near Acuity _____
16. Far Acuity _____
17. Depth Perception _____
18. Accommodation _____
19. Color Vision _____
20. Field of Vision _____

ENVIRONMENTAL CONDITIONS

ID NO. _____

Environmental Conditions		Comments
1. Exposure to Weather		
2. Extreme Cold		
3. Extreme Heat		
4. Wet and/or Humid		
5. Noise Intensity Level		
6. Vibration		
7. Atmospheric Conditions		
8. Moving Mechanical Parts		
9. Electric Shock		
10. High, Exposed Places		
11. Radiation		
12. Explosives		
13. Toxic/Caustic Chemicals		
14. Other Environmental Conditions		

Protective Clothing or Personal Devices

Analyst _____ Date _____

Field Center Reviewer _____ Date _____

Additional Reviewer _____ Title _____

CHAPTER 13

WRITING JOB SUMMARIES AND DESCRIPTIONS OF TASKS

A JAR is an organized presentation of the facts about a job; it distinguishes one job from all others. The report includes the purposes, tasks, responsibilities, and worker characteristics of a job. Job summaries condense into one sentence the information contained in job descriptions.

Job descriptions, the products of job analysis studies, are derived from the collection, organization, and presentation of job data in accordance with USES occupational analysis methodology. The analyst should arrange and describe tasks that comprise a job in either a chronological or functional order. Tasks are usually arranged functionally when a job has no regular cycle of operations.

The job summary should reflect: 1) the significant involvement(s) of the worker with Data, People, or Things and the level of such involvement(s); 2) the assigned Work Field(s); and 3) the assigned MPSMS. In some cases, MTEWA and the work setting or type of establishment should be reflected. Jobs should be summarized in a concise, general way.

PREPARING JOB SUMMARIES

For a Things job with a significant relationship to machines or equipment (Setting Up, Operating-Controlling, Driving-Operating, Tending, or Feeding-Off Bearing), apply the sentence analysis technique to the steps used to prepare a job summary.

Start the sentence with a verb. This verb expresses the worker's action and reflects the assigned Worker Function for Things. Remember that "the worker" is always the implied subject of the verb.

Example: "Tends. . ."

Follow the worker action verb with an immediate object, which will be the machine or equipment used.

"Tends injection molding machine. . ."

Next, indicate the purpose of the worker action. For jobs rated at levels 0 (Setting Up), 2 (Operating-Controlling), and 3 (Driving-Operating), an infinitive should be used to reflect the purpose of the job. For jobs rated at level 5 (Tending) and 6 (Feeding-Off Bearing), the purpose of the worker action is introduced by the word "that. . .". The purpose, thus stated, should reflect the assigned Work Field(s).

"Tends injection molding machine that molds. . ."

Next, indicate the materials or products, as the object of the infinitive. Materials and products must be appropriate to the MPSMS rating assigned.

"Tends injection molding machine that molds resin pellets into plastic bottles."

For a nonmachine, Things-significant job (Precision Working, Manipulating, or Handling), begin the job summary with a verb that states the worker action in terms of the job's purpose; then follow with the MPSMS. Next, include in some logical order the basic work devices used (including, when appropriate, the types of work instructions followed). If a limited number of work devices are used, each type should be specified, such as ". . . using tweezers, eye loupe, and hand soldering iron"; if a variety of work devices is used, only the general types should be indicated, such as ". . . using variety of metalworking machines, handtools, power tools, and precision measuring instruments." The summary of a Plumber job illustrates the latter style format:

Assembles, installs, and repairs heating, water, and drainage systems, using variety of machines, welding equipment, power tools, and handtools, and following blueprints, specifications, and plumbing codes.

"Assembles, installs, and repairs. . . " states both the worker actions and the job objectives, while "heating, water, and drainage systems" are the products (MPSMS). Because the job is also Data-significant, the Data function (Compiling) is substantiated by ". . . following blueprints, specifications, and plumbing codes". The work devices (". . . variety of machines, welding equipment, power tools, and handtools") and types of instructions also substantiate the Things-function (Precision Working), which would otherwise not be evident by the action verbs alone.

For a job that is essentially Data-significant, begin the job summary with the worker action verb that matches or is synonymous with the Data Worker Function, and follow with the object of the verb, which must reflect information of some kind. For example:

Evaluates credit information to investigate credit ratings of bank customers.

"Evaluates" places the job at the analyzing level. Unless the job is also People- or Things-significant, only the Data involvement need be included in the job summary, as in the above example. If the job is Data and People- or Things-significant, begin the job summary with a verb that states the worker action in terms of the job's purpose.

For a job that is People-significant, begin the job summary with the worker action verb that matches or is synonymous with the People Worker Function, and state the object of the verb, which is usually the people who are dealt with or served. In the example below, the worker action "instructs" denotes the job objective (to teach), which need not be separately stated; the object of the verb is "students".

Instructs students in social studies and English.

In sales jobs, the object of "sells" is the commodity or service sold rather than the customers.

Sells shoes in men's shoe store.

Using discretion, additional information can be included in the job summary to indicate the work setting or type of establishment. This information may or may not be important for a complete understanding of the job's objective or MPSMS. The previous examples are expanded as follows to show how the work setting and type of establishment can be incorporated into a job summary:

Tends injection molding machine that molds resin pellets into plastic bottles, working in container department of pharmaceutical-manufacturing firm.

Assembles, installs, and repairs heating, water, and drainage systems, using variety of machines, welding equipment, power tools, and handtools, and following blueprints, specifications, and plumbing codes, working for plumbing contractor specializing in new construction.

Evaluates credit information to investigate credit ratings of bank customers, working for credit-reporting establishment.

Instructs students in social studies and English in private, parochial junior high school.

PREPARING DESCRIPTIONS OF TASKS

The description of tasks is the main part of the JAR and lists, in order, the tasks that comprise the job. Each task statement is numbered and includes an estimate of the percentage of time allocated to that task. Detailed task descriptions are preceded by flag statements summarizing the work elements that follow.

The organization of job analysis data from notes and the selection of the number and scope of tasks to include in the job description is an integral requirement of job analysis. The primary consideration is to organize the data and to write the job description so that the uninformed reader can gain a clear concept of the work performed.

Identifying Tasks

From the definitions of task and element (Chapter 2), it is shown that they differ in scope; yet an identical activity may be a task in one job, an element in another, or an entire job in itself. The identification of tasks is based on a multifactor approach, using the following questions as guidelines.

Can the activity readily be discerned to be a discrete task or element? If an activity is sufficiently distinguishable from other activities of the job, this may be an indication that it is a separate task. If not, it should be treated as an element, integrally related to other elements of a task by common purpose, sequence of actions, or decision-making factors.

Does the activity differ significantly from other activities of the job observed? This may be determined by different levels of involvement with Data, People, and Things, for example, or by machine- or-nonmachine-oriented activities.

Is the activity performed frequently enough to be included as a distinct task? An activity performed a small percentage of the time may be consolidated as an element of a broader task or included with other infrequent activities as a separate task. On the other hand, if an activity requires a significant percentage of the worker's time, this is an indication that the activity should be identified as a separate task. It should be noted at this point that two analysts, studying the same job, are likely to write job descriptions with different task breakdowns; provided both descriptions are clear, complete, and accurate neither will be any more "correct" than the other.

Arranging Tasks

Once the tasks of the job are identified, the next step is to arrange them in a way that results in a clear, logical presentation.

For jobs that have specific cycles or sequences of operations, arrange tasks in the order in which they are performed. The sequential arrangement is often applicable to production jobs in manufacturing that have a definite cycle. For jobs having no established sequence of operations, arrange tasks according to their function. Tasks so described may be arranged either according to amount of time spent on them or according to their relative importance in the overall job. For a detailed explanation of identifying and organizing tasks and grouping work activities into tasks see Appendix A.

Flag Statements

A flag statement is a short summary of a task that precedes the complete task description. A flag statement consists of a verb and its object and orients the reader to the scope and content of the task, about to be described, by stating in general terms what the worker does. It is important that flag statements be sufficiently comprehensive to cover all basic activities of the task. If it is difficult to develop a concise flag statement for a prospective task, this may indicate a need to separate the activities into two or more tasks. Flag statements may be written in Worker Function terms, such as "Compiles data", "Instructs students", and "Tends machine", or they may have other verbs, such as "Maintains files", "Prepares report", and "Responds to customer inquiries". The task description which follows the flag statement elaborates on the flag statement through specific action verbs, as well as the other categories of job information.

For example, the following task description amplifies the flag statement "Sets up lathe:"

Sets up lathe: Examines blueprints to determine dimensions of part to be machined, and calculates unspecified dimensions and machine settings, utilizing knowledge of shop math and metalworking. Threads and locks chuck on headstock spindle, and sets and tightens toolholder in tool carriage, using setscrew and wrench. Positions and secures workpiece in chuck jaws, using dial indicator and chuckwrench. Selects cutting tool according to specifications for metal type and cut, and clamps tool at prescribed cutting angle in toolholder, visually judging angle of cut. Sets and adjusts control levers to regulate lathe speed, utilizing knowledge of metalworking and machine operation.

Estimating Time Percentages of Tasks

Estimating and recording the time percentage of each task is one of the last steps in preparing task descriptions. Indicate in parenthesis at the end of each task description an estimate of the time required for its performance. The percentage should be allocated on the basis of 100% for all the tasks performed. The assignment of time spent on tasks is an estimate, not a precise measurement; estimates are rounded to the nearest 5% interval.

WRITING DESCRIPTIONS OF TASKS

These guidelines provide a framework for preparing job descriptions and a technique for evaluating their adequacy.

AREAS OF INFORMATION: Every job description must tell what the worker does; what gets done; the MPSMS involved; and the MTEWA used. This is essentially an extension of the "what, how, why" concept of the job analysis formula in use prior to 1972 when the HAJ was published. In addition, each description should reflect the ratings for Work Performed and the Worker Characteristics and indicate the criteria for acceptable work. These six areas of information are necessary to: (1) ensure uniformity of description content; (2) make certain that the minimum essential information has been included; and (3) simplify and standardize review procedures. The areas are called:

1. Worker Action

2. Objective or Purpose

3. Machines, Tools, Equipment, and Work Aids

4. Materials, Products, Subject Matter, and Services

5. Work Performed and Worker Characteristics Ratings

6. Criteria for Acceptable Work

The areas are defined and applied as follows, at least for the body of a job description, i.e., the description of tasks. The job summary is a special case, however, and is treated separately.

1. Worker Action. This is an active verb in the present tense, third person singular that reflects a specific action taken by a worker. It tells what the individual does as distinguished from what gets done as a result of the action. (This ultimately leads to the rated Worker Functions.)

   a. Examples of adequate statements:

      1) *Demonstrates*. . . merchandise, such as. . . to sell. . .

      2) *Turns* valves to regulate coolant flow. . .

      3) *Feeds* material into machine that stamps out parts. . .

      4) *Talks* with supervisors to obtain information. . .

NOTE: These examples are intended only to illustrate worker actions. They are not the only ways to write such work elements.

In the first example, the worker *demonstrates* to sell. In the second example, the worker *turns* valves to regulate.

b. Examples of inadequate statements:

1) "Stamps out metal parts of toys with punch press."

The writer has failed to distinguish between the worker action and the purpose of that action. In this job, the verb "stamps" is a function performed by the machine, not the worker. The worker really "feeds," "tends," or performs some other action in relation to the machine, but this worker action has been omitted.

2) "Fills paper bags with flour, using machine that automatically fills bags to preset weight."

The worker action has been omitted. The word "fills" is a function performed by the machine, not by the worker. The phrase ". . . using machine. . ." neither states nor implies a worker action since the reader cannot be expected to know what are the specific actions involved.

a) If the worker keeps the hopper of the machine filled by shoveling flour into it, the sentence should read: "*Shovels* flour into hopper of machine that automatically fills. . ."

b) If the worker starts, stops, and observes the operation of the machine, occasionally making minor adjustments to ensure an even flow, the sentence should read: "*Tends* machine that automatically fills. . ."

c. The verb sometimes reflects both action and purpose. When both are reflected in the same verb, it is not necessary to express them separately as awkward or wordy sentences may result. For example:

"Instructs students in principles of engineering." The verb "instructs" implies both the *action* of the worker and the *purpose* of the action. It expresses the worker action adequately because the more specific actions involved in instructing are well known to most readers. It simultaneously expresses the purpose because, unlike "machine" or "tool" jobs, there are no intermediate instruments through which the worker's actions are transformed into achievement of their purpose. In this case, the instrument is the worker. This situation usually occurs when the worker is dealing with people or data, rather than with things.

d. Worker action is sometimes implied or understood. For example:

"Assembles parts of wooden packing crates, using hammer and nails." Although the purpose "Assembles" is specifically stated, the worker action "*hammers* nails" is not. It is implied by the phrase "using hammer and nails." In the context of the example, the actions involved in using hammer and nails are sufficiently well known to make specific expression of an action verb unnecessary.

e. Worker action rule: EACH ELEMENT SENTENCE MUST REFLECT A WORKER ACTION. This must be stated specifically or implied in such a manner as to be obvious to the reader.

2. Objective or Purpose. This is what gets done as a result of worker actions. It has been discussed under Item 1. Worker Action since the two are closely related. There are two types:

a. The overall objective or purpose of a job, indicated in the job summary, which reflects the assigned Work Field(s).

b. The intermediate purposes that are the objectives of specific worker actions in the description of tasks. For example:

1) Operates. . . machines to *drill and lap* channels in industrial diamonds for use as wire drawing dies. . .

2) Turns controls *to regulate* speed of revolution and reciprocating action of drilling machine. . .

3) Operates machine that rotates diamond as revolving wire rocks back and forth in channel, *to lap* inner wall of channel.

"Operates" is a worker action. The overall objective appearing in the job summary is "*to drill and lap* channels in industrial diamonds." "*To regulate* speed. . ." becomes an intermediate purpose because it is the objective of a specific worker action in the description of tasks and is a step along the way to the overall objective. "*To lap*," the purpose of the worker action "Operates" in the last sentence, is another intermediate objective.

c. Objective rule: EACH SENTENCE MUST REFLECT AN OBJECTIVE. This must be stated specifically or implied in such a manner as to be obvious to the reader. (Remember that a single verb may sometimes reflect both objective and worker action.)

3. MTEWA. These include the machines, mechanical equipment, handtools, and work aids, such as jigs, measuring devices, and graphic instructions, used to attain an objective or perform a worker action.

a. Examples:

1) Counts number of red blood cells. . . using *microscope*. . .

2) Operates *turret lathe*. . .

3) Tends *power generator*. . .

4) Assembles. . . using *electricians' handtools*.

5) Inspects. . . parts, using *plug gauges*.

6) Saws furniture parts. . . according to *blueprint specifications*.

7) Repairs radios. . . following *schematic diagrams*. . .

This area of information is essential to an understanding of the worker actions and ultimately the nature of the skills involved in performing a job.

b. MTEWA rule: THIS AREA OF INFORMATION MUST BE INCLUDED IN EACH STATEMENT WHEREVER IT IS PRESENT IN THE JOB ELEMENT CONCERNED.

4. MPSMS. These are the materials processed, products manufactured or handled, subject matter dealt with, or services rendered.

a. Examples:

1) Positions *aluminum shingles* on roof and nails. . .

2) Threads *steel wire* through rollers of machine. . .

3) Instructs students in one or more *modern or classical languages*. . .

4) Renders. . . *beauty services* to patrons. . .

b. MPSMS rule: THIS AREA OF INFORMATION MUST BE INCLUDED IN EVERY STATEMENT WHEREVER IT IS PRESENT. This requirement is necessary to place the job in its general occupational area and to contribute to an understanding of the basic knowledge required. Repetition of the identical item throughout the job description, however, should be avoided.

5. **Work Performed and Worker Characteristics Ratings.** The definition for these components and instructions for making the ratings are contained elsewhere in the HAJ. The discussion which follows is concerned primarily with their applicability to writing the description of job duties.

a. **Relationship to Data, People, and Things.** In most jobs the worker relates in some degree to data, people, and things. Workers deal with instructions and information (data); with supervisors, fellow workers, or the general public (people); and with material objects (things). In many instances the relationship may be so obvious that no special reference is required in the body of the job description. For example, every job involves a relationship to a supervisor or to a set of instructions. Where these relationships are not significant, they may be ignored. In all other instances, however, wherever such a relationship is *occupationally significant*, the analyst must provide an indication of that relationship.

1) Examples of relationship to data:

   a) Saws pieces. . . to *blueprint specifications*. . . using handsaw. (In this instance specifications are a work aid in the form of data.)

   b) . . . to adjust fluorescent penetration depth. . . *according to density of casting*.

   c) Drives automobile. . . noting performance of engine. . . *as indicated by instrument dials and gauges*.

2) Examples of relationship to people:

   a) *Instructs students* in principles of. . .

   b) *Negotiates with sellers* to purchase. . .

   c) *Supervises workers* engaged in. . .

   d) *Serves* food *to customers* in. . .

3) Examples of relationship to things:

   a) *Saws pieces*. . . to blueprint specifications. . .

   b) . . . to adjust fluorescent penetration depth. . . according to density of *casting*.

   c) *Drives automobiles*. . . noting performance of engine. . .

4) Example of a job description from which the worker's relationship to data has been omitted:

DRILL-PRESS OPERATOR (mach. shop)

Locates and marks points at which holes are to be drilled. . . Selects drill bit and secures it in chuck of machine. . . Verifies depth and diameter of hole, using plug gauges.

In the first sentence, since no indication is provided as to how the worker knows where to place the holes (relationship to instructions and information), no inference can be made as to the difficulty of the decision made. If a template is used, then the worker's basic decision is quite simple and the following qualifying phrase would cover the situation: "Locates and marks. . . using templates." If the holes are located when the worker ". . . measures surface area, using ruler, square, and triangle. . . according to blueprint specifications. . .", then a more difficult mental activity is involved and a phrase as above would be required to convey this information. Of all three relationships, the one referring to data is most often overlooked. It is a significant relationship since it provides an indication of the body of knowledge on which the worker's actions or decisions are based. Only through this type of data can inference be made as to the difficulty or complexity of the decisions made or actions taken.

5) When judgments are made: The relationship to data is extremely significant whenever a judgment is made by the worker. In cases when the worker "estimates, ascertains, classifies, grades, locates, recommends, develops, judges, describes, selects, determines, or makes any sort of decision", the basis for the judgment must be given. This reveals, in part, the level of complexity of the job.

b. Worker Functions. These summarize the activities performed by workers. Each job is rated for a function in each of the "Data-People-Things" hierarchies. Worker Functions are broader in scope than worker actions, which are verbs that describe specifically what a worker does. The sum total of all the worker actions in a description, however, should lead the reader to an understanding of the three assigned Worker Functions within the respective hierarchies.

1) Rate the job for its Worker Functions before preparing the job description. After the job description has been completed, evaluate it against the Worker Functions to ensure that the ratings and description reflect one another.

2) The Worker Functions establish the level at which the job description is written. If a job has been rated for "tending," the description should not imply that the worker usually performs at an "operating" level. If a job has been rated for "analyzing," it is not enough to describe "computing" or "compiling" elements without describing that aspect of the job which justifies the "analyzing" rating. The sentence analysis technique described earlier in the HAJ will assist in determining the most pertinent Worker Functions and in selecting the most specific worker action verbs.

3) When preparing the description of tasks, the analyst should avoid using Worker Function verbs assigned to one hierarchy to describe actions taking place in another, for example: "Manipulates electronic research data. . . " The word "manipulates" exists in the "Things" category and refers to a worker's relationship to a tool. It may not be used to describe a relationship to "data" as in the above example because of the confusion which it creates.

4) The assignment of Worker Functions cannot be justified unless there is sufficient information in the description of tasks to support the rating. This information can be expressed directly in the form of tasks or can be implied by the content of the job description. For example, such functions as Operating-Controlling or Computing cannot be assigned unless they are justified by information that the worker has a relationship to a machine at the operating level or is involved with adding, subtracting, or another type of mathematics.

c. Work Fields. These are specific methods characteristic of either MTEWA or techniques designed to fulfill special purposes. Work Fields are broader in scope than the intermediate objectives of specific worker actions. The sum total of all intermediate objectives contained in a description, however, should lead the reader to an understanding of the rated Work Field(s).

1) Rate the job for its most pertinent Work Field(s) before preparing the description of duties. After the description has been completed, evaluate it against the Work Field(s) to ensure that the rating and description reflect one another.

2) Work Fields assist in establishing the method of achieving the overall objective of a job and are related to the actions involved. For example: ". . . operates. . . *to machine* metal parts. . . " The method involved is "machining" and it is related to the function "operates."

d. Worker Characteristics. These refer to the ratings for Physical Demands, Environmental Conditions, GOE Subgroup, Temperaments, and Aptitudes discussed earlier in the HAJ. The reflection of this type of data in a job description provides a sharper focus on the type of work involved and nature of the individual worker concerned.

1) Rate the job for Worker Characteristics before preparing the description of duties. After the description has been completed, evaluate it against the ratings to ensure that each reflects and justifies the other.

2) A balance must be maintained between the ratings and the description of job duties. If Temperament factor J was rated as present, some indication should appear in the description that describes the nature of the worker's use of judgment and decision making. If Numerical Aptitude was rated at the 2 level, a computational element that justifies that level must appear in the description. If the job was rated for Atmospheric Conditions, some implication as to the nature of the condition should appear in the description.

3) In the event that a particular rating cannot be justified in the job duties, an explanation should be made in the General Comments section of the JAR.

6. Criteria for Acceptable Work. Most jobs have standards or measures by which the worker knows when work performed is acceptable. In the preceding job of Drill-Press Operator, the finished holes are tested with plug gauges. The worker knows when work is acceptable if it passes this test of accuracy.

a. Other criteria: These include performance tests of a product or a worker's self-evaluation of work performed.

b. Not always readily-discernible: Criteria of successful performance are frequently integral parts of and implied by the job objective. For example:

Observes operation of conveyor used to transport. . . and. . . to prevent jamming. . .

The ultimate objective is *to transport*, while an intermediate objective is to *prevent jamming*. The worker knows that work performance is qualitatively acceptable when a minimum amount of delay results from jamming.

c. Not always significant: Frequently the worker is not concerned with the criteria because they are applied at some later stage in the production process or because they are built into the machine itself.

d. Criteria rule: THE ANALYST MUST MAKE AN EFFORT TO DETERMINE THE CRITERIA AND TO INCLUDE THEM IN THE JOB DESCRIPTION IF THEY ARE OCCUPATIONALLY SIGNIFICANT.

NOTE: These guidelines are not to be construed as an attempt to force every sentence into a rigid mold or to specify a particular sequence of categories to which the analyst must adhere. Insofar as practical, however, work elements should begin with worker actions since job descriptions basically describe jobs in terms of what the worker is doing. Beyond that, the analyst should express the work performed in a natural manner, maintaining at all times standards of accuracy and good English.

STYLE CONVENTIONS FOR RECORDING DESCRIPTIONS OF TASKS

The style to be followed in recording task descriptions should conform to the following basic rules:

1. A terse, direct style should be used.

2. The present tense, third person singular should be used throughout.

3. Each sentence should begin with an action verb.

4. Each sentence must reflect a specifically stated objective or an objective implied in such manner as to be obvious to the reader. A single verb may sometimes reflect both objective and worker action.

5. All words should impart necessary information; others should be omitted. Every precaution should be taken to use words that have only one possible connotation and that specifically describe the manner in which the work is accomplished.

6. The description of tasks should reflect the assigned Work Performed and Worker Characteristics ratings.

7. Avoid excessive, technical language. The analyst's job is to make a technical subject understandable to persons unfamiliar with the subject. Where technical words are universally used throughout an industry, they become usable occupational data. In such instances, however, a definition of the term should be prepared for Item 17 of the JAR or a parenthetical phrase should be added immediately following the item.

8. Avoid being pompous. Use a one-syllable word rather than a four-syllable word if both convey the same meaning.

    "A superfluity of culinary assistance is apt to exercise a detrimental effect upon the consomme." A sentence such as "Too many cooks spoil the broth" is sufficient.

9. Avoid the use of slang and colloquialisms. The meanings of such terms are usually obscure. If they are universally understood throughout the industry, however, they may be included in the description of tasks with an explanatory phrase.

10. The use of poetic license is a barrier to precise communication and should be avoided.

    "This stroke requires great incubus of judgment in elevation and strength and betrays the hand of the master when successful." An incubus is a form of demon and no person was betrayed.

11. The word used must reflect exactly what is intended.

    "The engineer wrote a *partial* account. . . " (incomplete or prejudiced?)

    "Although the *proportions* of all males and females in ages 16-45 are essentially the same. . . " Does the analyst mean percentage?

    ". . . cattle usually and commonly *embraced* in dairying. . . "

12. Select the word that best reflects the thought.

    Judgment is held in suspense; a chemical is held in suspension.

    A problem is unsolvable; an ore is insoluble.

    Steam was discovered; the radio was invented.

13. Do not compress more than one or two thoughts into a single sentence. Such compression is usually accomplished at the expense of clarity and readability.

    "Mixes, blends, purifies, screens, and extrudes smokeless and plastic propellant powders, cast propellant charges, and high explosive powders on a small lot basis, including manual and machine operations for nickel mercury amalgam."

"Trims flash from rubber gaskets, rings, swim fins and goggles, handlebar grips, and other molded rubber products, using scissors, knives, and cutting die and mallet, by holding product against revolving abrasive wheel or trimming knives, or by means of a tumbling barrel in which flash is made brittle with dry ice."

14. Make active and positive statements rather than passive, negative, or conditional ones.

"An outline. . . may *be of* help to. . . " (Delete underlined words.)

"The ore is *not un*common in. . . " (The ore is common in. . .)

"*Makes* analysis of. . . " (Analyzes. . .)

15. Avoid superlatives and certain types of adverbs. Superlatives give a false emphasis and certain adverbs weaken the verb they modify.

Avoid "most", "best", and similar superlatives.

"*Very* straight" doesn't make the object any straighter.

"*Perfectly* perpendicular" fits the same category.

16. Do not use the definite or indefinite articles, "the", "a", or "an". Clarity and readability are not lost when they are not used.

"Inserts tubes into designated sockets of tube tester and observes meter readings. . . "

17. Never use "etc." or "and so forth." If there are no additional examples to be included, end the sentence at the last example. However, to denote an incomplete list, the analyst can use the expression "such as."

"Examines watch dials for defects, such as scratches, finger marks, dirt, and uncentered cannon and fourth wheel pinions, using loupe."

18. Avoid using attributes.

"*Complex* controls, *intimate* knowledge, *large* billet, *heavy* tool, *small* spring. . . "

The precise meanings of such attributes are a matter of individual interpretation. One cannot expect the reader to interpret them in the same manner as the writer. The job description itself must convey the desired impression.

"Transfers watch parts from. . . to holding fixture, using tweezers and magnifying lens."

The impression left here is that the watch parts must be "minute."

19. Pretend that such words as "necessary, proper, and appropriate" do not exist.

"Selects *proper* cutting tool to. . . "

The reader cannot be expected to understand what is "proper" or the extent of judgment that enters into the selection process. These must be explained; as soon as the explanation is made, there is no longer any need for the word "proper."

"Selects cutting tool depending on depth and diameter of hole to be drilled. . . "

20. Linking certain prepositions with certain verbs sometimes results in a looseness of language. Yet, certain prepositions idiomatically follow certain words.

account for	aware of	adhere to	differ from (quality)
differ with (opinion)	parallel with	preference for	perpendicular to

21. Word sequence can be important.

"These ladles *only* were filled with molten steel."

"These ladles were filled *only* with molten steel."

22. The word "may" is not considered synonymous with "occasionally" and is never used in a JAR. If a work element is performed occasionally or infrequently, it may be written as a regular work element which begins with the words "occasionally" or "periodically."

23. The Job Summary or Description of Tasks on the JAR, as opposed to an occupational definition, should not contain the phrase "Performs any combination of the following duties".

24. Do *not* hyphenate before these words when they are the last word in a title:

   Helper; Laborer; Maker; Mechanic; Operator; Tender; Worker; etc.

25. *Do* hyphenate before OPERATOR when HELPER is the last word in the title.

   Example: DRYING-UNIT-FELTING-MACHINE-OPERATOR HELPER

26. Always use a comma before "utilizing" and "using" in the body of a definition.

27. A comma is usually used before phrases beginning with "such as".

It is important that the style conventions for writing described in this chapter be followed in order that JAR's reflect accurately, factually, objectively, and in a reasonably standardized way the nature and content of jobs. Adherence to these conventions should help to achieve this objective for the benefit of the user of the data.

DETERMINING DETAIL NEEDED IN JOB TASK DESCRIPTIONS

The analyst should keep in mind the necessity for stating a task completely but should not allow the explanation to develop into a motion study. For example, it may be stated that an inspector of small parts "Slides fingertips over machine edges to detect ragged edges and burrs."

On the other hand, it would be absurd to state: "Raises right hand one foot to table height, superimposes hand over mechanical part and, by depressing the first and second fingers to the machine part and moving the arm slowly sideways about six inches, feels with fingertips for snags or pricks that are indicative of surface irregularities." For a detailed explanation of determining the detail needed in Job Task Descriptions see Appendix B.

LIST OF FREQUENTLY USED AND MISSPELLED WORDS

acid bath
airbag
airbrush
air-condition (all forms)
air duct
airflow
air gun
airhammer
airhole
airhose
air line (line for air)
airline (aviation)
align
armband
armhole
armrack
armrest

ball mill
bandcutter
bandsaw
barrelhead
bathhouse
bathroom
bench work
boiler room
boxcar
brake light
Btu
burr (deburred, deburrs)

caulk
c.o.d.
coworker
cutout (n,um)
cut out (v)
cutterhead

data base
date stamp
diecutter
diehead
die holder
die maker
die mold
diesetter
disk
dragsaw
drawbench
drophammer
drumhead

dustpan

ensure (guarantee)
envelop (v)
envelope (n)

faceplate
feedbin
feed line
feedrack
feed roll
fiberglass
forklift

gauge
gasline (auto)
gas line (people queue)
gas well
gearbox
gearshift
go-not-go
guardrail
guideline

handbrush
handcart
hand drill
handgun
hand held
handhold
handsaw
hand shears
handtool
handtruck
handwheel
heat-treating (um)
heattreat (v)

insure (protect)

judgment

layout (n,um)
lay out (v)
logbook
logsheet

makeup (n,um)
make up (v)
mathematics
movable

multi (all one word)
multiple-purpose

non (as prefix, one word)

off bear
off bearer
off bears
oilcan
oilcloth
oilcup
oil field
oilhole
oil line
oil well
over-the-counter (um)

panel board
photo mask
photoresist
photosensitive
pickup (n,um)
pipe line (in industry)
pipeline (in definition)
plaster of paris
power hammer
powerhouse
power line
power saw
power shears
power shovel
power tool
programmed
programmer
programming
pre (all one word)

railcar
railroad
rest room
right-of-way

sandpaper
screwdriver
setup (n,um)
set up (v)
sheet metal
smooths
staff hour
staff year

stockpile
stockroom
straightedge
straight-edged (um)

tabletop
takeup (n,um)
take up (v)
teamwork
time book
timecard
timesheet
touchup (n,um)
touch up (v)
trademark
trade name
TV (television)

water hose
waterproof
whiskey
whiskeys
woodstock
woodworking
workbench
workday
workflow
work load
work order
workpiece
worksheet
workshop
work site
workspace
worktable

x ray (n)
x-ray (um)

zigzag

(n) = noun

(um) = unit modifier

(v) = verb

THIS PAGE IS INTENTIONALLY BLANK.

CHAPTER 14

THE JOB ANALYSIS REPORT

The Job Analysis Report (JAR) serves a dual purpose as the basic tool for: 1) structuring the analysis and 2) recording data. All items on the report should be completed. When information is not available for a specific item, enter "none" by the item. Reference should not be made to another JAR for information, such as the definition of a term, a description of a machine, or a comment. All attachments, such as drawings and diagrams, should be attached with pages numbered in sequence. All establishment job titles mentioned in any section of the JAR should begin with initial capital letters, except where otherwise specified. Additionally, all codes, estimates, and ratings should be internally consistent and supported by narrative information where required. When it is necessary to present additional information, Continuation Sheets will be used and interspersed in such a manner so as not to interrupt the flow of reading the report.

PROCEDURE FOR PREPARING THE JAR

ID NO.

The identification number of the JAR consists of the Establishment Number appearing on the Staffing Table Face Sheet (Chapter 16) plus a sequential number, starting with number 1, identifying the JAR. For example, the first of 20 JAR's for establishment number 362-99-1145 would be 362-99-1145-1 and the last, 362-99-1145-20. This ID NO. is recorded at the top, left-hand corner of each page of the report to identify each page in a document.

Item 1. Establishment Job Title

Record all job titles by which the job is known in the establishment. Enter the most commonly used title in initial capital letters and all other titles in lower case letters. Separate the job titles with semi-colons. When an establishment job title is ambiguous, enter a descriptive title in parentheses and discuss the title under Item 18. General Comments. For example, a descriptive title of "drill press operator" recorded in parenthesis provides more information than a non-specific establishment job title of "machine operator".

Item 2. DOT Title, Industry Designation, and Code

When appropriate, all three blanks in this item will be completed; however, as noted in case 3 below, there are times when some of the blanks will not contain an entry.

Code the job according to the occupational classification structure used in the DOT. The Work Field and MPSMS components represent the primary basis for classifying the job according to the Occupational Group Arrangement (the first three digits of the code) in the DOT. Other considerations include generic occupational relationships and industry (*Standard Industrial Classification Manual*).

> OCCUPATIONAL GROUP (first three digits): Three steps are necessary to determine the first three digits. 1) Read the definition of the occupational categories to locate the proper one. 2) Read the definitions of the divisions within the category selected and choose the appropriate one. 3) Finally, read the definitions of the groups within the specific division.

> WORKER FUNCTIONS (second three digits): In the code, these digits reflect the relationships of the job to Data, People, and Things, respectively.

DOT TITLE and INDUSTRY DESIGNATION: Review definitions listed in the Fourth Edition DOT under the code selected for the first three digits. This review may reveal three situations which are described below.

1. When the description of duties for the job analyzed is identical in all significant aspects to a published definition, record the Title, Industry Designation, and 9-digit code shown in the DOT.

2. When the job is identical in all significant aspects to a published definition but the code assigned varies from the published DOT code, enter the DOT Title and Industry Designation as indicated above. Enter the 9-digit code from the DOT followed by the analyst's assigned 6-digit code in parentheses. Discuss the reasons for any variance in Item 18. General Comments.

3. When the job is not identifiable to a definition within the Occupational Group Arrangement, record the six-digit code. No entries are made in the DOT Title and Industry Designation spaces.

When a job is studied to obtain detailed information to support an Occupational Code Request (OCR), enter information in the blanks for DOT Title, Code, and Industry Designation as follows:

1. When the description of duties for the job analyzed is identical in all significant aspects to the OCR definition, record the Title, Industry Designation, and nine-digit code of the OCR in the appropriate spaces.

2. When the job is identical in all significant aspects to the OCR definition but the code assigned by the analyst varies from the OCR code, enter the OCR Title and the Industry Designation as indicated above. Enter the nine-digit code of the OCR followed in parentheses by the analyst's assigned six-digit code. Discuss the reasons for the code variance in Item 18. General Comments.

3. When the job is not identifiable to a definition within the Occupational Group Arrangement or to the OCR, record the six-digit code in the appropriate space and leave the DOT Title and Industry Designation spaces blank.

Item 3. DOT Industry Assignment

Enter the code and abbreviated title of the DOT Industry assigned for study. For those instances where the JAR is not generated from a DOT Industry study assignment, enter the DOT Industry for the job studied.

Item 4. SIC Code and Title

Enter the four-digit code and short title from the *Standard Industrial Classification Manual* (SIC) for the four-digit classification of the major activity of the establishment. The major activity is based upon the principal final product or service of the establishment and not upon a product or service that is consumed or used during the process(es) of obtaining the final product or service. The primary four-digit SIC Code and Title entered on the JAR must match the four-digit SIC Code and Title used on the Staffing Table Face Sheet. The short SIC Titles are listed in Part II of the SIC Manual.

Item 5. SOC Code and Title

Enter the four-digit code and title of the unit group definition from the Standard Occupational Classification (SOC) Manual that best describes the job. When the SOC classification structure is not defined to unit groups, enter the major or minor group code as a four-digit number by using trailing zeros. For example, when the establishment job is best represented by the major group of Registered Nurses, enter 2900 rather than 29.

Item 6. GOE Code and Title

Enter the six-digit code and title of the occupational subgroup that fits the job. See Chapter 11, Guide for Occupational Exploration.

Item 7. Job Summary

Enter a brief, yet comprehensive, statement to provide the reader with the purpose and nature of the job. The sentence must reflect the significant Worker Function(s); Work Field(s); MPSMS; and when applicable, must reflect MTEWA. See Chapter 13, Writing Job Summaries and Descriptions of Tasks.

Item 8. Work Performed Estimates

During the observation/interview, the analyst should relate all of the worker's activities to the definitions of the Work Performed factors. This process will facilitate further analysis and evaluation of the information about the worker's activities so that the subsequent analysis of a job fits the accepted structure. After determining those factors important for job performance, record the data in the appropriate spaces for this item. Compare these selections and ratings with the data presented in Item 16, Description of Tasks, to ensure that each reflects the other and that no essential information is omitted.

> WORKER FUNCTIONS: Select the Data, People, and Things Worker Functions that best character-ize the job as a whole, and enter the appropriate code in each space provided. Circle the captions, Data, People, or Things, to indicate those which are significant in the job. Worker Functions are fully discussed in Chapter 3.

> WORK FIELDS: Enter one or more of the Work Fields (Chapter 4) that most adequately encom-passes the specific methodology(ies) that reflect the major objective of the job-worker situation. Al-though it is possible to select more than one Work Field, this is not necessary when one is ade-quately comprehensive.

> MPSMS: Enter the code and title of one or more MPSMS classifications (Chapter 5) that reflect the major areas of worker involvement. Use the exact titles of MPSMS categories rather than the specific examples presented in the Alphabetical Listing of MPSMS. Group titles and codes (ending in zero) should be used when three or more categories of a group apply.

Item 9. Worker Characteristics Estimates

During the observation or interview, the analyst should identify the worker characteristics important in job performance. These estimates are expressed in terms of job characteristics or preferences, not worker qualifications. These selections should then be compared with the data presented in Item 16, Description of Tasks, to ensure that each reflects the other and that no essential information is omitted.

Enter in the spaces provided for the Worker Characteristic components of GED (Reasoning, Math, and Language), SVP, Temperaments, and Aptitudes the level or factor that the job requires of the worker. Transcribe from the PD and EC sections: 1) codes N, O, F, or C which represent the frequency (Not Present, Occasionally, Frequently, or Constantly) of each factor in the job; and 2) the noise intensity level which best represents the job setting.

Item 10. Formal Education

This is education of an academic nature required by the employer that is obtained in elementary school, high school, or college. Using the table below, enter the single-digit code that corresponds to the highest level of schooling required by the employer for the job.

Code	Level of Formal Education
1	less than high school
2	high school diploma/GED
3	one year certificate from college or technical school
4	associate's degree (A.A.) or equivalent obtained at a two-year college or technical school
5	bachelor's degree (B.A.) or equivalent obtained at a four-year college or university
6	fifth year teaching certificate from a college or university
7	master's degree (M.A.) or equivalent
8	Ph.D or equivalent

Item 11. Vocational Preparation

There are six modes of vocational preparation. Each item should be completed with the employer's requirements as follows:

College: Record the degree, major field of study, and subjects required and the number of years of college training. Include graduate and undergraduate work. Enter the amount of time typically required to obtain the degree.

Vocational Education: Enter the number of years and courses that are oriented towards a specific vocational objective. Include both public and private secondary and post-secondary vocational training offered in schools outside the traditional college setting.

Apprenticeship: Enter the length, name, and type of apprenticeship.

Inplant Training: Enter the length of the training time and the nature and content of such courses given by the employer in organized classroom study. (The classroom may or may not be physically located at the establishment.) Do not include orientation or break-in time required for a worker to become familiar with the work place.

On-The-Job Training: Enter the length of time spent training an inexperienced worker to become fully qualified. Again, do not include orientation time.

Performance on Other Jobs: Identify the job(s) in this or other establishments in which the worker acquires knowledge and training to qualify for the job being studied; specify the length of time required for this training. (If the employer has experience requirements that in the analyst's judgment are not related to vocational preparation, these requirements, including job title and length of experience, should be explained in the General Comments section.) Make sure that any experience requirements are reflected on the Staffing Table.

Enter "none" for items not applicable. See Chapter 8 Specific Vocational Preparation for instructions for calculating SVP.

Item 12. Certification

List licenses, certification, or registration which indicate attainment of a recognized level of competence and which meet Federal, State, or local requirements and are required for employment in the job.

Item 13. Relation to Other Jobs and Workers

Promotions: Through interviews with company officials and interviews with and observations of employees, ascertain the promotional policies of the establishment.

Promotion From: Record one of the following four entries:

1.   When there is an accepted policy, enter establishment job title(s) from which workers are promoted into the job studied.

2.   Enter "bid system" when the establishment uses a bid system for the job studied.

3.   Enter "entry job" when no experience is necessary in another job in that establishment. (When a worker is not required to have any experience in that establishment but is required to have occupational experience in another establishment or to have specific training, enter that information in Item 11, Vocational Preparation with an explanation in Item 18, General Comments.)

4.   Enter "none" when there is no establishment promotional policy.

When "bid system" or "none" is entered and the analyst can determine the promotional path most establishment workers follow to reach the studied job, also enter "see comments" and record explanatory information in the General Comments section.

Promotion To: Record one of the following three entries:

1.   When there is an accepted policy, enter establishment job title(s) to which workers are promoted from the job studied.

2.   Enter "bid system" when the establishment uses a bid system.

3.   Enter "none" when there is no establishment promotional policy.

When "bid system" or "none" is entered and the analyst can determine the path most establishment workers follow when promoted from the studied job, also enter "see comments" and record explanatory information in the General Comments section.

Supervision and Direction Received: Enter the establishment job title of the worker from whom supervision or direction is received. This title identifies the worker who has authority to issue specific, detailed instructions or is responsible for workers during job performance. When appropriate, also enter the title of the intermediary, such as group leaders or senior employees, from whom directions are received. (An entry for this item does not automatically require a Worker Function rating of Level 3 (Supervising) for the job of the worker who gives supervision or direction.)

Supervision or Direction Given: Enter the establishment job title(s) of the worker(s) to whom supervision or direction is given.

Item 14. Machines, Tools, Equipment, and Work Aids

Describe all machines, tools, equipment, and work aids used by the worker. Include the size, approximate weight, and identifying information. Those which are commonly known to the lay person must be listed, separated by a semicolon; but need not be described. For a sample Item 14 see Appendix C.

Item 15. Materials and Products

List the raw material(s) or finished product(s) with which the worker is involved. Define any of these which are not common or have a unique application as used in the job.

Item 16. Description of Tasks

Describe in concise form the tasks performed, following the concepts and procedures outlined in Chapter 13. Each description must designate the worker's actions and the results accomplished; the machines, tools, equipment, or work aids used; materials, products, subject matter, or services involved; and the requirements made of the worker. This description must provide a basis for and be compatible with the assignment of Work Performed and Worker Characteristics estimates.

Item 17. Definition of Terms

Define all terms which are not readily understood by the lay person who is not familiar with the job.

Item 18. General Comments

Enter any comments or explanations necessary to expand upon the information presented in any of the previous items. The analyst should keep in mind the following:

1. All comments should bear a cross-reference to the section to which they relate.

2. Statements of opinion as opposed to statements of fact must be stated as such. The reasoning on which such opinion is formulated must be explained.

3. The General Comments section should be reserved for pertinent information for which there is no specific space allotted; information which can appear under other items should appear there.

PROCEDURE FOR RECORDING ESTABLISHMENT JOB TITLES AND DOT TITLES

1. Unless specified to be in all lower case letters, Establishment Job Titles should be recorded in initial capital letters. This includes the JAR, Staffing Table, and Narrative Report. Initial capital letters should also be used in Narratives when referring to departments by name.

2. DOT Titles are always recorded in all capital letters wherever they are used.

3. Unless stated otherwise in the instructions for completing a specific item, wherever DOT titles are used, they are to include the Title; DOT Industry in parenthesis; and nine-digit Code. They also are to be entered in that order when used in Item 16, Description of Tasks.

The five next pages contain a sample Job Analysis Report

JOB ANALYSIS REPORT

ID NO. _____

1. Estab. Job Title(s) _____

_____

2. DOT Title _____

    Ind. Desig. _____ Code _____

3. DOT Ind. Assign. _____

4. SIC Code & Title _____

_____

5. SOC Code & Title _____

6. GOE Code & Title _____

7. JOB SUMMARY:

8. WORK PERFORMED ESTIMATES

    Worker Functions   Data _____ People _____ Things _____

    Work Fields _____

_____

    MPSMS _____

_____

9. WORKER CHARACTERISTICS ESTIMATES

    GED: R _____ M _____ L _____   SVP _____ Temperaments _____

Aptitudes	G	V	N	S	P	Q	K	F	M	E	C
Level											

	1	2	3	4	5	6	7	8	9	10	11	12	13	14	15	16	17	18	19	20
PD																				
EC																				

10. Formal Education _____

11. Vocational Preparation | Length

    a. College Courses _____

    b. Vocational Education Courses _____

    c. Apprenticeship _____

    d. Inplant Training_____

    e. On-the-job Training _____

    f. Performance on Other Jobs _____

12. Certification:

    Licenses, etc. _____

13. Relation to Other Jobs and Workers

    Promotion: From _____ to _____

    Supervision or Direction Received (title)_____

    Supervision or Directioon Given (titles)_____

    _____

    _____

    _____

14. Machines, Tools, Equipment, and Work Aids

15. Materials and Products

16. Description of Tasks

17. Definition of Terms

18. General Comments

CHAPTER 15

PROCEDURE FOR PREPARING FOR AND CONDUCTING A JOB ANALYSIS STUDY

This chapter contains an explanation of the rationale and the procedures for preparing Industry Study Planning Reports (ISPR's) and for conducting complete establishment studies. As noted in the previous chapter, a JAR is used to record information about a job. Jobs are studied in establishments as part of an establishment study. Establishments which are likely to have jobs targeted for study must be identified through some systematic method. One such method is the ISPR.

INDUSTRY STUDY PLANNING REPORT

The ISPR consists of two forms. The forms are designed to facilitate planning concurrent studies of several DOT Industries and to provide a report that outlines the range and depth of the study of each DOT Industry. The establishments included in the planning report are to be what the analyst considers sufficient to represent the range of processes and products or services within the industry. The listing of specific establishments in no way implies that these particular establishments will be studied. Seventy-five percent of establishments chosen for study should be outside the Field Center's metropolitan area, and fifty percent should be outside the Field Center's State to the extent this is practical and feasible.

DOT Industries group occupations with similar activities; the *Standard Industrial Classification Manual* (SIC) groups establishments with similar primary end products or services. Therefore, DOT Industries have a relationship to jobs that is similar to the relationship the SIC has to establishments.

Many jobs defined in the specific activity of a DOT Industry are found in establishments which have a similar end product or service as defined in the SIC classification. However, some jobs of a specific DOT Industry are found in establishments that have seemingly unrelated end products and services. Therefore, a thorough study of occupations in a specific DOT Industry, as outlined in an ISPR, may need to include establishments which appear to have unrelated primary activities.

Analysts usually study all jobs in an establishment identified with a specific DOT Industry. However, as sufficient data are collected for some jobs, it is possible that in the interest of time, analysts will limit their study to selected departments, sections, or jobs for which there is insufficient data. Further, it is possible that some employers will not allow all establishment jobs to be studied. Therefore, the priority of jobs to be studied within establishments is as follows:

1. Top priority will be given to jobs that have or will probably receive the DOT Industry designation of the current study.

2. Second priority will be given to all other production jobs that convert to (are essentially the same as) production-type, cross-industry DOT Industries, such as woodworking, machine shop, and heat treating.

3. The lowest priority will be given to administrative and support jobs that convert to the cross industry designations of any industry, clerical, and profess. & kin.

Preparing the ISPR

Before studying any job, identifying an establishment as one with jobs in the DOT Industry, or contacting personnel in the establishment to request permission to study jobs, an analyst must become familiar with the technologies of the jobs and characteristics of the industry. With knowledge obtained through advance planning, the analyst will be able to talk with management, supervisors, and workers using language understood by all. Further, background information will provide a basis for objective observation and evaluation of job tasks and processes without loss of time. Background information may be obtained from:

1. Books and periodicals on technical or related subjects available in libraries.

2. Technical literature on industrial processes, job descriptions, catalogs, flow charts, organization charts, and process descriptions prepared by trade associations, trade unions, professional societies, establishments themselves, and Occupational Analysis Field Centers as part of previous industry studies.

3. Pamphlets, books, and job descriptions prepared by Federal, State, and municipal government departments, such as health, agriculture, labor, or commerce, which have interests in the industry or occupational area.

4. Annual reports and product literature of establishments to be studied.

FACE SHEET

The Face Sheet contains 1) information that defines the DOT Industry covered in the ISPR and 2) an index of the segments of the Industry reported on individual Segment Analysis Sheets. Enter, for each item below, information according to the instructions which follow the item heading.

IDENTIFICATION SECTION

OAFC

Field Center preparing the report (including identification number). Example: NC - 362

Date

Date (MM/DD/YY) report submitted. Example: 11/14/88

Priority

Priority to be given to the study of this DOT Industry in relation to others assigned.

Assigned Analyst

List name of each and identify the lead analyst when there is more than one analyst. Example: J. Smith (Lead Analyst), J. Doe, J. Green

Date to Begin Study

The date DOT Industry research is to begin. Example: 02/01/88

Expected Completion Date

The projected date of completion. Example: 01/31/89

Dot Industry Title (long and abbreviated) and Definition

Name and definition of the DOT Industry.

Segment

Breakdown the DOT Industry into four-digit Standard Industrial Classification codes, using the conversion table in the DOT Industry manual and the 1987 SIC Manual. From these codes, designate segments of the Industry to be studied based on industry processes and products or services. Record the segments on this section of the ISPR. Segment titles can be broader or narrower in scope than those in the SIC Manual or can indicate specific products after a more general title.

SIC Code

Four-digit SIC Manual code of each segment listed.

Sheet No.

Sheet number appearing in upper right corner of each Segment Analysis Sheet attached.

Resources

Names of professional and trade associations, industry consultants, and other resource persons or agencies contacted or available for contact from which information about the DOT Industry or a major portion of it can be obtained. When Segments of the Industry are so varied that industry-wide resources do not exist, record "See Individual Segment Analysis Sheets".

Reference Publications

Bibliographic references to publications, such as books, pamphlets, and articles used (or available for use) in researching the DOT Industry or several segments. Record "See Individual Segment Analysis Sheets" when the DOT Industry is too broad to be covered in specific reference materials.

Continuation

If additional space is required, continue on another copy of the face sheet form with references to the appropriate item.

The following page contains a sample Industry Study Planning Report — Face Sheet.

INDUSTRY STUDY PLANNING REPORT—FACE SHEET

OAFC _____ DATE _____ PRIORITY _____

ASSIGNED ANALYST _____

DATE TO BEGIN STUDY _____ EXPECTED COMPLETION DATE _____

DOT INDUSTRY TITLE (LONG AND ABBREVIATED) AND DEFINITION

DOT INDUSTRY ASSIGNED		
SEGMENT	SIC CODE	SHEET NO.

RESOURCES:
PUBLICATIONS:

SEGMENT ANALYSIS SHEET

The analyst uses the Segment Analysis Sheet as the form on which 1) to record the definition of a segment of the DOT Industry, 2) to identify representative establishments identified for potential study, and 3) to comment upon the rationale for including the identified establishments. Establishments need not have been contacted to be listed in the report. Some of those listed may not be studied for various reasons. Other establishments may have to be added to the report at a later date to complete the DOT Industry study. Enter, for each item below, information according to the instructions which follow the item heading.

IDENTIFICATION SECTION

Sheet Number

Consecutive page number assigned to each Segment Analysis Sheet in the report. Must correspond to sheet number listed on Face Sheet.

Abbreviated DOT Industry Title

Abbreviated title of the DOT Industry designation as it appears on the Face Sheet.

SIC Code & Short Title

SIC four-digit title and code. Use SIC Manual short titles as printed on pages 427-443 of the 1987 SIC Manual.

Segment Description

Title of segment, as listed on Face Sheet, followed by a brief description of the types of products or services included in the segment.

PLANNED ESTABLISHMENT CONTACTS

Establishment to be Contacted

Names and addresses of establishments representative of the segment and recommended for study.

Number of Employees

Number of employees in establishment, when employment can be determined.

Products or Services

Names of specific types of products or services of each establishment.

Remarks

For each establishment, comments with rationale for inclusion in report, such as importance of product, change in technology, comprehensiveness of operations, or size in terms of numbers of workers.

RESOURCES AND REFERENCE PUBLICATIONS

Resources

Names of professional and trade associations, industry consultants, and other resource persons or agencies contacted or available for contact, and that you plan to contact to obtain information about the segment reported.

Reference Publications

Bibliographic references to publications, such as books, pamphlets, and articles used, or available for use, in researching the segment reported.

Approved/Date

Name of staff member approving report and date of approval.

Continuation

If more space is needed, continue on another copy of the form.

The following page contains a sample Industry Study Planning Report — Segment Analysis Sheet.

INDUSTRY STUDY PLANNING REPORTS
SEGMENT ANALYSIS SHEET

Sheet Number _____

ABBREVIATED DOT INDUSTRY TITLE: _____

SIC CODE & SHORT TITLE: _____

SEGMENT DESCRIPTION: _____

_____

_____

	Establishment to be Contacted	Number of Employees	Products or Services	Remarks

RESOURCES:

REFERENCE PUBLICATIONS:

Approved/Date_____

PROCEDURE FOR CONDUCTING A JOB ANALYSIS STUDY

This section describes: 1) the procedures usually followed by an analyst in conducting a job analysis study and 2) the techniques used to secure detailed, accurate, and comprehensive job information.

Arranging for the Analysis

Before beginning a job analysis study, the analyst must contact management to obtain permission for an establishment study. Frequently, approval for a study can be obtained by showing management completed Job Analysis Reports and pointing out possible uses for this information. Appealing to the manager's sense of altruism may also be helpful. If previous job studies have not been conducted in the establishment, contact will have to be made with the head of the establishment, the industrial relations director, the personnel director, or the company official who has jurisdiction over contacts with government agencies. These contacts can be determined locally.

Before the analyst conducts a study, the establishment must be visited to ensure that management understands the aims of the study and authorizes it. Frequently, approval for a study can be obtained by showing management how the results of the job analysis study can be applied directly to any personnel management or industrial relations problems the establishment might have.

The purpose and general plan of procedure for the establishment study should be discussed and agreed upon with management. It is often helpful to provide management with a statement outlining the objectives of the study and the techniques to be used. Upon receiving management's approval to conduct the study, the statement can be distributed to supervisory personnel to acquaint them with the purposes of the analyst's visit or can be placed on a bulletin board for the general information of all personnel. When establishments have organized labor, a complete explanation of the study should be made to the officials of the labor union.

Whenever possible, prior to the actual analysis of jobs, arrangements should be made for the analyst to receive: (1) an orientation tour of the establishment; (2) introductions to department heads and supervisors whose cooperation is needed for a successful study; and (3) a list of establishment job titles, together with an indication of the number of males and females employed in each job.

The orientation tour provides the analyst an overall picture of operations, the general processes, and the flow of work within the establishment. During the tour the analyst should be introduced to the supervisors or heads of the departments where the analyses are to be made. The analyst should take this opportunity to explain briefly the major objective of the study.

The analyst should request information regarding departmentalization, the titles of jobs in the various departments, and the number of workers employed in each job. This information will be used to prepare the Staffing Table and to make initial determinations about the processes and jobs involved within the scope of the study. Reviewing a copy of the company's current organization chart may also be of help.

Obtaining Information by Observation/Interview

The observation/interview method of job analysis involves analyzing jobs by: (1) observing workers performing their jobs and (2) interviewing workers, supervisors, and others who have information pertinent to the job. It is the most desirable method for job analysis purposes because it: (1) involves firsthand observation by the analyst; (2) enables the analyst to evaluate the data obtained and to sift essential from nonessential facts in terms of that observation; and (3) permits the worker to demonstrate various functions of the job rather than describing the job orally or in writing.

The analyst uses the observation/interview method in two ways: (1) The analyst observes the worker perform a complete work cycle before asking any questions. During the observation the analyst takes notes of all the job activities, including those not fully understood. When satisfied that enough information has been accumulated from observation, the analyst talks with the worker or supervisor or both to supplement notes taken while observing the job. (2) The analyst observes and interviews simultaneously by talking with the worker about the observations as well as the conditions under which the job is performed. Here, too, the analyst should take notes in order to record all the data pertinent to the job and its environment.

The interview process is subjective; it is a conversational interaction between individuals. Since communication is a twoway process, the analyst must be more than a recording device. The amount and objectivity of information received depends upon how much the analyst contributes to the situation. The contribution is one of understanding and adjusting to the worker and the worker's job.

A good background preparation will enable the analyst to obtain facts quickly, accurately, and comprehensively. The analyst must be able to establish friendly relations on short notice, extract all the pertinent information, and yet be sufficiently detached to be objective and free of bias.

SUGGESTIONS FOR INTERVIEWING AND NOTE TAKING

Opening the Interview

1. Put the worker at ease by learning the worker's name in advance, introducing yourself, and discussing general and pleasant topics long enough to establish rapport. Be at ease.

2. Make the purpose of the interview clear by explaining why the interview is scheduled, what is expected to be accomplished, and how the worker's cooperation will help in the production of occupational analysis tools to be used for placement and counseling. Assure the worker that the interview is not concerned with timestudy or wages.

3. Encourage the worker to talk by being courteous and showing a sincere interest in what is said.

Steering the Interview

1. Help the worker to think and talk according to the logical sequence of the duties performed. When duties are not performed in a regular order, ask the worker to describe the duties in a functional manner by taking the most important activity first, the second most important next, and so forth. Request the worker to describe the infrequent duties that are not part of the regular activities, such as the occasional setup of a machine, occasional repairs, or infrequent reports. Infrequently performed duties, however, do not include periodic or emergency activities, such as an annual inventory or the emergency unloading of a freight car.

2. Allow the worker sufficient time to answer each question and to formulate an answer. Ask only one question at a time.

3. Phrase questions carefully so that the answers will be more than "yes" or "no".

4. Leading questions should be avoided.

5. Secure specific and complete information pertaining to the two categories of information required for a complete analysis of a job.

6. Conduct the interview in plain, easily understood language.

7. Consider the relationship of the job under analysis to other jobs in the department.

8. Control the interview with respect to the economic use of time and adherence to subject matter. For example, when the interviewee strays from the subject, a good technique for returning to the point is to summarize the data collected up to that point.

9. The interview should be conducted patiently and with consideration for any nervousness or lack of ease on the part of the worker.

Closing the Interview

1. Summarize the information obtained from the worker, indicating the major duties performed and the details concerning each of the duties.

2. Close the interview on a friendly note.

Miscellaneous Do's and Don'ts for Interviews

1. Do not take issue with the worker's statements.

2. Do not show any partiality to grievances or conflicts concerning the employer-employee relations.

3. Do not show any interest in the wage classification of the job.

4. Show politeness and courtesy throughout the interview.

5. Avoid use of any manner or language that might be construed by the worker to be condescending. Be friendly, objective, and natural in your approach when communicating with the worker.

6. Do not be influenced by personal likes and dislikes.

7. Be impersonal. Do not be critical or attempt to suggest any changes or improvements in organization or methods of work.

8. Talk to the worker only with permission of the supervisor.

9. Verify job data, especially technical or trade terminology, with supervisor or department head.

Taking Notes

The analyst must develop a skill of combining note taking with the conversational aspect of the interview. One must be able to write intelligible notes while engaged in conversation or be able to intersperse writing with fluent conversation.

Often in deference to the analyst, the worker will stop talking while notes are being made. The analyst should make it clear whether the conversation should or should not be continued in these circumstances.

Some workers object to a record being made of what they say. The analyst must decide how much the interview may be affected by this attitude and must make modifications accordingly. A small loose-leaf book such as a stenographer's notebook is best suited for recording notes while observing and interviewing. Some helpful suggestions for effective note taking are as follows:

1. Notes should be complete, legible, and contain data necessary for the preparation of the JAR.

2. Notes should be organized logically according to job tasks and the categories of information required for a complete analysis.

3. Notes should include only the facts about the job with emphasis on the Work Performed and Worker Characteristics involved. Use only words, phrases, and sentences that impart necessary information.

4. Sketches of machines or equipment, their controls, brand names, model number, and approximate dimensions are useful.

Obtaining Information by Other Methods

In some instances it may be impossible to observe or interview workers. In these cases the analyst should consider: (1) using establishment job descriptions or specifications supplemented by discussions with administrative and technical personnel; (2) obtaining job descriptions, specifications, hiring requirements, and related data for certain jobs from associations, societies, and other similar organizations; or (3) interviewing supervisors or managers.

Conclusion

The analyst's purpose, regardless of the method used, should be to obtain all the information necessary for the job analysis. The principal techniques of interviewing outlined in the observation/interview method can be adapted to fit other interviewing situations. Information gathered during a job analysis study should be verified, if at all possible, with establishment officials. On completion of the study, a letter of appreciation should be sent to the establishment management to thank them for all courtesies and cooperation given to the analyst.

CHAPTER 16

PLANT CONTROL CARD AND STAFFING TABLE

The Plant Control Card provides a link between occupational analysis documents and the establishment in which the analyst obtains information. The Staffing Table is a graphic outline of the jobs in an establishment.

PLANT CONTROL CARD

The Plant Control Card contains information about establishments in which job analysis studies have been conducted. Since no occupational analysis documents, such as Job Analysis or Narrative Reports, contain the name of the establishment in which jobs are studied, a Plant Control Card is the analyst's only record of an establishment's identity and location. Therefore, regardless of the number of jobs studied or documents prepared, the analyst must complete a Plant Control Card for every plant study. An example of a completed Plant Control Card is presented later in this chapter.

PROCEDURE FOR PREPARING A PLANT CONTROL CARD

FC NO. (Field Center Number)

Enter the three-digit identification number of the State or Occupational Analysis Field Center which conducted the study. A complete list of all agency identification numbers is in Appendix E.

ESTB EMP (Establishment Employment)

Enter the number of employees in the establishment.

ESTB SN (Establishment Serial Number)

Enter the sequential number assigned to the establishment study by the Field Center.

> NOTE: When combined, the Field Center Number, Establishment Employment, and Establishment Serial Number are the establishment identification number.

COMPANY NAME

Enter the name under which the establishment does business.

ADDRESS

Enter the address of the company. If they are different, enter both the mailing and street addresses.

SIC CODE

Enter the four-digit SIC Industry Number from the *Standard Industrial Classification Manual* (SIC) of the major activity of the establishment. (The major activity is based upon the principal final product or service of the establishment and not upon a product or service that is consumed or used during the process(es) of obtaining the final product or service.)

DOT INDUSTRY

Enter the three-digit code of the DOT Industry assigned for study. (DOT Industry codes and abbreviated titles are listed at the end of this chapter.)

PRODUCT

Enter, in lower case letters, the specific products or services produced or rendered by the establishment.

STUDY DATES

From

Enter the date on which the study began.

To

Enter the date on which the study ended in the establishment. (This is not the date on which analysts complete preparation of all reports relating to the establishment study.)

NARRATIVE REPORT

Enter "Y" (Yes) if a Narrative Report was prepared for the establishment study or "N" (No) if a Narrative Report was not prepared.

WORKFLOW CHART

Enter "Y" (Yes) if a Workflow Chart was prepared for the establishment study or "N" (No) if a Workflow Chart was not prepared.

ORGANIZATION CHART

Enter "Y" (Yes) if an Organization Chart was prepared for the establishment study or "N" (No) if an Organization Chart was not prepared.

STAFFING TABLE

Enter "Y" (Yes) if a Staffing Table was prepared for the establishment study or "N" (No) if a Staffing Table was not prepared.

NO. OF JOBS

Enter the number of jobs listed on the Staffing Table.

NO. OF JARs

Enter the number of JAR's prepared as part of the study.

ANALYST

Enter the name of the analyst(s) who conducted the study.

OFFICIALS CONTACTED

NAME and TITLE

Enter the name and position title of all officials contacted during the process of arranging the establishment study.

DATE

Enter the date officials were contacted to arrange the establishment study.

REMARKS

Enter any information that will not fit elsewhere which is necessary to clarify entries on the Plant Control Card or to note any pertinent information concerning the plant or the establishment study.

NOTE: The following entries on the Plant Control Card must be identical to equivalent entries on all JAR's prepared for the plant study: Establishment Number, DOT Industry Name and Code, and SIC Code.

SAMPLE PLANT CONTROL CARD

FRONT

FC NO. ___362___ ESTB EMP ___354___ ESTB SN ___1145___

COMPANY NAME ___Monument Stand, Inc.___

ADDRESS ___123 East Main Street___

___Any Town, NC 27272___

SIC CODE ___2821___ DOT INDUSTRY ___237___

PRODUCT ___polyethylene compounds and phenolic resins___

STUDY DATES: From: ___Feb. 27, 1984___ To: ___March 26, 1984___

NARRATIVE REPORT: Y	WORKFLOW CHARG: N	ORGANIZ. CHART: N	STAFFING TABLE: Y	NO. OF JARS: 96	NO. OF JOBS: 132
ANALYST: J. Smith and B. Jones					

BACK

OFFICIALS CONTACTED		
NAME TITLE		DATE
John Green, Personnel Director		1/12/84
Alice Newton, President		1/16/84
Bob Clark, Production Superintendent		1/16/84

REMARKS: Studied all jobs to obtain information about chemical production process.

The Staffing Table is a systematic arrangement of data on the nature and distribution of all jobs and workers within an establishment. (In some cases, where it fulfills the objectives of a specific study, a Staffing Table may be limited to selected jobs, departments, or processes.)

An initial Staffing Table completed prior to an establishment study provides the analyst with an aid for planning the study. Establishment Staffing Tables also provide information on industry staffing patterns.

The Staffing Table consists of a Face Sheet and one or more Title Sheets. The Face Sheet contains space to record such information as establishment identification number, SIC title(s) and Industry Number(s), number of employees, analyst's name, date of the study, types of products manufactured or services rendered, and comments pertinent to the study. The Title Sheet contains, for each organizational unit, space to record establishment job titles; their equivalent DOT titles; and codes in the DOT, SOC, and GOE classification structures; and the number of workers, by sex, in each job.

PROCEDURE FOR PREPARING THE STAFFING TABLE

STAFFING TABLE FACE SHEET

Establishment No

Enter the establishment identification number, which consists of the OAFC or State agency code number, the total number of employees, and the serial number of the establishment study, such as 362-99-215.

Date

Enter the date (month, day, year) on which analysts complete the data-gathering phase of the study.

DOT Industry Code

Enter the three-digit DOT Industry Code, from the list at the end of this chapter, of the DOT Industry assigned for study.

Number of Employees

Enter the total number of employees in the establishment, regardless of whether analysts study all departments or jobs.

SIC Code

Enter the four-digit SIC Industry Number from the *Standard Industrial Classification Manual* which represents the major activity of the establishment. [The major activity is the principal final product or service of the establishment and not a product or service consumed or used during the process(es) of obtaining the final product or service.]

Secondary SIC Code

Enter the four-digit SIC Industry Number(s) that represent secondary activities of the establishment. If there are none, leave this item blank. Enter only the SIC Industry Numbers of secondary activities which represent final products or services of the establishment and not those of products or services which are consumed or used during the process(es) of obtaining the final products or services.

SIC Industry Name

Enter the SIC short title of the Primary SIC Industry Number. (The SIC short titles are listed in Part 2 of the *Standard Industrial Classification Manual*.)

Name of Analyst(s)

Enter the name(s) of the analyst(s) who conducted the study.

DOT Industry Name

Enter, in lowercase type, the abbreviated DOT Industry, from the list at the end of this chapter.

Products Manufactured or Services Rendered

Record information concerning the type, size, and other distinguishing characteristics of the product(s) or service(s) of the establishment.

Remarks

Explain briefly the scope or purpose of the study. For example, explain whether the study covers all jobs at the establishment, jobs peculiar to a specific industry, or selected jobs. Also include any restrictions, such as time limitations, imposed by establishment officials. Explain briefly factors which may affect the number and kinds of workers employed, such as the installation of automated equipment or changes in methods or procedures. Indicate hours of work shifts. Note any follow-up visits made to an establishment in this section and indicate changes that have occurred since the last visit to any of the information reported elsewhere on the Face Sheet.

> NOTE: The following entries on the Staffing Table Face sheet must be identical to equivalent entries on all JAR's prepared for the establishment study: Establishment Number, DOT Industry Name and Number, and SIC Code.

STAFFING TABLE TITLE SHEET

Page

Enter the consecutive page number of the Title Sheet.

SIC Code

Enter the four-digit SIC Industry Number which represents the major activity of the establishment.

Estab. No.

Enter the establishment identification number corresponding to the one used on the Face Sheet.

Dept. No.

Enter the sequential number, starting with "1", of the department identified in the "Department Name or Estab. Job Title" entry. Leave the item blank when recording an establishment job title in the "Department Name or Estab. Job Title" entry.

Job No.

Enter a zero in this column when recording a department name in the "Department Name or Estab. Job Title" entry. Enter a sequential number, starting with "1", for each establishment job title recorded in the "Department Name or Estab. Job Title" entry.

M/F Employees

Enter the number, by sex, of workers in each establishment job. Precede the number by an "M" or "F" as appropriate.

EX

Enter an "X" when the employer does not require a worker to have experience prior to placement in the establishment job.

DEPARTMENT NAME or Estab. Job Title

Enter either the name of a department or an establishment job title.

For a department, enter in all capital letters the name of the department, unit, section, or other organizational subdivision for which job titles are listed.

For a job, enter in initial capital letters the job title used by the establishment. When the establishment uses more than one title to identify the same job, enter the most commonly used or descriptive title. When the establishment title is ambiguous or nondescriptive, also enter a meaningful, descriptive title in parentheses. (For example, the establishment job title "Operator A" might be more descriptively titled "Turbine Generator Operator".)

DOT TITLE

When the analyst determines that the establishment job is identical in all significant aspects (basic job tasks and worker requirements) to a published definition, enter in all capital letters the published Base or Undefined Related (UR) Title. If the job is not identical in all significant aspects to a published definition, leave this portion of the item blank. (When the analyst is unable to study the establishment job, leave this and the next four items blank.)

(ind. desig.)

Enter the published industry designation(s) of the DOT title appearing in the previous portion of the entry. Leave the entry blank when there is no equivalent DOT Title.

Code

When the analyst determines that the establishment job is essentially the same as an occupation defined in the DOT, enter the published nine-digit DOT code of the similar occupation. When an analyst determines that the establishment job is not the same as an occupation defined in the DOT, enter the six-digit code assigned to the job.

SOC

Enter the four-digit *Standard Occupational Classification Manual* (SOC) code of the unit group that best represents the job. (When the SOC classification structure is not defined to unit groups, enter the major or minor group code as a four-digit number by using trailing zeros. For example, when the establishment job is best represented by the SOC major group of Veterinarians, enter 2700 rather than 27.)

GOE

Enter the six-digit code of the occupational subgroup from the *Guide for Occupational Exploration* (GOE) which best represents the job.

JAR SN-Type & Remarks

Enter the Serial Number and Type of the JAR. This space may also be used for brief comments about specific jobs. (JAR Type is an internal means of denoting the type of information contained on a JAR.)

> NOTE: The following entries on the Staffing Table Title sheet must be identical to equivalent entries on corresponding JAR's prepared for the establishment study: Establishment Number, JAR Serial Number and Type, SIC Code, Establishment Job Title, DOT Title, DOT Industry Designation, DOT Code, SOC Code, and GOE Code.

The two following pages contain sample Staffing Table Face and Title Sheets. Note that specific entries on the Staffing Table are identical to corresponding entries on the sample Plant Control Card, presented earlier in the chapter, for this establishment.

STAFFING TABLE FACE SHEET

Establishment No.:	362-354-1145	Date	3/26/84
DOT Industry Code:	237	No. of Employees:	354
SIC Code:	2821	Secondary SIC Code	—
SIC Name:	plastics materials and resins		
Name of Analyst(s):	J. Smith and B. Jones		
DOT Industry Name:	chemical		

Products Manufactured or Services Rendered:

(1) Polyethylene compounds for use in plastic products and especially for wire and cable insulations. (2) Phenolic resins used in bonding automobile clutch and brake linings, grinding wheels, wood bonding and impregnation, thermal and noise insulation, decorative and industrial laminates, and industrial coatings. (3) Polystyrene compounds used in packaging materials, appliances, housewares, toys, furniture, and containers. (4) Phenol, formaldehyde, and acetone, for sale and for establishment use in intermediate products.

Remarks:

This establishment study was undertaken to obtain information about occupations concerned with chemical processing. The study covers all departments. There are three plant shifts in this establishment. During the first two, the establishment operates at full production; scheduled maintenance, repair, and cleaning of equipment and facilities occur during the third. The first shift is from 7:00 am to 3:30 pm; the second shift is from 3:30 to 12:00 am; the third is from 11:00 pm to 7:30 am. All production shifts work five days per week from 7:00 am Monday through 7:30 am Saturday. The office staff works five days per week from 8:15 am Monday through 4:45 pm Friday.

Dept. No.	Job No.	M/F Employees		EX	DEPARTMENT NAME or Estab. Job Title DOT TITLE (ind. design.) Code SOC GOE	JAR SN-Type & Remarks
1	0				PULVERIZED RESINS	
	1	M1			Distribution Specialist MATERIAL EXPEDITER (clerical) 221.367-042 4752 05.09.02	1–V Team Leader
	2	M4	F1	X	Warehouse Attendant INDUSTRIAL-TRUCK OPERATOR (any industry) 921.683-050 8318 06.04.40	2–V
	3	M4	F5	X	General Operator (Grinder Operator) 558.362 7677 06.02.11	3–B
	4	M8			Still Room Operator A CHEMICAL OPERATOR III (chemical) 559.382-018 7676 06.01.03	4–V
2	0				BUTYL ROOM	
	1	M8			Chief Operator 559.132 7100 06.01.01	5–B
	2	F4			General Operator CHEMICAL OPERATOR III (chemical) 559.382-018 7676 06.01.03	See JAR No. 4–V
	3	M3			Process Unit Operator STILL-OPERATOR HELPER (chemical) 552.685-030 7666 06.04.11	6–V
	4	M2		X	Flaker FLAKER OPERATOR (chemical; smelt & refin.) 559.685-074 7676 06.04.11	7–V
3	0				PHENOL PLANT	
	1	M1			Production Department Head GENERAL SUPERVISOR (any industry) 183.167-018 1320 05.02.03	8–V (183.161)
	2	F1			Senior Chemist CHEMIST, ANALYTICAL (profess. & kin.) 022.061-010 1845 02.01.01	9–V

STAFFING TABLE TITLE SHEET   Page 1   SIC Code: 2821   Estab. No.: 362-354-1145

agric. equip. - 121

agriculture - 116

aircraft mfg. - 123

air trans. - 125

amuse. & rec. - 133

any industry - 138

auto. mfg. - 151

automotive ser. - 154

bakery products - 164

beverage - 168

boot & shoe - 176

brick & tile - 178

build. mat., nec - 186

business ser. - 187

button & notion - 191

can. & preserv. - 214

carpet & rug - 226

cement - 231

chemical - 237

clerical - 249

clock & watch - 251

comm. equip. - 725

concrete prod. - 264

construction - 271

cutlery-hrdwr. - 294

dairy products - 313

domestic ser. - 319

education - 335

elec. equip. - 341

electron. comp. - 343

electroplating - 345

engine-turbine - 351

engraving - 352

fabrication, nec - 366

financial - 375

fishing & hunt. - 381

food prep., nec - 385

forestry - 387

forging - 391

foundry - 393

fur goods - 399

furniture - 401

galvanizing - 405

garment - 409

glass mfg. - 411

glass products - 415

glove & mit. - 419

government ser. - 425

grain-feed mills - 427

hat & cap - 441

heat treating - 444

hotel & rest. - 453

house. appl. - 456

inst. & app. - 466

insurance - 473

jewelry-silver. - 484

knitting - 494

laundry & rel. - 516

leather mfg. - 518

leather prod. - 522

library - 524

light. fix. - 529

logging - 544

machinery mfg. - 557

machine shop - 561

machine tools - 563

meat products - 831

medical ser. - 573

metal prod., nec - 362

mfd. bldgs. - 568

military ser. - 574

millwork-plywood - 576

mine & quarry - 578

motion picture - 589

motor-bicycles - 592

motor trans. - 593

museums - 597

musical inst. - 595

narrow fabrics - 615

nonfer. metal - 632

nonmet. min. - 633

nonprofit org. - 634

nut & bolt - 636

office machines - 644

oils & grease - 646

optical goods - 648

ordnance - 651

paint & varnish - 657

paper & pulp - 661

paper goods - 664

pen & pencil - 671

personal ser. - 674

petrol. & gas - 677

petrol. refin. - 679

pharmaceut. - 323

photo. appar. - 683

photofinishing - 684

pipe lines - 687

plastic prod. - 364

plastic-synth. - 691

plumbing-heat. - 693

pottery & porc. - 696

print. & pub. - 699

profess. & kin. - 705

protective dev. - 673

radio-tv broad. - 724

railroad equip. - 542

real estate - 731

recording - 733

retail trade - 741

r.r. trans. - 751

rubber goods - 754

rubber reclaim. - 756

rubber tire - 761

sanitary ser. - 815

saw. & plan. - 817

ship-boat mfg. - 824

smelt. & refin. - 832

soap & rel. - 835

social ser. - 836

steel & rel. - 171

stonework - 845

struct. metal - 847

sugar & conf. - 851

svc. ind. mach. - 735

tel. & tel. - 869

tex. prod., nec - 873

textile - 875

tinware - 877

tobacco - 881

toy-sport equip. - 883

utilities - 532

vehicles, nec - 885

water trans. - 941

waterworks - 943

welding - 945

wholesale tr. - 948

wood. container - 957

wood prod., nec - 962

woodworking - 964

CHAPTER 17

ORGANIZATION AND WORKFLOW CHARTS

Organization Charts and Workflow Charts provide useful information in a limited space; therefore, a brief discussion of their construction is included here. Where such charts are used, cross-references should be made to them at appropriate points in the Narrative Report (see Chapter 18).

When preparing charts in the field, a clear, freehand pencil chart is adequate. In preparing finished charts, the analyst should concentrate on accuracy and clarity.

ORGANIZATION CHARTS

An organization chart shows graphically the organizational arrangement and the relationships among the subdivisions. Generally, one of two types of organization charts accompanies a narrative report. The first is an overall chart of the organization showing the relationship among subdivisions. The second is a chart of the subdivisions showing the relationship among jobs within each subdivision. Charts of the subdivisions are especially helpful when large establishments are studied. When the overall chart is used, it should be accompanied by chart(s) showing relationships among jobs. In no instance should a chart show a mixture of the names of jobs, departments, work processes, and subdivisions.

One method of developing charts is as follows: 1) write the titles of individual units that will appear on the chart on separate slips of paper; 2) arrange these slips of paper in descending order of authority; 3) place the units which have the same level of authority side by side; 4) sketch this layout in rough draft; and 5) connect the units with lines to show the appropriate relationship.

COMPONENTS OF AN ORGANIZATION CHART

In an organization chart, boxes represent the units of the organization. They depict: 1) jobs, positions, or groups of workers in one or more job titles; 2) divisions, departments, sections, or other organizational units; or 3) broad functions of workers or organizational units.

Lines indicate channels of authority, accountability, or cooperation. They must be straight and should be charted vertically or horizontally.

> **Solid** lines are used to indicate line authority (the authority to direct operations, supervise workers, give orders, or enforce compliance) and link units in a chain of command.

> **Dashed** lines are used to indicate functional authority. Functional authority is the authority to advise, assist, support, or inform management or operating staff but not the authority to direct and supervise.

> **Dotted** lines are used to indicate cooperation. Since nominal cooperation among units typically exists in any establishment and excessive use of lines only clutters the chart, cooperation should be indicated only when it is pronounced.

Captions are placed in boxes to identify job titles, divisions, departments, or sections.

Titles of Organization Charts consist of the identification number of the establishment, the name of the division or department covered by the chart, and the SIC Code of the establishment.

Simplicity and Clarity

The organization chart should be easy to follow and understand. It should show formal reporting relationships only. Do not attempt to show informal relationships nor convey other types of information by using footnotes, symbols, or elaborate devices; this will only cause clutter or confusion.

Balance

Arrange the chart so that the alignment and spacing of boxes and lines are reasonably balanced and uncrowded. To accomplish this, charting techniques often must be applied imaginatively. While few organizations can be charted symmetrically, most charts can be organized in an eye-appealing manner.

Recency

The chart should portray the organization as of the date of the study and not show projected jobs or unimplemented organizational changes.

Consistency

Unit and job titles and lines of authority on the chart should reflect official company titles and should be consistent with those used or indicated in other job analysis forms prepared in the current study. The content of chart captions should be consistent; for example, if the analyst includes the number of positions after each job title, all boxes must contain that information.

Purpose

The chart should show organizational structure and reporting relationships only. Do not attempt to show status, importance, or responsibility of jobs or subdivisions by any means, such as the relative size of the boxes.

A sample Organization Chart is included on the next page for illustration.

ORGANIZATIONAL CHART
Establishment No. 362-307-901
SIC: 9999

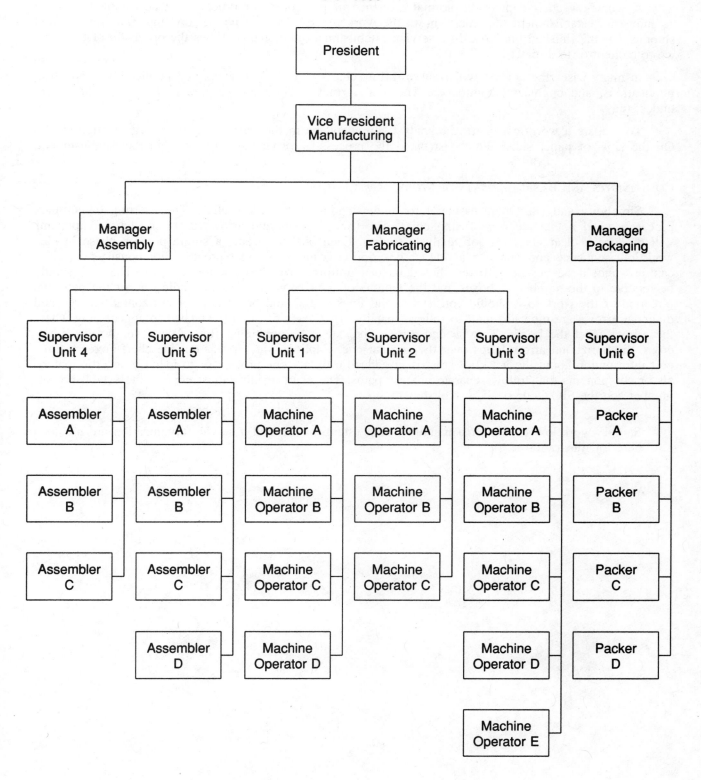

WORKFLOW CHARTS

A workflow chart depicts the normal sequence of procedures or processes at an establishment. In an industrial establishment, the chart shows the work process from arrival of raw materials through the shipment of the finished products. In a service establishment, the chart outlines the provision of the service to a client or to a material.

In many cases the analyst will find workflow charts in technical books and publications, industrial publications, and engineers' handbooks. The analyst may adapt these sources to fit the establishment under study.

To prepare a workflow chart, the analyst can adapt the method used to prepare organization charts. On the slips of paper substitute the steps in the process or service for the units in the establishment.

COMPONENTS AND BASIC FORMATS OF WORKFLOW CHARTS

Simplicity and clarity are essential for understanding a workflow chart. The charting of complex processes need not create a confusing chart. The use of boxes and arrows as basic chart components will produce a clear chart for job analysis studies. Each box represents a single process phase in the workflow sequence and contains a title or description (caption) of that process. For consistency, chart captions should be gerunds. Boxes should have a uniform size throughout the chart. The size should be relative to the number of boxes and the lengths of their captions. Arrows, indicators of the path and direction of the workflow, should consist of solid lines and should be vertical or horizontal. Curved and diagonal arrows are more difficult to follow visually. The heads of the arrows need to appear only where the arrows meet the boxes. Two-headed arrows indicate a bi-directional flow. Whenever arrows must cross, the horizontal arrow loops over the vertical one. Captions may appear outside chart boxes to impart information about the workflow that is not specific to any one process or to identify specific materials or components that follow separate process paths. The chart heading must contain the establishment number and the SIC Code of the establishment.

Sample workflow charts for a manufacturing establishment and a service organization are included here for illustration.

WORKFLOW CHART
Establishment No. 362-307-901
SIC: 9999

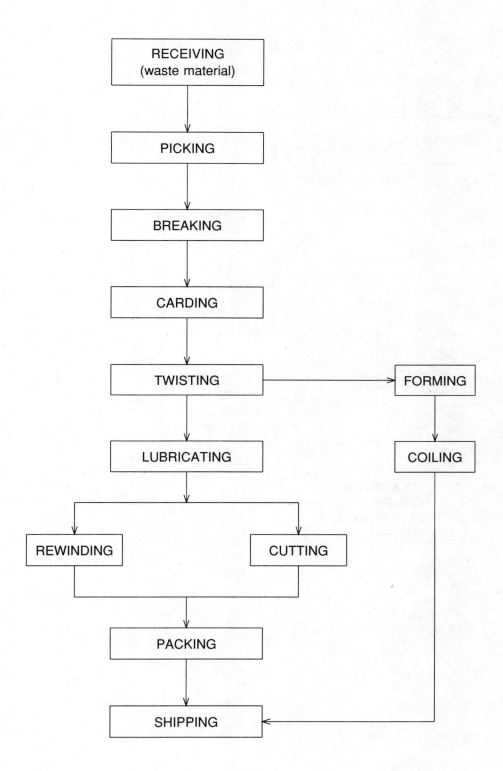

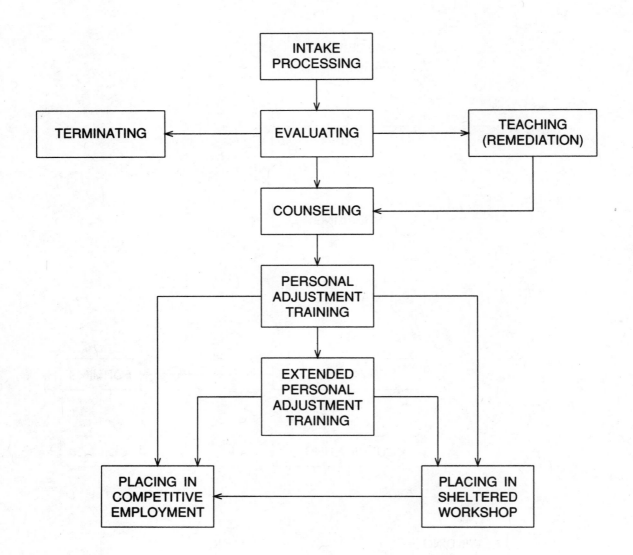

CHAPTER 18

THE NARRATIVE REPORT

The narrative report is an introduction to information about an establishment. A good narrative report provides background for the particular study and orients the reader to the jobs as they existed at that time. This information provides the reader with broad general occupational and industrial information which cannot be included in the JAR.

COMPILING DATA

The information in a narrative report is obtained from discussions with workers, establishment officials, industry experts, college or technical school personnel, and from a review of the technical literature of the industry. The information gathered during this process should relate to the structure or organization of the establishment, the interrelationships of the jobs, the workflow processes, personnel policies and practices, hazards, and other items which may contribute to job information. Much of this information can be obtained during the orientation tour (Chapter 15). The following list contains examples of questions the analyst should ask:

1. (For industrial establishments) What is the purpose of the establishment? What are the processes by which raw materials are converted to finished products? (For non-industrial establishments) What is the nature of the service rendered? What knowledge or technologies are required for adequate job performance? How is the service rendered? What are the general job duties or procedures?

2. What are the general environmental conditions of the work place? Are any hazards encountered by workers? Are any working conditions peculiar to the establishment?

3. Are the services or workflow of the establishment divided into departments or units? If so, how? How are these units interrelated? How are they arranged in the workflow process?

4. What are the personnel practices? Does a career lattice exist in this establishment? What are the entry jobs? Are training courses provided by the establishment?

5. Does this establishment have any unique characteristics in comparison to other establishments in the industry? What is the history of the development of the establishment? Has it been automated or has management initiated any progressive or unusual processes, equipment, or services? What effects have these new ideas or machinery had on the work performed and on the employment level of the establishment?

ORGANIZING MATERIALS

Generally, the data obtained through the discussions with establishment personnel or other technical experts can be placed under several major headings. Liberal use of headings and subheadings, even in a short report, will provide the reader with a reference to the particular sections of the report and will provide a text that is easier and more interesting to read. In addition, the use of headings will help the analyst organize materials and set limits on the amount of information to be included.

Since each analyst's report and presentation will include different types of data, a standard report outline cannot be established. However, a few general headings have been used in most reports. The outline below presents these headings and typical items in their contents. A report may not include all these headings or it may include additional ones as needed.

Introduction or Purpose of Establishment

    Purpose

    Scope and limit of study

    History and development of the establishment

Environmental Conditions

    Description of layout

    Description of equipment

    General environmental conditions and general working conditions

Organization and Operations or Activities

    Departmentalization of establishment

    Workflow

    Processes (industrial establishments)

    Services (non-industrial establishments)

Personnel Policies and Practices

    Hiring requirements

    Recruitment and sources of workers

    Methods of training

    Entry jobs

    Career lattices and promotional opportunities

    Job restructuring

    Effects of automation on personnel

Other Sections

    Comments

    Effects of automation on establishment or industry

Appendix and Glossary

WRITING THE REPORT

Introduction or Purpose of the Establishment

This section should begin with a statement about the product or service of the establishment. If the study is in an industrial plant, this section should include a general discussion of the raw materials and processes used and the range and variety of products produced. If a non-industrial establishment is studied, the section should include a description of the nature of the service and to whom and how the service is rendered. The establishment number which appears at the top of the first page beneath the words "Narrative Report" is used to identify the establishment. The primary SIC Code used on the Narrative Report should be identical to the one used on the Staffing Table form. The name of the establishment is not used in the report. Frequently, this section includes a history of the establishment, future plans of the establishment, and future trends in the industry.

Any restrictions which the employer imposes on the study and which affect the preparation of JAR's should be noted here. For example, the employer may limit or bar access to jobs involving secret processes.

Environmental Conditions

This section includes a description of the layout and size of the establishment. This gives the reader a picture of the physical arrangement of buildings, facilities, equipment, storage, or related areas as they affect workflow. The narration in this section includes information about working conditions and equipment, machines, or tools used. The description given here is concerned with the overall establishment picture and furnishes information not contained in the individual JAR's.

Organization and Activities

An explanation of the organization of the establishment gives an orientation to the individual reports. This section might begin with a discussion of the units of organization, the processes or major activities, and their relation to the workflow. This presentation could be followed by a more detailed description of the units, processes, or activities. This section should provide a visualization of the total work situation in which the worker fits.

Personnel Policies and Practices

This section contains information about the establishment's hiring requirements and methods of placement. Included are educational, physical, and other requirements; the employer's methods of recruitment; and the policy and practice in hiring. In addition, subsections may deal with methods of entry, training given or sanctioned by the establishment, the presence of union affiliation, apprenticeship programs, regulated occupations, and career lattices and promotional opportunities.

If the purpose of the study is to find job-worker situations which can be restructured or if the establishment has practiced some form of job restructuring, it should be noted here. Also, if the establishment has been automated and if the automation has had significant impact on employment, that information should be presented here. The discussion should include the effects of restructuring or automation on placement policies and practices, on employment statistics, and on any changes in educational and training requirements.

Other Sections

Sometimes a report needs to include a section or sections devoted to special or unique topics. For example, the analyst may include a section about the product market or about special factors affecting workflow in the establishment. The discussion of the history of the establishment or of future trends in the establishment or industry may appear here rather than in the introduction or purpose of the establishment section.

At times this section needs to include information about the effects of automation or mechanization in an industry or establishment. In these instances, a discussion of the effects of automation on personnel should appear in the personnel policies and practices section; all other aspects of automation or mechanization, such as changes in equipment, changes in processes or activities, or effects on working conditions and physical requirements, should be included in a section at the end of the report.

Appendix and Glossary

In the course of the study, the analyst may obtain materials such as brochures or forms, which might add to the report. These should be included in an appendix. Technical terms, processes, or equipment which need to be clarified should be included in a glossary at the end of the report.

GUIDELINES FOR REPORT WRITING

The writing of a narrative report is the process of converting the information secured into usable reference material. The report contains pertinent and essential information in the fewest possible words, and should be consistent with proper English grammar usage.

1. The analyst should distinguish between statements based on fact and those based on opinions. At times, statements of opinions enhance the value of the narrative by rendering an overall picture of the study. However, any sources of opinion should be identified as ''In the analyst's opinion'' or ''The personnel manager states. . .''. Crediting a statement thus, while indicating that the statement is not substantiated completely, gives authority for the opinion and lends weight to it.

2. A paragraph must be built around one central thought. Sentences not contributing to that specific thought do not belong in the paragraph. However, breaks between paragraphs serve as resting points for the reader and paragraphs of more than 200 or so words should not be used.

3. Suitable transition statements are necessary for the reader to follow the changing thought from paragraph to paragraph. Even when main headings and subheadings are used, the transition should be such that the reader understands that one thought has been completed and the next is beginning.

4. The emphatic position of the first sentence in a paragraph should not be wasted by the writer. Because of its position of emphasis, the opening sentence often is used to state a central thought which the remainder of the paragraph expands and supports. At other times, it points the direction in which the new paragraph will move away from the preceding paragraph.

5. The main headings may be centered. Secondary headings then can be placed at the left margin. Third-order headings (usually to be avoided) might be placed in the text. Label headings should be avoided. For example, while Plant Environmental Factors is adequate for a very broad heading, a subheading under it should say: Physical Layout of Departments rather than Layouts. The format should be consistent.

An example of a Narrative Report is included on the following pages.

NARRATIVE REPORT

Establishment No. 362-150-392

SIC: 2281

PURPOSE OF ESTABLISHMENT

This establishment is a processing plant within a synthetic yarn-producing division of a yarn and thread manufacturing corporation. It is engaged in spinning yarn from synthetic fibers for use in manufacturing such articles as hosiery, pile fabrics, and men's and women's outerwear. Basic yarn counts produced range from 6's to 30's both single and plied.

Prior to 1959, this plant was engaged in the manufacture of carded cotton knitting yarns of coarse to medium count. The transition to producing synthetic yarns was completed in early 1959 with the installation of machinery developed for manufacturing synthetic yarn. This continuous processing system is a variation of the cotton processing system eliminating the processes which involved opening, cleaning, and transforming cotton fibers into laps preparatory to the carding process. This development is due to the fact that synthetic staples do not require extensive opening and cleaning as do natural fibers. The establishment has 9,792 spinning spindles, producing in excess of 175,000 pounds of synthetic yarn weekly.

PERSONNEL POLICIES AND PRACTICES

Training for production jobs in this plant is usually on-the-job. Training periods extend from two weeks up to two years, the latter applicable to those persons engaged in setting up and repairing various machinery. No specialized training is required for entry jobs, only a general education being sufficient for communicating with coworkers and for learning the required tasks of the job. There are no definite lines of promotion; however, workers are upgraded into jobs that require more experience and skill as vacancies arise based on their industriousness and willingness to assume responsibility. This is an equal opportunity establishment. There are no restrictions on the employment, training, and promotion of minority groups, women, or the handicapped. This establishment works three shifts.

ORGANIZATION AND OPERATIONS

The Plant Superintendent coordinates production activities for the plant. Subordinate supervisory personnel include a Card Room Supervisor, Spinning Room Supervisor, Shipping and Outside Supervisor, and Machinist. A Shift Supervisor for both the second and third shifts works under the combined supervision of the Card Room Supervisor and Spinning Room Supervisor. This study was limited to the observation of production jobs.

Receiving

Synthetic fibers are shipped to the plant by manufacturers of synthetic staples in boxes weighing up to 650 pounds. Fibers are unloaded from trucks and stored in the warehouse according to type. Boxes of synthetic staples are drawn from stock and positioned near blending machines with steel bands and tops removed to facilitate feeding fibers into machine hoppers.

Carding

This process, as used in this establishment, involves blending synthetic fibers or reusable waste and feeding fibers through a distribution system into carding machines that produce sliver. Specified amounts of fibers fed into blending machines are deposited onto a conveyor from automatic weighing units attached to blending machines. Fibers are sprayed with fugitive dye tints and antistatic chemicals for identity as to type and to reduce friction in fibers during processing, and are conveyed through a piping system to automatic feeding units containing aprons with pins that feed fibers on a controlled basis to carding machines. Carding machines are equipped with several cylinders covered with metallic spikes that work in conjunction with carding drums to remove impurities from fibers, arrange fibers parallel, and produce sliver which is coiled in cans for use in the drawing process.

Drawing

This involves combining and passing several strands of sliver through two or more pairs of rollers, each of which rotate at a higher speed than the preceding pair, to attenuate the sliver.

Two phases of this process are used; namely, breaker and finish drawing. In the initial step, eight slivers are fed into drawing machines that combine and straighten the fibers to produce a strand of uniform weight and size. The second phase combines eight breaker strands of sliver into one, thus improving the quality of the sliver processed. Sliver formed during the drawing process is coiled into cans for feeding into roving frames.

Roving

The purpose of this process is to combine and reduce sliver received from drawing frames into a continuous, slightly twisted strand called roving and to wind roving into bobbins for use in the spinning process. The drafting rollers of the roving frames draw out the sliver and flyers slightly twist the roving as it is wound into bobbins.

Spinning

In this process, ring spinning frames are used to reduce roving to yarn and to wind yarn onto bobbins. Roving from bobbins placed in the creels of spinning frames is drawn to its final size by sets of drafting rollers, twisted by travelers on the rings of spinning frames, and wound onto spinning bobbins.

Winding

This involves transferring yarn from spinning bobbins onto cones and spring coils through use of winding machines. A technique for joining broken ends together in specified yarn types is employed in addition to the use of hand knotters. This process, called "splicing" by management, involves gluing broken yarn ends together with a latex base compound, producing a knotless yarn.

Inspecting and Packing

Yarn packages are examined for finishing defects, such as knots, soils, loose or tight winding, and absence of labels and specified color tip of cones. Ultraviolet lamps are used for detecting packages failing to meet blending specifications and for separating faultily mixed lots. Following inspection, yarn packages are wrapped in paper to prevent damage to yarn during shipment and packed in shipping cartons. Cartons are stenciled with identifying information, weighed, strapped with steel bands, and moved to the shipping area by a conveyor.

Shipping

Customer order shipments are loaded onto trucks and transported to a central warehouse for consolidation of orders and delivery to customers of subsidiary plants, following priority of orders.

ENVIRONMENTAL CONDITIONS

The physical plant was constructed during the 1920's but has been remodeled in the past seven years. It is adequately lighted and ventilated and is clean. A cafeteria containing a coin-operated food-and-beverage dispensing machine is available for use by workers during breaks and lunch periods. Smoking areas are also provided and so designated to minimize fire hazards.

The noise level is considered critical as a result of the constant operation of machines throughout the plant. Automatic vacuum piping systems and overhead traveling cleaners reduce the amount of lint and other foreign matter in the carding and spinning rooms that could result in worker discomfort.

Workers handling cartons of yarn and fibers or other heavy objects work together as team members or use lifting devices and handtrucks to prevent personal injury while moving materials and supplies.

Though the possibility for injuries exists for personnel working with or around machines, strict observance of safety rules and regulations rarely results in serious injury. Selected workers from each shift are trained in rendering first aid treatment when minor injuries occur.

SPECIAL COMMENTS

The processing of synthetic fibers into sliver using the system outlined eliminates the picking process which involves transforming fibers into laps for use in the carding process. The replacement of revolving flats with a series of rolls containing metallic spikes reduces the grinding and stripping operations, usually accompanying the carding of natural fibers, as synthetic fibers do not require extensive cleaning. As a result, such tasks as feeding blending machines and tending carding machines have been added to the carding process.

GLOSSARY

6's to 30's: coarse to medium yarn.

Hoppers: Units containing aprons with spikes that remove compression from synthetic fibers. Several types of fibers and waste can be blended into this unit with unusable waste fibers removed by piping system.

Sliver: Loose, untwisted strand of synthetic fibers produced on carding machines and drawing frames.

Fugitive Dye: A dye which is not fast.

Attenuate: To make slender or thin.

Cans: Large, cylindrical containers used to receive and hold sliver delivered from drawing frames for feeding into roving frames.

Drafting Rollers: Two or more pairs of rollers, each pair of which rotates at a higher speed than the preceding pair, serving to attenuate the roving passing between them.

Carding Machine: Machine used to remove impurities from synthetic fibers, arrange fibers parallel, and produce sliver for drawing process. The machine consists of several cylinders covered with metallic teeth that card the fibers.

Drawing Frame: Machine used to combine several strands of sliver and draw out strand to produce one of uniform weight and size.

Spinning Frame: Machine used to draw out and transform slightly twisted roving into yarn and wind yarn onto bobbins.

Roving Frame: Machine used to draw out strands of sliver and loosely twist them together to form roving.

Winding Machine: Machine used to transfer yarn from bobbins onto cones and spring coils.

Traveler: A small, free-running metal ring sliding on a bar through which thread passes into other textile machine to impart a twist to the thread.

APPENDIX A

BREAKING A JOB DOWN INTO TASKS

IDENTIFICATION AND ORGANIZATION OF TASKS
ARE CRITICAL TO WRITING EFFECTIVE JOB DESCRIPTIONS

Organizing job analysis data from notes and deciding on the number and scope of tasks to include in the job description is one of the most difficult aspects of job analysis. The primary consideration is to organize the job description so that the uninformed reader can gain a clear understanding of the work performed.

From the definitions of task and element in the HAJ, it is shown that they differ in scope; yet an identical activity may be a task in one job, an element in another, or an entire job in itself. For example, the activity of typing addresses on envelopes could be an element of a task for a Secretary, an entire task for a Correspondence Clerk, and a complete job activity for an Envelope Addresser. For the Envelope Addresser, the activity can be further subdivided into tasks: 1) Prepares envelopes and address lists and adjusts typewriter; 2) types addresses from lists onto envelopes; 3) counts, bundles, and packs addressed envelopes.

CONSIDERATIONS FOR IDENTIFYING TASKS

A job is a conceptual rather than a physical entity and, as such, cannot be neatly subdivided like a sliced pie or a stack of cards. Two analysts studying the same job are likely to write job descriptions with different task breakdowns; neither description being any more ''correct'' than the other, provided both are clear, complete, and accurate.

Except for the simplest of jobs, identification of tasks is based on a multifactor approach using the following questions as guidelines:

1. Can the activity potentially be assigned to another worker?

    If an activity is sufficiently divisible from other activities of the job so that it can be done by another worker, it may be considered as a separate task. If, on the other hand, it is not practical to assign the activity to another worker, it should be treated as an element integrally related to other elements of a task by common purpose, sequence of actions, or decision-making factors.

    In the example below, some activities of a Physical Therapy Aide working in a hospital are arranged in their usual order of performance.

    a. Assists or lifts patient to transfer patient between wheelchair and treatment equipment, following instructions of Physical Therapist.

    b. Observes patient during transfer for correct application of learned transfer technique and gives direction and encouragement as needed.

    c. Informs Physical Therapist of adverse patient reaction during transfer.

    d. Obtains and positions equipment for treatment.

    e. Supports, guides, and stabilizes patient as directed while Physical Therapist administers treatments.

    Activities a, b, and c, all relating to the transfer of patients, are inseparable. The performer of activity ''a'' must also make concurrent observations ''b'' and take immediate action (notifying Physical Therapist) ''c''. Therefore, a, b, and c constitute a task. Activities d and e, however, could each be written as a separate task because they are distinct activities assignable to other workers.

2. Do certain key job analysis components (GED, SVP, Worker Functions, Work Fields, MTEWA, and MPSMS) of the activity differ significantly from those of other activities included in the job?

This is determined by informally rating the various job activities and considering those with similar ratings for possible treatment as distinct tasks. Differences in GED, Worker Functions, and Work Fields usually justify treatment as separate tasks; differences in SVP, MPSMS, and Work Devices may justify such treatment, depending on other considerations. For example, because of different Worker Functions, the copying of data is almost always treated as a task distinct from the analysis of data; and because of different Work Fields, the polishing of metal parts is a task separate from the assembly of those parts. However, the cutting of plastic sheets using Handtool A and Machine B may or may not be a task distinct from the cutting of metal sheets using Handtool X and Machine Y depending on the extent to which the required SVP, skills, knowledges, and abilities differ. A 3-month difference in SVP would of course be more significant when comparing activities with 1- and 4-month training times than when comparing those with 9-and 12-month training times.

3. Is the activity performed frequently enough to be written as a distinct task?

A noncritical activity performed a small percentage of time, i.e., less than 5 percent, can be consolidated as an element of a broader task or included with other infrequent activities of a "miscellaneous" task.

4. Is the activity sanctioned by the establishment and performed by an accepted method?

Activities that are not recognized by management as part of the job are not included in a job description. Tasks performed in a nonstandard or unacceptable manner are described as they are expected to be performed.

5. Is the activity sufficiently broad in scope to be ratable for key job analysis components?

For example, "Turns control to regulate flow of material into machine" alone could not be meaningfully rated for GED and Worker Functions, but would have to be combined with other elements to collectively form a ratable task. Although only the entire job will eventually be rated, each task should have the potential to exist as a distinct activity, separately ratable and potentially assignable to another worker.

6. Is the activity self-contained to the extent that it does not include elements that overlap or duplicate other tasks?

For example, see the following element description and task summaries of the same job:

Element: "Wipes machine dies after clearing jammed metal, using rags and solvent, to clean die surface of metal dust and fragments."

Task A (summary):   "Monitors machines and clears jams."

Task B (summary):   "Cleans machines and work area."

If the analyst feels that cleaning of the die is an integral element of clearing jams, it should be included in Task A but not in Task B. If it were included in both, an overlap would occur.

Below is an example of an element that duplicates a task of the same job:

Task X: Inspects raw material: Visually inspects raw materials for surface defects, such as scratches, creases, and coating imperfections; sets aside defective batches and notifies supervisor of defects.

Task Y: Conveys raw material to job site: Reviews production order to determine types and amounts of raw materials needed for job order. **Examines raw materials for defects** prior to conveyance to machine and notifies supervisor of defective batches. Conveys materials from storage area to machine area, using handtruck. Stacks materials in designated areas near machine. Periodically conveys additional materials to replenish supplies during production run.

NOTE: The bolded element of Task Y is repetitive of the entire Task X. The analyst must decide whether to retain Task X as a separate task or as an element of the broader Task Y based on the integrity of the element with other activities performed prior, concurrently, or subsequent to the element.

ARRANGING TASKS FOR JOB DESCRIPTIONS

Once the tasks of the job are identified, the next step is to arrange them in a way that results in a clear, logical presentation.

Sequential or chronological presentation of tasks. For jobs that have specific cycles or sequences of operations, list tasks in the order in which they are performed. The sequential arrangement is often applicable to production jobs in manufacturing, especially jobs in which the significant relationship is to Things and the Worker Function involved is machine/equipment related. For example, the tasks of a machine-operating job may be arranged as follows:

1. Sets up machine
2. Operates machine
3. Removes workpiece
4. Inspects workpiece
5. Maintains tools
6. Maintains machine

Functional presentation of tasks. For jobs having no established sequence of operations, arrange tasks according to their function. Tasks, when broken out according to function, are arranged in one of the following ways:

1. In descending order of the **percentage of time** spent in performing each task.

2. In descending order of **importance** or criticality to the job as a whole.

3. In descending order of **skill level**, difficulty, or responsibility.

Decide which of the three arrangements presents the clearest picture of the job and is the most appropriate for the intended use of the job description.

The amount of time spent by the worker in performing a task is sometimes the sole determinant of its relative importance to the overall job, especially if all tasks are at about the same skill level. For example, the tasks of the following job are properly presented in order of frequency:

1. Plants, fertilizes, prunes, and waters flowers and shrubbery. (40%)

2. Rakes and disposes of leaves. (30%)

3. Shovels snow from walkways. (20%)

4. Paints fences and outside structures. (10%)

In most cases, however, functional tasks of a nonsequential job vary to some degree in skill level or importance. By presenting the most important or skilled tasks first in the job description, those which are vital to the job as a whole (regardless of the percentage of time spent in performing them) are highlighted so that the reader understands the job more quickly.

Important tasks are usually, but not always, the most highly skilled. The importance of a task is estimated by assessing the degree to which successful performance is necessary to meet the job's overall objective. The complexity of a task is determined by evaluating the skills, knowledge, abilities, judgments, and degree of responsibility required of the worker. To do this, the analyst informally rates each task for certain job analysis components, such as GED and Worker Functions, and compares the ratings to establish relative levels of complexity.

GROUPING SIMILAR WORK ACTIVITIES INTO TASKS

Activities similar in purpose or function are often separated by intervals of time, during which dissimilar activities are performed. For example, a Lunch-Counter Attendant serves several customers at once and shifts rapidly from one activity to another. An analyst, taking notes, might list the activities for serving each customer in the order observed:

1. Greets customer.

2. Provides customer with menu.

3. Positions napkin and glass of water on counter in front of customer.

4. Takes customer's order and fills out check by recording name and price of each item ordered.

5. Selects proper eating utensils according to items ordered and places on napkin.

6. Prepares beverages, such as coffee, tea, and soft drinks.

7. Prepares sandwiches, salads, and hamburgers.

8. Prepares ice cream products, such as floats and sundaes.

9. Serves food, beverages, and ice cream products to customers.

10. Takes orders for additional items, such as desserts.

11. Computes and records tax on check and totals check.

12. Collects payment from customer.

13. Operates cash register to record payment, deposit payment, and remove change.

14. Returns change to customer.

15. Clears away used dishes and utensils.

16. Wipes counter or booth with damp cloth.

One way to organize these activities into tasks is as follows:

(1 & 2)   Greets customer and provides menu. (A distinct activity, performed in some establishments by a host or hostess. Worker Functions: Comparing, Serving, and Handling. Work Field: Accommodating.)

(3 & 5)   Provides customer with napkin and water prior to taking order and with appropriate utensils after taking order. [Both activities are arranging the place setting; the fact that some items are placed before the order is taken and some afterwards does not justify separating the arranging of the place setting into two tasks. The Worker Functions Comparing, Serving, and Handling and the Work Field Accommodating are similar to those of Task 1.) Tasks 1 and 2 could be combined into a single task if the time percentage of one or both is too low to justify separating them as shown here.]

(4 & 10)   Takes initial customer order and additional orders, such as order for dessert, and records name and menu price of each item on customer check. (Identical activities although performed at different times. Worker Functions: Compiling, Serving, and Handling. Work Field: Numerical Recording-Record Keeping.)

(6, 7, & 8)	Prepares food requiring short preparation time, such as sandwiches, salads, hamburgers, and ice cream sundaes; and beverages, such as coffee, tea, and soft drinks. (Since the preparation of various types of food and beverages, although involving different techniques, procedures, and equipment, is similar enough in function and purpose to be assigned identical work performed ratings, all food-and-beverage-preparation activities can be combined into a single major task. Worker Functions: Compiling, Serving, and Manipulating. Work Field: Cooking-Food Preparing.)
(9)	Serves food and beverages to customer. (Retained as a distinct task; this activity can be performed by another worker. Worker Functions: Comparing, Serving, and Handling. Work Field: Accommodating.)
(11)	Totals prices on check, computes tax or determines tax from chart, records total amount, and hands check to customer. (Retained as a distinct task. Worker Functions: Computing, Serving, and Handling. Work Field: Numerical Recording-Record Keeping.)
(12, 13, & 14)	Collects payment from customer, operates cash register to record sale, and returns change. (Integrally related activities that form a distinct task; not consolidated with previous Task 6 because many establishments have separate workers performing these activities, e.g., Cashier and Waiter/Waitress. Worker Functions: Computing, Serving, and Operating-Controlling. Work Field: Numerical Recording-Record Keeping.)
(15 & 16)	Clears away used dishes and utensils and wipes countertop or booth table with damp cloth. (Both activities are elements of an overall cleaning function and form one task. Worker Functions: Comparing, Taking Instructions-Helping, and Handling. Work Field: Cleaning.)

The above task descriptions while based largely on functional considerations are arranged more or less sequentially to reflect the work cycle for serving an individual customer. This arrangement presents a clear picture.

GROUPING SEQUENTIAL WORK ACTIVITIES INTO TASKS

In order to identify the tasks of sequential, short-cycle jobs, it is necessary to determine the points in the work cycle where activities or groups of activities can be separated into tasks. The example below shows the sequential elements of a Power-Press Tender and one way in which they can be grouped into tasks. The rationale for each task is stated based on some of the considerations for task identification previously discussed.

1. Picks up metal ring from tray.
2. Picks up wood mop handle from carton.
3. Examines ring and mop handle for obvious surface irregularities and discards defective ones.
4. Inserts ring onto narrowed tip of mop handle.
5. Positions ringed end of mop handle onto jig of power press.
6. Depresses treadle to actuate power-press ram that crimps ring to handle and forms partial thread on ring.
7. Rotates mop handle one-half turn to position ring for completion of thread.
8. Depresses second treadle to actuate power-press ram that forms remainder of thread on ring.
9. Removes mop handle from jig and places into cart.
10. Reads counter on press at end of workshift and records readings on production ticket.
11. Sweeps floor around press at end of workshift, using broom and dustpan.

12. Oils press once daily, using oilcan.

These activities could be grouped as follows into a three-task description:

Task 1: (Elements 1, 2, 3, and 4) Inserts metal ring onto end of mop handle. (Rationale: The fitting of the ring onto the end of each mop handle is an activity that prepares the product for a machine operation; it could be done by another worker as a nonmachine activity. The elements are integrally related and inseparable.)

Task 2: (Elements 5, 6, 7, 8, and 9) Tends power-press to stamp threads on metal ring and to crimp metal ring onto end of mop handle. (Rationale: The elements beginning with the feeding of the mop-handle assembly into the machine and ending with the removal of the finished handle comprise the machine-related part of the job: tending the power-press. The elements of this task are performed in rapid succession during which time the worker's hands never leave the product.)

Task 3: (Elements 10, 11, and 12) Performs miscellaneous activities. (Rationale: These infrequently performed activities are incidental to the main purpose of the job, fabricating mop handles, and are best consolidated into a "miscellaneous" task, thus placing the two more important tasks in better perspective in the final job description.)

APPENDIX B

DETERMINING DETAIL NEEDED IN JOB AND TASK DESCRIPTIONS

CONSIDERATIONS

Job descriptions vary in detail from brief, generally worded task statements to element-by-element task descriptions that approach but fall short of the specificity of a motion study. Insufficient detail leaves the user with broad statements too vague to be useful. Excessive detail forces the user to sift through superfluous facts for pertinent data. Not everything in an analyst's notes needs to go into the job description. By eliminating, summarizing, or selectively highlighting data, the job descriptions can be more usable. Considerations in deciding how much detail to include are:

1. Type of job studied.

   Descriptions of factory, clerical, service, technical, and craft jobs are usually written in terms of specific actions performed. Professional and managerial jobs typically require carefully selected Data/People action verbs in order to reflect adequately the responsibilities and duties performed.

2. Relative time percentages of tasks.

   A task that is performed a significant percentage of the worker's time is usually written in more detail than it would be if it were performed infrequently. For example, an occasional machine-feeding task (performed 5% of the time) may be described as follows:

   > Feeds machines: Feeds stacks of paper blanks into feed racks of automatic cup-forming machines to maintain supply of blanks in each machine of battery.

   The same task performed a significant percentage of time, perhaps 20% or more, would require more descriptive detail as shown below:

   > Feeds machines: Grasps stack of paper cup body blanks from bin and carries blanks to feed rack of cup-forming machine. Examines blanks for curvature and defects, such as short size, missing print or ink color, cracks, creases, wrinkles, and dirt. Bends curved blanks in opposite direction to straighten, if necessary, to prevent jamming in machine. Holds stack of blanks in one hand and fans edges with other hand to separate stuck edges and to dislodge loose paper scrap. Removes and discards defective blanks and notifies supervisor if quantity of blanks affected exceeds specified amount. Places stack onto machine feed rack behind previously fed blanks and brushes line of liquid emulsion along top and bottom edges of stack, using paintbrush and container of emulsion located next to feed rack, to soften top and bottom edges of cup bodies, to facilitate formation of rims and bottoms, and to prevent paper from cracking. Patrols work area and repeats feeding procedure to maintain sufficient supply of blanks in feed racks of machines.

3. Relative importance or skill level of tasks.

   Important job tasks often require more detail than less important tasks, even when they take but a small percentage of the time. A worker may spend 80% of the time watching a machine for warning lights and automatic stoppage caused by problems with machine or raw material, but only 10% of the time adjusting the machine settings to prepare for operation and 10% on diagnosing malfunctions and taking corrective action. The latter two tasks, because they involve a higher degree of skill and are more important to successful performance, require detail comparable to that in the first task.

Another example is that of two workers performing the same activity: duplicating printed material on a photocopy machine. For one worker, Duplicating Machine Operator, who spends virtually 100% of the time on the activity, a detailed task description would be warranted; for the other worker, General Office Clerk, who only occasionally performs the activity, less detail would suffice.

4. Type of work activity.

Some work activities are commonplace and need not be described in specific detail to convey a clear picture of what is being done. In such tasks as, "Sweeps sawdust from floor, using broom and dustpan", and "Hammers nails to seal lid on crate, using hammer", the actions involved are obvious. However, a specialized task, such as "Measures thrust-load capacity of ball bearings, using mechanical preload gauge", gives no clear depiction of how the worker does this; more detail is needed to enable the reader to understand the specific skills and actions involved, such as "Manually places ball bearing into fixture of preload gauge. Lifts and releases handle of gauge to allow attached weight to fall onto bearing. Reads dial indicator on gauge to determine if bearing's capacity to withstand impact is within prescribed tolerance range. Places acceptable and rejected bearings into separate trays."

EXAMPLES OF EXCESSIVE DETAIL IN WORK-ACTIVITY DESCRIPTIONS

Once it is decided that a detailed job or task description is needed, care must be taken to avoid creating a motion study description. For example, an element in a description of a Small-Parts Inspector might read: "Feels edges of machined metal part to detect burrs." It would be giving an excessive amount of detail to state: "Raises right hand one foot to table height, superimposes hand over metal part, and by depressing first and second fingers onto part and moving arm slowly sideways about six inches, feels with fingertips for snags and rough spots that are indicative of surface irregularities."

A job description is not a motion study, nor is it a training manual to teach a worker to perform the job through step-by-step work instructions. Excessive detail overwhelms the reader and obscures the features that distinguish that job from all others. The following example shows how one task of a Wire-Cloth Weaver can be written either as part of a job description or as a work procedure.

For Job Description in the DOT perhaps, or in a Job Summary Statement:

Installs specified arrangement of cams in loom for production of twilled-weave wire cloth, using handtools and following written instructions.

For Job Procedure:

To produce twilled-weave in loom:

1. Install a #1 cam on the #1 treadle centered above the cam follower.

2. Install a #2 cam on the #2 treadle, rotated 90 degrees to the rear of the #1 cam.

3. Install a #3 cam on the #3 treadle directly opposite the #1 cam.

4. Install a #4 cam on the #4 treadle opposite the #2 cam and toward the front the loom.

5. Repeat above cam-installation procedures on the other side of the heddle frames.

6. Connect #1 to #3 heddle frame by means of support chains.

7. Connect #2 to #4 heddle frame by means of support chains.

It is evident that most of the detail in the above work procedure is superfluous in a task description. Training manuals are available to evaluate job data, but the specificity of the final task description needs to be based on the considerations just discussed. A detailed account of every step of the job or movement of the worker in a photographic or documentary fashion is not a useful description of tasks for a JAR.

APPENDIX C

MACHINES, TOOLS, EQUIPMENT, AND WORK AIDS

The importance of Machines, Tools, Equipment, and Work Aids (MTEWA) cannot be overemphasized. Often an analyst brings confusion to JAR-users by neglecting to enter information here which helps place the job in perspective. The analyst is urged to include information in this item needed to give JAR users the best understanding of the job and its relation to the process or service in which it was observed.

All MTEWA which are commonly known to the general population, such as saws, hammers, and adding machines, should be listed but do not need to be defined.

Considerable latitude is allowed in preparing descriptions of MTEWA, but ordinarily the descriptions must include the following information:

1. Statement of the function of the device.

2. Description of the physical appearance of the device and its essential parts.

3. Description of the operation of any machines or equipment as they relate to the worker.

Only essential features of mechanical equipment should be included in these descriptions. Structural details, such as gear ratio, types of power drive, and similar technical features, need not be included unless the worker has some specific task to perform in relation to them. The analyst should assume the place of an observer who stands beside the machine, and should tell what the observer sees and what would have to be known to understand what was being done on the machine. The description of an automatic machine should be simpler than the description of one that requires a worker's constant attention.

To clarify certain operations that are mentioned in the description of duties, it is often desirable to follow a piece of work through the machine or equipment. The description in Item 14 should be written in a manner that presents a clear picture of the relationship between the MTEWA and the performance of the worker's tasks. Any special features of, or attachments to, the machine or equipment should be mentioned if they have any definite relationship to the worker.

For simpler devices, particularly handtools, it is only necessary to include a definition of the device rather than a complete description. However, the purpose for which the device or machine is used must be explained.

In the description of the job, it is better to use the generic names of machines and other devices than to use their trade names unless there is no appropriate, commonly understood generic name. For example, "automatic screw machine" should be used in preference to "Acme Machine". When describing the machines in Item 14 of the JAR, the generic name should be followed by a parenthetical explanation, giving the trade name of the machine, the name and address of the manufacturer, and any other identifying information that can be obtained, such as model number or size. This enables persons who may later write from the data contained in the JAR's to request catalogs and photographs from the manufacturers, if necessary. Where a drawing has been included with the JAR and where it is practicable and desirable, an equipment or machine description may be tied in with the drawing by placing letters appearing on the drawing in parentheses after the parts of the device mentioned in the description.

A convenient technique for composing the best type of description or definition of an item (MTEWA) is for the analyst to be guided by the following general outline:

1. State the name of the item.

2. Place the item in its general category, e.g., a floor-mounted, electrically powered machine.

3. State the function of the item.

4. Describe its physical appearance, makeup, and essential parts.

The following is an example of an MTEWA thus described:

Edging Machine (Sommer & Maca Glass Machinery Co.; Chicago, Illinois; Auto Edger Model 4A): Floor-mounted, electrically powered machine approximately 30' long, 5' wide, and 7' high. An automatic, straight line, conveyor-type machine that grinds and polishes the bottom edges of rectangular glass by means of a series of spindle-mounted grinding and polishing wheels. The five spindle assemblies include four diamond wheels for grinding and seaming, and one rubber composition wheel for polishing. The diamond wheels use a water soluble coolant and the rubber composition wheel uses pumice and water as a polishing agent. The wheels are adjusted by turning a calibrated crank to control inward and outward movement. Ammeters indicate grinding loads of individual grinding wheels and need for grinding pressure adjustment. Glass is placed upright against an upper guide support on the endless conveyor belt. As glass advances toward grinding unit it is gripped and held by rubber blocks on parallel, endless chains. These blocks support glass as it is conveyed through grinding and polishing units. Glass is washed automatically as it advances beyond grinding unit and dried by blown air as it leaves washing unit.

folded cardboard strip; pumice; pallet; water hose; shovel; cleaning solution; rag

All MTEWA noted in Item 14 of the JAR must be mentioned in the description of tasks. For example, if a micrometer is defined in this section and if it does not appear in Item 16 of the JAR that the worker measures anything, the presumption is that the task of measuring has been omitted from the description of duties.

APPENDIX D

BIBLIOGRAPHY

Dictionary of Occupational Titles, Fourth Edition (1977). U.S. Department of Labor, Washington, DC: U.S. Government Printing Office. For sale by the Superintendent of Documents, U.S. Government Printing Office, Washington, DC 20402, Stock Number 029-013-00079-9.

Dictionary of Occupational Titles, Fourth Edition Supplement (1986). U.S. Department of Labor, Washington, DC: U.S. Government Printing Office. For sale by the Superintendent of Documents, U.S. Government Printing Office, Washington, DC 20402, Stock Number 1987-169-678.

Guide for Occupational Exploration (1979). U.S. Department of Labor, Washington, DC: U.S. Government Printing Office. For sale by the Superintendent of Documents, U.S. Government Printing Office, Washington, DC 20402, Stock Number 029-013-00080-2.

Occupational Outlook Handbook (1988). U.S. Department of Labor, Bureau of Labor Statistics, Washington, DC. For sale by the Superintendent of Documents, U.S. Government Printing Office, Washington, DC 20402.

Selected Characteristics of Occupations Defined in the Dictionary of Occupational Titles (1981). U.S. Department of Labor, Washington, DC: U.S. Government Printing Office. For sale by the Superintendent of Documents, U.S. Government Printing Office, Washington, DC 20402, Stock Number 029-014-00202-0.

Standard Industrial Classification Manual (1987). Executive Office of the President, Office of Management and Budget. For sale by the National Technical Information Service, 5285 Port Royal Road, Springfield, VA 22161, Order number PB 87-100012.

Standard Occupational Classification Manual (1980). U.S. Department of Commerce, Office of Federal Statistical Policy and Standards. For sale by the Superintendent of Documents, U.S. Government Printing Office, Washington, DC 20402, Stock Number 1980 0-332-946.

United States Government Printing Office Style Manual (1984). U.S. Government Printing Office. For sale by the Superintendent of Documents, U.S. Government Printing Office, Washington, DC 20402, Stock Number 021-000-00120-1.

APPENDIX E

AGENCY IDENTIFICATION NUMBERS FOR OCCUPATIONAL ANALYSIS

The following table contains numbers used within the cooperative Federal-State Occupational Analysis Program to identify the originator, State Employment Security Agency or Occupational Analysis Field Center (OAFC), of source material for Job Analysis Reports.

010	Alabama		280	Montana
020	Alaska		290	National Office
030	Arizona		300	Nebraska
040	Arkansas		310	Nevada
050	California		320	New Hampshire
060	Colorado		330	New Jersey
070	Connecticut		340	New Mexico
080	Delaware		350	New York
090	District of Columbia		360	North Carolina
100	Florida		362	North Carolina OAFC
110	Georgia		370	North Dakota
120	Guam		380	Ohio
130	Hawaii		390	Oklahoma
140	Idaho		400	Oregon
150	Illinois		410	Pennsylvania
160	Indiana		420	Puerto Rico
170	Iowa		430	Rhode Island
180	Kansas		440	South Carolina
190	Kentucky		450	South Dakota
200	Louisiana		460	Tennessee
210	Maine		470	Texas
220	Maryland		480	Utah
230	Massachusetts		482	Utah OAFC
232	Massachusetts OAFC		490	Vermont
240	Michigan		500	Virginia
242	Michigan OAFC		510	Virgin Islands
250	Minnesota		520	Washington
260	Mississippi		530	West Virginia
270	Missouri		540	Wisconsin
272	Missouri OAFC		550	Wyoming

Other Titles Available from

JIST publishes a variety of books on careers and job search topics. Please consider ordering one or more from your dealer, local bookstore, or directly from JIST.

Orders from Individuals: Please use the form below (or provide the same information) to order additional copies of this or other books listed on this page. You are also welcome to send us your order (please enclose money order, check, or credit card information), or simply call our toll free number at **1-800-648-JIST** or **1-317-264-3720**. Our FAX number is **1-317-264-3709**. **Qualified schools and organizations** may request our catalog and obtain information on quantity discounts (we have over 400 career-related books, videos, and other items). Our offices are open weekdays 8 a.m. to 5 p.m. local time and our address is:

JIST Works, Inc. · 720 North Park Avenue · Indianapolis, IN 46202-3431

QTY	BOOK TITLE	TOTAL ($)
_____	***Getting the Job You Really Want***, J. Michael Farr · ISBN 0-942784-15-4 · **$9.95**	_____
_____	***The Very Quick Job Search:*** *Get a Good Job in Less Time*, J. Michael Farr · ISBN 0-942784-72-3 · **$9.95**	_____
_____	***America's 50 Fastest Growing Jobs:*** *An Authoritative Information Source* · ISBN 0-942784-61-8 · **$10.95**	_____
_____	***America's Top 300 Jobs:*** *A Complete Career Handbook* (trade version of the *Occupational Outlook Handbook*) · ISBN 0-942784-45-6 · **$17.95**	_____
_____	***America's Federal Jobs:*** *A Complete Directory of Federal Career Opportunities* · ISBN 0-942784-81-2 · **$14.95**	_____
_____	***The Resume Solution:*** *How to Write and Use a Resume That Gets Results*, David Swanson · ISBN 0-942784-44-8 · **$8.95**	_____
_____	***The Job Doctor:*** *Good Advice on Getting a Good Job*, Phillip Norris, Ed.D. · ISBN 0-942784-43-X · **$5.95**	_____
_____	***The Right Job for You:*** *An Interactive Career Planning Guide*, J. Michael Farr · ISBN 0-942784-73-1 · **$9.95**	_____
_____	***Exploring Careers:*** *A Young Person's Guide to over 300 Jobs* · ISBN 0-942784-27-8 · **$19.95**	_____
_____	***Work in the New Economy:*** *Careers and Job Seeking into the 21st Century*, Robert Wegmann · ISBN 0-942784-19-78 · **$14.95**	_____
_____	***The Occupational Outlook Handbook*** · ISBN 0-942784-38-3 · **$16.95**	_____
_____	***The Career Connection:*** *Guide to College Majors and Their Related Careers*, Dr. Fred Rowe · ISBN 0-942784-82-0 · **$15.95**	_____
_____	***The Career Connection II:*** *Guide to Technical Majors and Their Related Careers*, Dr. Fred Rowe · ISBN 0-942784-83-9 · **$13.95**	_____

Subtotal _____

Sales Tax _____

Shipping: ($3 for first book, $1 for each additional book.) _____

(U.S. Currency only) **TOTAL ENCLOSED WITH ORDER** _____
(Prices subject to change without notice)

❑ Check   ❑ Money order   Credit Card: ❑ MasterCard   ❑ VISA   ❑ AMEX

Card # (if applies)_____ Exp. Date _____

Name (please print) _____

Name of Organization (if applies) _____

Address _____

City/State/Zip _____

Daytime Telephone ( ) _____ — _____

Thank-you for your order!